Business English

Lisa Förster, Ian Lewis, Annette Pattinson, Sander Schroevers,
Stephanie Shellabear, Jaquie Thomas

Business English

Alle wichtigen Vokabeln und Redewendungen für den Job

1. Auflage

Haufe Group
Freiburg · München · Stuttgart

Bibliografische Information der Deutschen Nationalbibliothek

Die Deutsche Nationalbibliothek verzeichnet diese Publikation in der Deutschen Nationalbibliografie; detaillierte bibliografische Daten sind im Internet über http://dnb.dnb.de abrufbar.

Print: ISBN 978-3-648-12133-7 Bestell-Nr. 10292-0001
ePub: ISBN 978-3-648-12134-4 Bestell-Nr. 10292-0100
ePDF: ISBN 978-3-648-12135-1 Bestell-Nr. 10292-0150

Lisa Förster, Ian Lewis, Annette Pattinson, Sander Schroevers,
Stephanie Shellabear, Jaquie Thomas
Business English
1. Auflage 2018

www.haufe.de
info@haufe.de
Produktmanagement: Jürgen Fischer

Satzvorstufe: Agentur: Satz und Zeichen, Karin Lochmann, Buckenhof
Satz: kühn & weyh Software GmbH, Satz und Medien, Freiburg
Umschlag: RED GmbH, Krailling

Inhaltsverzeichnis

Teil 1: E-mails in English 17

1 **An E-mail's Anatomy** 19
1.1 Subject Lines That Work 19
1.2 Common Salutations and Openings 20
1.2.1 Salutations 20
1.2.2 Opening sentences 23
1.2.3 Small talk 24
1.3 Ending an E-mail 25
1.3.1 Closing remarks 25
1.3.2 Correct closing expressions 26
1.4 Signatures and Disclaimers 27
1.4.1 Signatures 27
1.4.2 Disclaimers 28
1.4.3 Out-of-office assistant 29
1.5 E-mail Techniques: about CC and BCC 29

2 **A Reader-friendly Approach** 31
2.1 When to Use E-mail and When Not? 31
2.2 Structuring the Information 32
2.2.1 Writing effectively for the monitor 32
2.2.2 Less is more 32
2.2.3 Techniques to make e-mails better structured 33
2.3 Formal or Informal? 35
2.3.1 Colloquial language 36
2.3.2 More personal style 36
2.4 Netiquette Guidelines 37
2.5 How to Deal with Attachments 38
2.5.1 Best ways to deal with attachments 38
2.5.2 Useful phrases 39
2.5.3 Avoiding attachments 40

3 **Common Business Situations** 43
3.1 Requesting Information or Favours 43
3.1.1 Useful phrases 44
3.2 Hotel or Conference Enquiries 45
3.2.1 Useful vocabulary 46

3.3 Giving Enquiries 48
3.3.1 FYI: for your information 48
3.3.2 Answering requests 48
3.3.3 Useful phrases 49
3.4 Change of Address 50
3.5 Appointments 50
3.5.1 Useful phrases 51
3.6 Invitations 52
3.6.1 Useful phrases 53
3.6.2 Indicating date and time 54
3.7 Sending Agendas and Minutes 57
3.8 Refusing a Request 59
3.8.1 Useful phrases 59
3.8.2 Stylistic stand back: negative – positive 60
3.9 Complaints 60
3.10 Apologies 61
3.10.1 Useful phrases 61
3.11 Congratulations and Season's Greetings 62
3.12 Thanks 63
3.13 Payments and Reminders 63
3.13.1 Useful phrases 64
3.13.2 Useful vocabulary 65
3.14 Making Offers 65
3.15 Delivery and Incoterms 66
3.16 Numbers and Currency Symbols 67
3.16.1 Indicating larger numbers 68
3.16.2 Monetary and currency symbols 68

4 Practical Reference 71
4.1 Useful Vocabulary and Key Terms 71
4.1.1 Digital vocabulary 71
4.1.2 Vocabulary: function keys 71
4.1.3 Key terms: e-mails 72
4.2 Abbreviations and Acronyms 72
4.3 E-mail Features 78
4.3.1 Formatting e-mail for foreign screens 78
4.3.2 Templates 79
4.3.3 Identifying international e-mails 80
4.3.4 Legal implications of e-mail 81
4.3.5 Responding to e-mail 82

Teil 2: Phone Calls in English 83

5 Getting Started and Ending a Conversation 85
5.1 Calling according to plan 85
5.1.1 Beginning a call 85
5.1.2 Telephone scripts 86
5.2 After the greeting 87
5.2.1 Small talk 90
5.2.2 Getting past the secretary 91
5.2.3 Obtaining information 91
5.3 I beg your pardon? 93
5.4 Connecting people 94
5.5 Answering the phone 95
5.6 Ending a conversation 95

6 Typical Situations and How To Deal with Them 99
6.1 Taking and leaving messages 99
6.2 Appointments 100
6.3 Telephone spelling 102
6.4 Taking down names and numbers 105
6.5 Electronic addresses 107
6.6 Answering machine and voice mail 109
6.7 Mobile telephones 111
6.7.1 Recognising mobile numbers 112

7 Special Situations 113
7.1 Conference calls 113
7.1.1 Hours for international business calls 119
7.2 International trade 120
7.3 Sales and finances 126
7.4 Travel enquiries 129
7.5 A job interview by telephone 132

8 Practical Reference 135
8.1 Intercultural communication 135
8.2 Pronunciation 136
8.2.1 Speech 138
8.3 Telecommunications terminology 138
8.4 Key terms: the company 140
8.5 Telephone sources on the Internet 141
8.5.1 National telephone numbering plans 142
8.6 Country codes and dialling codes for well-known cities 143

Teil 3: Presentations in English ... 145

9 Preparation ... 147
9.1 Developing an international viewpoint ... 147
9.1.1 Things can be different ... 147
9.1.2 Accept that differences exist! ... 148
9.1.3 Opposite behaviour may not mean opposite values ... 148
9.1.4 Use cultural generalisations with care ... 149
9.1.5 When and how to adapt to others' cultural style? ... 150
9.2 Preparing yourself, the person ... 152
9.2.1 How to deal with nerves ... 152
9.2.2 Dealing with »language« nerves ... 154
9.2.3 Your English isn't good enough? ... 154
9.2.4 Everyone else speaks better English than you? ... 154
9.2.5 What if you forget the words? ... 155
9.2.6 What if you can't understand the audience? ... 157
9.3 Putting yourself in your audience's shoes ... 158
9.4 Organising facilities ... 161
9.4.1 Be prepared ... 161
9.4.2 Organising the setup ... 161
9.5 Your presentation structure ... 163
9.5.1 Circular vs. linear structure ... 163
9.5.2 Timing ... 164
9.5.3 Structure – main components ... 165
9.5.4 Structure in detail ... 166
9.6 How to prepare good slides ... 167

10 Greetings and introductions ... 169
10.1 What to say when you enter ... 169
10.1.1 Meeting people for the first time ... 170
10.1.2 Making conversation ... 170
10.2 Introducing your presentation well ... 171
10.3 Introduction components ... 173
10.3.1 Openings ... 173
10.3.2 Objectives ... 174
10.3.3 Overview ... 175
10.3.4 Organisation ... 175
10.4 Dealing with handouts ... 175
10.5 Taking care of technical problems ... 176

11 Main section: skills and techniques 179
11.1 Fixing your body language 179
11.1.1 International viewpoint 179
11.1.2 Body language basics 180
11.2 Using your voice well 181
11.2.1 International viewpoint 181
11.2.2 Two key techniques 181
11.2.3 Advanced techniques 182
11.3 Making transitions 183
11.3.1 Between slides 183
11.3.2 Between sections 184
11.3.3 Between breaks 185
11.3.4 After the break 186
11.4 Explaining slides and diagrammes 186
11.4.1 Text slides 187
11.4.2 Charts and diagrammes 187
11.5 Business English terms 189
11.5.1 Reasons behind events 189
11.5.2 Results 190
11.5.3 Change and development 191
11.5.4 Problems 192
11.5.5 Making comparisons 195
11.5.6 Plans and goals 196
11.5.7 Useful Vocabulary 196
11.6 Dealing with questions 197
11.6.1 International viewpoint 197
11.6.2 English language points 201
11.6.3 Preparation and procedure 202
11.7 Handling interruptions and disturbances 207
11.7.1 Getting attention at the beginning 208
11.7.2 Audience member working on laptop 208
11.7.3 Interruptions from people coming in 209
11.7.4 Useful comments 209
11.7.5 Audience member on a telephone call 209
11.7.6 Outside noise 210
11.7.7 Audience members talking 210
11.7.8 Unwelcome interruptions from audience 211
11.7.9 Heating and light disturbances 211

12 **Ending your presentation** ... 213
12.1 Making a good finish ... 213
12.1.1 International viewpoint ... 213
12.1.2 English language points ... 214
12.2 Ending components ... 214
12.3 Saying goodbye ... 216
12.3.1 International viewpoint ... 217

13 **Useful examples** ... 219
13.1 Basic outline – non-specific content ... 219
13.2 Product presentation ... 220

Teil 4: Meetings in English ... 223

14 **Preparing a meeting** ... 225
14.1 Inviting people to a meeting ... 225
14.1.1 Suggesting a meeting ... 225
14.1.2 Responding to a request for a meeting ... 226
14.2 Making meeting arrangements ... 226
14.2.1 Who would like to meet when? ... 227
14.3 Rescheduling, cancelling or confirming a meeting ... 228
14.3.1 Rescheduling ... 228
14.3.2 Cancellation ... 229
14.3.3 Confirming a meeting ... 229
14.4 Making the agenda ... 231
14.4.1 Compiling the agenda ... 232
14.4.2 Submitting items for the agenda ... 232
14.4.3 Circulating the agenda ... 233
14.5 Hands-on organisation ... 234
14.5.1 Giving travel directions ... 235
14.5.2 Giving information on local accommodation ... 235
14.5.3 Finding out about visitors' special dietary requirements ... 236
14.5.4 Finding out about visitors' technical requirements ... 237
14.5.5 Booking meeting facilities ... 237
14.5.6 Intercultural considerations ... 238

15 **Arriving at the meeting** ... 243
15.1 Arriving in reception ... 243
15.1.1 Receiving visitors on arrival ... 243
15.1.2 Lift talk ... 244

15.2 Introducing oneself and others 245
15.2.1 »How do you do?« and »How are you?« 246
15.2.2 Introducing others 246
15.3 Small talk 247
15.3.1 How's business – and life? 248
15.3.2 Effortless small talk 249
15.4 Setting up the meeting room 250

16 Conducting a meeting 251
16.1 Opening the meeting 251
16.1.1 Introductions and apologies 252
16.1.2 Introducing the agenda and the objectives of the meeting 252
16.1.3 Initiating the discussion 253
16.2 Guiding the discussion 253
16.2.1 Dealing with dominant participants and interruptions 253
16.2.2 Encouraging quiet participants to contribute 254
16.2.3 Reminding participants to be brief 254
16.2.4 Keeping to the agenda 255
16.2.5 Summarising and concluding an item 255
16.2.6 Moving on to the next agenda item 256
16.3 Bringing about a decision 256
16.3.1 How to reach consensus 256
16.4 Closing the meeting 257
16.4.1 Initiating further action 257
16.4.2 Bringing the meeting to a close 258
16.4.3 Thanking the attendees 259

17 The meeting itself 261
17.1 Roles at a meeting 261
17.1.1 Assigning and accepting roles 261
17.2 Active participation and asking for more information 262
17.2.1 Interrupting politely 262
17.2.2 Asking for more information 263
17.2.3 Active listening 264
17.2.4 Responding to questions 265
17.3 Expressing agreement and disagreement 266
17.3.1 Agreeing with an opinion 266
17.3.2 Diplomatic disagreement 267
17.3.3 Expressing criticism 270
17.3.4 Straight talking 271
17.4 Making suggestions and having your say 272
17.4.1 Expressing your opinion 272

17.5 Enquiring and resolving misunderstandings ... 274
17.5.1 Asking for repetition ... 274
17.5.2 Summarising for clarification ... 275
17.5.3 Recapping and confirming ... 275
17.6 Diplomacy and politeness ... 276
17.6.1 It's bad news, I'm afraid 276
17.6.2 Polite questions ... 277
17.6.3 A diplomatic game of give and take ... 278
17.7 What to do in case of language problems ... 280
17.8 Voting ... 280

18 After the meeting ... 283
18.1 Making the minutes ... 283
18.1.1 Tips for minute-taking ... 284
18.2 Following up the meeting ... 286

19 Special types of meetings ... 287
19.1 Meetings with customers ... 287
19.1.1 Getting in touch ... 287
19.1.2 Identifying your client's needs ... 287
19.1.3 Explaining your proposal in detail ... 288
19.1.4 Anticipating objections ... 288
19.1.5 Ending the visit ... 288
19.1.6 Attentive hosts ... 289
19.2 Negotiations ... 289
19.2.1 Useful phrases ... 291
19.2.2 Useful grammar ... 293
19.3 Briefing and brainstorming ... 294
19.3.1 Briefings ... 294
19.3.2 Brainstorming sessions ... 295
19.4 Jours fixes and kick-offs ... 296
19.4.1 Jours fixes ... 296
19.4.2 Kick-off meetings ... 297
19.5 Telephone conferences ... 297
19.5.1 Agenda ... 297
19.5.2 Starting a conference call ... 298
19.5.3 Controlling the meeting ... 299
19.5.4 Ending a telephone conference ... 301
19.5.5 Feedback on the TC ... 301
19.6 Literature ... 302

Teil 5: Negotiations in English ... 303

20 Negotiating skills ... 305
20.1 Preparation and planning ... 305
20.1.1 BATNA: Best Alternative To a Negotiated Agreement ... 307
20.1.2 Parameters ... 308
20.1.3 A negotiation agenda ... 308
20.1.4 Promoting the climate ... 310
20.1.5 Knowing the participants ... 311
20.2 Getting acquainted ... 311
20.2.1 Introducing oneself and others ... 313
20.2.2 Business cards ... 314
20.2.3 Addressing others ... 315
20.2.4 Socialising and small talk ... 316
20.3 Opening phase ... 317
20.3.1 Stating the purpose ... 318
20.3.2 The agenda ... 320
20.4 Main phase ... 320
20.4.1 Bargaining ... 320
20.4.2 Marking transitions ... 323
20.4.3 Linking words ... 324
20.4.4 Interrupting ... 325
20.4.5 Rephrasing ... 326
20.4.6 Referring back ... 326
20.4.7 Making your point clear ... 327
20.4.8 Summarising ... 327
20.4.9 Adjourning ... 329
20.5 Agreement phase ... 330
20.5.1 Reaching an agreement ... 330
20.5.2 Ensuring agreement ... 331
20.5.3 Disagreeing ... 332
20.5.4 We agree, but... ... 333
20.5.5 No subdivided agreement ... 333
20.5.6 Closing remarks and next steps ... 333
20.6 Asking questions ... 334
20.6.1 Clarifying ... 335
20.6.2 Question categories ... 335
20.6.3 Question the facts ... 337
20.6.4 Avoiding asking questions ... 338
20.7 The art of listening ... 338

20.8 When things get tough ... 339
20.8.1 Reducing tension ... 339
20.8.2 Anger management ... 340
20.8.3 Dealing with impasses ... 341
20.9 Tables, graphs or charts ... 342
20.10 Telephone negotiating ... 344

21 Cross-cultural negotiations ... 347
21.1 Relation orientation ... 347
21.2 Sociolinguistic influences ... 348
21.3 Negotiating internationally ... 351
21.4 Local negotiation techniques ... 353
21.5 Strategic negotiating framework ... 354

22 Country-specific negotiating ... 357
22.1 Introduction ... 357
22.2 China ... 357
22.3 Czech Republic ... 359
22.4 France ... 360
22.5 India ... 361
22.6 Italy ... 362
22.7 Japan ... 364
22.8 Netherlands ... 365
22.9 Poland ... 366
22.10 Russia ... 367
22.11 Spain ... 369
22.12 United Kingdom ... 370
22.13 United States ... 371
22.14 Cross-cultural differences ... 372
22.15 Practical reference ... 375
22.15.1 Financial numbers ... 375
22.15.2 Language transfer ... 377
22.15.3 British and American English ... 378

Teil 6: False Friends in Business English 381

23 False friends for beginners 383
23.1 Different types of false friends 383
23.2 Degrees of confusion 384
23.3 Applying for a job 385
23.4 Your CV 386
23.5 The interview 388
23.5.1 Some typical questions 388
23.5.2 What's wrong? 389

24 False friends in business communication 391
24.1 On the telephone 391
24.2 In e-mails 392
24.2.1 Find the false friends 392
24.3 In letters 393
24.4 In meetings 394
24.4.1 Typical phrases in meetings – with false friends 394
24.5 Making presentations 396
24.6 Negotiating 397

25 False friends on a business trip 399
25.1 At the airport 399
25.2 At a restaurant 400
25.2.1 Typical phrases in restaurants – with false friends 400
25.3 When shopping 401
25.3.1 Better phrases for shopping 402
25.4 Small talk 404
25.4.1 Phrases for business situations 404

26 False friends in different departments 407
26.1 Human resources 407
26.2 Logistics 408
26.3 Finance and accounting 410
26.4 Sales and marketing 411
26.5 Production 412

27 Useful false friends to know 415
27.1 Internet resources 448

Teil 7: Appendix ... 451

28 Practical Reference ... 453
28.1 Linguistic Characteristics ... 453
28.1.1 The proper use of capital letters ... 453
28.1.2 Using apostrophes ... 454
28.1.3 Using the spelling check ... 455
28.2 Linguistic Differences: UK-USA ... 456
28.3 English around the world ... 459
28.4 Tables and Overviews ... 460
28.4.1 Types of companies ... 460
28.4.2 Official holidays and translations ... 462
28.4.3 Country-specific holidays ... 463
28.4.4 Translated geographical names ... 465
28.4.5 Temperature conversion table ... 466
28.4.6 Weights and measures ... 466
28.5 Electronic Guidelines on Internet ... 467

29 False friends game ... 468

Die Autoren ... 471
Weitere Literatur ... 472

Teil 1: E-mails in English

Autor: Sander Schroevers

Zweifellos sind E-Mails nach wie vor das wichtigste Kommunikationsmittel im Berufsleben. Durch sie bleiben wir in Kontakt mit unseren Unternehmen und bekommen die Möglichkeit, über unterschiedliche Zeitzonen hinweg zu kommunizieren. Dieses Kapitel »E-mails in English« soll Ihnen dabei helfen, das Kommunikationsmedium auch in der Fremdsprache gerne zu nutzen. Wenn Sie das umsetzen, was Sie hier lesen, können Sie die elektronische Kommunikation produktiver in Ihren internationalen Geschäftskontakten einsetzen.

Dieses Kapitel deckt alle wichtigen Bereiche des Geschäftslebens ab und ist in thematische Einheiten gegliedert, um Ihnen einen schnellen Zugriff zu ermöglichen. Sie bekommen einerseits das nötige Handwerkszeug, um geschäftliche E-Mails effektiv verfassen zu können, und bauen andererseits systematisch Sprachsicherheit und somit Selbstvertrauen auf.

1 An E-mail’s Anatomy

This paragraph focuses on the specific elements of English business e-mails, that we don’t always pay attention to, but can make all the difference.

1.1 Subject Lines That Work

The subject line is one of the two most critical parts of an e-mail message. Most people (approximately 80%) make decisions on reading and responding based on the subject line and the identity of the sender, not on a first-in – first-out basis. Nevertheless a subject line seems to be one of the most neglected lines in e-mails.

How to make subject lines in English

The first step is to consider what your reader needs or wants to know from the subject line:

- Ideally, it is a summary of your message.
- Just like in journalism or direct mail: the more active and informative phrases are, the quicker they result in action. That’s why mentioning essential information like who, what, when already in the subject line is advisable. Try to keep it short and simple (›k-i-s-s‹) and avoid vague indications like *project* or *update* etc.
- Always try to write subject lines that stimulate the reader to open your message. Should you need anything specific from the addressee, then introduce this in the subject line.
- Subject lines are also handy for people who wish to archive messages. Therefore make sure that they aren’t left blank and that the subject line relates to the subject of the message. Avoid lines like: *one more thing* or *on second thoughts*, if you think that your message might be archived.

Examples !

☑	Good news Schaffhausen project
☑	Action needed by 4 p.m.
☑	November 27 committee meeting
☑	Update
☑	Status report

RE: automatically inserted
Another thing is that when choosing ›Reply‹ most e-mail programs automatically insert ›RE:‹ (short for *regarding* or *reply*).

The same happens after choosing ›Forward‹ when ›FW:‹ is inserted. The problem is – and certainly you know this from your e-mails in German – that when a message goes back and forth several times, it might lead to unnecessary automatically expanded subject lines. This can easily result in subject lines such as: »Fw: Re: Aw: Re: Aw: Feedback on seminar Julle«. You may therefore simply want to change subject lines sometimes. This also allows you to show the progression in an e-mail correspondence.

!

Example

I: Request for finance Hamburg project
II: Feedback requested – financing Hamburg project
III: Feedback provided – Hamburg project
IV: Hamburg project – finance request approved

1.2 Common Salutations and Openings

1.2.1 Salutations

Salutations or greetings can be formal or informal, depending on the situation or the relationship. And of course e-mail doesn't always follow the rules of formal business correspondence.

First name or last name?
Do bear in mind however that many English-speaking people will be quicker on first-name terms, whereas for German-speaking people it is less common to use one's first name in an e-mail message. Therefore be careful not to appear too distant in a culture which moves to first names easily because in addressing people with a more formal address, you do. And this could indicate you don't consider being friendly to your correspondent. Perhaps the reason lies in the fact that in the English language there is no difference between *Sie* and *Du*, as they both are translated with *you*.

!

Important

A clear indication that it's all right to move to the first-person familiar is when a person signs her or his e-mail with the first name only. You may also wish to take the first step yourself by writing something like: *»Dear Helen (if I may)«*.

Formal or informal?

Which salutation to use may also depend on your company's e-mail policy. The table below gives an overview of the possible salutations:

Type	English	German
You do not know who you are writing to:	▪ Dear Sir or Madam ▪ Dear clients ▪ Hi everyone	Sehr geehrte Damen und Herren,
You know the person but you've never written to or met this person	▪ Dear Mr Smith ▪ Dear Mrs Wade ▪ Dear Dr Young	Sehr geehrter Herr Müller, Sehr geehrte Frau Reusch,
The person is a little bit closer	Dear Sophie Reusch	Liebe Frau Reusch,
The person is a close business contact or she/he has signed her or his e-mail with the first name	▪ Dear Sophie ▪ Hello, Sophie * ▪ Hi, Sophie * ▪ Sophie ▪ Hi, ▪ Hello,	Liebe Sophie,
Several person/ closer contact	Hi everyone	Hallo zusammen

* Please note the extra comma!

!

Important

Ms or *Mrs*? *Ms* is used more frequently in the meantime as this term does not disclose the marital status. Only if the addressee refers to herself as *Mrs*, do you assume this salutation. The English *Miss* is out of date just as is the German *Fräulein*. *Dear Sirs* or *Dear Gentlemen* also seems old fashioned nowadays.

Professions or positions in salutations

Just like it is possible in German to mention a profession or position in the opening without using a person's name, this can also be done in English. In this case, the specific word must be written with a capital. For instance as in: Dear Colleague, Dear Webmaster, etc.

Non-gendered salutations/several persons

When sending bulk e-mail invitations, try to use non-gendered salutations like *colleagues* or *friends*. *To whom it may concern* still seems to function in e-mails, though its use appears to be on the decline. Nowadays e-mail writers prefer to use salutations like: *Hi all, Hi there, Dear All, Dear Team, Dear Co-workers* and so on.

Woman or man?

With certain languages you may not always be sure whether you are writing to a man or a woman. In cases where you aren't sure, it is acceptable to write the full name in the salutation. For example: *Dear Moriko Kira* (this is a Japanese name, where *Moriko* is the female first name, and *Kira* is the family name). In Asian cultures (e.g. Japan, Korea, Vietnam, but also in Hungary) the family name comes first. Thus: *Mrs. Kira Moriko.* Family names in Slavic languages often have masculine and feminine versions. The latter can be recognised by the female suffix, often ending with ›a‹ or ›e‹.

No salutations?

Is it necessary to always use a salutation or greeting? Not always, although it usually is. But in back-and-forth e-mail correspondence, for instance, salutations quickly seem to be disappearing. And perhaps there is no need to identify or reinforce the parameters over and over again. The same applies for a quick answer to a short question for people who know each other well. Also e-mails among colleagues that are part of an ongoing conversation do not require a salutation or greeting.

Checklist: formal or informal salutations

1	Is the addressee outside the organisation? Then you usually need a formal salutation.
2	Is the addressee a colleague or a friend? Then you can use an informal salutation, or even begin with the person's first name.
3	Have you had previous contact? Then choose between formal and informal, depending on that contact.
4	Note how the sender addressed you. You probably want to return the same salutation.

Punctuation marks and abbreviations

Should there be a colon, a comma or no punctuation after the salutation? The right answer depends on the country you are e-mailing to.

!

Important

no punctuation: Dear Mr Smith

colon: Dear Mr Smith:

In other English speaking areas a comma is used: Dear Mr Smith,

When using abbreviations there is another important difference you should pay attention to:

Important !

Contractions in British English are generally written without a full stop, e.g. *Mr, Mrs* and *Ms* – American English usually uses a full stop however, called *period* in North America, e.g. *Mr., Mrs.* and *Ms.*

🇬🇧 *Mrs/Mr*

🇺🇸 *Mrs./Mr.*

Vocabulary:
colon: Doppelpunkt
punctuation: Satzzeichen
contraction: Zusammenziehung
🇬🇧 full stop/ 🇺🇸 period: Punkt

1.2.2 Opening sentences

Use one of the following phrases to refer to earlier contact or to give the reason why you are writing.

Formal: referring to earlier contact

- I am writing with regard to your recent e-mail.
- Referring to your request for information, …
- I'm writing with reference to order number KULIP-1.
- Further to your last e-mail, …
- I am mailing this via the ›Contact us‹ link on your web shop. I would like to ask you …
- Your name was given to me by …

Informal: referring to an earlier contact

- Just a quick note to say I really appreciated …
- I got your name from Dr Stampstaaf.
- Re your e-mail … (*instead of formal:* Further to your last e-mail …)

Giving the reason for writing

- Our reason for contacting you is the following: …
- *Informal:* I'm writing about …
- As discussed this morning in our telephone conversation,
- It is our pleasure to inform you of …

- As we agreed during …
- As requested in your e-mail of …
- I am writing in connection with …
- We would like to inform you about …
- We would like to draw your attention to the following: …
- Thank you for your e-mail and your interest in ...
- Thank you for the enquiry you made via our website.

! **Important**

Note that in English the first phrase after the salutation always starts with a capital letter, whereas in German it starts with a small letter.

1.2.3 Small talk

Although the German translation for small talk is *Geplauder*, this social skill can have an important function in Anglophone cultures because small talk is not only the ability to conduct a conversation, but also a method of showing some friendliness. This naturally influences the way e-mails are written. People in North America tend to add a bit more of a personal or emotional note in their correspondence than people in German-speaking areas, although the actual choice of words depends of course on the social and professional hierarchy.

! **Example**

Dear Thomas
I hope you had a pleasant trip and that your accommodation is fine. Although the weather can be quite cold at this time of year, I'm sure you will like the old city. I'm writing to tell you how happy I am to hear the good news on the new business deal. My congratulations on the contract. I'm sure that it's only the beginning of our work in the Baltic market. And how are Aynur and the kids? Please give them my warmest regards.

- I hope you had a great weekend?
- I'm writing to tell you how happy I am to hear your good news. My congratulations on your recent marriage.
- I hope you're well, and give my regards to your family.
- It would be so nice to have you over one day here in Munich.

1.3 Ending an E-mail

1.3.1 Closing remarks

In English e-mails it is common to include a closing remark to let readers know that they have reached the end of a message. A closing may also be used to express your gratitude, or what you expect the reader to do (e.g. answer, provide information, etc.).

Standard closing remarks

- I look forward to hearing from you soon.
- We look forward to welcoming you to Düsseldorf.
- I look forward to receiving your advice on this matter.
- We should be glad to receive this information.
- We hope we have been of help to you.
- We trust to have furnished you with all the necessary information.

Timed closing remarks

In certain situations your choice of words might be influenced by the pressure of time. The phrases below show an increasing amount of pressure:

- We hope for an early reply
- I look forward to receiving this information as soon as possible.
- I would appreciate a reply asap.
- Please deal with this matter urgently. Can I expect a reply from you by tomorrow morning, please?

Vocabulary:

increasing: wachsend
asap: schnellstens (as soon as possible)

Offering further information or service

- Should you need any further information about … we will be happy to assist you.
- If you'd like any more details, just let us know.
- Should you have any further questions, we stand readily at your disposal.
- If we can be of service in any way?

Thanks

- Finally, we wish to express our appreciation for the cooperation we received from your company's employees during the audit.
- Thank you again for your interest in our company.
- Thank you in advance for your cooperation.

Announcing activities

- I hope I may contact you later on this matter.
- Mr/Mrs ... will contact you at an early date to explain the details.
- We'll inform you on a weekly basis about ...
- We will forward the report as soon as possible.
- We'll be glad to provide you with further details.
- We shall inform you as soon as we have the requested products in stock again.

Informal

- I'm looking forward to ... (+ ~ing).
- Please feel free to contact me.
- If you'd like more details, let me know.
- Just give me a call if you have any questions.
- Have a nice weekend.
- Speak to you soon.

1.3.2 Correct closing expressions

The closing or ending of an e-mail should correspond to the salutation. Informal salutation means informal closing; formal salutation means formal closing; no salutation means no closing.

Type	Salutations	Closings
You do not know who you are writing to:	Dear Sir or Madam Dear clients	Yours faithfully
You know the person but you've never written to or met the person:	Dear Mr Smith Dear Mrs Wade Dear Dr Young	(UK) Yours sincerely (US) Sincerely (yours) (US) Cordially yours
The person is a little bit closer:	Dear Sophie Reusch	Best regards With best regards
The person is a close business contact or she/he has signed her or his e-mail with the first name:	Dear Sophie Hello, Sophie Hi, Sophie Sophie Hi, Hello,	Best regards With best regards If the person is also a good personal friend: Kind regards Best wishes

Punctuation

As mentioned earlier there is a punctuation difference between British English and American English. But besides this, the order of the two words is also reversed:

Important

no punctuation: Yours sincerely

comma: Sincerely yours,

1.4 Signatures and Disclaimers

1.4.1 Signatures

Make sure that your signature follows the international standards. Mention telephone and fax numbers with the appropriate country codes. Also note that the way of using spaces in numbers may differ from country to country. Sometimes city names must be translated to English. Foreign addresses can be difficult for someone who doesn't speak the language, or has a different database structure. Therefore it is best to write street names out in full without abbreviations. For the same reason it is advisable to translate the word *Postfach* to P.O. Box (an abbreviation of Post Office Box). Signatures often include a one-line description of the service the company provides. It is a subtle form of marketing.

Example

Thorsten Wächter
Muster GmbH
Musterstrasse 10 (*or* P.O. Box 123)
10100 Berlin
Germany
tel. +49-(0)30-123 4567
fax +49-(0)30-123 4589
e-mail thorsten.waechter@muster-gmbh.de
www.muster-gmbh.de

Leadership Symposium 20XX – To be held at the Muster College of Art and Design, Muster University, London.

Create an English version

Most e-mail programs allow you to make several signatures, usually by going to ›Preferences‹ and then into ›Signature‹. This way you can make a specific English version besides your German one. You can set the preferences of the program so that the signature you use most is the standard version.

1.4.2 Disclaimers

A disclaimer is a statement intended to specify or delimit the rights and obligations in connection with a dispatched e-mail. Although the legal status of e-mail disclaimers is relative in some countries, you may want to use one or more of the sample texts below.

!

Examples

This message and any attachments are intended for the named addressee(s) only and may contain information that is privileged and/or confidential. If you receive this message in error, please delete it and immediately notify the sender. Any copying, dissemination or disclosure, either whole or partial, by a person who is not the named addressee is prohibited. Virus scanning software is used, but any liability for viruses or other devices which remain in this message or any attachments is disclaimed.

This e-mail may contain confidential and/or privileged information. Any unauthorised copying, disclosure or distribution of the material in this e-mail or of parts hereof is strictly forbidden.

For legal and security reasons the information provided in this e-mail is not legally binding. Upon request ABC GmbH would be pleased to provide you with a legally binding confirmation in written form.

Nothing in this e-mail message amounts to a contractual or any other legal commitment on the part of ABC GmbH unless confirmed by a communication signed on behalf of ABC GmbH.

Because it can be annoying to see a long signature block repeated with back-and-forth messages, you may just want to use a hyperlink with a short phrase. This is especially helpful for people who want to print e-mail messages. To avoid the extra texts you may want to use a phrase like:

- Please visit our e-mail disclaimer for further details.
- For further information visit www.abc.de/disclaimer.

Vocabulary:

disclaimer: Ausschlussklausel
liability: Haftung, Verantwortlichkeit
disclosure: Offenbarung
commitment: Verpflichtung

1.4.3 Out-of-office assistant

You can create a customised message to inform people to contact someone else, or otherwise advise them on when you will be available again.

Examples !

Thank you for your message – this is an automated response.
I am currently away from the office, and will return on Monday morning, 26 June.
I will respond to your message upon my return. For any urgent matters during my absence, please call the office's general number (below).
Thank you for your message. I will be out of office until 25 April included. For urgent matters please contact my colleague Chiara Chessa on +39(0)4916314 or chiara@chessa.it.

1.5 E-mail Techniques: about CC and BCC

In daily life lots of people tend to send CCs or BCCs too easily. It's probably better to think a little bit about who should really get the message. A copy is best sent to people when they need the specific information for their work. But there is another disadvantage of sending too many CCs. When you send an e-mail to one person there is a big chance that you will get a reply, but if you send the message to many people the actual response rate drops to approximately five percent. If you think someone needs or doesn't need to be Cc'd on messages you can mention this as seen in the examples below.

Examples !

Let me know if you still want to be Cc'd on everything, or if you'd prefer we don't clog your inbox.
I have Cc'd Maryam Salehi, who handles all translations, as well as Mr. Bagherian, the CEO.

By the way, the term BCC might be referred to differently in other languages: CCI in French or CCO in Spanish.

2 A Reader-friendly Approach

Most of us receive around fifty e-mails a day, but many of these messages simply fail to communicate. Writing reader-friendly e-mails means thinking about your readers and their needs.

2.1 When to Use E-mail and When Not?

Some people can get so used to e-mailing, that they also use it in situations where they simply shouldn't. Already in German daily business life, the choice between a phone call or an e-mail is substantial, all the more in an international context. And although there aren't any explicit differences between the German and Anglophone business cultures, certain southern cultures are still inclined to be more personal. As a result a phone call might be more effective than a written message there. On the other hand, a telephone call with certain Asian cultures might prove difficult at times. In such cases, an electronic message could be easier. The following general checklist can be helpful when choosing between e-mail and telephone.

Checklist: to send or not to send?

Send an e-mail	▪ if you need a written record to document the correspondence.
	▪ if your primary reason for writing is to pass on information or ask a question.
	▪ if you need to inform a larger group of people at once.
Don't send an e-mail	▪ if an e-mail seems too difficult to write.
	▪ if you are answering more complex e-mails.
	▪ if you think the content of your message is: personally sensitive, potentially embarrassing, contains confidential information or legal implications, e.g. trade secrets, job performance or hiring and firing.
	▪ if you need direct feed-back, brainstorming, inspiration or a serious discussion. Hold a conference call or plan a meeting instead.
	▪ if you have a quick question that needs an answer right away. Then make a phone call, or walk down the hall (if possible).

2.2 Structuring the Information

People who receive larger numbers of e-mails probably won't have the time to read each mail word for word. They will scan messages instead of reading them. Another thing that you should realise is that people often deal with e-mails in combination with other activities. A third point is that an inbox offers a great deal of competition. A writer of an e-mail needs to convince a reader twice: firstly to click on the message, and secondly to continue reading the content.

2.2.1 Writing effectively for the monitor

E-mail is usually read from a computer monitor or PDA screen. Studies have shown that people read slower on a screen by about 25%. Below are some recommendations for readability of e-mails:

- E-mail content has half the word count of a printed letter.
- Get to the point in the first sentence.
- Write in inverted pyramid style (conclusion before details).
- Use short sentences in a simple and direct style because when people are indeed scanning a message ›less is more‹.
- Organize your content into logical paragraphs. Avoid long blocks of texts. Vary the length of both sentences and paragraphs. Leave extra space (between the lines) after each paragraph. Think about using short two or three-word subheadings at the beginning of paragraphs.
- Try to keep short messages within one screen, and long messages within a maximum of four screens.
- Try using bullet lists, which are easy to scan and read.
- Avoid using italics as they quickly become illegible.
- However, don't overdo it. Try to find the right balance between emphasis and readability.

2.2.2 Less is more

E-mails have made business correspondence more compact and most of all faster. Paragraphs in e-mail have become smaller.

- The effectiveness of e-mails is maximised by keeping them short and simple.
- That's why the language is simple, clear and direct.
- Sentences are generally short. An advantage of short sentences is that they are easier to read on-screen.

- There is more use of contractions (I've *instead of* I have, *etc.*) than in paper letters.
- If you make the reader scroll, it better be worthwhile.

Example: e-mail too long and badly structured !

Dear Mrs Salehi

Following our pleasant meeting at Jamshidiyeh, I am pleased to inform you about our specific needs for the Farsi version of our on-line brochure. Firstly we will be needing adaptations of the profile page (where we could use the beautiful image from ›Keynoosh‹ you suggested), secondly a general introduction text concerning our publications, thirdly, idem for the workshops, and last but not least, a contact information overview. We have decided to accept your offer. If you are indeed interested in participating in this project, please e-mail us, sending your e-mail to the attention of Miss Maryam at maryam@muster-gmbh.de. She will send you all specific details. She is also the contact person should you need additional information. Thank you in advance for your cooperation in this matter.

Yours sincerely

Vocabulary:
emphasis: Nachdruck
contraction: Zusammenziehung
worthwhile: der Mühe wert

Example: e-mail short, simple, well structured !

Dear Mrs Salehi

I am pleased to confirm our interest in your offer.

For the Farsi version of our website we'd need:

- a profile page,
- an introduction for the publications,
- an introduction for the workshops
- and contact information.

May I ask you to contact Miss Maryam at maryam@muster-gmbh.de for further details. I'm delighted that our meeting at Jamshidiyeh has had such results.

Yours sincerely

2.2.3 Techniques to make e-mails better structured

One technique is using specific linking words or expressions, indicating to the reader what the connection is between descriptions, situations or for instance, actions.

Enumerations

- First(ly)
- Second(ly)
- Third(ly)
- In the first place
- To begin with
- First of all
- Another
- Then there is
- Next
- Finally
- Last(ly)
- Last but not least

Extra remarks

If you want to add an extra argument or remark it looks nicer not only to use words like *and* or *also*. but to varv a bit. The table below offers some alternatives.

- Furthermore, …
- Additionally, …
- What is more, …
- Moreover, …
- …as well as …
- On another point, …
- In addition, …
- Besides, …
- On top of that, …

Temporal indications

- Then, …
- Later, …
- In the end, …
- Prior to this, …
- Subsequently, …
- Eventually, …

Summarising

If you want to give an overview of the points mentioned, you can indicate this to the reader bv using one of the following expressions.

- To conclude, …
- To sum it up, …
- In conclusion, …
- Summarising, …
- To recap briefly, …
- All in all, …
- In other words, …
- i.e.
- That's to say, …

Miscellaneous linking words

Below are some other useful expressions for structuring the information in correspondence or reports.

- For example, …
- For instance, …
- e.g., …
- As a result, …
- For this reason, …
- Therefore, …
- Actually, …
- As a matter of fact, …
- In fact, …
- In relation to, …
- With reference to …
- Regarding, …
- In general, …
- On the whole, …
- Usually, …

Vocabulary:
linking: Koppelung
prior to this: zuvor
subsequently: anschließend

2.3 Formal or Informal?

Without wanting to revert to stereotypes, it is fair to say that the British tend to be polite, whereas North Americans can be direct and optimistic in their communication. Intercultural research clearly shows that German communication can be characterised as more direct than British communication. Let's take a closer look at such different ways of expressing ourselves, and focus our attention on the differences between formal and informal, as well as the differences between direct and indirect or polite writing styles.

Informal, direct	Formal, indirect
I'm writing about …	I am writing with regard to…
Re your e-mail, …	Further to your last e-mail, …
Just a quick note to arrange a day to meet. When would it suit you?	I'm writing to arrange a date for our meeting. What day would be convenient for you?
Don't forget …	I would like to remind you that …
So see you in Chemnitz, and do give me a call if anything changes.	I look forward to meeting you in Chemnitz. Please let me know if you need to change the arrangements.
Please send me	I'm interested in receiving
But …; Also …; So …	However …; In addition …; Therefore …
Shall I … ?	Would you like me to … ?
What about ... (+ ~ ing)?	Have you thought of ... (+ ~ ing)?
Just give me a call if you have any questions. My number is +49-12345.	Please feel free to contact me if you have any questions. My direct line is +49-12345.

Shorter words – more informal

It is also said that loan words of Latin origin sound quite formal, whereas shorter English words sound more informal. Below you can compare the alternatives (the words of English origin are in brackets).

- assistance (help),
- possess (have),

- inform (tell),
- requirements (needs),
- obtain (get),
- request (ask for),
- verify (check),
- provide (give),
- repair (fix),
- enquire (ask).

2.3.1 Colloquial language

E-mail can feel like face-to-face conversation, which is usually shorter and more to the point. Whether a colloquial choice of words is appropriate, has to do with the relationship with the person to whom you're writing. And as vocabulary is situational; you will need to make a judgment about the company culture and your relationship to the person with whom you're communicating. Research shows that readers of e-mails are more tolerant of a spoken-language writing style than readers of printed letters. Besides, short sentences are easier to read on-screen.

Useful phrases

- Just letting you know that I'll be arriving late.
- Could you ...? *(instead of formal:* I was wondering if you could ...)
- Just a short note about ... *(instead of formal:* I am writing in connection with)
- That's good for me. *(instead of formal:* I would like to confirm)
- I'm leaving for Shanghai, but I'll try to be there.

2.3.2 More personal style

Contemporary English business letters tend to be written slightly more personally then their German counterparts. You may notice this in the three examples below, where pronouns have often been used like *we*, *us* or *our*. Although the language that is used is personal, its style is less direct than speech.

Useful phrases

- We very much enjoyed meeting you in Berlin last Friday. I have now talked to Mrs Funk about our meeting and I am pleased to say ...
- Following our discussion earlier this month, I regret to inform you ...
- As we agreed on the phone this afternoon, I am mailing you a PDF file with ...

- Please feel free to contact me if you have any questions.
- I think your idea would work really well.
- May I suggest that I call you at your convenience to discuss the matter further?

2.4 Netiquette Guidelines

By their nature, e-mail conversations tend to be rather informal and quickly typed messages. During the evolution of e-mail certain basic rules of conduct have developed, which is generally referred to as *netiquette*. Below is a selection of these guidelines:

- Unless you are using encryption, you should assume that mail is not secure. Never write in an e-mail anything you wouldn't want to write on a postcard.
- Don't send emotional messages (called *flames*) even if you are provoked. It is better to calm down first.
- It is not always permissible to forward just anything. Sometimes forwarding may be in violation of copyright laws.

Delivery and read receipts

A delivery receipt informs someone that an e-mail message was delivered to the recipient's mailbox. A second option, the so-called read receipt, informs that the message has been opened as well. The point is that the recipient has the option to decline sending read receipts, and certain e-mail programs also don't support read receipts. In daily life, you should keep in mind that asking for receipts means you are in fact freezing someone else's computer until they click on a dialogue box.

Electronic humour

When you are communicating orally, you have the advantage of vocal variety and other non-verbal communication. All of that is absent in e-mail. It is therefore important to be careful with jokes. It is better to save anecdotes for in-person gatherings. Electronic humour can be a risk especially when corresponding with other cultures because jokes don't like to travel. On the other hand, it is good to realise that in Anglophone business cultures, jokes are much more accepted and can often play an important role in creating the right professional atmosphere.

Emoticons :-)

Although e-mails often tend to be more informal, the smiley created from a colon-hyphen-close pare probably has no place in a business document. Therefore, to keep e-mails professional simply avoid all frivolous emoticons.

Gender-neutral language

With gender-neutral language one can avoid the usage of masculine pronouns. Especially in the USA and Canada many people find the usage of masculine language inaccurate or even offensive.

- Using a term like chairperson instead of chairman is a good example of acknowledging that a woman in authority will also read the e-mail in question.
- Other options for gender-neutral language are to recast sentences into plural, to use the generic pronoun *one*, to replace typical masculine words like *his* or *he* with articles (*a, an, the, this, these*, etc.), or to use plural pronouns (*they, them, their*).

Errors

Due to the nature of e-mails occasional errors (while undesirable) are not uncommon. Research has shown that readers have become much more permissive in that aspect compared to the days of paper communication. Nevertheless, errors in style, punctuation or spelling influence a professional image or, to some extent, a company's reputation. Therefore, spell-check your e-mail. Most software packages (also webmail) have an automated feature for this. Proofread e-mails, too before sending them.

2.5 How to Deal with Attachments

People don't always expect and/or welcome the information given in attachments. Besides, attachments may transmit destructive viruses and worms. It is therefore not surprising that people have become reluctant to open attachments, unless of course, they trust the sender and are informed in the message itself.

2.5.1 Best ways to deal with attachments

- Inform the addressee about attachments by indicating this in the subject line and/or in the beginning of the message. This is even more important since attachments aren't always indicated as such, and can only be seen after scrolling to the end of the message. This is caused by the way different software programs react on each other.

!

Examples

Itinerary Berlin conference – 2 files attached.
The first line might say: Two files attached.

- When an attachment is long and complex, you might consider summarising it briefly in the body of the e-mail message.
- If the purpose of a message is to simply forward an attached file, then the cover e-mail should be written very briefly, and should explain where the recipient should focus her or his attention on.
- And finally always try to give instructions to the recipient about what to do with an attachment. Do you expect the reader to file or forward it, or do you need comments?

Examples !

Example: summarising the attachment:
Dear Mrs Kawashima
I am pleased to attach the new final report for Cargill Brazil. This report shows the outcome of …
Example: indicate the addressee to forward the attachment:
Attached is the proposal for our new website. Can you forward it to all your managers?
Example: instructions on what to do with the attachment:
I've attached the draft of the final report. Thanks for using the ›track changes‹ feature to comment. I would specifically like to draw your attention to the section on Kyoto and Maya Bay. I will be interested in hearing your thoughts about this report's findings at our next Brazil summit.

2.5.2 Useful phrases

Indicate attachments

- Enclosed please find the necessary technical specifications.
- We are happy to enclose …
- You will find particulars of …
- A route description has been enclosed.
- For the general terms please refer to the attachment.
- Please see our prices on enclosed price list.
- Enclosed please find our latest catalogue.
- Please find enclosed some low resolution jpg images.
- Please find attached my report.
- I'm sending you our general conditions as a PDF file.

Important !

Make it a habit to attach the file before composing the message.
And double-check whether you attached the right file.

Instructions

- That document is stored in PDF format. You need the free Adobe Acrobat Reader to open the PDF file.
- By clicking on the hyperlink, you will be directed to the appropriate information on our website.
- Because the attached document is a bit complex, I have briefly summarised it below.
- All documents have been scanned for viruses and are compatible with Mac and PC.

Say what to do with the attachment
I've attached the draft of the final report. Please use the ›track changes‹ feature in MS Word for any comments.

Here is the design for the new Swiss brochure. We'd like to know your comments by Wednesday next week.

I have attached the revised quarterly budget. Could you forward it to all the Düsseldorf managers?

Explaining errors when sending attachments

- I'm sorry to say that I forgot to attach the attachment in my previous mail. Here it is.
- Did you mean to send me the minutes? They weren't attached. Would you mind sending them again?

2.5.3 Avoiding attachments

You can avoid attachments by simply pasting the content of short files into the body of an e-mail message. This always works unless formatting is important. In this way you also save people downloading time because business travellers may have to use slow phone connections in hotels. Also users of smart phones may be charged per Mb. And they don't want to download a file for many minutes to discover there is a picture they never wanted anyway.

Vocabulary:
general terms and conditions of trade (GTCT): allgemeine Geschäftsbedingungen (AGB)

Checklist: e-mail basics

- Are the correct addressees in the To, Cc or Bcc fields?
- Think of the reader's specific information needs.
- Know which key points must be covered.
- Decide upon a good subject line.
- In the event of attachments: add these first and indicate them in the subject line or first sentences. When an attachment is complex, summarise it briefly in the body of the e-mail message. Give instructions to the recipient about what to do with an attachment.
- Announce the main point of the e-mail in the beginning.
- Write paragraphs in the ›most-important-first structure‹ (the so-called inverted pyramid).
- Write in an active and direct way.
- Try to use short paragraphs.
- Make use of headers and bullet points.
- Avoid jargon, specific abbreviations or technical language unknown to readers.
- Never forget that an e-mail might have unseen readers: do not send an e-mail containing confidential information or one that has legal implications.

3 Common Business Situations

The business situations which follow are intended to cover a wide range of interactions typical of international correspondence. The material in this paragraph is intended as a sort of phrase bank and as a basis for further expansion.

3.1 Requesting Information or Favours

E-mails in which information is requested or given are among the most common topics in inboxes. When requesting information, it is well-advised to explain things clearly. Start for instance by explaining how you obtained the addressee's contact data and then write what particular information you would like to have or are interested in.

Bear in mind that writing in a foreign language doesn't mean simply translating a text from German. Different cultures can use other ways of asking for things. As mentioned, British English formulates requests in a slightly more indirect way. For instance, by using modal auxiliaries, or using the word *please* more often. This is shown in the examples below:

Examples !

Formal: to an unknown addressee

Dear Sir or Madam

During my last visit to the GDS trade fair at Messe Düsseldorf, I saw a sample of your products. Our company specialises in the manufacture of shoemaker's machines and we are looking for a reliable supplier.

May I ask you to send us full information and details of your latest models? If possible quote prices in euros please.

Yours faithfully

Silke Mertens

Formal: to a known addressee

Dear Mr Roll

I'm writing with regard to booking one of your workshops. As we are organising an in-company conference at our firm ›Innovate Consulting‹ this March, we'd be interested in finding out whether you are able to give a presentation of about 45 minutes? Our focus is on creating value through a company-wide branding approach.

We would be grateful for some information about your prices and availability.

Should you have any further questions, do not hesitate to contact me.

Yours sincerely

Mr Pirouz Malekzadeh

Managing Director

Informal: to a colleague
Dear Pirouz
Could you send me the latest material on Mahram ketchup please? I will need it to prepare the pitch in Milan next week. I'd appreciate your help on this. Let's talk next week and see how things are going.
Best regards
Sander

Vocabulary:
modal auxiliaries: Modalverben
supplier: Lieferant
to quote: ein Angebot machen

3.1.1 Useful phrases

Formal: introductions

- I was interested to see your advertisement in the latest issue of ›Deutschland‹ magazine.
- I understand you are manufacturers of ...
- We have read about your company in the trade press.
- Mrs. Zeurpiet, we have not met; however, I would be grateful for your advice.

Formal: request for information

- I wonder if you could ... ?
- Do you think I could have ... ?
- I'd be grateful if you could ...
- I would like to know ...
- We're interested in finding out ...
- We would like to receive ...
- I wonder if you could ...
- Could you perhaps attach your current catalogue and price list as a MS Word or PDF file?
- Please send us information about your product range and prices.
- Please send full details of your prices, discounts, terms of payment and delivery times.

Informal: request for information

- Can you tell me a little more about ... ?
- Can I have ... ?
- Please could you ... ?
- Please send me ...

- Just a quick note to remind you to …
- Your name and address were passed to me by …
- We met last Thursday at the Leipzig Trade Fair.

Scales of politeness

British English uses different scales of politeness depending on the familiarity between people. The examples below are ascending:

- Why don't you send me the attachment?
- Send me the attachment, won't you?
- Send me the attachment, will you?
- Send me the attachment, would you?
- Won't you send me the attachment?

It isn't really possible to make such distinctions in the German language system. But when writing in English it nevertheless matters. It is therefore advised to use the polite or indirect form when you're not exactly sure about which form to use. This means that you should use *might* instead of *may*, or *could* instead of *can*. For the same reason you should be careful with translating *ich möchte* with *I want*.

Important !

Anglophone cultures don't often use a direct *no*. Therefore a phrase like:
I wonder if this is the best solution translates best with *Nein …*

3.2 Hotel or Conference Enquiries

Examples !

Reservation: hotel and technical equipment

Dear Sir or Madam

For our company Muster GmbH from Düsseldorf, I would like to make a group booking for 10 guests. It concerns a three day meeting including accommodation. The date of arrival is Friday, June 13. We'll need two double rooms and six single rooms on a half board basis. There are no special requests.

The rooms will be paid for by the participants, and the meeting can be billed to the organiser: Muster GmbH, Düsseldorf.

For the conference, we'd like a meeting arrangement of: coffee (10:30 AM) and lunch (1:00 PM). We are looking for a medium-sized conference hall with three separate meeting rooms.

Each equipped with WLAN, whiteboards and flipcharts.

Could you please inform me on availability and prices? Thanking you in advance.

Yours faithfully

Jule Funk

Muster GmbH

Reservation: Restaurant
Dear Sir or Madam
I would like to reserve a table for four people in your non-smoking area, for tomorrow April 1st at noon. Please make the reservation in the name of Muster GmbH from Düsseldorf. Thanking you in advance.
Yours faithfully
Jule Funk

Useful phrases

- Please reserve a single room with bath for Mr James Bond during his visit in Aachen from April 25th through May 2nd (date of departure).
- Can you offer a discount for a group of twenty-five?
- May I ask you to please quote the inclusive price?
- I attach a copy of my intended itinerary.
- Layla Kawashima will settle the bill on behalf of Cargill.
- Unfortunately I have to cancel our reservation at your hotel.
- I should like to reserve a conference hall for approximately thirty people. Is it possible to have seating in a U-shape?
- Please send us details of available conference equipment, as well as simultaneous interpretation and translation services.
- Could you inform us how much the charge per half day is for a second beamer, flip-chart and white-board?
- We would like to be picked up from the conference by coach.

3.2.1 Useful vocabulary

Hotel

queen-size bed 🇺🇸	1,5 m breites Bett
king-size bed 🇺🇸	2 m breites Bett
settle (the bill)	begleichen
booking request	Buchungsanfrage
executive class	Businessclass
double bed	Doppelbett, französisches Bett
double room	Doppelzimmer
single room	Einzelzimmer
half board	Halbpension
high season	Hauptsaison

low/off season	Nachsaison/Vorsaison
itinerary	Reiseroute, Wegbeschreibung
B and B, bed and breakfast	Übernachtung mit Frühstück
full board	Vollpension
no. of rooms	Zimmeranzahl
twin-bedded room	Zweibettzimer

Conference equipment

meeting room	Besprechungsraum
seating	Bestuhlung
stage	Bühne
fax service	Fax-Service
flip chart	Flip-Chart
big screen	Großbildschirm
Internet access	Internetanschluss
air conditioning	Klimaanlage
conference room	Konferenzraum
photocopier	Kopiergerät
laser pointer	Laserpointer
integrated loudspeaker	Lautsprecheranlage
microphone facilities	Mikrofonanlage
flip-over	Präsentationsmappe
lectern	Rednerpult
reach 25m.	Reichweite 25 m
rows	Reihen
wireless presenter	schnurlose Computerfern-bedienung
secretarial support	Sekretariatsarbeiten
room dividers	Stellwände
meeting and accommodation as flat rate	Tagung und Übernachtung als Pauschale
U-shape	U-form
dimming	Verdunkelung
video conference	Videokonferenz
whiteboard	Weißwandtafel
wireless local area network, WLAN	W-Lan

3.3 Giving Enquiries

3.3.1 FYI: for your information

One of the most commonly sent e-mails is the FYI. This acronym stands for *for your information*. FYI is commonly used in e-mail or memo messages to flag the message as an informational message that does not require a response. This is typically indicated in the subject line: »FYI: annual sales meeting«. Sending people an e-mail without informing them you are actually sending it as an FYI might trick them into opening a mail, they didn't want to open as generally an FYI doesn't require someone's immediate attention. Because busy readers might not always read all the subject lines, it is also recommendable to repeat the FYI again in the first line of the body of the text.

Useful phrases

- For your information ...
- This is to inform you...
- Just so you know...
- I wanted to let you know that...
- This is just to tell you...
- For your files I attach ...

3.3.2 Answering requests

The phrases below offer content for those e-mails in which information is given based upon e-mail requests.

!

Examples

Formal

Dear Sir or Madam
Muster GmbH from Linz in Austria, is seeking bids for the production of several trade fair stands. May I ask you to send us your bid if you are interested?
Detailed specifications are attached. Also please note that Muster GmbH doesn't wish to work with products that are in anyway associated with environmental hazards in the production, manufacturing or maintenance of materials.
The deadline for bids is June 26.
Feel free to contact me should you need more information.
Yours faithfully

Less formal
Dear Mr Sanchez
I was wondering if I could ask you something regarding the new product development analyst. I believe you have known him for some time and I would be grateful for any information you could give us. This will of course be treated with strictest confidence. Thank you in advance for your help in this matter.
Yours sincerely

Informal
Hi Betty,
I wanted to get the June 26 business unit notes to you as soon as possible. Please get back to me if there's any information that I can supply.
Regards

3.3.3 Useful phrases

Formal: enterprise and product information

- Thank you for your e-mail of 14 July enquiring about ...
- Your enquiry/query concerning our products ...
- You will note that our ... is on special offer.
- We are also happy to send you full details of our prices, discounts, terms of payment and delivery times.

Informal: enterprise and product information

- John, it's been a while since we have spoken. I'm attaching a document that gives you full details of ...
- I took the liberty to attach a list of some of our clients, which you will see include ...
- I understand that you are looking for ...
- In reply to your e-mail, here ...
- Allow us to draw your special attention to ...
- Our products are carefully tested to ensure quality.
- All our products carry a one-year guarantee.
- Of course we replace all defective parts free of charge.

Formal: more time needed

- We are behind with production.
- Because of problems with our supplier ...
- We therefore cannot guarantee delivery by June 26.
- We offer you our sincere apologies for this.
- We shall do our utmost to ...

Informal: more time needed

- I might need some more time after all.
- I'm sorry to inform you that we will not make the deadline. But we're doing everything we can to sort it out.
- I hope you will understand my position.
- I'll be in touch again soon with more details.

3.4 Change of Address

These days, more and more changes of address come by way of e-mail. When informing foreign relations, always try formatting address information according to international standards. By the way, the so-called *Landeskürzel* (e.g. D) should no longer be used.

Useful phrases

- Change of address notification: ...
- Our head office has moved to Hanover.
- We have now opened a new branch in Vienna.
- Our address has changed and is now as follows: ...
- May we ask you to please forward any correspondence to our new address?
- Change of address: as of July 1: ...
- Change of address as of May 2nd: Devon House, Devon Centre, Manchester, M4 5KC.
- Our telephone numbers remain unchanged.
- Our telephone number now is: ...

3.5 Appointments

Making appointments for meetings, teleconferences or lunches are the order of the day. In general such messages can be brief, but make sure that you don't cancel appointments too abruptly. As already mentioned, all too direct communication might be misunderstood.

!

Examples

Informal

Dear Sara Lou,

Could we meet in the next few days? I'm open this Thursday and Friday for lunch or in the afternoons.

Cheers,

Sander

Refusing
Sorry Sander, I'm not available then. I've got an offsite client meeting. How about next week? Bisoux, Sara Lou

More formal
Dear team managers
I'm setting up a meeting at 10 a.m. on Nov. 27, together with the Marketing Department from head office. It's to review and evaluate the performance of the brand against competitors. Please let me know if you will be able to attend as soon as possible, so I can circulate the agenda.
Best regards
Martin Saunders

Refusing
Dear Martin
Thank you for your kind invitation. Unfortunately, I have another appointment on that day. But please let me know how it went.
Best regards
Sara

3.5.1 Useful phrases

To ask for an appointment

- I'm writing to arrange a time for our meeting. Could we meet on Friday, June 26, in the afternoon at 3 p.m.?
- Would be very pleased if you could come to a meeting here on 1 April.
- The meeting will last all morning and will have an informal agenda.
- Your presence at the meeting will be most useful.
- Please everyone let me know if you will be able to attend by next Wednesday at the latest.

Confirming proposals

- Yes, I think I should be able to make next Friday morning at The Savoy.
- I'll get back to you later today to confirm our appointment.
- Just to confirm my visit to you, on Friday 13 at 10 a.m. ET (Eastern Time Zone).
- Looking forward to meeting you next week.
- Please let me know if there's anything I can prepare.

Refusing/postponing an appointment

!

Example: Example: refusing an invitation (formal style)

Thank you for your kind invitation.
Unfortunately, I have another appointment on Friday. Please accept my apologies. In the case any reports arise from the discussion on Central Europe, I would be most grateful to receive a copy. I hope we will have the opportunity to meet on another occasion in the near future.

- I'm afraid I can't manage next Friday.
- I‹m not available for lunch on either day, but would 3 p.m on Friday suit you?
- I'm out of the office until 11 p.m., but any time after that would be fine.
- This is to let you know, that I will not be able to attend the meeting in Berlin.
- Please accept my sincere apologies for cancelling our appointment on such short notice.
- I had an unavoidable emergency that prevented me from keeping our appointment.

3.6 Invitations

When accepting or declining invitations, note that in English one often tends to use adjectives like: *happy*, *delighted* or *pleased*, which in German might sound somewhat exaggerated at times. Nevertheless, it is advisable to express enthusiasm or regret with slightly more emphasis.

!

Examples

Invitation for a conference

Muster GmbH has the pleasure to invite you to the Conference ›XYZ‹, organised in Lucerne on 22 May 20XX, in association with ABC-AG. The conference will take place at Auditorium KKL Luzern (Zentralstrasse 9) from 9 a.m. to 5.30 p.m. The programme will be updated regularly on the website of Muster GmbH. Please complete the attached form and return to …

Invitation for lunch

Dear Mr Haas
I would like to take this opportunity to invite you for our monthly business unit lunch at Tantris, on Johann-Fichte-Strasse 7. Friday, 13 February at 13:30 o'clock. Your attendance will be very welcome.

3.6.1 Useful phrases

Inviting and RSVP

- We would very much like to invite you for a presentation given by Mrs. Maryam Salehi on May 22 in the Khajeh Nasir Hall, which starts at 11 a.m.
- It would be a pleasure to receive you at our annual trade exhibition.
- I would like to take this opportunity to invite you for our monthly sales manager meeting.
- The pleasure of your company is requested at the ...
- Would you please send an answer to our invitation as soon as possible.
- We would very much appreciate it if we could receive your decision before 26 June.
- RSVP (regrets only): presentation@muster.de

Route descriptions and other information

- We hereby attach a route description as a PDF file.
- If this information is not accurate or if you need additional information about your travel plans or information on our company, please call, e-mail or fax me directly. That way, we will receive your message in time to make the appropriate changes or additions.
- When you arrive, just ask for me at reception.
- Again, we are very honoured that you will be visiting us, and we look forward to a successful business relationship between our two companies.

Formal: accepting/declining an invitation

- May I thank the board for their kind invitation to ... on May 22 and I take great pleasure in accepting it.
- Thank you for your kind invitation. I would be delighted to attend the ...
- I'm very sorry that I will miss the meeting. Please accept my apologies.
- Mrs Funk thanks PressEasy Ltd for their kind invitation but due to a previous engagement she regrets she is unable to accept.

Informal: accepting/declining an invitation

Example: accepting an invitation !

Thanks a lot for inviting me. I'd love to come to the meeting.
Would it be okay to bring Silke Mertens as well? She's in charge of the whole series.
I met her in Frankfurt last year.

- Thanks a lot for your kind invitation.
- Unfortunately, I have something else on my agenda on that day.
- I'd really love to come to your lecture.

Canceling an appointment

When you deem it necessary to cancel an event and inform the participants by e-mail, it is important to find the proper tone of voice and courtesy.

!

Example

Dear Sirs,

Due to circumstances beyond the control of Muster GmbH, the banquet unfortunately had to be cancelled. Muster GmbH apologises for any inconvenience caused.

Sincerely yours

Useful phrases

- Owing to circumstances beyond our control, we will unfortunately need to …
- Regrettably, due to unexpected events Dr. Doğan must cancel the lecture of June 26.
- Mr Jorritsma sends his sincere apologies for his absence from the conference, and …

3.6.2 Indicating date and time

While trying to arrange an appointment, pay attention to using the proper expressions concerning date and time. Take special precautions if your message will be sent internationally to prevent misunderstandings: Spell out dates, as in Germany, 02/05/XX means May 2, 20XX; but in the United States this means February 5, 20XX. There are more specific differences between German and English, e.g. the twelve-hour clock. In case of doubt try to double check appointments; some people ask for confirmation by e-mail or fax. Electronic agendas like MS Outlook offer practical functionalities that automatically send reminders per e-mail.

Months

January	Januar	July	Juli
February	Februar	August	August
March	März	September	September
April	April	October	Oktober
May	Mai	November	November
June	Juni	December	Dezember

Dates

26 June, reads as: the twenty-sixth of June.
June 26, reads as: June twenty-sixth.
26th June, reads as: June, the twenty-sixth.
2019, reads as: two thousand and nineteen.
2019, reads as: two thousand nineteen.

Please note that years are usually pronounced in pairs: e.g. nineteen ninety-nine (1999).

Ordinal numbers

1st – first	8th – eighth (only one ›t‹)
2nd – second	9th – ninth (no ›e‹)
3rd – third	10th – tenth
4th – fourth	11th – eleventh
5th – fifth	12th – twelfth (›f‹ not ›v‹)
6th – sixth	20th – twentieth
7th – seventh	21st – twenty-first etc.

Days

Monday	Montag
Tuesday	Dienstag
Wednesday	Mittwoch
Thursday	Donnerstag
Friday	Freitag
Saturday	Samstag, Sonnabend
Sunday	Sonntag

today	heute
tomorrow	morgen
yesterday	gestern
the day before yesterday	vorgestern
the day after tomorrow	übermorgen
as from today as of today	von heute an

this Thursday	diesen Donnerstag
next Tuesday	nächsten Dienstag
by Friday	bis Freitag
on Saturday	am Samstag, Sonnabend
a week on Monday	Montag in einer Woche
a week from Monday	
in a fortnight's time in two weeks' time	in vierzehn Tagen
every Monday	jeden Montag, montags
on Mondays	
in 6 days' time	in sechs Tagen
last/next month	im letzten/nächsten Monat
last week	letzte Woche

Times of the day

in the morning	morgens, am Morgen
early morning	der frühe Morgen
morning	Morgen, Vormittag
midday	Mittag
lunchtime	Mittagszeit
before lunch	vor dem Mittag
after lunch	nach dem Mittag
in the afternoon	nachmittags, am Nachmittag
afternoon	Nachmittag
late afternoon	Spätnachmittag
evening	Abend
in the evening	abends, am Abend
in the morning	am Vormittag

What time?

Perception of time may differ from culture to culture. In the UK, for instance, people tend to give each other a margin of several minutes. The Irish saying ›When God created time, he created plenty of it' is of course only a generalisation, it nevertheless indicates that punctuality might be looked upon differently from country to country.

Therefore, always plan meetings with a sufficient margin because they may start a little bit later than expected. And also don't let yourself be too much guided by what you are used to in Germany. Apparently, six out of ten American managers are late for their appointments, according to research. This »CEO's quarter of an hour's grace« also costs companies a lot of money.

at 8 (o'clock) in the morning/8 a.m.	um 08:00 Uhr
at 8 (o'clock) in the evening/8 p.m.	um 20:00 Uhr
till 5 (o'clock) in the evening/5 p.m.	bis 17:00 Uhr
after three (o'clock)	nach 15:00 Uhr
before three (o'clock)	vor 15:00 Uhr
(UK) as from 3 p.m. (US) as of 3 p.m.	ab 15:00 Uhr
between three and five (o'clock)	zwischen 15 und 17 Uhr
a quarter past nine	viertel nach neun
a quarter to nine	viertel vor neun
three thirty	halb vier
(UK) half eight (half past eight)	halb neun (*not*: halb acht!)
twenty-five minutes past ten	zehn Uhr fünfundzwanzig
five to twelve	fünf vor zwölf
noontime	Mittag
half an hour	eine halbe Stunde
quarter of an hour	eine Viertelstunde
three quarters of an hour	eine Dreiviertelstunde

3.7 Sending Agendas and Minutes

There are certain standard items that belong to an agenda: like a title, followed by the date, time and venue of the meeting and a list of the people who will be attending it. In English the minutes always follow the agenda exactly. Each section of the notes is identified by the number of the item on the agenda, or the heading taken from the agenda. Below are some useful hints for making summaries.

Checklist: summary of a meeting

- **Include the date**: avoid vague descriptions like *yesterday* or *last week's meeting*.
- **List the participants**: as members of a department change from time to time, it is better to list people by name.
- **Indicate action points** to the discussed topics. Also designate responsibility, mention the possible deadline and describe each action. This ensures the action and serves as a record.

!

Examples

Agenda

Muster GmbH Management Team Meeting
Tues. Nov. 27, 20XX at 10-12 a.m. Rm. 69, 2nd floor
1 Confirmation of minutes
2 Matters arising from Oct. 25 meeting
3 Reports from task groups
4 Late items, AOB (any other business)
5 Closing

Minutes

Dear all
Below are the minutes from the April 1, 20XX board teleconference. Attendees: Sylvia, Udo, David and Chiara. Absent with regrets: John, Etsuko. Staff: Truus.
1 Approval of agenda as published: carried unanimously.
2 Motion F:04.10 to approve the Frankfurt bid for 20XX
3 Date of next teleconference: May 10, 20XX.
4 The meeting was adjourned at 5:30 p.m. EST.

Useful phrases

- Attached are the approved meeting minutes for the October annual meeting held October 2, 20XX.
- Minutes of Berlin team meeting, 27th May 20XX, 11-12.30 a.m., be approved and signed. (Noted)
- The next meeting for the London Project Management meeting will be on Fri. Nov. 13, 11 a.m,. in room 69-C.
- Could you please check the agenda, and be in touch with your questions and concerns? Thanks in advance.
- Attached is the report from our last meeting in Berlin, which was held on July 14. Should anyone miss anything, than please notify me before next Friday.

- It was decided to delay action until the next meeting.
- Please find below the agenda of …
- The notes from the February 13 Business Unit meeting include …
- Please take time to consider the minutes …

3.8 Refusing a Request

The actual task of refusing someone something and yet maintaining goodwill is not the easiest one. But in the business world it simply does not suffice to refuse a request politely. There are methods however that will ensure that customers will want to continue doing business. Let us look at the four-step format below:

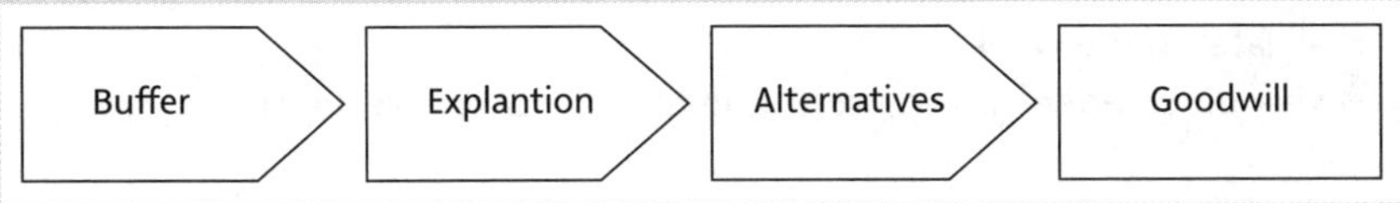

Checklist: negative messages

- **Buffer statement**: the first two sentences contain general neutral and positive remarks. They must be related to the refusal in the next paragraph.
- **Explanation**: in the second part of the e-mail explain why you cannot fulfil the request. Give logical reasons before you mention the negative message at the end of paragraph two. Also make sure the refusal is clear to avoid further debate on this topic.
- **Alternatives**: in the third paragraph try to demonstrate your concern for the reader. This way the reader also regains the psychological freedom after your refusal.
- **Goodwill ending**: which comes last is often remembered best. Therefore pay attention to a friendly ending.

3.8.1 Useful phrases

Buffer

- Thank you for bringing this matter to my attention.
- We regret to inform you that …
- With regard to your request, unfortunately we are not able to …

Explanation

- There appears to have been a misunderstanding.
- I have spoken to my line manager, and unfortunately we aren't able to ...
- As we are bound by regulations of the ...

Alternatives

- But I am sure we can find an acceptable compromise. I suggest you contact a@b.c to arrange this matter.
- We are however prepared to let you have the requested goods on credit.
- We could replace the damaged goods with ...

Goodwill ending

- We offer you our sincere apologies for this.
- I have arranged for a member of our customer services team to give you a call later in the week.
- I very much hope you will continue to use our services in the future.

3.8.2 Stylistic stand back: negative – positive

Sometimes a negative phrase can sound much more positive by replacing the negative element which is in the word *not* by an alternative word. The table below gives some examples of this.

Implicitly negative	Explicitly negative
unable	not able
impossible	not possible
insignificant	not significant
irrelevant	not relevant
different	not the same
lacks	does not have
prevented	did not allow
unless	if ... not

3.9 Complaints

Complaints can be best dealt with in a neutral polite tone. To maintain a good working relationship, you might need to make a useful suggestion to solve the problem brought to your attention. Especially North American customers can be used to higher levels of personal service. In that sense a defensive approach might shut down effective communication. Providing rational explanations for a complaint probably gives better results.

Examples !

Polite request

There seems to be an error in the invoice we received for goods delivered on May 22. As I discussed this morning with your associate Pete Johnsons, Muster GmbH notified you on May 16 of this matter.
May I ask you kindly to revise the billing statement by removing items ABC and sending us a cancelled invoice please? Thank you for your prompt attention to this matter.
Regards

Urgent

I am writing in connection with our order A-01, which arrived this morning. You sent us 11 ... instead of the 110 which we had ordered. This has caused us considerable difficulties, as our production unit needs the goods urgently. Unless we receive the goods by this Wednesday, we will have no choice but to cancel our order. I hope that ABC-AG will deal with this matter promptly.

Useful phrases

- We regret to write you that the products we received Friday, 13th were below the standard we expected.
- Please replace the broken goods as soon as possible.
- We wish to point out an error in the consignment we received yesterday.
- I hope that you will deal with this matter promptly, as it is causing us considerable inconvenience.

3.10 Apologies

When writing a formal e-mail to express regretful acknowledgement of a failure, you can choose from one of the alternatives listed below.

3.10.1 Useful phrases

Formal style

- I was very concerned to learn about your problems.
- We're doing everything we can to resolve this issue.
- Please accept our apologies for the inconvenience caused.
- This was due to circumstances beyond our control.

- I will look into the matter immediately and get back to you within the next few days.
- To compensate for the inconvenience caused by this, I would like to suggest ...
- We realise this is disappointing news to hear, and we apologise for the inconvenience we have caused you.
- We are sending you a ... as a gesture of goodwill ...

More personal style

- Please accept my sincere apologies for cancelling our appointment on such short notice.
- I had an unavoidable emergency that prevented me from keeping the appointment.
- An urgent matter at the head office came up that I just had to deal with immediately.
- On behalf of ABC GmbH, I offer sincere apologies to you for ...
- I'm afraid I had completely misunderstood the situation.
- The fault was entirely mine and I really regret that it occurred.
- I do hope we shall be able to put this unfortunate misunderstanding behind us.
- Once again, my sincere apologies.

Vocabulary:
inconvenience: Unbequemlichkeit
resolve: lösen, beikommen
circumstances: Umstände

3.11 Congratulations and Season's Greetings

In business, personal relationships will benefit from sending greetings on appropriate occasions.

Congratulations

- I was very happy to hear about your promotion to business unit manager. I congratulate you heartily.
- I would like to convey my sincere congratulations on winning the Prix de Rome.
- I am delighted to see that all your work has been recognised in this way.
- Please accept my warmest congratulations on your promotion to business unit manager.
- Once again my very best wishes.

Season's greetings

- We wish you a Merry Christmas and a happy New Year!
- Here is wishing you a happy holdiday season and all the best in the New Year.

Informal: congratulations

- Well done!
- I'm so glad to hear the news about …
- Our sincere congratulations

3.12 Thanks

Formal style

- Our company is very grateful for the trouble you have taken to …
- I'm writing to let you know how pleased Muster GmbH was with …
- If the occasion arises, I hope you will allow us to return the favour.

More personal style

- I wanted to thank you again for such an enjoyable lunch yesterday.
- I am just writing to say what an excellent job you did of the Cologne project.
- Many thanks again for your help yesterday. If we can return the favour sometime, please let us know.

Short informal thanks

- Just a quick note to say many thanks for …
- We really appreciate it.
- Thanks a lot/a million

Vocabulary:
convey: überbringen
favour: Gunst, Gefallen

3.13 Payments and Reminders

This paragraph is intended for anyone who is faced with the task of sending English e-mails in the financial world. Given the fact that some conventions are different (see the paragraph on numbers and currency symbols), it is good to know about such differences in advance.

!

Example

Dear Mr Holzbauer

We can confirm that we shipped your items, and that this completes your order. You can track the status of this order, online at: www.muster.de. Please note that tracking information may not be available immediately.

A copy of our invoice is attached as a PDF file. We kindly request you to remit the invoice amount within 14 days after invoice date.

Sincerely

Customer Service Department

3.13.1 Useful phrases

Sending invoices

- Please find enclosed a PDF copy of the invoice for our services.
- The total amount payable is: …
- We request your remittance of the following balance by payment in advance: € 1,963.
- We request you to make remittance for the amount stated on the invoice to our account no later than 27 November 20XX.
- We request you to make payment within 14 days to one of our accounts.
- We enclose a copy of our invoice for the goods delivered to you on … against order number …
- We ask you to settle the invoice by May 2.

Reminding payments

Intercultural text analyses have shown that differences exist between German and English in the way debt collection correspondence addresses readers. But although the tone might seem polite, the legal consequences are perfectly identical. Below are some useful phrases.

- We refer you to our conditions of payment.
- The outstanding invoices however must be paid by the end of this month.
- We should like to kindly remind you that our invoice no. 09-01 is due.
- In case you might have settled the account in the meantime, please ignore this e-mail.
- We kindly ask for early settlement of our invoice.
- We request payment of the invoice to account number …
- We would be grateful if you could adjust the invoice accordingly.
- We have as yet had no reply to our request for payment.
- We must now insist on immediate payment.
- We need to take steps to collect the amount due.
- We hope you will understand our position.

Confirmations, inquiries and thanks

- We acknowledge receipt of the consignment.
- Could you please send us an amended invoice?
- At the current rate of exchange ...
- We have instructed our bank to pay you the sum owed.
- We have given instructions to our bank to make payment of € 1,963 against your invoice.
- We have transferred the sum of ... to your account.
- We thank you for your prompt payment of our invoice.

3.13.2 Useful vocabulary

bank connection	Bankverbindung
concerns	Betreff
BIC	BIC
date	Datum
foreign currency	Devisen, Fremdwährungen
total amount	Gesamtbetrag
fee	Honorar
IBAN	IBAN
bank account number	Kontonummer
Value Added Tax	Mehrwertsteuer
VAT	MwSt.
incidental expenses	Nebenkosten
invoice no.	Rechnungs- Nr.
amount of the invoice	Rechnungsbetrag
from	von
ATTN	z. Hd.
at the current rate of exchange	zum Tageskurs

3.14 Making Offers

Useful phrases

- We thank you for your enquiry about ...
- We are pleased to submit the following quotation ...
- We offer you the goods you specified as follows: ...

- Enclosed please find a sample of …
- The prices are inclusive/exclusive of VAT.
- We can give you a discount of 13%.
- As long as supplies last.
- The offer/quotation excludes transportation costs.
- We hereby confirm your telephone order of …
- This offer is non-binding and valid while supplies last.
- The goods will remain our legal property until full payment has been received.
- The prices and terms of delivery mentioned are binding until 27 November.
- Please refer to our conditions of sale for further particulars.
- You may rely on a quick and careful execution of your order.

3.15 Delivery and Incoterms

Useful phrases

- Delivery will be made immediately on receipt of your remittance.
- The goods will be transported by air.
- The merchandise is delivered ex factory (EXW).
- The consignment consists of: …
- We take extra care in the packaging of our goods.
- We have booked your order and will do our best to carry out your request to your satisfaction.
- The products were sent to you today; the tracking number is: …

Vocabulary:
remittance: Überweisung
consignment: Versand
tracking: Sendungsverfolgung

Incoterms

The Incoterms 2000 (International Commercial Terms: Internationale Regeln für die Auslegung von Handelsklauseln) are a series of international sales terms which serve to divide transaction costs and responsibilities between buyer and seller. They are usually mentioned in an abbreviation-city combination (e.g. our prices are FOB Hamburg).

Abbreviation	English	German
Group E		
EXW	Ex Works	Ab Werk
Group F		
FCA	Free Carrier	Frei Frachtführer
FAS	Free Alongside Ship	Frei Längsseite Schiff
FOB	Free On Board	Frei an Bord
Group C		
CFR	Cost and Freight	Kosten und Fracht
CIF	Cost, Insurance and Freight	Kosten, Versicherung, Fracht
CPT	Carriage Paid To	Frachtfrei
CIP	Carriage and Insurance Paid To	Frachtfrei versichert
Group D		
DAF	Delivered at Frontier	Geliefert Grenze
DES	Delivered Ex Ship	Geliefert ab Schiff
DEQ	Delivered Ex Quay	Geliefert ab Kai
DDU	Delivered Duty Unpaid	Geliefert unverzollt
DDP	Delivered Duty Paid	Geliefert verzollt

3.16 Numbers and Currency Symbols

When writing decimals or amounts of money, the English language observes a few other conventions compared to German.

- The most important difference probably is the reverse use of commas and full stops (periods):
  19,95% (German) → 19.95% (English)
  16.090km (German) → 10,000 miles (English)
- Amounts in round figures don't necessarily need a comma with two decimals behind it:
  25,00 EUR (German) → EUR 25 (English)
- The position of the currency can be placed before or behind the amount, depending on the local linguistic convention. There is no space between the pound sign and the amount in English.

- Another option is to use the ISO abbreviations for currencies in stead of the euro or pound sign. Notice the different position of the currency abbreviations:
  12.904,90 EUR (German) → GBP 10,000 (English)
- Please note that Australian texts may use a space instead of a comma, and Swiss texts often use an apostrophe to separate the thousands.

3.16.1 Indicating larger numbers

For describing larger amounts or numbers in the English language you may come across the following abbreviations:

- thousand: K
- million: M
- billion (*in German:* Milliarde): bn *or* B
- trillion (*in German:* Billion): T

Expressing numbers in alphabetic characters, such as *forty-three billion Canadian Dollars'*, finds application in official documents and in a formal or contractual context. But for sending e-mails around the globe, it's better to use figures.

3.16.2 Monetary and currency symbols

Monetary units, such as dollars or pound sterling, are often abbreviated with their own currency symbols. Note that in the United Kingdom a middle dot is often used as the decimal point on price stickers (e.g.: £6·95). Besides the currency symbols, you may also wish to write the international monetary abbreviations as stated in the list of currencies from the International Organization for Standardization (ISO 4217: Currency names and code elements).

List of currencies

Country	Currency	Sign	ISO	Fract.
Australia	Australian dollar	$	AUD	Cent
Bahamas	Bahamian dollar	$	BSD	Cent
Canada	Canadian dollar	$	CAD	Cent
Cyprus	Cypriot pound	£	CYP	Cent
Gibraltar	Gibraltar pound	£	GIP	Penny
Hong Kong	Hong Kong dollar	$	HKD	Ho
India	Indian rupee	Rs	INR	Paisa
Ireland	Euro	€	EUR	Cent
Malaysia	Malaysian ringgit	RM	MYR	Sen
Malta	Maltese lira	₤	MTL	Cent
New Zealand	New Zealand dollar	$	NZD	Cent
Nigeria	Nigerian naira	₦	NGN	Kobo
Pakistan	Pakistani rupee	Rs	PKR	Paisa
Singapore	Singapore dollar	$	SGD	Cent
South Africa	South African rand	R	ZAR	Cent
United Kingdom	British pound	£	GBP	Penny
United States	United States dollar	$	USD	Cent

Please note the differences in writing the word *euro*:

- The word *euro* is written in small letters in English.
- EU legislation prescribes using the words *euro* and *cent* both in singular and plural. But common usage in the rest of the English-speaking world is to use the natural plural in -s. Also most financial media in the UK prefer *euros* and *cents* as the plural forms.

4 Practical Reference

4.1 Useful Vocabulary and Key Terms

4.1.1 Digital vocabulary

to	an
attachment	Anlage
@ (at sign)	At-Zeichen, Affenschwanz
subject	Betrifft, Betreff
hyphen	Bindestrich
file	Datei
e-mail	die E-Mail (D), das E-Mail (A, CH)
wireless	drahtlos
hard disk	Festplatte
to download	herunterladen
dot	Punkt
slash	Schrägstrich
back slash	umgekehrter Schrägstrich
underscore	Unterstrich
to forward	weiterleiten

4.1.2 Vocabulary: function keys

PgUp (page up)	Bild hoch
PgDn (page down)	Bild runter
PrtSc (Print Screen)	Druck
Insert	Einfg
End	Ende
Delete	Entf
Home	Post
Ctrl (control)	Strg
Shift	Ums

4.1.3 Key terms: e-mails

ASCII	American Standard Code for Information Interchange. A standard set of codes used for representing text and keyboard-control characters. Pronounced as: [aski]
Auto responder	A prewritten reply to an e-mail message, which is sent automatically
Bounced message	An e-mail that is returned to the sender because it cannot be delivered
Compression	File management technique that shrinks data for easy transportation. For instance: ZIP or RAR
Emoticons	Electronic symbols indicating emotions, e.g.: smileys
Encryption	Encoding or scrambling of an e-mail message or attachment for privacy reasons
Filter	A feature of an e-mail program to sort incoming messages
Flame	Angry or insulting e-mail messages
Forward	Retransmitting an e-mail message to other recipients
Group list	A group of e-mail addresses that can be addressed as a single recipient
Instant messaging (IM)	Direct exchange of messages with other people online
MIME	›Multipurpose Internet Mail Extensions‹: automatic recognition and display of file types
Priority	Designates an e-mail message's importance: high, normal or low priority
Signature	A personal identifier at the end of an e-mail message, informing on other contact data
Subject line	Topic of an e-mail message
Thread	An ongoing e-mail conversation
Word wrap	A feature in e-mail programs that allows insertion of soft returns at the right-side margins of an e-mail message

4.2 Abbreviations and Acronyms

Because in e-mails people tend to write very quickly, many electronic acronyms have found their way into e-mail messages. In the table below you can find a selected overview of electronic acronyms and/or abbreviations that have found their way into business e-mail messages.

Only use abbreviations yourself if your readers (the intended as well as the hidden readers) will recognize and understand them. And don't use too many abbreviations, as they can make a sentence hard to read. Furthermore, it's advisable to clarify an uncommon abbreviation by writing it out on the first reference and citing the abbreviation in parentheses.

A/P	Accounts Payable
AA	Author's Alterations
abbr	Abbreviation, Abbreviated
abr	Abridged
abt	About
acc	According
acct	Account
acq	Acquired, Acquisition
ACWP	Actual Cost of Work Performed
Afaik	As Far As I Know
agg	Aggregated
AGM	Annual General Meeting
AKA	Also Known As
ANI	Automatic Number Identification
ans	Answer
apt	Apartment
ASAP	As Soon As Possible
ASL	Above Sea Level
ASP	Average Selling Price
ASR	Automatic Speech Recognition
asst	Assistant
AST	Atlantic Standard Time
Att	Attorney
Attn	Attention
Av	Avenue, Avenida
AWB	Air-Way Bill
AY	Academic Year

AYR	At Your Risk
B4	Before
BC	Before Christ
BE	Bill of Exchange
BKA	Better Known As
BL	Bill of Lading
bldg	Building
Bn	Billion
BP	Bill Payable
BPO	Business Process Outsourcing
BS	Bill of Sale
BSI	British Standards Institution
bsmt	Basement
BTW	By The Way
BW	Black and White
C&F	Cost And Freight
c/o	Care Of
c/w	Coming With
CAP	Customer Administration Panel
CBD	Cash Before Delivery
CBI	Confidential Business Information
CC	Carbon Copy, Customer Copy
CC	Chamber of Commerce
CCC	Customer Care Center
CDT	Central Daylight Time
CEO	Chief Executive Officer
CET	Central European Time, Centraal Eur.Tijd
CFO	Chief Financial Officer
CFP	Call For Proposals, Call For Papers
CFV	Call For Votes
ch	Chapter, Chapitre

chmn	Chairman
CIO	Chief Information Officer
cmte	Committee
Co	County
co	Care Of
Corp	Corporation
CPI	Consumer Price Index
CST	Central Standard Time
CT	Central Time
ctr	Center
DIY	Do It Yourself market
dna	Does Not Apply
DoB	Date Of Birth
e.g.	Exempli Gratia
EDT	Eastern Daylight Time
Esq	Esquire
EST	Eastern Standard Time
ewt	Elsewhere Taken
F	Floor
F2F	Face to Face
FAO	For the Attention Off
FAQ	Frequently Asked Question(s)
ff	Following
FMCG	Fast-Moving Consumer Goods
FOB	Free on Board
FSS	Financial Services Sector
FTC	Free Trade Committee
FY	Fiscal Year
FYI	For Your Information
GA	General Average
GL	Ground Level

GMT	Greenwich Mean Time
H&S	Health And Safety
HR	Human Resource
i.e.	Id Est
i/c	In Charge
ICT	Information & Communication Technology
Imho	In My Humble Opinion
imo	In My Opinion
IOW	In Other Words
ITT	Invitation To Tender
JIT	Just In Time
KISS	Keep It Short and Simple
L/C	Letter of Credit
LL	Lines
M/F	Male or Female
MD	Managing Director
mfg	Manufacturing
misc	Miscellaneous
MoM	Minutes Of Meeting
mph	Miles Per Hour
MSGS	Messages
n/a	Not Applicable
NB	Nota bene
NDA	Non-Disclosure Agreement
NLT	No Later Than
NOTA	None Of The Above
o/a	On Account
PA	Personal Assistant
pct	Percent, Procent
pkwy	Parkway
PLS	Please

PM	Post Meridiem, Past Mid-day
PM	Prime Minister
pp	Pages
PPI	Producers Price Index
PS	Pound Sterling
PT	Part-Time
PTO	Patent and Trademark Office
Pty	Property, Proprietary
REC'D	Received
RGDS	Regards
RoI	Return On Investment
SMB	Small or Medium Business
SME	Small and Medium-sized Enterprises
SOHO	Small Office, Home Office
Spec	Specification
SSN	Social Security Number
T/B	Top and Bottom
TBC	To Be Considered
THX	Thanks
TIA	Thanks In Advance
TS/SI	Top Secret/Sensitive Information
TWIC	To Whom It Concerns
USASI	USA Standards Institute
USPTO	United States Patent and Trademark Office
VSB	Very Small Business
w/	With
w/o	Without
WRT	With Regards To

A special e-mail style

Besides such expressions another form of abbreviated words in e-mail developed. In this style, the vowels are often deleted, or parts of words are replaced by homonyms:

! **Example**

Subject: Thx for yr msg
Re your msg on our ans machine: gr8 you've got a back-up :-)
Hv 2 work now. CU,
Silke

Although you may occasionally come across this kind of new abbreviation, it is nevertheless discouraged from using them in formal business correspondence.

Full stops or periods?

There is a tendency in Great-Britain to write abbreviations without a full stop (period). British usage favours omitting the full stop in abbreviations which include the first and last letters of a single word, such as *Mr, Mrs, Ms, Dr* or *St* – American usage on the contrary prefers: *Mr., Mrs., Ms., Dr. and St.*, with full stops. Two other common abbreviations are *a.m.* and *p.m.*, like in: *11.00 a.m.* or *five p.m.* Note that these are not capitalised in British usage. Funnily enough American usage here prefers capitals and no full stops, so *11:00 AM* or *five PM*.

4.3 E-mail Features

4.3.1 Formatting e-mail for foreign screens

A common problem is the way e-mails look on the screen of the receiver. I tested this once by sending an e-mail to five different people, whom I asked to print and fax the message to me. Not one of them looked like the original. Some of the main differences that appeared: specific German letters (ß, Ü, Ä, etc.) were replaced by strings of other characters; Internet addresses no longer worked like hyperlinks; italicised letters didn't show; word wrap influenced the look and feel of the text. The average line length is 75 characters (screen width).

To avoid such discordances in international business you could use the following techniques:

- In your options you can choose ›MIME encoding‹, instead of ›BinHex‹ or ›Uuencode‹. In the ›Options window‹ you can also set lines to wrap automatically at 65 to 75 characters.
- Probably it's best to choose ›plain text‹ (also known as ASCII) in stead of ›HTML‹ in the settings of your e-mail program. Then once you know that the addressee's software is capable of interpreting all symbol codes correctly, you can always opt for fancier settings. One problem with ASCII however, is that the only characters that are sure to be properly transmitted are those with ASCII/ANSI numbers between 32 and 126. Thus, an outgoing German character (usually falling outside the range 32-126) transmitted from a German QWERTZ keyboard is likely to be converted into something else. To be on the safe side you can replace the following typical characters with alternative keyboard combinations.

Character	Alternative	Majuskel	Minuskel
Ä	ae	Alt-142	Alt-132
Ö	oe	Alt-153	Alt-148
Ü	ue	Alt-154	Alt-129
ß	ss	Alt-225	Alt-225

- Another point is the downloading of images that are connected to the content. It might look great before sending, but many people have set their mail software to block automatic picture downloads and other external content in messages (if the content is linked to a server). In the recipient's inbox this results in sloppy areas showing messages that the content needs to be downloaded first. Not necessarily the best first impression.

4.3.2 Templates

Form letters or templates are reusable letter elements. They were invented for a reason, namely because they can save people a lot of time if used properly. In certain jobs people probably need to write the same type of e-mail over and over again, as both purpose and content are essentially the same. The following situations lend themselves to templates:

- Meeting announcements, agendas and minutes,
- Common requests and responses to common questions,
- Sales letters or other marketing messages.
- Regular reports and project updates

In the example below you can see a typical message that is qualified for a template. The fields between square brackets can be typed in manually, but also be connected to an excel spreadsheet (containing product or address information e.g.).

!

Example

This is a reminder of the weekly meeting: [date, time and location].
May I ask you to please send me any additions and/or corrections at least two days before the meeting.
Also, please let me know if you won't be able to attend.
Thanks,
Aynur

Checklist: using e-mail templates

- First analyse your existing e-mails or responses to see what the essential elements are.
- Keep the template files up-to-date over the years.
- Besides features like ›Autotext‹ there are also specific (free) software programs available on Internet to help you streamline the writing process.
- Try to make a habit of always proofreading the mails you create from templates before sending them out.

4.3.3 Identifying international e-mails

People who are used to electronic addresses ending with dot-de or dot-com might have some difficulties with the type of addresses that use a second level domain (SLD). Usually such extra codes indicate an activity (*co* for companies, *gov* for governments, etc.). Such an address contains an extra dot and the specific code, e.g.: www.bbc.co.uk. In fact, quite a number of countries use this type of electronic address. In addition to most Commonwealth countries and South America, countries like Austria, Sweden, Turkey or Japan, also use such URLs.

When trying to locate a website it can be practical to know the suffix of the country in question. The list below gives an overview for Anglophone countries.

Code	English	German
sld*.au	Australia	Australien
.ca	Canada	Kanada
sld.hk	Hong Kong	Hongkong
sld.in	India	Indien
.ie	Ireland	Irland
sld.nz	New Zealand	Neuseeland
sld.za	South Africa	Südafrika
sld.uk	United Kingdom	Großbritannien
.com, .gov *etc.*	United States	Vereinigte Staaten
* *sld.* means *second level domain*, e.g.: www.independent.co.uk		

4.3.4 Legal implications of e-mail

The first publicised case, in which an e-mail was used as evidence, was the Iran-Contra scandal, which involved the White House and Lt. Col. Oliver North. In the past few years, e-mails have often made the news headlines. The lesson learned is that e-mails, written in a certain way, can result in companies being confronted with legal liability. This can happen in three ways basically:

- When the content of the mail involves exaggerations, guarantees, leaking of sensitive information and/or the spreading of rumours.
- People can be presumed to have knowledge of the contents of an e-mail once it arrived on their workstation. E-mail can create a responsibility to report in this way.
- Forwarding electronic clippings in an e-mail implies a possible violation of copyright laws.

Vocabulary:
liability: Haftung
presume: annehmen
violation: Übertretung, Verletzung

4.3.5 Responding to e-mail

Recent surveys reveal that we now spend between 30 minutes and four hours or more a day on e-mail-related activities. What tactics can you use to manage the e-mail interruptions? If you compare e-mail to let's say phone calls, then why do we use our precious times replying to certain information? I ask this because on the phone you probably wouldn't respond. However, quite a few people can click on the reply button probably faster than they can pronounce the word *reply*. And they do so despite the fact that many of these messages may need no response at all. Therefore, when a sender is only passing along information and has not asked for a reply, probably just reading, filing or deleting the e-mail suffices.

Quite often it's possible to summarise the key points or questions from several individual messages. Combine your responses into one e-mail that includes answers to questions, provides the necessary details, and so on. Also don't open e-mails you don't really need to read.

By using the questions below you can see whether you respond appropriately and efficiently to the e-mails you receive.

Checklist: responding to e-mail

- Wouldn't it be quicker to reply on the phone or in person than in an e-mail?
- Is a response really necessary? Or can you just file, print out, forward or delete the e-mail?
- Do you need some time to think or calm down first? In this case, don't respond immediately.
- Do you need to inform others by Cc or Bcc?
- In case you decide to copy people, do they really need to have that information, and will they think of it as useful?
- Did you run a spell check?
- Is it necessary for you to respond at this very moment?

Teil 2: Phone Calls in English

Autor: Sander Schroevers

Dieses Kapitel ist konzipiert für Menschen, die im Beruf internationale Telefonate führen müssen. Obwohl jeder weiß, wie man am Telefon erfolgreiche Gespräche führt, fällt dies in einer Fremdsprache um einiges schwerer. Wie reagiert man angemessen auf einen Anruf aus dem Ausland, wenn man darauf nicht vorbereitet ist? Wie hinterlässt man Nachrichten auf Anrufbeantwortern?

Von derartigen Herausforderungen lassen sich viele verunsichern, insbesondere in einer fremden Sprache. Die Telefonsituationen in diesem Kapitel decken weite Bereiche des Geschäftslebens ab. Sie sind in thematisch unterteilt, damit man sich schnell zurechtfindet, wenn man englische Telefonate in der Praxis führen will. Damit Sie mit Sicherheit einen guten ersten Eindruck machen!

Die Texte und Beispiele in diesem Kapitel sollen Ihnen das nötige Grundwissen für effektive Geschäftstelefonate an die Hand geben und somit Ihr sprachliches Selbstvertrauen systematisch aufbauen.

5 Getting Started and Ending a Conversation

When calling in another language it is often difficult finding the right words to start or end a conversation. Do your best to make a good first impression and to end your call in a friendly way.

5.1 Calling according to plan

Making phone calls in another language can be difficult at first, especially for someone who doesn't speak the language fluently yet. That is why important business telephone calls should never be made on the spur of the moment. Because telephone conversations tend to be short and you do not have eye contact, it is difficult to adjust what you are saying as you go along. Advance preparation can be a big help.

Check-list: advance preparation

1. Look up international dialling codes.
2. Decide who the best person is to talk to.
3. Decide who the next best person is to talk to.
4. Decide the objective(s) of the call.
5. Think of specific desired information.
6. Make a list of key points to be covered.
7. Write down what to say in the opening sentences.

Vocabulary:
on the spur of the moment: spontan
objective: Zielsetzung

5.1.1 Beginning a call

When you call someone it is important to observe the following: identify yourself and your company clearly, because there is only one first impression. But also try to make a positive closing, as that is usually best remembered.

Always let the caller hang up first. It is helpful to prepare some expressions for the following situations during the start of a telephone conversation:

- how to introduce yourself with your name and company name,
- how to ask for a specific person, if the phone is answered by someone else,
- how to explain the reason for your call, and ask whether your call is convenient,
- how to leave a message in case the person you wish to talk to isn't available.

In English-speaking cultures it is common to exchange a few polite phrases about unimportant or uncontroversial matters at the beginning and ending of a conversation. This is called ›small talk‹ and considered an important part of building business relationships. For further details please refer to the specific paragraph.

Vocabulary:
observe: beachten
desired: erwünscht
elaborate: näher eingehen

! **Example**

A: Good morning. Tulip Technology. Ali speaking.
B: Hi Ali, this is Jule at Oberbilk Computing
A: Oh, hi Jule. How are you?
B: Good, thanks. Have I rung you at a busy time?
A: No, now is fine. What can I do for you?
A: Hello. Accounts.
B: Hello. It's Czeslawa. Is Albrecht there?
A: No, he isn't. Shall I try someone else for you?
B: No, I think I'd rather leave him a message.
A: Right, one moment. I'm just getting a pen. OK. Go ahead.
B: Well, I need Albrecht to submit an estimate by Thursday.
A: OK, Czeslawa. I'll give him the message. Anything else?
B: No that's it. Thank you very much. Goodbye.

5.1.2 Telephone scripts

In order to make their call more goal oriented, people often work with so-called telephone scripts. These allow a caller to structure a conversation and think in advance about possible answers and changes of topic. Telephone scripts are best printed in a readable size (13 points or more). Also write down some specific translations, the spelling of a name or website etc. It will lead to telephone calls (in another language) with better results.

!

Example

Name and contact details	Mrs. Shizuka Moriwaki 51 E.42nd Street, New York +1-212 661 5151
Own name (in English spelling)	Heiko. That's H for Harry, E for Easy, I for Item, K for King and O for Oliver.
Own (international) telephone number	+49-211-712257
Opening phrase	My name's Heiko Broschek of Train AG. I'm calling about our next meeting.
Is it convenient?	*No:* shall I call back at 2 PM or 4 PM?
Did you receive my report?	*Yes:* can I ask your opinion? *No:* would you like me to e-mail it to you now?
Ending phrase	Thank you for your time. It has been very nice talking to you again.

Vocabulary:
telephone script: Dialogschema

5.2 After the greeting

Try to identify yourself and your company clearly because there is only one first impression. But also try to make a positive closing, as that is usually best remembered. Always let the caller hang up first. At the beginning of a call there are a number of different ways of clarifying who you are. These follow a similar pattern:

Introducing yourself
- Good morning. It's Franziska Hauser here, from head office.
- Hello. My name's Andreas Obermaier from sales.
- Good afternoon, this is Chris from Tulip Technology.

- Hi, Jule speaking, from the Düsseldorf office.
- This is Antje. Is that Jack? Speaking.

Vocabulary:
speaking: am Apparat

! **Important**

Don't say ›hello‹ or ›hi‹, unless you already know a person well. Don't call *yourself* ›Mr‹; however, ›Mrs‹ is fine for women.

Using first names

In contact with Americans, Australians, New Zealanders or Irish, it is normal to switch quickly to using first names. People from cultures that use family names in combination with Mr and Mrs may feel a bit uneasy perhaps. But the social consequence of not being on first-name terms with a person is the risk of appearing distant or even unfriendly. So simply follow the approach of your conversation partner. It would probably sound exaggerated to suggest saying ›Du‹, as there is no difference between ›Du‹ and ›Sie‹ in English.

Many Americans or other English-speaking people commonly use nicknames in business contacts. To address them with their full first name could even look somewhat exaggerated. In the same way as names like Maximilian and Gabriele may be shortened to Max and Gabi, the English language shortens first names. Examples of common nicknames are: Harry for Harold, Tony for Anthony, Bob for Robert, Gene for Eugene, Jack for John, Bill for William, Frank for Francis and Ted for Edward. Irish nicknames can also be spelled in Gaelic sometimes (for example: Seán for John, Liam for William).

Vocabulary:
be on first-name terms with somebody: duzen
nickname: Spitzname
Gaelic: gälisch

What's in a name?

In certain countries other words than first and ›last name‹ may also be used. For instance, in the Republic of Ireland the word ›Christian name‹ is often used in official papers. Also note that ›first name‹ may refer to any forename, not just the very first.

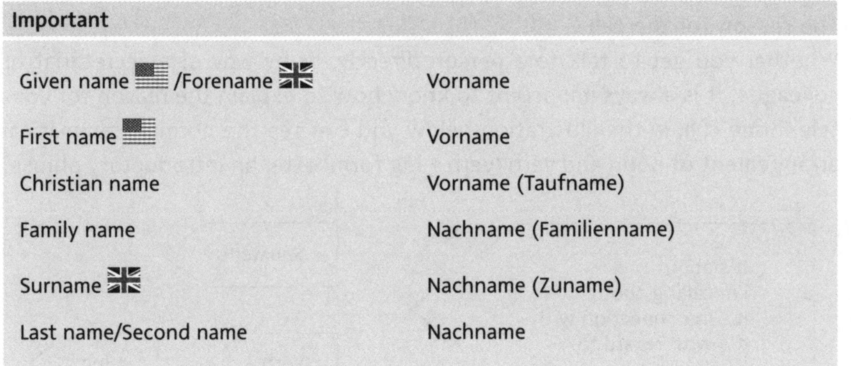

Important

Given name /Forename	Vorname
First name	Vorname
Christian name	Vorname (Taufname)
Family name	Nachname (Familienname)
Surname	Nachname (Zuname)
Last name/Second name	Nachname

Most married women (still) adopt their husband's family name. When a woman decides to use both names (e.g. Hillary Rodham Clinton), the second last name (unlike the practice in German-speaking areas) is the husband's family name. However, when two last names are written with a hyphen, this indicates that it is a double last name.

Asking to speak to someone

When asking to speak to a person it is best to use politer expressions such as: ›could I‹ or ›I'd like to speak to‹ instead of a too direct phrasing like ›I want to speak to‹.

- Could I speak to Jack Miller please?
- Could you put me through to Mrs Schätzing, the import department, please?
- I should like to speak to Mr. Staebel, please.
- I'd like to speak to the head of the purchasing department, please.
- Can I speak to his secretary/assistant, please?

Who's calling please?

- Sorry, who's calling/speaking, please?
- I'm sorry, who shall I say is calling?
- Yes, of course. And your name again?
- Sorry, what did you say your name was?
- Are you one of our suppliers?
- What would you like to speak to him/her about?

Vocabulary:

phrasing: Formulierung
supplier: Lieferant

The reason for the call

Whether you get to talk to a person directly, or by way of a secretariat or colleague, it is always important to know how to explain the reason for your telephone call. In the illustration below you can see the normal grammatical arrangement of noun and verb (verb + ing form) after an introductory phrase.

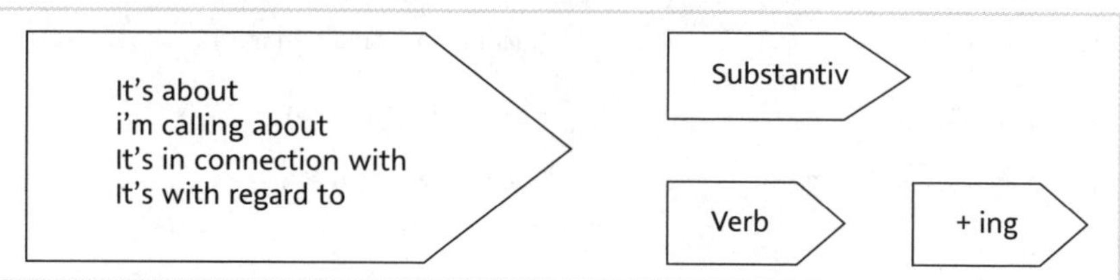

- It's/I'm calling in connection with Friday's conference.
- I'm phoning/ringing about the PowerPoint presentation.
- I'm calling to discuss the conference of next Friday.
- I'm phoning to inform you about the changes.
- It's about placing an order.
- The reason I'm phoning is Friday's conference.

Is it convenient?

To check if the person who answers the phone has time to talk can be done with the following phrases:

- Are you busy right now?
- Do you have a sec/second?
- Is this a good moment to talk?
- Have I rung you at a bad moment, Christa?
- Can we talk now or perhaps later?
- What time do you want me to call you back?
- Do you mind calling back this afternoon?
- Sorry, can you call again later?

5.2.1 Small talk

Small talk is used in English-speaking cultures, to influence conversations in a positive way. Small talk is very functional to introduce or end a conversation, with a few phrases about friendly and risk-free topics. Please note that the question ›How do you do?‹ is best answered with ›How do you do?‹ or ›I'm fine, thank you. How are you?‹. Below are some more phrases to begin or end a call:

- It's ages since we spoke.
- We haven't spoken since the Frankfurt Book Fair.
- How is business for you?

- So how have you been?
- So how old are the kids now?
- When are you coming to Europe?
- We must really speak again soon.
- I look forward to hearing from you again.

5.2.2 Getting past the secretary

One cannot always reach a contact directly, and sometimes it might even be necessary to ›get past the secretary‹. If it comes to that, it is always good to have one or two phrases prepared that quickly explain the connection or reason for the call.

- Well, it's a bit technical/complicated. Can I have a quick word with Mrs Funk to explain briefly?
- Well, Mrs Albrecht rang me this morning, and I was asked to call her back.
- My name is Jochen, Jochen Stäbel. We met at a conference in Amsterdam last week.
- It's Jule Funk. I'm phoning to check on the new design.
- It's with regard to placing an order.
- I'm phoning to request a schedule of rates and prices.
- I would like to offer some background information on ...
- I found your company on the Internet and I'd like some information about ...
- It's confidential.

Vocabulary:
check on: überprüfen
place an order: einen Auftrag erteilen
schedule of rates and prices: Preisverzeichnis

5.2.3 Obtaining information

Using the telephone for obtaining information can be very useful, provided that the true purpose of such a call is information gathering and not selling. The three paragraphs below give example phrases for asking contact details, asking for the right contact and obtaining additional information.

Contact details

- May I have his contact details, please?
- Could you give me the direct telephone number and e-mail please?
- I wanted to ask you some detailed address information.

- What's your full address/postal address?
- Just give me your PO box address please.
- What is the postal code/ZIP code please?
- Where is your company located?
- I'm afraid I didn't catch your name?
- What's the department manager's name?
- Would you be so kind as to give me Mr Fischer's e-mail address?
- Who have I been speaking to?

Vocabulary:
contact details: Kontaktdaten
direct telephone number: Telefondurchwahl
postal code/ZIP code: Postleitzahl

Asking for the right contact

- I was given your name by Mrs Funk.
- I would like to ask information on the latest software update. Who is dealing with this matter?
- We want to upgrade the European version. Which department is responsible for this?
- I'd like to speak to the person in charge of ..., but I don't know his or her name. Can you help me?
- Could you tell me who's responsible for the Austrian market, please?
- Who do I need to contact for information about ...?

Obtaining additional information

- In addition, I would like to ask you for a valid price list.
- Could you send me a catalogue of your products?
- We would like to receive a copy of your terms of sale.
- How much is the annual turnover approximately?

Vocabulary:
upgrade: aktualisieren
catalogue/catalog: Katalog
terms of sale: Verkaufsbedingungen
in addition: zusätzlich
annual turnover: Jahresumsatz

5.3 I beg your pardon?

Well, if I called the wrong number, then why did you answer the phone?
James Thurber (1894 – 1961).

When communication doesn't go smoothly, or when you need a few seconds to switch over to another language, the following phrases may help:

Technical problems
- Your line was busy 🇺🇸 /engaged 🇬🇧.
- I couldn't get through./There was no reply.
- Sorry, I can't hear/understand you.
- Could you speak a little louder, please? The connection is quite bad.
- This connection is pretty bad, I can hardly hear you. Let me just hang up and call you back immediately, OK?
- Can you hear me alright?

Language problems
- Could you speak a little slower please? I don't really speak English that well.
- Sorry, I didn't catch that. That was too fast for me.
- Could you repeat the last sentence once more, please?
- Would you mind saying that again?
- I'm sorry, I don't know that word. What does it mean?
- I'm very sorry. I don't understand. Could you explain that please?
- I can't understand you properly.
- Perhaps you could e-mail it to me, in case I didn't write it down correctly.
- May I connect you with someone who speaks English/German?
- Is there anyone in your office who speaks German?

Wrong number
- Sorry, wrong number. Please, excuse my mistake.
- Oh, sorry to have bothered you. I must have gotten the wrong extension.
- I'm afraid you have the wrong connection.
- I'll put you through to the operator again, hold on.

Vocabulary:
the wrong connection: falsch verbunden
call the wrong number: sich verwählen

5.4 Connecting people

Whenever you need to connect someone speaking English, or need to be connected yourself, there are many phrases to do so in a friendly and polite way. The examples below cover such situations as when a line is busy or when someone is not available.

Please hold the line

- Hold the line, please./Could you hold please?/Just a moment/minute, please.
- I'll put you through 🇬🇧 /I'll connect you 🇺🇸.
- It's ringing for you 🇬🇧.
- Putting you through to accounts now./I'll connect you with the person in charge.
- I had best directly connect you with Mrs Neigel.
- Our specialist, Mr Fischer, can take your call now.

Vocabulary:

person in charge: zuständiger Mitarbeiter
It's ringing for you: ich habe Sie durchgestellt
I had best directly connect you with ...: ich verbinde Sie am besten direkt mit ...

Person not available

- I'm sorry, but he's on another call/on the other line at present. Would you like to hold or call back later?
- Mrs Funk is having a meeting and I can't disturb her. Can I connect you with her colleague Mr Lorentz?
- I'm afraid Mrs Hausner is not available at the moment. Can I pass you to her assistant/colleague?

Person not in

- Mrs Heitz is not in at the moment. She said she would be back at eleven o'clock.
- Mr Fischer is in a meeting at the moment. Shall I try someone else for you?
- I'm sorry but Gisela is not in the office today.
- I'm sorry, but Jutta is no longer with the company.

Asking when someone is available

- Do you know when she's free?
- When will he be available?
- When is the best time to reach her?
- Could you tell me what time she will be back?

- Could you try again, please?
- Has he got a deputy?
- Can I speak to his secretary?

Vocabulary:
deputy: Stellvertreter
suits: passt

5.5 Answering the phone

When answering a business telephone call in English, it is common practice to start with a greeting, not to simply mention one's last name or company name. Receptionists will usually ask: ›How can I help you?‹ In private phone calls however, people might answer with just their telephone number or a simple ›hello‹. Then the caller is expected to identify him or herself.

- Good morning. ABC Text & Redaktion.
- Tulip Technology. Good afternoon.
- Presseasy. Jule Funk here. How can I help you?
- Marketing Department. Julia here.
- Good morning. Andreas Obermaier speaking.

5.6 Ending a conversation

It is important to close a conversation properly before saying ›good-bye‹. By using phrases as in the following examples you are assured of a polite closing and you leave a good impression.

Example !

A: It was nice talking to you, Mr. Murphy.
B: Yes, indeed. Well, I'll have my secretary schedule an appointment. And thanks again for the information.
A: You're welcome. Bye.

C: Could I contact you by e-mail?
D: Yes, let's keep in touch by e-mail.
C: Good. Well, thanks for taking the time to talk with me.
D: That's alright. Bye then.
C: Goodbye.

E: Well John, it's been nice talking to you.
F: Can I call you if I have any questions?
E: I'm very sorry, I have another call waiting.

Pre-closing

One can't just launch into closing without a preamble. Here are some ways to introduce getting out of a conversation:

- Is there anything else I can help you with today?
- So, I think that's everything then?
- It was nice to make contact at last.
- Good to speak to you again.
- It's been nice talking to you. – Yes, nice to talk to you, too.

Thanks for calling

- Thank you for phoning/calling (me) back/ringing.
- Thank you for getting back to me.
- Thank you for your time.
- OK, fine. Well, thanks, Mr Kauner.

Thanks

Expressing thanks or appreciation in English is usually done with more adverbs or adjectives then one would expect.

- Thank you ever so much.
- I can't thank you enough.
- It's been most kind of you to help us.
- Thanks very much for your help.
- Thank you for the information.
- Many thanks.
- That's very kind of you.

No thanks

After people have expressed thanks, it is customary to give a short equivalent of ›gern geschehen‹. Any of the following phrases will do:

- You're welcome.
- Don't mention it.
- Pleasure.
- That's alright.
- Not at all./No trouble at all.

Follow up

Below are some phrases that give a call to (future) action:

- When can I expect to hear from you?
- Speak to you soon/next week then.
- Could I call you again in a week's time?
- That's agreed then, until Friday.
- I look forward to seeing you soon/hearing from you.

Saying good-bye

Usually a simple ›bye‹ or ›good-bye‹ is enough, because a polite closing has been made in the phrases before. Below are examples of slightly different parting phrases:

- Alright. Bye then.
- Bye for now.
- Have a good weekend.
- Goodbye. And give my regards to Claudia.

I'll have to stop

As mentioned elsewhere in this book, the British tend to communicate in a bit more indirect way. The examples below offer a decent way of ending a call with the proper respect.

- Can I phone you later, when I have some spare time?
- I'm sorry, but I really must get on now. I'll e-mail you a summary of the discussed point. Is that alright?
- I'm very sorry, but I must hang up now.
- I'll have to stop you there. I'm expecting a visitor.
- I'm sorry, I have another call waiting.

6 Typical Situations and How To Deal with Them

6.1 Taking and leaving messages

When people are not available a message can still inform the other party. This does not only apply to your own phone, but also when answering someone else's phone. Therefore, don't forget to offer to take a message.

Good messages include information such as:

Check-list: leaving messages

1. The date and time of the call
2. The name of the caller and/or company
3. Contact data of the person (if necessary) and what time they can be best reached by phone
4. The details of the call: question, problem, solution, proposal, follow-up, etc.
5. An indication which next steps you expect

Taking messages
- Would you like to leave a message?/You can leave a message if you want./ May I take a message?
- Can I get him to call you back?
- May I take your name and number?
- No problem. I'll find a notepad. Hold on please./Could you wait a minute?
- Let me just get a pen. Right, what's the message?
- Alright. I'll leave that on his desk./Fine, I'll see that he gets that.

Asking to leave a message
- I'd rather leave a message.
- Could I leave a message for Mr Ferdinand Ilahi please?
- Could you ask him to call me back? My number's 012-3456-789.
- Could you tell her that I will call back later, please?
- Could you please tell him Dr Schroeder called?

Leaving specific messages
- Can she call me as soon as she gets in?
- Could you ask him to phone me on Tuesday afternoon?

- Yes, tell Romeo that Julia would like him to e-mail the confirmation before 5 o'clock tomorrow.
- Could he e-mail his report to me by Monday, please?
- I need her to phone me as soon as possible. My name's Kopfkaas, that's K-O-P-F-K-double A for Amsterdam-S.

Vocabulary:
by Monday: spätestens bis Montag

Responding to messages
- Thanks for your message about the postponement.
- Thanks for phoning back/calling me back, Peter.
- I'm just returning your call.
- I've just got your SMS/e-mail and I ...

6.2 Appointments

The essence of making appointments is of course finding a convenient date and time for a meeting. Besides arranging the right moment, it might be practical to think about a realistic time period for the meeting in advance. The following example phrases can be used when making appointments.

!

Examples

A: Hello Jochen, Klaus here. I'm calling about arranging a meeting with Moritz. Can you make Thursday after lunch; at three thirty?
B: Yes, that's fine.
A: Shall we meet in our office?
B: Yes, that seems a good idea.
A: Our office is on the second floor (US third floor). But just ask for me at the reception desk. I'll fax you a map.
B: That's very kind of you. Let me just confirm: Thursday the 25th, 3:30 at our office.
A: That's right. I look forward to it. Goodbye.
B: Bye.

A: Sorry for interrupting you again Jochen, but it's about the date we arranged for our meeting. I'm calling to fix another date because apparently Moritz is busy all week. Can we postpone it to Friday?
B: I'm just looking at my diary. OK, here we are. Hm, I'm afraid I'm unavailable on Friday. What about Monday afternoon?
A: Alright, I'll put that in my agenda. So that's Monday the 29th at 3.30. I'll confirm it by e-mail.
B: Thank you.
A: Not at all. Goodbye.
B: Goodbye.

Vocabulary:
third floor: im zweiten Stock
reception desk: Empfang
map: Wegbeschreibung
apparently: offenbar/anscheinend

Introducing an appointment

- I'm calling to arrange/fix a time for that conference call with Munich.
- Could I make an appointment to see her sometime this week?
- I need to make an appointment with Mr Weischenberg as soon as possible.
- I've just spoken to Fabian and apparently he can attend the meeting next Monday at ten o'clock German time.
- Let's meet in the restaurant at a quarter past twelve.
- Hello S.M., Jule here. I just wanted to check the time of our meeting tomorrow.

Vocabulary:
fix a time: Zeit ausmachen
attend a meeting: an einer Besprechung teilnehmen

Arranging an appointment

- Which day would be convenient for you?/Which day would you prefer?
- How about next Friday or the following Monday?/Are you free on Monday?
- What about Thursday instead?
- Would the morning/Monday afternoon suit you?
- Is two thirty OK?
- Anytime next Thursday sounds fine.
- I'm afraid I can't manage Monday.
- I've got another meeting at four thirty.
- Well, it won't take more than an hour.
- So that's Monday at three o'clock./Monday at three is confirmed.

Cancelling appointments

- I'd like to cancel/put off/postpone our appointment/interview.
- I am afraid I will not be able to keep the appointment I made for Friday, June 26th.
- I'm afraid I can't make it by 3 o'clock on Friday.
- Would it be possible to put off our meeting until tomorrow?
- I'm afraid Professor Krämer must change his appointment for the afternoon. Could we make another one?
- I'm sorry but an urgent matter has come up at the very last moment.
- I'm sorry but I haven't been able to get in touch with you before.

Vocabulary:
put off: verschieben
postpone: aufschieben
get in touch with you: Sie erreichen können

Indicating date and time
When trying to arrange an appointment, pay attention to using the proper expressions concerning time and date. The fact is, that there are not only specific differences between German and English (e.g. the twelve-hour clock), but also some variations between British and American English. In case of doubt, always try to double check appointments or ask for confirmation by e-mail.

For the correct vocabulary refer to the chapter »Invitations« in the first part of the book.

6.3 Telephone spelling

When speaking in another language, it can sometimes be difficult spelling family or street names. That's why it is practical to develop a skill at spelling. Try to practice the pronunciation of all individual letters. It is also important to use the same spelling consistently, otherwise people might get confused. Tell callers in advance that you intend to spell a name. This gives them a chance to get a hold of pen and paper.

In the past, it was customary to first mention a letter, followed by ›as in‹ or ›for‹ and then a full word, but nowadays it is recommended not to use such phrases because they take more time and may even confuse a caller. Start spelling with an introduction phrase like: »The name is Bonn, James Bonn. I'll spell that for you: Berlin – Ottawa – double New York.«

!

Example

A: Can I have your name please?
B: That's Oxfoord.
A: Could you spell that please?
B: Oxfoord is spelt O-X-F-O-O-R-D.
A: Sorry, was that X for Xylophone?
B: Yes, that's correct, and then double O (or: Oliver Oliver).
A: I see. Thank you so much.

Check-list: spelling

1. Notify your calling partner before you start spelling.
2. Pronounce the alphabet words quickly.
3. Try to avoid the use of phrases like ›for‹ or ›as in‹.
4. It is not necessary for the other side to repeat each letter.
5. Many countries use a regional telephone alphabet.
6. Double letters are repeated in the US, but in the UK preceded by: ›double‹.
7. The German ›e‹ sounds like the English ›a‹.
8. In the US the ›z‹ is pronounced like [zii] and in the UK like [zed].

Useful phrases

- I'm afraid I didn't catch the last name. Would you mind spelling it for me?
- Would you like me to spell the company name?
- Can you spell that using a telephonic key, please?
- Is that ›I‹ as in Italy, or ›E‹ as in Edison?
- Did I hear you correctly: MYER, not with EY, just with Y?
- I'd better read that back to you.

Vocabulary:
catch: verstehen
spell: buchstabieren
telephonic key: Telefonbuchstabiertafel
read back: aufsagen

Telephone alphabets

The following table shows the regional differences in spelling. You can use the British alphabet for countries of the Commonwealth. The American alphabet can be used in both the North and South American continent. For all other countries the international alphabet is recommended.

Letter	English	American	International
	for, as in	as in	
A	Alfred	Able	Amsterdam
B	Benjamin	Baker	Berlin
C	Charles	Charlie	Casablanca
D	David	Dog	Denmark

Letter	English	American	International
E	Edward	Easy	Edison
F	Frederick	Fox	Florida
G	George	George	Greenland
H	Henry	Harry	Havana
I	Isaac	Item	Italia
J	John	Jack	Jerusalem
K	King	King	Kilogram
L	London	London	London
M	Mary	Mary	Madrid
N	Nellie	Nancy	New York
O	Oliver	Oliver	Ottawa
P	Peter	Peter	Paris
Q	Queen	Queen	Quebec
R	Robert	Roger	Roma
S	Samuel	Sam	Sydney
T	Tommy	Tom	Tripoli
U	Uncle	Uncle	Upsala
V	Victoria	Victor	Valencia
W	William	William	Washington
X	Xylophone	X-ray	Xantippe
Y	Yellow	Yellow	Yokohama
Z	Zebra	Zebra	Zuerich

Pronunciation alphabet

A	ee	N	en
B	bii	O	oo
C	sii	P	pii
D	dii	Q	kju
E	ii	R	ar
F	ef	S	es

G	djii	T	tii
H	eetsch	U	ju
I	ai	V	vii
J	dzjee	W	dàbbel ju
K	kee	X	eks
L	el	Y	wai
M	em	Z	zed /zii

Specific German letters

The umlaut is a specific German diacritic which looks like a dieresis (trema), or a pair of dots above a vowel. An umlaut is used for vowel mutation and can be replaced by an extra ›e‹ after the vowel. The German letter ›ß‹ (Eszett or scharfes s) can be replaced by a double ›s‹.

Example !

A: What was the address again?
B: That's Kantstraße number 5; the second last letter [ß] is called Eszett in German. But you can simply replace that with double ›s‹.
A: I understand, how interesting.
B: Thank you. Well, goodbye.
A: Bye.

Vocabulary:
second last: vorletzter

6.4 Taking down names and numbers

Telephone numbers

Telephone numbers are much easier to understand, when pronounced in groups and divided by a pause. Therefore try to use single numbers when saying telephone numbers, and group them with pauses (e.g. 96-69 = ›nine six – six nine‹, not ›ninety-six sixty-nine‹). However, prefixes or extensions of phone numbers are never grouped. Note that double numbers like 66 can be spoken as ›six – six‹ or ›double – six‹. The number 0 is usually pronounced ›oh‹ or ›zero‹, never as ›nought‹.

!

Example

A: What's your phone/fax number?
B: 5678 9330 – five six seven eight [pause] nine double three oh.
A: Sorry, could you repeat the last part?
B: Yes, it's nine double three zero.
A: And what's your area code again?
B: 0-2-0, that's oh two oh, for London.

Useful phrases

- Call me on 0123 456, or try my mobile: 987 654 321.
- What's the international code?/What's the country code?
- It might just be that fax numbers in Germany can have a variable length, sir.

Vocabulary:

area code: Ortsvorwahl
international code: internationale Fernkennzahl
country code: Landeskennzahl

Numbers on the phone

To pronounce numbers on the phone in another language can be harder than one would expect. In English the numbers after twenty have a different order then they do in German. For instance, einundzwanzig becomes twenty-one. Furthermore, the American ›billion‹ means ›Milliarde‹. There are also some differences concerning the pronunciation of amounts or fractions. We just saw that there are different translations for the number ›0‹ (null). But when pronouncing a telephone number, always use ›oh‹, as in: ›double oh, forty-nine‹ (00-49). In figures, however, it is better to use the word ›nought‹ or ›zero‹. For instance, ›an amount with six noughts/zeroes‹.

Decimals

Decimals are divided by either a comma or a point. The consequence of this is that amounts need to be pronounced with the word ›point‹. For example, 0.2 is read as: nought (zero) point two, and the amounts in the examples below are all pronounced as: ›twenty point fifty euros‹ or ›twenty euros fifty‹. By the way, note that the currency sign for Britain and Ireland is typed in front of the amount, and without a space.

!

Example

United Kingdom: £20.50
Germany: 20,50 €
Ireland: €20.50

Large numbers
100 – one hundred
200 – two hundred
101 – a hundred and one
900 – nine hundred
1,000 – a thousand
100,000 – a hundred thousand
1,000,000 – a million
1,000,000,000 – a billion (eine Milliarde!)
10^{18} – trillion, quintillion – eine Trillion

In American English there is a tendency to pronounce figures like 180, as one hundred eighty. Whereas in British English, this is pronounced as one hundred *and* eighty.

Fractions
1/2 – one half
¼ – one-quarter, one-fourth (ein Viertel)
1/3 – one-third
2/3 – two-thirds
1 1/2 – one and a half

6.5 Electronic addresses

Giving an electronic address in another language can be difficult. The main reason for this is that not everybody always knows the translations for unusual punctuation marks. As a matter of fact, the first programmers who designed electronic communication looked for the least used characters on a key-board. That was because in e-mail and Internet addresses it was impossible to use spaces. The following paragraph gives you an overview of all essential phrases and vocabulary you need to communicate an electronic address with ease.

Digital vocabulary

@ (at sign)	At-Zeichen/Klammeraffe
attachment	Anlage
back slash	umgekehrter Schrägstrich
dot	Punkt

e-mail	die E-Mail (D), das E-Mail (A, CH)
file	Datei
hard disk	Festplatte
hyphen	Bindestrich
slash	Schrägstrich
subject	Betrifft/Betreff
to	an
to download	herunterladen
to forward	weiterleiten
underscore	Unterstrich
wireless	drahtlos

Useful phrases

- What's your e-mail address?
- My e-mail address is: info@bfai.de. That's info at B for Berlin, F for Florida, A for Amsterdam and I for Italia, dot D-E.
- That's all lower case and no capitals.
- All details can be found on deutsche-boerse.com. That's DEUTSCHE with C-H-E, then a hyphen followed by BOERSE with O-E and ending with E for Edward, dot COM.
- The Internet address is: www.austria.gv.at/english. Please note that the address contains a second level domain. So there is a dot before and after G-V. Then it's dot A-T slash ENGLISH.

Electronic country codes

People, who are used to electronic addresses ending with dot-de or dot-com, might have some difficulties with the type of addresses that use a second level domain (SLD). Usually such extra codes indicate an activity (›co‹ for companies, ›gov‹ for governments, etc.). Such an address contains an extra dot and the specific code. An example is: www.bbc.co.uk.

In fact, quite a few countries use this type of electronic address. For a list of examples please refer to paragraph »E-mail Features« in the first chapter of this book (»E-mails in English«).

Computer variations

The QWERTY keyboard layout of English-speaking countries differs somewhat from the QWERTZ layout in German-speaking countries. Not only are the Z and Y keys interchanged, but also the separate keys for characters such as ä, ö, ü or ß are missing. Furthermore, the function keys have different names or abbreviations.

The table below gives an overview:

Ctrl (control)	Strg
Delete	Entf
Shift	Ums
Caps Lock	Umsch. Tastst
PgUp (page up)	Bild hoch
PgDn (page down)	Bild runter
Insert	Einfg
Home	Post
End	Ende
PrtSc (Print Screen)	Druck

Keyboard combinations
Sometimes it can be useful to give someone a so-called alt-code, allowing them to type a specific letter. The table below gives an overview for the most common letters.

Letter	Alternative	Upper case	Lower casel
Ä	a e	Alt-142	Alt-132
Ö	o e	Alt-153	Alt-148
Ü	u e	Alt-154	Alt-129
ß	s s	Alt-225	Alt-225

6.6 Answering machine and voice mail

Although Willy Müller already invented the first automatic answering machines in 1935, many people still seem to hang up on recorded messages. Is it a fear of microphones or of disembodied voices? It probably hasn't been investigated yet, but one can imagine that people find it difficult to improvise while being taped, especially when it concerns leaving messages in a second language. The section below gives you examples for making your own recorded messages in English, as well as leaving messages.

Check-list: leaving messages

1. Be prepared for voice mail: know in advance what to say.
2. A message contains six Ws: who, what, where, when, why, what way.
3. Write down some keywords or specific English vocabulary.
4. Always mention your first, last and company name; people may not recognise your voice due to technical reasons.
5. Specify the next steps: do you need to be called back?
6. Try to mention two different times at which you will be available.
7. Pronounce telephone or fax numbers slowly because who wants to listen to messages twice?

Answering machines

- You are connected with the voice mail of Črt Perović. Please leave a message after the tone.
- You're connected with 12 34 56 78. Please leave a message after the tone.
- Welcome to Oberbilk Computing. Our offices are open from 9 to 12 and from 1 to 5.
- Hello, you're through to Oberbilk Computing. We are now closed for the holidays /vacation until August 21st. In an emergency call 0800-123 456. Thank you.
- Leave your message or send a fax after the tone.

Private answering machines

- Hello, I'm afraid I'm not in at the moment. But please leave your name and phone number after the beep ☺/bleep and I'll get back to you as soon as possible.
- Hello, this is Aynur. I'm sorry I cannot take your call right now, but if you'd like to leave your name and number, I will be happy to get back to you.
- Hello, this is Jack. I'm sorry, but there is currently no one here to take your call. Please leave a message. Or you can reach me on my cell phone at 1234 5678.

Leaving a message

When leaving messages, it is important to speak slowly and clearly state your contact information. Despite all advances in technology it still is advisable to leave your telephone number, as not all international connections will indicate your caller ID.

- Hello, this is Claudia/my name's Claudia I work for ABC in Graz.
- This is a message for Julius Neigel. Could you please give me a ring tomorrow morning? I'll be in my office until 11. Thank you.
- I won't be in this afternoon but you can normally reach me between nine and twelve on 01-234, that's 01-234.
- My phone number is 1234 5678. Could you call me back, please? Thank you. I look forward to speaking to you. Goodbye.

Important !

Try to talk slowly and clearly, because the sound quality of a reproduction is no more than 25% of the original.

Recorded information

- If you want to speak to XYZ, press 1, for ABC, press 2, to speak to the operator press the star key (star button).
- To go back to the menu, please press the pound sign (hash key).
- Your call is being diverted to the voice mail service.
- The person you have called is unavailable. Please try again later.

Example !

Welcome to Oxfoord Summer Academy. If you require service in English, please press one. If you require service in German, please press two. For information on this month's summer academy please press three. If you wish to return to the main menu, please press four. If you are unsure of which option to choose, please hold and you will be connected to one of our operators as soon as possible. Thank you for calling Oxfoord.

6.7 Mobile telephones

In some dictionaries you will have a hard time finding the specific words used in mobile telephony. The table below offers a selection of that terminology.

cellular (phone), mobile (phone), cell phone	Handy, Mobiltelefon
network operator	Mobilfunkbetreiber, Mobilfunkanbieter
prepaid, Pay As You Go (PAYG)	Prepaidkarte, Guthabenkarte, Wertkarte (A)
ring tones	Klingeltöne, Töne
voice mail	Mailbox, Voicemail

6.7.1 Recognising mobile numbers

In many countries it is easy to recognise a mobile telephone number from the first digits. In the United States and Canada, however, mobile numbers cannot be recognised because they use the normal area codes. But since both outbound and received calls are being charged, the difference isn't so important from a cost point of view. The selection below allows you to verify whether a telephone number is a landline or not.

Australia	4
Austria	6
Belgium	4
China	13
Cyprus	99
Czech Republic	60, 72, 73, 77
France	6
Gibraltar	54, 58
Hong Kong	3, 6, 8, 9
India	9
Ireland	8
Italy	3
Japan	70, 80, 90
Liechtenstein	7
Malta	79, 99
Netherlands	6
New Zealand	21, 25, 27, 29
Russia	50, 51, 90, 91, 92
Singapore	8, 9
South Africa	7, 8
Spain	6
Sweden	7
Switzerland	76, 77, 78, 79
United Kingdom	7

7 Special Situations

For those maintaining close connections with foreign business partners, it might sometimes be necessary to take part in more specific telephone calls.

7.1 Conference calls

Conference calls offer an alternative for travelling or overseas meetings because one doesn't have to go out of office for a particular meeting. Conference calls are becoming more and more popular, now that digital telephony (e.g. VoIP: Voice-over-IP) offers such cost-effective solutions. Combined with computer technology, it even allows us to share applications, making it possible to give a long-distance presentation, including the possibility to interact with the audience. Most conference calls, however, are still made by telephone. This can be done with a so-called group call, where several parties are phoned by an operator, or each party calls a specific telephone number and enters a pin code. For larger groups there are also special conference telephones. These are professional meeting telephones, with so-called duplex connections. Such machines ensure that the sound of all voices at a meeting table is at an understandable level.

Practical tips
Non-verbal communication isn't possible over a telephone, therefore be careful with sarcastic or ambiguous remarks. Not everybody may recognise each other's voice. Therefore it is sometimes protocol to mention one's name before talking. This is also helpful for the person taking the minutes of the meeting. When you are attending a conference call, it is important that you understand key English phrases and expressions related to meetings. Also practical skills like keeping to the agenda, or knowing how to refocus, are components of an effective telephone meeting. This may sound simple in German, but it requires some preparation in another language. This paragraph will help you to hold or attend conference calls in English with success.

Vocabulary:
conference call: die Telefonkonferenz/das Sammelgespräch
agenda: die Tagesordnung
the chairman: die (der) Vorsitzende(r)
participant: der Teilnehmer

! **Example**

Good morning everybody, my name is Kevin Johnson, I'm the chairman of this conference call and I would like to welcome you all as participants to our telephone strategy meeting.
Let me start by reminding you that our call ends around 12 a.m. Also, I would like to inform you that the necessary conference documentation is called ›teleconf_report_3.doc‹ and that an audio recording of this conference call will be e-mailed to you as a mp3 file, together with a written summary. I will now quickly introduce you to all the other participants. May I ask you to greet the other members after your name is mentioned? This allows us to check that everyone is connected properly and that the technology is working smoothly. Thank you.
Then I would like, firstly, to welcome Mrs. Milena Albrecht from Munich, Germany. She will recapitulate the SWOT-and PEST analyses and will be available for questions. But that's item number three on our agenda. So let me first inform you of the sequence of today's discussion topics. As you can see from ... etc.

Vocabulary:
audio recording: Tonaufnahme
summary: Zusammenfassung
connected: angeschlossen
recapitulate: resümieren

Welcome

To create a proper meeting atmosphere a chairperson welcomes the participants. In case new people join a conference, the welcome offers a good chance to introduce them to the other participants.

- Hello, everyone. Thank you for dialling in today./First I'd like to welcome you all.
- Firstly, I want to thank you all for being punctual, despite this early hour for our colleagues from Washington.
- Thank you all for attending at such short notice.
- I know most of you, but there are a few unfamiliar ›voices‹.
- As chair, it is my pleasure to introduce to you: Mrs Claudia Hausner./I'd like to take a moment to introduce Claudia.
- You can request the help of our operator by using the hotkey *0.
- Well, since everyone is present, we should get started./We have a lot to cover today, so we really should begin./I declare the meeting opened/adjourned.

Vocabulary:
chair: Vorsitzende(r)
adjourn: schließen

Absences

- The treasurer is absent due to unforeseen circumstances.
- Unfortunately, Jack cannot join us today, as he has been called away to Cologne.
- I have received apologies for absence from Julia, who is in London.

Vocabulary:
absence: Abwesenheit
unforeseen circumstances: unvorhergesehene Umstände

Agenda

- Let me inform you of the sequence of discussion topics.
- There are six items on the agenda. First ..., second ..., third ..., lastly ... Shall we take these points in this order?
- Let's quickly go through the minutes from the previous meeting. Claudia, can I put you in charge of reviewing the minutes from the last meeting for us?
- Our agenda allocates ten minutes for this item, but I think ...
- Has everyone received a copy of the design proposal from Mrs. Cortez?
- But this matter is not on today's agenda.
- Well, the next item on our agenda is: questions and reminders.
- I think we've covered everything on the agenda.

Chairperson

- Could I have your attention, please?
- I've called this meeting in order to ...
- I think we've spent enough time on this topic.
- I'm afraid we've strayed from the task at hand.
- I think we're steering off topic a bit with this.
- We've been arguing back and forth over this issue for some minutes now.
- It sounds like you've found some common ground; can you work that out bilaterally?
- We're running short on time. I suggest we skip the next item.
- We'll have to come back to this at a later time.
- I suggest that we address this matter again in our next conference call.

Procedures

- If you have a comment, please introduce yourself by name, rather than simply speaking out.
- Peter, you may have the floor!
- Getting back to item number four, I'd like to propose ...
- I'd like to hand over to Julia Funk, who is going to lead the next point: marketing.

- As I mentioned in my opening remarks, we have to end this group call before the end of the hour.
- We'll have to keep each item to five minutes. Otherwise we'll never get through.
- We cannot speak all at once, please.
- Could you repeat that?
- If there are no further developments, I'd like to move on to today's topic.
- I suggest we go round the table.
- Jack, would you like to kick off?
- Gisela, would you like to introduce this item?

Vocabulary:
have the floor: das Wort ergreifen
go round the table: die Meinung aller Anwesenden einzeln einholen
kick off: anfangen

Negotiations

! **Example**

A: Well, hello, everyone. My name is Horst, I am the Managing Director at the Paris office and I'm chairing today's meeting. We've organised this conference call to decide collectively by vote on Frankfurt's proposition. I hope you've all had a chance to look at Carsten's report. I suggest we go in the same order as last week's meeting and each say what we think, and afterwards we vote. Berndt, what is your opinion on the proposal?
B: Yes. Well, personally, I think the best solution is simply to wait. Despite Carsten's analyses.
C: Carsten here; I'd like to comment on that. I'm not sure I agree with that because as time passes the value also decreases.
B: Well, in my opinion, that loss is not decreasing proportionately.
C: I really think it would be better to act now, Berndt.
A: We've been arguing back and forth for some minutes now, and we're running short on time. However, we'll have to come to a consensus here, so I suggest we put it to a vote now. Those of you in favour of the proposition please push the star key; all opposed, please push the pound key. Thank you.
A: Gentlemen: the outcome of the vote is that the proposal has been adopted. Good, the next item on our agenda is: Berndt's report on outsourcing.

- We'd be willing to comply/agree with your counter proposal if you can reduce the insurance costs.
- The Berlin branch accepts a delay of one week, but that's their bottom line.
- We are very far apart on this issue.

- Shall we summarise the points of agreement?
- Do you accept these terms?
- I will send the proposal to you for your comments.

Vocabulary:
I'm chairing: ich präsidiere, sitze vor
decreasing proportionately: anteilmäßig abnehmend
comply: sich fügen in, einwilligen, nachkommen
counter proposal: Gegenvorschlag
branch: Niederlassung
bottom line: letztes Angebot
apart: auseinander
terms: Bedingungen
for your comments: zur Stellungnahme

Personal opinion
It is important to realize that British tend to use polite expressions to take a strong stance. When you are taking part in a conference call, try to express yourself accordingly, and use one of the following phrases:
- I really think it would be better to ...
- The way I see things .../From my perspective .../Well, in our opinion, ...
- If you look at it from our point of view, then ...
- That's not exactly how I look at it.
- Well, personally, I think the best solution is ...
- I feel that ...

Agreeing
The same indirectness as mentioned in the last paragraph applies to agreeing.
- I certainly agree to that./I agree with you entirely.
- That sounds like a very good idea to me.
- We agree with you, as far as this is concerned.
- That's right/correct/possible.
- Can you agree to this proposal?
- We feel exactly the same way.
- We are agreed on this matter.

Disagreeing
Telling another party that you disagree is usually softened with indirect elements as can be seen in the phrases below:
- We're not sure we agree with that.
- I'm afraid I'd have to disagree about that.
- That is not entirely correct.

- I'm afraid we cannot accept your statement.
- That's absolutely impossible/not possible.
- That's incorrect/not correct.
- The information seems insufficient/not accurate.
- I don't agree with that ...

Providing feedback

- Mister/Madam chairman?
- Excuse me for interrupting, my name is ...
- I'd like to comment on that.
- Tom here, could I just say one thing?
- I'm glad you brought that up, Peter.

Voting

- Since we cannot come to a consensus, I suggest we put it to a vote. All in favour please push the star key, all opposed can push the pound sign (hash key).
- The motion moved/suggested by Claudia is carried/agreed upon.
- There is a tie vote; I will therefore cast the deciding vote.
- I'll have Leonie Kootstra send out a group e-mail with the voting results.

Vocabulary:
pound sign/hash: Rautentaste
tie vote: Stimmengleichheit
deciding vote/casting vote: ausschlaggebende Stimme

Closing/adjourning

As a chairman, one is responsible for the official closing of a telephone meeting. Use any of the following phrases:

- I just have a few closing remarks and then you will all be free to return to your desks.
- Before we close this meeting, let me just summarise the main items.
- If there are no further comments, we will adjourn the meeting here. Thanks for your participation.
- It looks like we've run out of time, so I guess we'll have to adjourn our conference call here.
- I'm afraid we're going to have to cut this meeting short.

Final remarks

- Can we set the date for the next meeting, please?
- We'll meet again on the twenty-seventh of next month, same time. The minutes from today's meeting will be posted as of tomorrow morning.

- If anyone has any questions about what we discussed today, feel free to send me an e-mail. I neglected to mention that anyone who wants can receive a digital recording of this call.
- I'd like to thank Milena and Kevin for calling in from Amsterdam.
- Again, thank you all for taking time out of your busy schedules to be present.

7.1.1 Hours for international business calls

What is the most convenient time to make conference calls with participants from different continents? The example table below shows the best possibilities, based upon German business hours. Because of the influences of daylight saving time, the times mentioned in August may differ from those in March.

UTC	Friday 14 March	Thursday 14 August
Berlin	Friday 17:00	Thursday 17:00 *
London	Friday 16:00	Thursday 16:00 *
New York	Friday 12:00 *	Thursday 11:00 *
San Francisco	Friday 09:00 *	Thursday 08:00 *
Chicago	Friday 11:00 *	Friday 10:00 *
Denver	Friday 10:00 *	Friday 09:00 *
Los Angeles	Friday 09:00 *	Friday 11:00 *
Hong Kong	Thursday 15:00	Friday 14:00
Sydney	Thursday 17:00	Friday 17:00 *
Hobart	Thursday 17:00	Friday 18:00 *
* means the place observes daylight saving time (DST)		

Know that certain countries (e.g. Thailand, Iceland etc.) or even states (e.g. Arizona) don't observe daylight saving time. A very practical website to compare international time zones is: www.timeandedate.com

Vocabulary:
Daylight Saving Time (DST): Sommerzeit
CET, Central European Time: MEZ, Mitteleuropäische Zeit
UTC, Coordinated Universal Time: Koordinierte Weltzeit

7.2 International trade

This paragraph is more directly concerned with tasks in the field of international trade. It discusses and illustrates how to tackle various everyday situations, such as enquiries, deliveries or legal matters. Besides containing many model phrases to suit your business needs, this chapter also informs you about idiomatic expressions and intercultural differences, in order to give you the best chance of communicating effectively.

!

Example

A: Extension 213.
B: Hello, Mr Beer?
A: Yes, speaking.
B: Jolanda Bouman here.
A: Oh, yes, Mrs Bouman. How can I help you?
B: Well Mr Beer, I'm ringing to change our order number JB-07-03.
A: Can you refresh my memory and tell me what it was for?
B: It concerned that chicken delivery for October 1st.
A: Of course, I also see it on my computer now.
B: I would like to change the delivery date to October 8th if I may?
A: Naturally, but can I ask you to send me a note on that?
B: That's no problem. I'll fax it to you this afternoon.
A: That would be fine. In the meantime I'll arrange all necessary changes.
B: Thank you very much for your help.
A: Don't mention it. Bye for now.
B: Bye.

Making enquiries

Below are some useful phrases for making an enquiry.

- We saw your stand at the Leipzig trade fair.
- I read about your firm in the trade press.
- Is your catalogue also available in German?
- Can you send me a copy of your catalogue and a price list?
- The prices you quote are without discount?
- Could I ask if you allow trial purchases?
- Can you supply from stock? I ask this because we require the goods by June 26 at the latest.
- The quality of the goods is of prime importance.
- Provided quality and price are satisfactory.
- The point is that we are working already at a reduced profit margin.
- We grant a discount of 69% on all catalogue prices.

Vocabulary:
enquiry: Anfrage
trade press: Fachpresse
trade fair: Messe
from stock: ab Lager
by … at the latest: bis spätestens
provided: vorausgesetzt
quote: angeben
at a reduced profit margin: mit verringerter Gewinnspanne
grant a discount: Rabatt gewähren
trial purchase: Kauf mit Rücktrittsrecht/Kauf mit Option auf Rückgabe

Ordering

- I placed an order with you this morning on the Internet and I'd like to change something. Who should I speak to?
- We'll get your order processed in the next few days.
- Could you please let me have some samples? It is rather urgent!
- Is there a discount for quantity?
- Please send us a note cancelling the initial order.
- Dominik Weischenberg here. I'm ringing to confirm receipt of our order number 2007/SR.
- Could your sales manager confirm this order in writing for us please?
- Would you confirm this conversation in writing please?

Vocabulary:
confirm receipt: Empfang bestätigen
processed: erledigt
samples: Warenprobe
discount for quantity: Mengenrabatt
initial order: ursprünglicher Auftrag
sales manager: Verkaufsleiter
confirm in writing: schriftlich bestätigen

Example !

A: The Travel Company, Jill Smith speaking. How can I help you?
B: I should like to order a copy of »Paris City Guide« please.
A: Certainly sir, putting you through.
C: Good morning bookshop.
B: Hello, could I order one copy of »Paris City Guide« please?
C: Yes, of course, we have it in stock, so I can send out your order this afternoon.
B. That would be great.

C: Good, what name shall I put on the invoice, or do you perhaps have a customer number here?
B: Yes I do, it's 1001-MD.
C: Sorry, could you spell that?
B: One-double oh-one-M for Mary and D for David.
C: Thank you, anything else?
B. No, that will be all, thanks very much. Goodbye.
C: Goodbye Mrs Funk.

Delivery

- Can you supply these products by June 26?
- I'd like some information about a shipment of boxes weighing 2,000 kilos each to New York City next week.
- You can send the goods directly to our premises in the Kantstraße in Berlin, carriage paid 🇬🇧 /freight prepaid 🇺🇸.
- May I ask who takes care of customs duties and insurance cover for this shipment?
- Who I should speak to about a delivery problem?
- Please let us know the current freight rate for sea/rail/air/road transport.
- What is the delivery time?
- I can promise you prompt delivery.
- Delivery may be delayed by 24 hours.
- When were the goods sent/dispatched?
- But I suppose the carrier issued a bill of lading?
- We'd like to know whether you can dispatch 1,999 books to Düsseldorf next Wednesday.
- We decided to send this consignment by general cargo.

Vocabulary:
by: bis zum
premises: Gebäude/Gelände
carriage paid: frachtfrei
freight prepaid: Fracht im Voraus bezahlt
customs duties: Zollgebühren
current freight rate: derzeitiger Frachtpreis
delivery time: Lieferfrist
prompt delivery: pünktliche Lieferung
delayed by 24 hours: um 24 Stunden verzögert
bill of lading: Konnossement
to dispatch: senden/schicken
general cargo: Stückgutladung

Incoterms

The Incoterms 2000 (International Commercial Terms: Internationale Regeln für die Auslegung von Handelsklauseln) are a series of international sales terms which serve to divide transaction costs and responsibilities between buyer and seller. They are usually mentioned in an abbreviation-city combination (e.g. our prices are FOB Hamburg).

For a list of common abbreviations please refer to paragraph »Delivery and Incoterms« in the fist chapter of the book (»E-mails in English«).

Complaints

- I regret to have to complain about your consignment ...
- The goods delivered on the 27th of this month, were not the ones I had ordered.
- The goods that we ordered arrived damaged by water.
- Does your guarantee cover this damage?
- I must ask you to send a replacement as soon as possible.
- In accordance with the terms of the contract, I suggest ...
- We think you shouldn't have disregarded such a detail.
- I must point out to you, that the delay is causing us serious problems in the field of ...
- I believe a mistake has been made in invoice number 69C.

Example !

A: Good morning, AZ Werbeagentur. Can I help you?
B: Hello. Can you put me through to the service department, please?
A: Certainly. Putting you through now.
C: Service department, good morning.
B: Good morning, my name's Obermaier from Tulip Technology. I regret to have to complain. I rang last week about the fact that our customer database doesn't work properly, and I was promised full functionality by last Friday. However, we are still waiting for improvement.
C: I'm sorry Mr Obermaier, let me just check. ... It's due to circumstances beyond our control. But I'll see what I can do right now. Let me call you back by three o'clock, to let you know what the situation is.
B: Very well, three o'clock. But I must point out to you that this delay is causing us serious problems.
C: We are very sorry and I'll start calling right away to try and find a solution.
B: That would be fine. Thank you. Goodbye.
C: Goodbye, Mr Obermaier.

Vocabulary:
consignment: Sendung
replacement: Ersatz
terms of a contract: Vertragsbedingungen
disregard: missachten, nicht beachten

Apologise

- I'm really sorry.
- We do apologise for the delay, but it's due to circumstances beyond our control.
- I'm afraid that we have made an error.
- I want to offer you an apology for this misunderstanding.
- Don't worry; we'll settle the matter as soon as possible.
- We are very sorry; apparently a mistake was made when the goods were shipped.
- I must admit that your complaint sounds totally justified.
- I must apologise again for the incorrect calculation of these costs.
- I must excuse myself on account of illness.
- I beg your pardon; I must have dialled a wrong number.

Vocabulary:
calculation of the costs: Kostenberechnung
on account of: auf Grund

Legal matters

When referring to a contract or an agreement, it is important to use the right vocabulary. Legal language often has a specific meaning. The examples below also include some phrases in the field of international contract law.

!

Example

A: Hello Klaus, I wanted to discuss a few details before entering into a contract.
B: Sure, Volkmar. So I understood.
A: It mainly concerns section 3, paragraph 4.
B: Yes, what about it?
A: It says here that unless we deliver within three working days, we are in breach of contract and the order can be cancelled.
B: That's part of our general agreements.
A: The point is we find three days very restrictive. Would you have a problem with one week?
B: No, under the circumstances that sounds fair. I'll have the changes made and e-mail you the draft contract this afternoon.
A: That's very kind of you Klaus. Thank you, and speak to you soon.
B: You're welcome. And give my regards to Rüdiger

- Shall I have Peter draft an outline agreement in the meantime?
- Naturally it is our intention to create legal relations.
- Can you have your lawyer prepare a written contract?
- ABC must simply fulfil (UK) /fulfill (US) the obligations under the terms of the contract.
- Hamburg was deemed venue of jurisdiction in the case of disputes between the parties.
- But you did sign the invoice ›EOE‹ (errors and omissions excepted), if I'm not mistaken.
- Did the contracting parties agree on this particular forfeiture clause?
- We think that the shipping company has certainly not performed its contractual duties.
- We therefore claim that the deadline has been exceeded.
- The board specifically issued a power of attorney for me, to negotiate this matter.
- Our lawyer will file a lawsuit for breach of contract.

Vocabulary:
contracting parties: Vertragspartner
forfeiture clause: Verfallsklausel/Verwirkungsklausel
EOE/E & OE: Irrtümer und Auslassungen vorbehalten
venue: Gerichtsbezirk/Gerichtsstand
perform: erfüllen
exceed: überschreiten
terms of the contract: Vertragsbedingungen
power of attorney: Vollmacht
file a lawsuit: eine Klage einreichen
breach of contract: Vertragsverletzung

Marketing

- Our marketing consultant is conducting a pilot survey.
- Will we have our normal modular stands available on the trade fair grounds?
- Does the stand rental also include all utilities and set-up?
- The report forecasts market leadership as of next year.
- Capturing a market share in Canada is the main objective.
- Sales have increased by 15% since we introduced more competitive pricing.
- We hope to maximise sales after this promotion scheme.
- Can your company cater to all potential customers in this market niche?

Vocabulary:
trade fair: Handelsmesse/Fachmesse
set-up: Aufbau
pilot survey: Pilotumfrage
forecast: vorhersagen, voraussagen
capture market share: Marktanteil erobern
objective: Zielsetzung
competitive pricing: konkurrenzfähige Preise
promotion scheme: Werbekampagne
cater to: ausgerichtet oder eingestellt sein auf
market niche: Marktlücke

False friends
False friends are words that look similar, but mean something quite different in the other language. Below are some examples of German-English and English-German false friends.

German	English	False friend	Translation
Konzept	draft, plan	concept	Begriff, Idee
Konkurrenz	competition	concurrence	Einverständnis
Messe	fair; mass	mess	Unordnung
Bedeutung	meaning	Meinung	opinion
Marke	brand	mark	Note
Aktion	campaign	action	Handeln
Fotograf	photographer	photograph	Foto
Objektiv	camera lens	objective	Ziel

7.3 Sales and finances

Selling a product or service
Making a telephone call with a potential customer is a difficult communication moment. However, with good preparation it may prove successful. Therefore prepare the right questions, listen as well as possible, and try to make notes during the conversation.

!

Example

A: Could I ask you a few short questions?
B: What's it about?

A: It's about our brochure which we sent you last week. May I ask you what your initial reason was to ask for that information?
B: The main reason was to compare delivery times.
A: And why is this so important to you, Mrs. Funk?
B: Because we have to supply our customers.
A: I fully understand that's important to you. That's why I can propose to deliver all materials directly to your customers. In that way, I can even guarantee delivery within two days. Would that be a good solution for you?
B: Well, if you can actually guarantee that, it might.
A: Would you like me to send you some details per e-mail, or shall I show you some examples next week in your office?

- I would like to ask some short questions on ..., is that alright?
- We have branches throughout Europe.
- Our head office is located in Freiburg.
- It will only take about 14 minutes to see if we can help.
- I'll be in your area next week; could I make an appointment to see Mr Fischer on, say, Monday at 11 a.m.?
- What are the (dis)advantages of the present product, if I may ask?
- We provide free consultancy service for the duration of the contract, and our product is reasonably priced.
- I can offer you a discount of 5% off list prices. That is our final offer.
- Can you prepare a draft contract?
- So may I conclude that you accept our discount/payment terms?

Vocabulary:
branches: Filialen
head office: Hauptsitz
reasonably priced: preiswert
list prices: Listenpreise
draft contract: Vertragsentwurf
final offer: letztes Angebot
discount/payment terms: Rabatt/Zahlungsbedingungen

Important !

A human being has two ears and only one mouth. Try speaking accordingly in sales calls: listen twice as much.

Financial matters

International trade partly has to do with international finance. Recently some new financial vocabulary has been introduced. This paragraph illustrates various situations:

- I will need to mention your VAT number as well.
- I don't need the bank's number, but if you could give me your exact IBAN number and BIC code, please?
- Can you tell me where the nearest ATM (automated teller machine) is?
- Our portfolio manager makes day-to-day decisions about such investments.
- Did you receive a fax from us last week, reminding you about the outstanding account you have with us?
- I've been told by the accounts department that the invoice due on 27th November hasn't been settled yet.
- When was the bank transfer made?
- What are your usual terms of payment?
- Our trading partner demands a confirmed and irrevocable L/C (letter of credit).
- We offer a discount of 15% on orders exceeding 1,500 euros.
- These goods are paid in kind.
- I have instructed our bank to send a remittance every month.
- It's a standing order 🇬🇧, automatic transfer 🇺🇸.
- The point is: that price will be below our MSRP.

Vocabulary:
VAT (value-added tax) number: MwSt-Nummer
bank account number: Bankkontonummer
bank code number: Bankleitzahl
ATM: Geldautomat/Bankomat (A)
portfolio manager: Vermögensverwalter
outstanding account: unbezahlte/offenstehende Rechnung
accounts department: Buchhaltungsabteilung
due: verschuldet
settle: zahlen/begleichen
irrevocable: unwiderruflich
letter of credit: Akkreditiv
discount: Rabatt
remittance: Überweisung
in kind: Bezahlung in Naturalien/Sachspende
standing order/automatic transfer: Dauerauftrag
MSRP (manufacturer's suggested retail price): empfohlener Richtpreis
terms of payment: Zahlungsbedingungen

!

Important

Bankleitzahl, IBAN and BIC

A ›BLZ‹ is called ›sort code‹ in the United Kingdom and Ireland, ›routing transit number‹ in the USA, ›bank transit number‹ in Canada, and ›BSB number‹ in Australia. This code or number serves to identify a branch of a bank for internal purposes. Nowadays specifying your **IBAN** account number (International Bank Account Number) is usually enough (China and the United States do not participate in IBAN at present). IBAN formats for the United Kingdom and the Republic of Ireland both use 22 characters. A **BIC** code (Bank Identifier Code) may also be called SWIFT address or SWIFT code.

7.4 Travel enquiries

One often needs information about travel opportunities. The phrases in this section will help to plan when travelling.

Hotel/conference

- I'd like to book a single room with a bath for Friday, 13th January please./ Do you have a double room with twin beds for three nights?
- Would you be so kind as to book a conference room accommodating 45 people?
- How much is that per day, please?/How much does it cost, please?
- How much is the charge for a second beamer, flip chart, white board?
- I'd like to rent a studio as from next October.
- What are your rates during the Frankfurt Book Fair?
- Can you recommend a hotel near your office?
- Could you let me have a confirmation by e-mail?
- I have a reservation in the name of Anneke Hut.

Vocabulary:

as from: von ... an

in the name of: auf den Namen

!

Example

A: Hello. The Ritz hotel, this is François speaking, how may I help you?

B: Hello, Julia Funk here, I'd like to book a room please.

A: Certainly, may I have your name again please?

B: That's Mrs Funk.

A: Sorry, could you spell that?

B: Funk: F-U-N-K.

A: Thank you, how many nights is that for?

B: Two, please.
A: When is it for, Mrs Funk?
B: October 3rd and 4th.
A: Would you like a single or a double room?
B: I'd like a double non-smoking room, please, as well as a conference room accommodating twelve people for October 4th.
A: May I ask for your credit card number to secure your reservation?
B: Yes, it is: Master 1234 567 8910.
A: And what is the expiry date?
B: It is October 20XX.
A: Good, and could you give me a contact number Mrs Funk?
B: Yes, certainly my mobile number is 49-172 3456 789.
A: OK, I think that's everything. I have reserved a double non-smoking room for you on October 3rd and 4th, and a conference room for October 4th. Would you like a confirmation in writing perhaps?
B: No, that's alright, thanks.
A: Well, we look forward to having you here and hope you will enjoy your stay with us. Thank you, and goodbye.
B: Bye.

Useful vocabulary

American plan	Vollpension
B and B, bed and breakfast	Übernachtung mit Frühstück
double bed	Doppelbett/französisches Bett
double room	Doppelzimmer
full board	Vollpension
half board	Halbpension
high season	Hauptsaison
low/off season	Nachsaison/Vorsaison
king-size bed	2-m breites Bett
queen-size bed	1,5-m breites Bett
single room	Einzelzimmer
twin-bedded room	Zweibettzimmer
conference room	Konferenzraum
sound technique	Tontechnik
Internet access	Internetanschluss
secretarial support	Sekretariatsarbeiten

Restaurant

- I'd like to book a table for six for tonight, please.
- What time is that for exactly, sir?
- Do you also serve vegetarian dishes?
- What time does your kitchen close, if I may ask?
- Sorry, can I change the reservation for Ms Frist?

Car rental

- I'd like to hire/rent a mid-range car, please.
- Is unlimited mileage included?
- How much is passenger insurance, comprehensive insurance or full insurance, please?
- Don't you have a manual/stick-shift available?
- I'd prefer to drive an automatic transmission.
- Do I have to pay a deposit?

Vocabulary:

mid-range car: Mittelklassewagen
unlimited mileage: uneingeschränkte Kilometerzahl
full insurance: Vollkasko
passenger accident insurance: Insassen-Unfallversicherung
automatic transmission: Automatikgetriebe

Booking a flight

- I'd like to book a direct flight from Southampton to Düsseldorf on October 3rd please.
- Is there a connecting flight to Hamburg?
- Could you reserve an aisle/window seat, please?
- There are no domestic flights/internal flights available.
- I'd like to change my reservation on flight number 007.

Vocabulary:

connecting flight: Anschlussflug
change a reservation: eine Reservierung umbuchen
aisle/window seat: Gang- Fensterplatz
domestic/internal flight: Inlandflug

Important !

single ticket 🇬🇧, one-way ticket 🇺🇸: einfache Fahrkarte
return ticket 🇬🇧, round trip 🇺🇸: Rückfahrkarte

7.5 A job interview by telephone

Nowadays, more and more North American companies employ phone interviews to save time and travel expenses. In this way, human resources managers or job recruiters actually use telephone interviews to narrow their selection of application letters. All too often, European job applicants aren't prepared for such job interviews by telephone. Try preparing for a phone interview just as you would for an in-person interview. Don't be afraid to use silence or an intentional pause when you need some time to think. Be prepared to give a quick description of your background, skills and knowledge. Always make sure that you have a copy of your résumé and cover letter at hand.

! **Example**

A: Good morning Mr Snorremans. I hope we are calling you at a convenient moment?

B: Yes, I expected your call.

A: First let me introduce you to Lynne Carter, who is listening on the other line.

B: Good morning. How do you Ms Carter.

A: Well, the first question I want to ask you is if you could tell us why you want this particular post?

B: As I wrote in my application, I'm very motivated to be a part of your new design team in Paris.

A: So, tell me about yourself Jorryt.

B: I'm currently senior designer for Jorritsma Controls which focuses on automotive and industrial design.

A: That's very interesting. We are considering inviting you to talk about the content and requirements of the position.

B: Can we schedule to meet in person over the next few days?

About your curriculum vitae/résumé

- Could you describe your previous occupation, duties/tasks and the length of your experience?
- When did you encounter the greatest challenge of your career to date?
- I attended the University of Graz from 2001 to 2005.
- I graduated in the following subjects ...
- I was promoted to department manager in 2007.

About your current position

- I'm currently working as a ... for X AG, focusing on ...
- I am more interested in a full-time position. However, I would also consider a part-time position.
- My promotion prospects were limited in that company.

- I am looking for a similar position.
- I am looking for a position with more responsibility.
- I hope to improve my career prospects in your company.
- What's the salary range you're offering for the position?
- Let's talk about the content and requirements of the position first, so that we can better discuss compensation
- I want to thank you for the interview.

When you are calling

- Good morning. Could you put me through to Human Resources, please?
- I'm calling in connection with your job advert in the Rheinische Post.
- It says I can get more information about the vacancy by calling this number.
- Good afternoon I'm calling about the job on your website.
- I have some questions about the content and requirements of the position.

Vocabulary:

curriculum vitae/résumé: Lebenslauf
letter of application/cover letter: Bewerbungsschreiben

Questions to ask about a vacancy

- What are the day-to-day duties involved in this job?
- Why has this vacancy arisen?
- What challenges is the organisation currently facing?
- How quickly are you looking for someone?
- How will the performance be measured?
- Are you looking for anything in particular from the person who will fill the vacancy?
- What training and development possibilities exist for employees?

8 Practical Reference

8.1 Intercultural communication

For successful international communication, just speaking the other language is not always enough. It is also necessary to have some basic understanding of the other culture. Certain behaviour is (also with respect to telephone calls) culturally defined, and misunderstandings can arise easily.

Using names

For example, many English-speaking people will quickly be on first-name terms, whereas German-speaking people are more hesitant to mention their first names in a telephone conversation. Perhaps the reason lies in the fact that in the English language there is no difference between ›Sie‹ and ›Du‹, as they both are translated with ›you‹. Another difference is that in the English language it is unusual for a man to call himself Mr Johnson on the telephone. For a woman, however, it's no problem to call herself Mrs Johnson, Miss Johnson or Cathy Johnson.

Who identifies first?

In Britain it is not that uncommon to answer the phone by simply mentioning one's number or extension. For instance, ›extension 1013 speaking‹. By the way, extension numbers are always pronounced digit by digit.

In many other cultures the telephone is answered in an impersonal way. Like the Italian ›pronto‹ (ready) or the Spanish ›dígame‹ (tell me). Their true function is only to let a caller know that the line is working and the caller can identify him or herself. It is simply a matter of different telephone etiquette.

Directness

Intercultural studies by Hall, and more recently by Hofstede and Trompenaars, have shown that people from cultures like Germany, the United States, the Netherlands and Scandinavia have quite a direct way of communicating. People from Britain have a more indirect way of expressing ideas or feelings.

Important !

Be aware not to express your wishes or criticism too directly when calling with people from more indirect cultures.

In order to communicate successfully, some knowledge of such culturally defined patterns seems necessary. It is certainly useful to mention the word ›please‹, in as many phrases as possible. On the other hand, certain German operators have been known to get irritated by the fact that not every Englishman always introduces himself when asking for an extension or a person. Effective intercultural skills probably imply that one has to accept certain differences.

In the business world, one has to deal with people and not with generalisations. Nevertheless, there are some generalisations worth keeping in mind. For instance, the fact that British tend to use more humour in business life. This is often seen as a professional opening to a conversation. On the other hand, British people don't like to show emotion, either in a business context or even in society in general. As a word of warning, it should be mentioned that there are also differences between the English, Scottish, Welsh, Northern Irish and Irish and that this can be quite a sensitive issue. Mixed feelings also exist about being part of the European Union, as essayist Richard Hill discovered when he heard the pilot say: ...›we're now leaving Europe, and the weather in Britain is fine‹...

8.2 Pronunciation

Although it can be very challenging for you to listen to someone speaking English over the telephone, some of us forget that listening to a non-native speaker may be even more difficult for the person on the other side of the line. Try, therefore, to pay attention to your weaker pronunciation areas.

Emphasized syllables
Not every syllable is pronounced in English with the same force or strength. If you compare the words ›photograph‹, ›photographer‹ and ›photographic‹, they look very much alike when written, but when pronounced they actually sound quite different. This is because the accentuated syllable changes in each of the three words. Native speakers of English are used to concentrating on the accentuated syllables. If you are able to remember the right emphasis, people will understand you much better. The diagrams below help you to visualise the changes meant.

Word pronunciation	Graphically	Number of syllables	Accentuated syllable
PHO-to-graph	▮ ▬ ▬	3	1st
Pho-TO-graph-er	▬ ▮ ▬ ▬	4	2nd
Pho-to-GRAPH-ic	▬ ▬ ▮ ▬	4	3rd

There are two simple rules that will help you remember accentuated syllables:

1. Each word has only one accentuated syllable.
2. Only vowels can be accentuated, not consonants.

Tongue twisters

If you feel that you want to improve your pronunciation skills, try practising with the tongue twisters below. A tongue twister is a phrase that is difficult to pronounce correctly even for native English speakers, and are a popular form of wordplay. Try to say them as fast as possible, but correctly.

- Mixed biscuits, mixed biscuits.
- She sells sea shells on the seashore.
- Peter Piper picked a peck of pickled peppers.
- Around the rugged rocks the ragged rascals ran.
- We surely shall see the sun shine soon.
- I can think of six thin things and of six thick things too.
- Swan swam over the pond, swim swan swim.
- Three grey geese in green fields grazing.
- Cows graze in groves on grass which grows in grooves.
- Red leather, yellow leather, red leather, yellow leather.
- The sixth sick Sheik's sixth sheep is sick.
- A proper copper coffee pot.
- Comical economists.

Vocabulary:

tongue twisters: Zungenbrecher
word play: Wortspiel

8.2.1 Speech

Intonation has been called the music in a person's voice. Or as the French saying goes: ›C'est le ton qui fait la musique‹. And indeed, according to American psychologist Mehrabian, a good forty percent of our communication is influenced by the tone of our voice. This is, by the way, much lower than the fifty-five percent which is influenced by non-verbal communication, but then again; telephone calls aren't influenced by that. There are more elements besides intonation that can influence the way a phone call is perceived. We take a closer look below at: speed, volume, timing and articulation.

Professional telemarketers, for instance, try to talk slower on the phone, because people are then supposed to listen longer. The key to retaining a listener's attention is to also use clear, compact, fact-filled sentences when you speak. Try interjecting short responses like ›yes, I see‹, ›aha‹, ›that's interesting‹ etc., to show that you're engaged in the conversation. Timing is another effective skill in telemarketing: when a pause is made just before an important word or phrase, the impact is much greater. People who talk too loudly run the risk of making an aggressive impression. But people who talk too softly might sound hesitant, and this is also supposed to make listeners tired. Articulation: try to use your jaws, tongue, lips etc. to pronounce everything clearly. Especially when talking in another language, audibility is an important factor. It can be effective to ask a colleague to listen to your own calling style. Or even better, record a few telephone conversations in order to evaluate yourself.

Homophones

Homophones are words that have the same sound but a different spelling and meaning. Especially for non-native speakers these can sometimes be difficult. For a selection of some relevant business homophones please refer to paragraph »Linguistic Characteristics« in the first chapter of this book (»E-mails in English«).

8.3 Telecommunications terminology

This paragraph contains specific telephone terms and words for use in a business context. It explains, for instance, how to ask someone for their fixed line number as well as other distinctive vocabulary, which often cannot be found in an ordinary dictionary.

area code	Vorwahl
battery charger	Ladegerät
ex-directory, unlisted	geheime Telefonnummer
be on hold	in der Warteschleife sein
call forwarding	Rufumleitung
cellular, mobile, cell phone	das Handy, das Mobiltelefon
collect call	R-Gespräch, Rück-Gespräch
conference call	Konferenzschaltung, Telefonkonferenz
dial	Wählscheibe
dial-direct number, STD number	Durchwahl(nummer)
emergency call	Notruf
landline, fixed line	Festnetz
international dialling code	Landeskennzahl
key lock	Tastensperre
key pad	Tastatur
pound sign, hash	Rautentaste, Rautenzeichen
receiver, handset	Hörer
redial	Wahlwiederholung
star key	Sterntaste, Sternchen
subscriber's number	Rufnummer
switchboard	Telefonzentrale, Vermittlungsstelle
telephone book/directory	Telefonbuch
telephone booth/box	Telefonzelle
text messages	Textmitteilungen, SMS
toll-free	gebührenfrei, zum Nulltarif
voice message	Sprachmeldung
Yellow Pages©	Gelbe Seiten, Branchenverzeichnis

8.4 Key terms: the company

The following tables provide a quick reference source when trying to describe elements or divisions of a company.

Departments

orders	Bestellungen
accounting	Buchhaltung
purchasing	Einkauf
finance department	Finanzabteilung
research and development, R&D	Forschung und Entwicklung, F&E
information technology	IT-Abteilung
customer service	Kundenberatung
after-sales service	Kundenbetreuung
warehouse	Lagerhalle
logistics	Logistik
marketing	Marketing
assembly	Montage
public relations, PR	Öffentlichkeitsarbeit
human resources, personnel department	Personalabteilung
production	Produktion
legal department	Rechtsabteilung
sales department	Verkaufsabteilung
out-of-office sales	Verkaufs-Aussendienst
sales support	Verkaufs-Innendienst
sales management	Verkaufsleitung
despatch, dispatch	Versand
sales and distribution	Vertrieb
administration	Verwaltung
advertising department	Werbeabteilung

Company positions

shop floor worker	Arbeiter/-in
assistant	Assistent/-in
staff	Belegschaft
office staff	Büropersonal
director	Direktor, leitender Angestellter
managing director, CEO	Generaldirektor/-in
manager	Manager/-in
personnel	Personal
management	Unternehmensleitung
vice president	Vizepräsident/-in
supervisor	Vorgesetzter
chairman	Vorsitzender
board of managers	Vorstand

Company divisions

department, section	Abteilung
branch	Filiale, Niederlassung
business unit, division	Geschäftsbereich, Sparte
head office, headquarters	Hauptsitz, Zentrale
holding company	Holdinggesellschaft
parent company	Muttergesellschaft
subsidiary	Tochtergesellschaft

8.5 Telephone sources on the Internet

The following list gives the Internet addresses for business telephone directories in Anglophone countries.

Australia	www.whitepages.com.au
Canada	www.yellowpages.ca
	www.maplepages.com

Cyprus	www.cytayellowpages.com.cy
Gibraltar	www.gibyellow.gi
Hong Kong	www.yp.com.hk
	www.cwhkt.com
India	www.indiacom.com
Ireland	www.eircomphonebook.ie
	www.goldenpages.ie
Malta	www.yellowpages.com.mt
	www.maltacom.com
New Zealand	www.whitepages.co.nz
South Africa	www.phonebookonline.co.za
	www.easyinfo.co.za
United Kingdom	www.thephonebook.bt.com
	www.yell.com
United States	www.yellowpages.com
	www.att.com
	www.verizon.com

8.5.1 National telephone numbering plans

Calling another country is no longer simply a matter of leaving the first zero off the area code. Many countries have been changing their national numbering plans. Unfortunately, these changes were not always uniform. Certain countries, for instance, stopped using a zero completely, others stopped using area codes, and many countries now require area codes to be used for local calls (e.g. Switzerland, Spain, Denmark, Poland etc.). Some countries even created differences between international calls to a land line or to a mobile telephone. The company International Numbering Plans from Apeldoorn offers a free up-to-date database with specific details on its website: www.numberingplans.com.

In addition, the length of a number may vary: American phone numbers have a standard seven digits, very unlike German phone numbers which may have between three and eight digits. In other countries, mobile telephone numbers might have more digits than landline telephone numbers.

8.6 Country codes and dialling codes for well-known cities

Use the table below for international country codes or the city dialling codes of English-speaking countries.

Country/code	City code
Australia 00 61	Adelaide 8, Albury 2, Brisbane 7, Cairns 7, Canberra 2, Darwin 8, Gold Coast 7, Hamilton 3, Hobart 3, Melbourne 3, Newcastle 2, Perth 8, Sydney 2.
Canada 00 1	Alberta 403, British Columbia 250, British Columbia (Lower) 604, New Brunswick 506, Newfoundland 709, Nova Scotia 902, Ontario (London) 519, Ontario (Ottawa) 613, Ontario (Toronto Metro) 416, Ontario (Toronto vicinity) 905, Quebec (Montreal) 514, Quebec (Quebec City) 418, Quebec (Sherbrooke) 819.
Cyprus 00 357	Famagusta 3, Kyrenia 357, Larnaca 4, Lefkonico 3, Limassol 5, Nicosia 2, Polis 6.
Gibraltar 00 350	
Hong Kong 00 852	
India 00 91	Bengaluru (Bangalore) 80, Bhopal 755, Chennai (Madras) 44, Delhi 11, Hyderabad 40, Jaipur 141, Kolkata (Calcutta) 33, Mumbai (Bombay) 22, New Delhi 11, Pune (Poona) 212, Surat 261.
Ireland 00 353	Cork 21, Donegal 77, Dublin 1, Galway 91, Killarney 64, Limerick 61, Sligo 71, Tipperary 62, Waterford 51.
New Zealand 00 64	Auckland 9, Hamilton 7, Hastings 6, Invercargill 2, Nelson 3, New Plymouth 6, Tauranga 7, Wanganui 6, Wellington 4, Whangarei 9.
South Africa 00 27	Bloemfontein 51, Cape Town 21, Durban 31, East London 431, Johannesburg 11, Pietermaritzburg 331, Port Elizabeth 41, Pretoria 12, Uitenhage 41, Welkom 57.
United Kingdom 00 44	Aberdeen 1224, Belfast 2890, Birmingham 121, Blackpool 1253, Brighton 1273, Bristol 1272, Cambridge 1223, Cardiff 2920, Coventry 2476, Dover 1304, Dundee 1382, Edinburgh 131, Glasgow 141, Ipswich 1473, Jersey, Channel Islands 1534, Leeds 1532, Leicester 1533, Liverpool 151, London (city 207) (around 208), Londonderry 1504, Manchester 161, Newcastle 1632, Northampton 1604, Norwich 1603, Nottingham 191, Oxford 1865, Plymouth 1752, Portsmouth 2392, Sheffield 114, Southampton 2380.

Country/code	City code
United States of America 00 1	Atlanta 404, Atlantic City 609, Austin 512, Baltimore 410, Boston 617, Cape Cod 508, Charlotte 704, Chicago 312, Cincinnati 513, Dallas 214, Denver 303, Detroit 313, Hawaii: 808, Hollywood 213, Houston 713, Indianapolis 317, Kansas City 816, Las Vegas 702, Long Beach 562, Los Angeles 213, Memphis 901, Miami 305, New Orleans 504, New York City (Bronx) 718, New York City (Brooklyn) 718, New York City (Manhattan) 212, New York City (Queens) 718, Palm Springs 760, Philadelphia 215, Phoenix 602, Pittsburgh 412, Salt Lake City 801, San Diego 619, San Francisco 415, Seattle 206, Washington 202, Yonkers 914.

Teil 3: Presentations in English

Autorin: Jaquie Mary Thomas

Präsentationen vor Publikum sind bereits in der eigenen Sprache eine Herausforderung. Ungleich stärker steigt der Adrenalinspiegel, wenn man das sichere Terrain seiner Muttersprache verlässt und auf Englisch präsentiert: Ist mein Englisch gut genug? Was, wenn ich nicht auf das richtige Wort komme? Was, wenn meine Zuhörer mich nicht verstehen – oder ich sie nicht? Das sind nur die ersten Hürden, die viele bei einem Vortrag auf Englisch sehen.

Mit dem Handwerkszeug in diesem Kapitel werden Sie nicht nur diese Hürden überwinden. Sie finden Werkzeuge, mit denen Sie Ihren gesamten Vortrag meistern – von der Vorbereitung, über die Begrüßung, die Präsentation selbst, bis zur Verabschiedung des Publikums. Auch auf die Diskussion mit Ihren Zuhörern können Sie sich gezielt vorbereiten – und dadurch sicher in die Präsentation gehen. Ich zeige Ihnen, worauf es beim Vortragen auf Englisch ankommt, und stelle Ihnen zahlreiche sprachliche Techniken und Beispiele vor. Ganz nebenbei eignen Sie sich nützliche Sätze, Wendungen und Key Words an.

Die Sprache ist das eine, die Herkunft Ihres Publikums das andere – und nicht weniger wichtig. Denn die kulturellen Unterschiede in der Art zu kommunizieren, sind groß. Und der beste Vortrag nützt nichts, wenn man seine Zuhörer schon bei der Begrüßung vor den Kopf stößt. Ich zeige Ihnen, wie Sie sich auf Ihr internationales Publikum einstellen und es so für sich gewinnen.

9 Preparation

Whether you have five minutes, five hours or five months to prepare, these are the most important points:

- developing an international viewpoint,
- preparing yourself, the person,
- putting yourself in your audience's shoes,
- organising facilities,
- your presentation structure,
- preparing good slides.

9.1 Developing an international viewpoint

You have to do a presentation in English, maybe abroad or in your home country. Your audience may be from another country, or from many. What will they be like? What will they expect?

9.1.1 Things can be different

You want to do a good (or at least reasonable) presentation. You know your own idea of a good presentation but what's their idea of a good presentation? From an international viewpoint, a great many things can be different to presenting to a »home« audience. These can include:

- timing,
- content detail,
- how people listen,
- how/if they ask questions,
- eye contact (if any),
- conversation making,
- clothing,
- body language or
- even the question of whether a presentation is at all suitable or if everybody should have a good discussion over a 3-hour lunch with a bottle of wine instead.

It's a question of culture. A question of the way things are done in that situation, in that place, with those people.

!

Example

Chinese and other cultures, where the group is more important than the individual, may come to a presentation as a group of ten to twenty or more people, depending upon the importance to them. They may then be surprised to see only you (with maybe one or two colleagues) and wonder where the others are.

The best way you can develop an international viewpoint and avoid a lot of misunderstandings, is to always keep the following four points in mind.

9.1.2 Accept that differences exist!

Think perhaps of a bottle standing next to a glass. From your point of view, the bottle may be in front of the glass. From someone on the other side it is behind the glass. From another person's viewpoint it's on the right. And, yes, from another person's viewpoint it's on the left.

Everybody can have a different viewpoint, a different view, but everybody can be right. Compare this to different places in the world. Presentations are done differently in France, in Germany, in Japan, in the US. Each of these ways of doing presentations is right, in those places, in those situations, with those people.

!

Examples: Starting a presentation

Presentations in the US often start with a joke, in the UK with an apology, in Germany with the background details.

This does not mean that you should start with a joke in the US or an apology in the UK. It does mean that you need to think about the differences. How does your style suit the setting you are dealing with? You can then decide if you shorten the introduction and/or reduce the number of slides in total. You may then need to be more prepared to »go with the flow« – letting your audience point you in the direction they want to go to with their questions.

9.1.3 Opposite behaviour may not mean opposite values

Realise that differences in behaviour and differences in the importance of values can lead to a lot of misunderstanding. Opposite behaviour does not necessarily mean opposite values.

Example: Direct and indirect speech

!

Germans tend to speak directly: »You made a mistake.« This direct behaviour is often based on values of openness, honesty and the desire not to waste the other person's time.
The British tend to speak indirectly: »It seems that something wasn't quite right«: This indirect behaviour is often based on values of politeness and respect for the other person and the desire not to hurt the other person's feelings.
The Chinese may say nothing at all.
The translation »opposite behaviour = opposite values« here often leads to Germans thinking that the Chinese and the British are not open, not honest and waste time and, conversely, to British and Chinese thinking that the Germans are impolite, lack respect for other people (arrogant!) and don't care if they hurt other people's feelings.

This means that you shouldn't always let your reactions be led by how you interpret specific behaviour. Keep more of an open mind during a multinational or international presentation.

9.1.4 Use cultural generalisations with care

A generalisation is something that applies to 55% or more of a group of people – not a stereotype (100% of the people in that group, all of the time) and not a prejudice (a stereotype plus positive or negative judgment). A group can be a nationality group (e.g. French, Italian, Japanese), a regional group (e.g. north German, south German), a gender group (men, women), a professional group (IT people, sales people, commercial people, marketing people), as well as corporate, religious or age.

Example

!

»All French people interrupt presentations to ask questions« is a stereotype. »All French people interrupt presentations to ask questions – this is very rude« is a prejudice. The French people that you present to may not interrupt at all, and if they do, they will probably see it as positive.

You can use generalisations to help you prepare for your presentation, if you think of them as »most of the people do this most of the time«. So you can expect interruptions from Italians in general or active listening (nodding, verbal agreement or disagreement) from Americans in general but, if the people you deal with don't do that, then you shouldn't be too surprised. Everyone is an individual, with their own unique history – you can only identify tendencies that may or may not apply.

9.1.5 When and how to adapt to others' cultural style?

People often ask »Why should I change, why don't they?« and may feel that they are not being »themselves« if they change their style.

First and foremost, we all change our style depending on whether we are talking to our colleagues, our managers, our partners, our friends, our children, etc. It doesn't mean we are not being »ourselves« if we change style. We just have different roles.

This is the same in business. Sometimes you present to your colleagues, sometimes to your managers, maybe to your team members, as well as suppliers, customers, collaboration partners – again you have different roles and adapt often quite naturally, without thinking about it too much. Presenting in English can mean you are presenting to any of those just mentioned – maybe two nationalities, maybe twenty nationalities, maybe in your own home country, maybe abroad. All of these situations are different and, if you want to do a good presentation every time, you may need to adapt in every situation.

When to adapt: situation, surrounding and individuals
This decision of when to adapt to others' cultural style can only be made by you (or you and your colleagues when working as a group). There are no clear black and white guidelines, but you can make the decision easier by considering the situation, the surrounding and the individual.

- **situation:** This is your first factor when deciding to adapt. What is the business situation and what does the distribution of power look like? Are you making your presentation as customer or supplier? Are you an engineer presenting technical information to a potential buyer or transferring information to other people on your international project team? Are you a financial controller presenting to your board or to your team? People are generally more motivated to switch styles when they need something.
- **surrounding:** Where are you? This is your second factor when deciding when to adapt. Are you presenting in your home country or abroad? Are you in your own company or in theirs? Are you in the boardroom or on the factory floor?
- **individuals:** Who are you presenting to? This is your third factor when deciding when to adapt. Who are the people you are dealing with? Are they men, women, older or younger than you? Are they board members, sales or marketing people, human resource experts, accountants, engineers? Do they have a lot of international experience?

How to adapt: cultural dimensions

If you don't know or are unsure about any of the above three points – e.g. who you are dealing with – then you need to do some thinking (see »Putting yourself in your audience's shoes«). Once you have made the decision of **when** to adapt, you need to think about **how** to switch style. You need to consider the possible cultural influences regarding the situation, surroundings and individuals according to cultural dimensions. When you present internationally, the following cultural dimensions are usually the most important:

- **time orientation** – how is time likely to be seen? Could your audience be more, the same or less punctual than you? Do you think they see time as money or do they treat it as something that will continue endlessly? Intercultural researchers talk about monochronic and polychronic cultures. People belonging to monochronic cultures prefer to do one thing at a time and place importance on deadlines and time schedules. You need to be aware of your natural style in comparison to the people you are dealing with. Then you can decide how to switch style by becoming more or less punctual, for example.

Example !

When planning a presentation to a Spanish audience, you may find that they could probably be less punctual than yourself, and that they don't cut time into specific numbered pieces as much as you do.
This means that for a presentation scheduled to start at 09.00, you don't need to worry if half of the people are not there and you start later than originally scheduled. Also, that your presentation may go well over schedule. This may not matter to them as much as it does to you – again no need to worry.

- **People vs. task orientation** – how important to your audience is the personal relationship compared to the task? Do they split or mix the two more or less than you? In Germany, people tend to separate business and pleasure – »Dienst ist Dienst und Schnaps ist Schnaps«. Germans generally do the business first, and then maybe get to know the people. Other nationality cultures, such as the Japanese, will want to get to know the people before doing business.

Example !

When presenting to an audience more person-oriented than yourself, make sure you allow time for relationship building – getting to know each other – e.g. dinner the evening before the presentation or coffee and cookies before you start.

- **Communication style – direct vs. indirect** – how directly or indirectly does your audience communicate? Again, you need to be aware of your natural style, so that you can choose to »soften« your English language with phrases such as »I think«, or »perhaps« or »maybe«, as well as opposites »not easy« instead of »difficult«, or rephrasing »challenge« instead of »problem«.

!

Example

When formulating objectives, don't say »you will ...« but »I hope you will ...«. For example, »By the end of this presentation, I hope you will have a clear picture of progress on the project.«

9.2 Preparing yourself, the person

Most people have nerves before making a presentation – in fact, you're unusual if you don't. On top of any normal nerves comes the fact that you need to do a presentation in a foreign language – English. Finally the uncertainty about the international audience: How will they react?

9.2.1 How to deal with nerves

First, you need to fundamentally accept how much you like making presentations or not. That's the way it is. You need to remember that you are an expert in your specific field. Communicating specific information to others is part of your job. Doing that well means doing part of your job well. You have probably already given other presentations and they went well enough. Or at least, you didn't lose your job.

Three golden principles to remember

1. **You don't need to be perfect to succeed.**
   You can be average, or below average, you can make mistakes, too. As long as you give the audience something of value, it doesn't matter. They will be thankful if they walk away with something of value.
2. **Your audience is usually not sitting and waiting for you to fail.**
   Most of them are scared to death of public speaking. A slip of the tongue or a mistake of any kind may seem big to you, but it's not usually very meaningful or important to your audience. Their judgments of you will be much more easy-going than your own. It's useful to remind yourself of this point, especially if you think you performed poorly.

3. **You are unlikely to please 100% of the audience.**
   That's okay. Even if you would like to please everybody, no matter how good a job you do, there is likely to be at least one person in your audience who will disapprove of you or your content. That's human nature!

!

Important

Think back to the last few presentations you watched. Were the mistakes that the presenters made important? Do you even remember any mistakes?

Techniques to reduce some of your nerves

Choose between one and three of these techniques and use them for your next presentation. If they don't work for you, then try others. It's unlikely that you will be able to eliminate your nerves completely – indeed, having some nerves is positive, providing you with the necessary adrenalin.

- Make sure you have the key English words for each slide either in the slide itself, or on numbered cards. Have one or more solutions ready, if you forget the words (see »What if you forget the words?«).
- Learn the first few sentences and last few sentences of your presentation word for word.
- Visualise yourself starting your presentation well – close your eyes and see the first few steps – e.g. walking to the front, calmly setting up your laptop, checking the image, turning to the people, taking a deep breath, saying good morning and outlining the purpose of the talk today
- Visualise yourself ending your presentation well – close your eyes and see the final few steps – e.g. looking at the audience and thanking them slowly and clearly, gathering your papers/equipment calmly and returning to your place.
- Remember your audience are people – just like you, they eat, breathe and sleep. No more, no less. Just people.
- Remember past experience – somehow, somewhere, you've been through this type of thing before. You know this feeling, you got through it and you survived. You can do it again.
- Let go of »I can't« – research shows that if you focus on »I can't do it«, you reduce your chance of success. Logical really, isn't it? Stop telling yourself you can't do it and focus on doing things differently. That's one of the reasons you're reading this book.
- Just do it! – no comment needed here.

9.2.2 Dealing with »language« nerves

First, you need to fundamentally accept that you have to do the presentation in English. Even if you don't like it, even if you wish that you could do it in your own native language. There's probably nothing you can do about it, so just getting on with it is the easier policy.

»My English isn't good enough.«, »Everyone else speaks better English than me.«, »What if I forget the words?« and »What if I can't understand them?« are typical thoughts running through people's minds.

9.2.3 Your English isn't good enough?

Second, you need to accept however good or bad your English is. That's the way it is at the moment. Most non-native speakers always feel that their English is not good enough. Whether they are at an advanced, intermediate or elementary level, their attitude is still the same – not good enough. People would like their English to be as good as their mother tongue. This is unrealistic and illogical.

Just think of the number of conversations you have had, the number of books and newspapers you have read, the number of television programmes you have seen, the amount of work you have done in your mother tongue and compare it to the same in English. Don't create stress for yourself with negative guilt feelings that you really should attend an English course, learn more vocabulary, practise more, etc. Work and information flows have become much faster over the last couple of decades. Business trips by air, leaving and returning the same day are commonplace. Internet information sourcing means people process huge amounts of information very quickly. Process steps are performed much more quickly than before via e-mail, Netmeeting and other electronic methods of communication. All of these put demands on people's time. They are often left with the feeling of not having enough free time. Therefore, if you do manage to attend an English course, that's fine. If not, don't worry about it. Just get on with the job.

9.2.4 Everyone else speaks better English than you?

Next, think of your audience. If you have non-native speakers, it is highly unlikely that they will notice your mistakes. It could even be that their English is not as good as yours and you may need to simplify your English (use shorter, not longer words) and speak more slowly than usual (i.e. with pauses between phrases). If you have native speakers, they are probably impressed with the fact that you can speak a foreign language. The majority of native English speakers cannot speak a second language. Switch your attitude and try to be proud of the fact that you can speak English (if you aren't already proud).

If you think that your colleagues speak better English than you, remember again that you, too, are an expert in your field. Don't hesitate to consult them whenever a word is missing.

Don't feel inferior language-wise if presenting to Scandinavians, a great many of whom can speak fluent English. This results from the fact that their television films are shown in English, with subtitles in their native languages. They have a huge advantage. Try and put them in the category of native speakers.

> Listeners absorb information differently to readers. You need to speak using the »spoken word« – not the formal more complicated »written word«.

Checklist: dealing with »language« nerves

- Make your presentation Concise, Clear and Complete (C.C.C.).
- Use short sentences.
- Use simple words.
- Avoid phrases that are difficult to say.

9.2.5 What if you forget the words?

A person forgetting their words completely is extremely unusual. Truly unusual. The chances are minimal. If, however, you are one of the people who have the experience of drying up completely in the past and not being able to say a word, well, even if it was horribly embarrassing, we are all human at the end of the day and the audience most probably sympathised with you. One of the best techniques is to learn the first and last few sentences of your presentation by heart. Have it checked, if you have time, by a native speaker (colleague, another department, friend) and then learn it so that you can say it off by heart. This means you have to practise saying it. Not just in your head. Do make sure you speak the words aloud, again and again, in the car, on the train or bus, in the bathroom, until you know them inside out. It is more likely that you will not be able to think of a specific word(s) during the presentation. You have a selection of alternatives:

Solution 1

If other people in your audience are native speakers of the same language as you, then the immediate solution is to say:

- I'm looking for the word »zeitraubend« in English.
- What's »zeitraubend« in English?

Either someone will give you the answer and say »time-consuming« or will try and explain »takes a long time«, or nobody will be able to help you. At the very least, you will not be alone. This solution really works very well and needn't interrupt the flow of your presentation.

Solution 2

If the word doesn't come to mind, close your mouth (to prevent an »err«, »umm« or »aah«) and just give yourself a little time to find the word or rephrase or start another sentence. Most people speak too quickly during presentations and your audience will welcome a break to think or to let your last point sink in or to even just relax for a moment or two. Don't be afraid of a silence.

Solution 3

If you can't find the word and have no native speakers of the same language as you, try involving the audience:

!

Example

You: This new process is much more ... what's the word? It won't break down so often, it's much more ...
Audience: Safe?
You: Not exactly
Audience: Reliable?
You: Yes, exactly, thank you – it's much more reliable than the old system.

You can substitute »What's the word?« with »I'm looking for a word ...« or »I can't think of the word ...« If the audience doesn't know the word either, stay calm and move on to the next sentence. Use the words »anyway« and/or »well« to link or thank the audience:

- Anyway, what I want to say is that it really is a very good system.
- Well, the main point is that this system really is very good.

9.2.6 What if you can't understand the audience?

People often worry that they won't be able to understand the audience. English, Scottish, Welsh, Irish, west coast American, east coast American, Australian, etc. all have extremely different accents. It's not uncommon for native speakers to misunderstand each other. Again, the key is to stay calm and get others people's help if necessary. Don't appear aggressive by telling someone to speak more clearly – always take the problem away from the speaker.

Useful phrases
Acoustic problem: Sorry? I couldn't hear that. Could you say it again a little louder please?

Too fast: Sorry? I'm afraid that was a bit too fast for me. Could you say it again a little slower please?

You didn't understand: Sorry? I didn't get that. Could you say it again?

Then check by repeating the statement/question:
- You're saying/asking ...
- What you're saying/asking is …
- What you want to know is …

!

Example

A: What do you think it all boils down to in the end? Are there really any significant differences between all three options at the end of the day?
B: Sorry? I didn't quite get that. Could you say it again?
A: Sure. What I want to know is whether it really makes a difference which option we take here, or if they are all pretty much the same.
B: So you're asking about the differences between the three options?
A: Yes, that's right.

- If you still don't understand, try to get the audience to help: I'm sorry, I still don't quite understand. Perhaps someone could translate for me?
- Or ask the person if you could talk together in the break or at the end, depending on the situation. Be specific – »in ten minutes« or »at 10.30« – otherwise you may sound like you don't mean it: »I'm sorry I don't understand right now. Can we meet in the break in ten minutes and talk together? I'd like to take some more questions before we finish.«
- Another solution could be to use a flipchart to visualize the statement/question, if suitable: »Let me put that on paper, to be sure it's clear. Your idea is to do A first, then B, followed by C and D. Is that right?«

! **Important**

In situations where it is important not to lose face (e.g. Japan and most Asian countries in general), it may be a good idea to give an answer (some general comments) even if you don't understand the question. In this way, the questioner is not embarrassed, you don't lose face either and you can always speak to the questioner.

See the section »Dealing with questions« for more details.

Understanding non-native English speakers better

It's often difficult for native English speakers to understand each other. The differences between American, Australian, British and Indian English are huge. Even differences within a country (Oxford English and Scottish English, for example) make things difficult. The next two points can be helpful.

- A lot of Asian languages are made up of »consonant, vowel« pairs – e.g. »Mi – tsu – bi – shi.« This often makes it difficult to say consonants at the end of English words – e.g. »foo« could be food, fool or foot, which are all »consonant, vowel, consonant« patterns. Listening is made easier if you know this fact. Speaking is made clearer by adding a »weak« vowel after the final consonant – e.g. »foo – t«
- Indian people in general often speak fast, in a sing-song voice without pauses. Either you get used to it within a couple of days, or you »gently force« the person to make breaks. Interrupt carefully by lifting your hand(s) up and repeating the keywords of their last phrase then put your hands down to »let« them carry on. If you know them well enough, you could ask them to make pauses.

9.3 Putting yourself in your audience's shoes

Try to see things from your audience's point of view. Not yours. This is vitally important – whether for 6, 60 or 600 people. »What do **they** want to know?« is usually different to »What do I want to tell them?« You cannot start to prepare a presentation without having at least some idea of who your audience is. If you start preparing before you know who they are, it means that you are telling them things from your point of view only. Not theirs.

Imagine you are sitting in the audience, watching and listening to your presentation. In your mind's eye, go and sit in a chair and be part of the audience:

1. Who are you?
2. Why are you there?
3. What do/don't you want to know?

If you don't already know the answers, even the smallest amount of research or thinking will show large benefits. Ask the person who requested you to do the presentation. Ask your colleague who was with the same people last month. Ring and ask a department secretary. Find out the following: Are they younger or older than you? What are their jobs? What are their management levels? Are they more or less technically-minded, sales-oriented, commercially-minded than you? You may need to acknowledge these points.

Examples !

If presenting to older people, recognise their experience to start with:
»Good morning everybody. It's good to be here in our Berlin office this sunny morning. For those who don't know me already, my name is James Harrison from the Frankfurt sales office. During the next thirty minutes, I'd like you to see how we gained a new key customer last month. I do realise that a lot of the people in this room today have a great number of years' experience in this field already. The idea is to share this case study with you.«

If presenting to a multi-disciplinary audience, recognise this fact, too:
»During the next thirty minutes, I'd like you to obtain a basic overview of the new process you will start using this June. I know that we have technical, financial, sales, legal and quality assurance people in this room today. That means that some parts of the presentation will be more interesting than others depending on who you are. The main point today is that everybody has a basic overview – specialised training for each department will take place next week.«

You need to formulate objectives and plan content for the presentation, based on your audience's needs as well as yours. Your audience's interests can be very different.

Examples !

1. **Who are you?**
A: a board member, listening to the fourth presentation from a project manager that day (27th that month)
B: engineers on your project team who have a lot of other meetings booked this week.
C: company trainees
2. **Why are you there?**
A: here to make sure the project is going well.
B: here to be updated on the project progress.
C: here because the overview of your work in your department is part of the training course.

3. **What do/don't you want to know?**
A: wants to know the main points of how the project is going, including how difficulties are being dealt with. Doesn't want to have to »search« for the difficulties. Doesn't want to waste time. An interesting real-life story might be of interest.
B: wants to know only your main points, especially any potential interfaces with their work. Doesn't want too much irrelevant background detail.
C: wants to hear what they could really be doing in your department. Wants to know the most interesting and most boring parts of the work.

- Use »you« or »we« but not »I« (more interesting): »You will be able to see.« not »I will show you.«
- Use »need« but not »must« (very direct, stressful): »Today we need to plan a rough time schedule.« not »Today we must plan a rough time schedule.«

Useful phrases

- In the next twenty minutes, you should get a good idea of the progress made in the main areas of the project, plus an overview of how we are dealing with current difficulties.
- So, here we are again for you to get the latest update on our project, specifically concentrating on any areas of overlap.
- Our main aim today is to compare current and projected performance with the targets. I can tell you now, fourteen out of twenty-six regions are on or over target and twelve are either just under or struggling. The total balance is slightly less than target, although 3% up on last year. Let's start with ...

Checklist: preparation international viewpoint

If you have to present to people from only a couple of other countries then you can research as follows:
▪ Find a cultural insider who can give you main »do's and don'ts« – a person from that country who now lives in your country or works in your company or a contact you already have abroad or a colleague who was there before.
▪ Consider the cultural dimensions mentioned in paragraph »How to adapt: cultural dimensions« in chapter »Developing an international viewpoint« (time, person vs. task orientation, etc.).
▪ Don't forget to ask yourself, when dealing with a more person-oriented culture, whether a presentation is really suitable? Should you be starting with dinner the night before? Or planning a long lunch? Or is a factory tour followed by lunch/dinner more appropriate?
▪ Search for »How to do business in ...« on the Internet.
▪ Buy a book.

If you have a multi-national audience from many different countries:
▪ Consider the cultural dimensions as above.
▪ Make sure you have both a clear and flexible starting time! For example, 08.45 Coffee and greetings, 09.15 First talk.
▪ Make sure you have both a clear and flexible agenda – for example, five points written in a circle with a total start and finish time, clear for the monochronic people, with the option to change the order for the polychronic people.

9.4 Organising facilities

If you're going to make a presentation in another country, be prepared to be flexible. Don't expect to always have the same standards everywhere.

9.4.1 Be prepared

- Have a backup of your PowerPoint presentation on a (second) USB stick or even printed out on overhead projector transparencies, depending on where you are going. Carry it with you in a different place (not both in your briefcase).
- Consider the power supply and take your own international adaptor or two (usually on sale at airports).
- Take your own pens with you, if you want to use a flipchart or white-board. Better still, take your own flipchart paper and masking tape (plastic cylinder carriers are light and very cheap).

9.4.2 Organising the setup

How much of the setup you can influence depends, of course, on the situation and whether you are the customer or supplier, guest or host, etc. If you need to make the arrangements yourself, the main requirements you may need to consider are:

- room size and room set-up – U-form or hollow square for small groups, theatre or classroom style for large groups
- equipment – projector, flipcharts, pinboards
- acoustics – microphone, lectern
- refreshments – water, tea, coffee

Even if you clearly requested specific arrangements, these may not be considered suitable and the organisers may be culturally unable to refuse the request without offending.

! **Example**

Requesting a semi-circle of chairs with no tables for a training course in China may be pointless due to the necessity of tables for the supply of tea. You may not know this until you arrive, because the organisers are unlikely to want to disagree with you beforehand and may feel certain you will understand when you see that the tables are there.

Useful telephone phrases

- Good morning, this is Klaus Schmidt calling from ABC.
- I'm coming over to hold a presentation on the 15th of March and I need to speak to the person responsible for the organisation. Is that you?
- I just wanted to ask a few questions. Is now a good time? Okay. I understand that there will be about 15 people, is that right?
- And could you tell me how big the room is?
- Could we possibly have the chairs and tables in a U-shape?
- And do you have a projector I can attach to a computer or should I bring one myself?
- And is there a flipchart in the room?
- That sounds fine. And my final question is about refreshments. Will there be any drinks and snacks?
- How are the acoustics in the room? Will everyone be able to hear me, or should I have a microphone?
- Can you tell me wether here is a stage or a podium? And do you have a lectern or does the presenter move around?
- Could I have your e-mail address and then I can just send you a short e-mail to confirm?
- I think that's all for now. Can you let me know if anything changes?
- Okay then, thank you very much for your help.

! **Important**

»Beamer« in English means a BMW car. You need to use »projector« or »data projector«.

E-mail examples !

Re: Presentation, March 15, 10.30

Dear Ms Woods

With reference to the above presentation, I would appreciate it if you could organize the following:

- 15 places in a U-shape
- 1 data projector (to attach to my laptop computer)
- 1 flipchart plus pens
- refreshments for the break
- as well as a table for lunch in a nearby restaurant for 15 people at approx. 13.00.

Please let me know if the above is possible.

I look forward to hearing from you.

Best regards

Re: Presentation, March 15, 10.30

Dear Peter

It was good to talk to you this morning. I'd just like to confirm the requirements as follows:

- seating for 35-40 people
- 1 data projector (to attach to my laptop computer)
- refreshments for the break
- 45 hard copies of the presentation

I'll send you a soft copy of the presentation 2-3 days beforehand, as agreed.

Thank you for your help.

Best regards

Important !

You yourself may prefer e-mail, but a lot more person-oriented countries prefer to communicate by telephone. Doubling up (or even tripling) can be more effective – e.g. call the organiser in Greece, then confirm by e-mail and perhaps ring again the day before, depending on the situation.

9.5 Your presentation structure

9.5.1 Circular vs. linear structure

International presentations need to be both circular and linear, because some nationalities are polychronic and others monochronic. The following could happen to you when presenting to an international audience. You may plan carefully and logically according to your preferred system – first, background detail and history, then the problem itself, next, possible options and, finally, your recommendation. You find, however, that your audience wants to know your final recommendation first and asks you a lot of questions, forcing you to jump back and forth from point to point in a circular fashion. Maybe they're not interested in either the background or the details, but want to concentrate on the outcome.

Five golden structure rules
This means you should

- show an agenda slide but be ready to move between sections as required,
- provide background and details in the slides for the analysis-oriented people (e.g. Germans), but watch the audience's reactions and skip over them if you think suitable,
- not »hide« any recommendations at the end but state them right at the beginning, if possible. Example: »So, we need to find a solution to problem A today. I recommend B and want to show you what the problem was, the different options and why I recommend B, so that you can then make a decision.«,
- definitely not say »I'd like to come to that point later« (that can seem very offensive) but give an answer »I think option B is better because of X, Y and Z. The problem we had was ...« and go back to where you were, or just spring forward and leave out the details,
- don't always ask your audience to keep questions to the end – but ask for questions during the presentation, in order to suit their style as necessary.

If you have your agenda written on a flipchart (which you can prepare beforehand and take with you, or printed cards/A4 sheets, with sticky tape), you can refer to it and people can see it all the time. This can help you and others keep track when needed.

9.5.2 Timing

If your presentation is scheduled to start at 10.00 and you expect it to start at 10.00, 10.01 or 10.02, latest 10.07, then you could get frustrated working internationally. Remember the most important thing – what is your overall aim for the audience? It's not to follow your time schedule. Most people try and pack too much into a presentation – whether for an international audience or not.

Allow breathing space
Most situations need a plan with a lot of breathing space because of the following three points:

- People might just not yet be there at the time you're due to start. This can be due to the concept of time which is viewed differently worldwide.

Some cultures consider time to be a never-ending, constant quantity. »If we don't use the time and do it now, we can always do it later«.

- Others view time as an event-related concept: if something more important happens, that takes priority. You need to expect this. »Feel« the situation – if it starts to feel uncomfortable, ask the person in charge if/how long you should wait.
- People might be drinking coffee and chatting, not ready to start. This can be due to different person/task orientation at work. Some cultures need to get to know the person first, before they can do the business.

Again, you can expect this from polychronic cultural groups. You need to »feel« the situation, go with the flow, depending on the distribution of power. Alternatively, plan coffee and informal introductions at the start, if you can. Don't become stressed about your time plan – remember your aim. People might want less input from you and more discussion. Again, adjust accordingly – remember your aim. Put »approx.« (short for approximately) or »circa« in front of times, prepare an agenda with few details – that way you can be more flexible.

!

Example: agenda

08.45 Coffee and refreshments, informal introductions
09.30 BSN Motorparts, James Holloway
circa 11.00 Break
BSN Motorparts (continued)
circa 12.30 Lunch
14.30 PCR Chemistry, Annette Rowlings
circa 16.00 Break
18.00 Close

9.5.3 Structure – main components

1. Introduction: Tell them the point and the plan (1-2 minutes max.).
2. Main body: Tell them the details, including any difficulties and proposals or next steps.
3. Summary: Tell or remind them of what you just said, including the point and next steps (should be shorter than introduction).

Questions are ideally taken all the way through, depending on the situation.

9.5.4 Structure in detail

Structure	Elements
introduction	
opening	▪ greeting and name (slowly and clearly) ▪ company and/or department ▪ reference to place and time (here and now)
objective	point of presentation (from audience point of view)
overview	one slide agenda (ideally three main points)
organisation	time available, questions welcome throughout or afterwards, refreshments, etc.
Main body	
starting signal	Say that you are starting: »So, let's start with ...«
three main sections	People remember three things best – split your presentation into three parts, with sub-divisions later if needed. For example: ▪ new regulations in export paperwork ▪ main differences to current paperwork (details section by section) ▪ future references and assistance
realia	real-life relevant pictures of product, site, people and interesting stories
graphs, charts, diagrammes	Explain »big picture« first, then details second.
Summary (introduction in reverse)	
ending signal	Say that you are ending: »So, that brings us to the end.«
review	Show agenda slide again.
objective achieved	Re-state objective: »So, I hope you now have a clear picture of ...«
open discussion	depending on time
next steps	State next steps or action required: »Our next meeting will be on ...«
thank the audience	Say: »Thank you everybody.«
Question and answer	
	throughout your presentation or at end: ▪ listen ▪ pause ▪ repeat (part of) question ▪ answer ▪ link to a main point

9.6 How to prepare good slides

Most important of all – you really don't need to spend most of your time preparing perfect, detailed slides for an international audience. Remember that person orientation is likely to be at least, if not more important than task orientation. For the French and Belgians, for example, the objective is to be creative and provoking – make the audience think and reason. You need to know exactly the aim and the key messages of your presentation and be prepared to talk about those with the audience. Discussion and interaction are most usually more important than perfect slides.

Good slides are clear and to the point. They help show something to people, so that they can understand better. You need to ask yourself:

- What's the point of this slide?
- What do the people need to know?
- Can it be clearly read?

Checklist: preparing slides

The slides in your international presentation need to be in »international English« – you should avoid long, complicated words.
▪ Always get the slides checked by a native speaker for spelling and grammar – at the very least, use the »spell-check« function.
▪ Make sure you have a note of the English keywords for the main message of every slide. Ask a colleague or use an online dictionary. Don't spend hours on it – stay realistic.
▪ Use the »six-pack« rule: six words per line, six lines per slide are ideal.
▪ Bullet points with key words are easier to read and remember than long texts.
▪ If your company working style means you must make long sentences, then don't pack them all together, but spread them out on more than one slide.
▪ Keep it simple – three colours maximum and the minimum of font styles (preferably one only) and sizes (preferably two, maximum three) make the slides much less confusing and much easier to read for your audience.
▪ Pictures speak one thousand words – use photographs of real products, systems, locations or people whenever possible, to bring your presentation to life and make it memorable.

Important !

German language speakers often use too many capital letters – especially in headings. Capital letters should be used in business English only at the beginning of sentences and for specific names, e.g. Reservation system overview, not Reservation System Overview.

10 Greetings and introductions

What you say and do when meeting the people and getting started with your presentation all counts towards the first impression. This chapter will help you to find the right phrases and feel confident about making a good start.

10.1 What to say when you enter

We all know that greetings are not the same the world over. If you choose to match style, points to watch for are:

- whether handshakes are made or not (less common after the first meeting)
- strength of handshake: you should mirror, strong with strong and gentle with gentle
- amount of eye contact or looking away: again, mirror – don't force someone to look in your eyes if they don't want to
- distance between persons: could be much further or closer than you are used to
- use of first or last names: this often causes uncertainty. Listen carefully and then match the style. Americans, Australians and British tend to use first names very soon, if not immediately – »You can call me Robert.« Other cultures use »Mr« and »Ms« to start with and may or may not switch to first names later. Chinese often have an additional western first name, which you should then use. Japanese often add »san« at the end of the name
- conversation making: be prepared to do it!

Example !

When doing business with the Far East, watch out for card exchanging when greeting. Koreans, for example, will stand apart, approach each other, bow, exchange business cards using both hands, step back and then read each other's business card aloud, with appropriate remarks »I see you are the Business Director ...«. This shows respect for the persons and their positions. As a foreigner, you are not expected to know how exactly to bow (different depths show different levels of respect), but you should not write on the business card and definitely not put it into the back pocket of your trousers. Watch to see what the other does.

10.1.1 Meeting people for the first time

!

Example

»Hello, good morning. My name's Heinrich Melke. Nice to meet you.« – »Hello. It's nice to meet you, too. I'm Alexander Thompson. Call me Alex, it's easier.« – »Okay then Alex, I'm Heinrich, or Henry, whatever you prefer.« – »Henry's easier for me!« – »I'm not surprised, Heinrich is a bit of a mouthful if you don't speak German.« – »Yes, I'm always impressed by how well Germans speak English.« – »Oh, it's not easy, you know. We are perfectionists – it's never good enough!«
»Hello, good afternoon. I'm Wolfgang Steinecke from ABC GmbH.« – »Ah, yes, good afternoon. I'm Roger Silvestre and this is Sylvie Dalmar.« – »Nice to meet you.« – »Nice to meet you too.« – »Did you find the way here okay?« – »Yes, it was no problem at all. It's a very nice place. Is it new?« – »Well....«

Useful phrases

- Hello, I'm Andrew, Andrew Smith. It's good/nice to meet you.
- Hi, I'm David Jones. (I'm) pleased to meet you, too.
- Hello, I'm James Morrison. It's good/nice to meet you, too.
- Hi, I'm Mary Thompson. Pleased to meet you, too.

»It's good/nice to meet you.« and »(I'm) pleased to meet you« are interchangeable. »How do you do?« is rather more formal British English. It means »Pleased to meet you« and does not mean »How are you?« The answer is simply »How do you do« or »Nice/good/pleased to meet you.«

Most people all over the world use »Good to **meet** you« for the first meeting, then say »Good to **see** you again« for further meetings. Americans, however, often use »Good to see you« for the first meeting, too.

10.1.2 Making conversation

Making conversation is often a very important part of the business. Try not to fire questions »bullet style« but say a little yourself first before asking.

Phrases like »It's a nice day, isn't it?« are usually not really invitations to talk about the weather, but an opening to see if the other person wants to talk. A suitable answer if you want to talk is »Yes, it's lovely. Much nicer than when I left home in Kiel, northern Germany yesterday. Where do you come from?«

If someone asks »How are you?«, you should not only give an answer, but also ask back. You shouldn't directly translate into German and answer with a list of your latest illnesses, but think of it as meaning »Good morning«.

Important !

Avoid talking about politics, sex or religion.

Useful phrases

- So, here we are. This is my first trip to ... I have heard so much about it. Do you live nearby?
- I come from ..., myself. Have you ever been to Germany? /Did you ever go there?
- There are a lot of trees just starting to flower at the moment. Is it the beginning of the cherry blossom season?
- I'm really looking forward to trying the food/wine/beer here. I have heard so many good things about it.

Examples !

Good subjects for Americans can be sport – baseball, basketball or American football – ask about the local teams e.g. »What are the main sports around here?« Chinese people often love to talk about food e.g. »We have a lot of Chinese food in Germany, but I'm really looking forward to a real Chinese restaurant here in Beijing.«

10.2 Introducing your presentation well

This is the start – get it right! A good guideline to make sure your presentation will be acceptable for the whole world is to make very sure you clearly (and quite slowly) state who you are and the point of your presentation, with some reference to »here and now« to make it »real« and interesting, together with a few details of the plan. The title and plan should be visualised in simple English – either on a slide or a flipchart (advantage – it remains in view).

Examples !

Presentation 1

Good morning ladies and gentlemen, I'm Benno Donauer from the electronic engineering department at Opus GmbH and it's good to be here in Rio on this very sunny Friday morning. By the end of this presentation you should be able to see why A, B and C are so very important to you and your company, Omega. First we'll look at A, then move on to B and finish with C. We have forty minutes altogether. If you have any questions at any time, do please just ask.

Presentation 2
Good morning everybody!
For those who don't already know me, my name's Bernd Huber. I'm from the Electronics Assembly Systems Department at Drive Technologies AG in Berlin. Here we all are in Madrid, today, October 5th, 20XX, and by the end of this presentation (*show title slide, read name of presentation*) »Serrano Limitido and Drive Technologies« I hope you will know how technologically advanced, reliable and flexible our machines are for you, and be able to see why we at Drive Technologies are the very best partner for you.
We'll look at the X-machine technical functionality to start, then move on to possible adaptations for you, Serrano Limitido, and finish with our service offer – how we can work well together.
We have three hours scheduled, with a break halfway through for coffee. If you have any questions at any time, please do ask me. Good. Let's get started.

Checklist: introducing your presentation

- Be sure to formulate your objective(s) carefully from your audience's point of view – who they are and what they need (see »Putting yourself in your audience's shoes«).
- If you know that problems are likely to arise, you can either talk to people about them beforehand or name them at the beginning of your presentation.
  - »So, we are here today to obtain a common understanding of A, B and C. I know that D and E happened this morning and that a lot of people here would probably also like to go over F and G, but the plan right now for the next twenty minutes is A, B and C.«
  - »I realize that the situation regarding … could change next week or next month – who knows, it may not change at all – and I realize that this would mean that we would immediately change the product, no question. Today, however, I want to use our time to deal with the present situation, the conditions that we have now, at the moment and not spend time speculating. If things change, then we will need to change, too.«
- A rhetoric question, real-life story or example can be a good opening if you want to do a little more.
- Be as authentic as possible. If you are not »happy to be here today«, then use another phrase – don't say it.
- Avoid humour if you have a multi-national audience. Test your funny stories with cultural insiders beforehand if you have a single nationality audience. Humour can be very »unfunny« or even offensive if it falls flat. People may feel unsure or even stupid if they don't understand. If you're not sure, don't do it.
- Also avoid apologies (»I didn't really have enough time to prepare the slides«) or making yourself appear less significant than you really are (»I'm not really the boss, I just let people do their thing«) – these are both typical for the UK but could be seen as »losing face« in a lot of Asian countries.

10.3 Introduction components

An introduction needs four components: an opening, objective, overview and some information about organisation.

10.3.1 Openings

- Good morning, I'm ... (*name*), from ... (*department and/or company*).
- Good afternoon everybody. For those who don't already know me, my name's ..., from ...
- Hello everyone. I know most people here already, for those I don't, my name is ... and I'm from ...
- I'm pleased to be here in ... (*place*) with you today, ... (*date*).
- It's good to be here in ... with you on this sunny Friday morning.
- Here we all are in ... this Wednesday afternoon.
- So, let's get started. (*More informal with no name, if you all know each other.*)

Important !

Typical German English mistake: »Good morning altogether« – should be »Good morning everybody« or »Good morning everyone«.

Opening with a question

- So, everybody, why are we here? We are here because you need an update on the changes to the booking process. It's important because you will need to use it next week, starting Monday morning at 08.30. My name's ..., from ... and ... (*objective*).
- Good morning everybody. The question now is why are we at Schneider GmbH the best partner for Millwards Systems? The answer is because we really do meet your needs. For those who don't already know me, my name's ..., I'm the technical director at Schneider and ... (*objective*).
- How reliable is our service and maintenance system? The answer is 100 percent over the last six years. That, ladies and gentlemen, is what I'd like to show you today. My name's ..., from ... and ... (*objective*).

Opening with a story

Be as specific as possible, with a couple of dates and times, numbers and background details.

- On the 31st of March this year, we put in our XYZ system at AB Consulting, with over 1,200 users worldwide. There were the minimum of start-up problems and AB Consulting can definitely recommend us and the XYZ system. For those who don't know me, my name's ...

- Hello everyone, I was on site last Wednesday, Thursday and Friday in Kiev. The weather was absolutely freezing, but work went well. There were over 130 workers that week and this week we will have over 160. Things are going well on the whole (*objective*).

Opening with an example or picture

- Next week, we will have a six-figure reference number instead of four figures. This is one of the changes to the invoicing process that we need to look at today. My name's ... from ... and (*objective*).
- This (*illustration on slide*) is my favourite of the new posters in our new marketing campaign (*objective*).

10.3.2 Objectives

- By the end of this presentation, I hope you will ...
- By the end of the next twenty minutes, you should ...
- We now have sixty minutes for you to ...
- ... know why A, B and C are important for you in your job.
- ... have a clear picture of progress on the project including the main challenges.
- ... be able to see why we at Schneider GmbH are the very best partner for you.
- ... have a clear overview of the financial/technical/sales/marketing aspects.
- ... have an update on the changes to the existing system/product/method.
- ... be updated on the latest marketing campaign/sales figures for the third quarter.

When more than one objective:

- ... and, as well, ...
- ... and on top of that ...
- ... and in addition ...
- ... be able to implement this information starting next week.
- ... have enough information to reach a decision regarding supplier/time schedule.

!

Important

A typical German English mistake is to always say »my presentation« – should be »the presentation« or leave it out. For example, »This is the overview of my presentation – should be »This is the overview«.

10.3.3 Overview

- First, we'll look at A, then move on to B and finish with C.
- A is our first point, followed by B and then C is last.
- First, the present status, next, the present challenges and proposed solutions and finally, the next steps.

10.3.4 Organisation

- We have forty minutes in total.
- We have one and a half hours, with a ten-minute break halfway through.
- If you have any questions at any time, do please ask.
- If you have any questions, please could you hold them till the end, when we will have time for a discussion – except questions for understanding, of course.
- Coffee will be served in the break/at the end on the tables outside the doors.
- Matthias has reserved a table at the Hard Rock Café for us all for lunch afterwards.
- Can we all switch our cell phones off? Or at least have them on silent mode?
- If anybody needs to take a phone call, I'd be grateful if they could leave the room.

Important !

Many person-oriented cultures, especially the Middle East including Saudi Arabia, Kuwait and others may find it unthinkable to be unreachable during your presentation. Don't even ask them to switch off the phones; if you are important enough they will do it without asking (see »Handling interruptions and disturbances«).

10.4 Dealing with handouts

Providing handouts very much depends on the situation and content of your presentation. Remember that a lot of cultures will be very interested in you as a person, as well as the facts and figures. If the handouts are designed to be used during the session then you obviously need to give them out beforehand.

Example !

People from specific countries, such as Japan, will expect handouts in a presentation. Research the Internet when presenting to one or two nationalities.

Handouts at the beginning

- Finally, before we start, there are handouts for everyone to make notes if they wish. Do we need some more? I can see a man at the back waving his hand – could you pass this back to him? Thank you.
- Everybody should, with a bit of luck, have already seen the presentation slides. I sent them out last week. There are some additional hard copies here for anyone who needs one.
- There are handouts for everyone to make notes if they wish.
- There are handouts at the back of the room if anyone would like to take notes.
- Does everybody have a handout? If not, I have some more here.
- Does anybody *not* have a handout?
- Do we need more handouts? If we need them, we can have more copies made.

Handouts at the end

- There are handouts by the door for you to take on your way out.
- If you would like a copy of the presentation, please leave your e-mail address on the list by the door.
- I'll send everybody a copy of the slides for future reference.

Requesting copies

- Could you make us another 20 copies please?
- Could you staple them together with holes? That would be great.
- ... Double-sided would be fine as well.
- ... Hmm, double-sided won't quite work because the print on the diagrammes will show through.

10.5 Taking care of technical problems

When something goes wrong you should do what you want your audience to do – stay calm. Use some or all of these steps:

- Keep the audience informed at all times, even if nothing happens.
- Name the problem.
- State the options (depending on the situation).
- Decide on action (any decision is better than none).
- Follow that action including adhering to time limits.
- Stay calm and don't stop communicating!

!

Examples

»My computer doesn't want to start right now. I can change the power supply and try again or use someone else's laptop with my USB stick. (*Member of audience offers laptop.*) Great. Okay then, I need two or three minutes to set up again. You can have a coffee, make a phone call, etc. ... Okay, let's get started. Thank you for your patience everyone.«

»We don't seem to have a connection to the computer. Let me switch off and start again. Can you bear with me? It'll take a minute or two and then we can see if it works ... Okay, I'm afraid it's still not working. Let's take a ten-minute break and meet again at 11.15. I'll try and find another projector in the meantime, otherwise we can do without one ... Unfortunately, we couldn't solve the problem. We can do one of three things now – either postpone the meeting or all crowd round my laptop, or find another room in the next building, maybe. (*Audience wants to crowd round laptop.*) Okay, for those who don't know me ...«

Computer problems

- Well, my computer doesn't want to start.
- It looks like my computer is having problems.
- I'm afraid my computer will need another two or three minutes to restart/boot up.
- My computer is very slow today.

Projector problems

- The projector doesn't seem to be plugged in. Could you check the socket for me?
- We don't seem to have a connection to the computer. Let me start again.
- It looks like there's no signal. Does anyone know how to scan for a signal on this projector?

Sound and light problems

- We don't have any sound. I can't find the command/button – can anyone help?
- Could somebody close the blinds?
- Does anyone know where the switch is?
- Could you close the curtains?
- Can we switch the lights off at the front?
- Can we keep the lights on at the back?

11 Main section: skills and techniques

You can use a few or all of the clearly-explained process steps in this chapter, together with the lists of useful phrases to improve your presentation delivery, question handling and disturbance management.

11.1 Fixing your body language

11.1.1 International viewpoint

When presenting to different nationality audiences you need to be aware of three main body language points: eye contact, smiling and the audience's body language.

Example !

When presenting to the Japanese, make sure you know who the most senior person is and address your presentation to them. Japanese respect for hierarchy is usually very high. Do not try to motivate others to ask or answer questions; this could be embarrassing for them. Discussion, if any, should take place with the senior manager or, most often, after the presentation out of work hours, during perhaps karaoke evenings.

Eye contact

If the people you are speaking to don't look you directly in the eye, don't force them to do it by trying to move into their view. Direct eye contact in Western European countries most often means honesty and friendliness, but not always in other parts of the world. In Japan and other Asian countries it can mean a lack of respect. Men and women looking at each other directly in the eye can also mean different things in countries such as Turkey, for example.

Smiling

Smiling at the beginning and during your presentation is seen differently in different countries. Americans are likely to smile more than Germans, who are likely to smile more than Russians. Indeed, in Russia a smile is not a sign of politeness, nor is it common to smile when meeting a person for the first time, or at the beginning of a presentation. A Russian saying goes: »To smile without reason is the mark of an idiot.« Important to know, too, is that Chinese and a lot of Asian cultures will smile or laugh if embarrassed. Inform yourself beforehand for presentations to one nationality; otherwise use your smile sparingly. Try mirroring others – smile if they smile at you.

Audience's body language

Don't be put off if your audience doesn't react the way you expect. Indeed, German audiences can be seen as non-smiling immobile or motionless »stones« by UK/US presenters. Indian audiences may »waggle« their heads – from a western European point of view, as if they are disagreeing, but they are in fact probably agreeing. The UK/US and others may nod their heads from time to time, smile, throw in »agreement« comments or noises – if they sit completely still and unsmiling, this could mean disagreement or even hostility. Some Japanese may look as if they are falling asleep – it could be that the presentation itself does not have the same value as in Western Europe, more important could be the talks later, outside the presentation room.

!

Important

Be careful of differences in body language. You can watch the TV, if presenting in that country or research for »taboos« from books, the Internet or a cultural insider. Don't sit with the soles of your feet showing in the Arabic world, don't point directly at people in Britain, the finger and thumb »okay« sign in Germany means you are going to kill someone in Tunisia, to name but a few.

11.1.2 Body language basics

When you make international presentations, it really is very difficult to know all of the culture-specific body language rules of your audience. Even if you do, you then have the dilemma of a mixed nationality audience – which rules should you follow? The answer is to stay as natural and as neutral as possible. The following tips are the most important.

Checklist: body language basics

Preparation	When preparing for a presentation, stand up and say it at least once. No time? Then, at the very least, the words of the beginning, introduction and the summary should come out of your mouth at least once before you do the real presentation. This will help you feel and therefore look much more confident.
Clothing	If unsure, go overdressed. Again, watch for the way things are done. In the UK and US, no tie, taking a jacket off and rolling up sleeves might be okay, but Japan and Saudi Arabia usually expect suits and ties.
Hands	Do hold your hands at waist height or above to start and finish your presentation – waist and above looks strong, below waist looks weak. Again, watch for the way things are done – e.g. Belgians and French may move their arms from the shoulders upwards and not just from the elbows. Be aware and choose what you do.

Eyes	Don't look at the slides and the walls, do look at the people (or in their direction, if they avoid eye contact). Don't focus on one person you like or who looks most interested – you might appear to be excluding the others. Do look at the audience zig-zag style for a couple of sentences at a time.
Feet	Don't stand with your feet tightly together – this looks unnatural and stiff and can be interpreted as nervousness about the subject. Do keep your feet a little apart; one can be further forward than the other – then you look balanced and solid. Don't point your feet away from the audience – this can be seen as not wanting to be there, or even not liking the people. Do point your feet towards the audience in an open »v«, like clock hands at five to one (12.55) – this usually looks natural and friendly.
Movement	Don't stand still, rooted to the same spot the whole time – it's unnatural. But don't dance around constantly – it can be tiring for the audience to concentrate on your words if you move all the time. Do make definite movements, from one specific place to another, then stop and talk. Move again, stop and talk again.

11.2 Using your voice well

11.2.1 International viewpoint

Speak more slowly than usual and watch your audience's reactions, if you are presenting to an audience of non-native English speakers. Make breaks between phrases. This is easier than speaking more slowly over a length of time. Watch the audience carefully and repeat yourself using other words, if necessary. Watch for differences in volume – Greeks, for example, tend to be louder than Scandinavians – and switch style if you choose.

11.2.2 Two key techniques

We are sure you must have seen sentences that go on and on without any full stops or commas or capital letters and are so long that they are difficult to understand and sometimes even go over three lines or more and use a lot of difficult long words and phrases that are not needed and just go on and on and on and on and on ... Do you see what we mean?

Basically, two techniques are enough for you to be sure your voice sounds interesting in English. If your spoken English is at elementary level and not intermediate or advanced, using these two techniques can make you sound much better.

Use pauses

Firstly, use pauses. Pauses are quite wonderful for a lot of different reasons:

- they give you time to think,
- they give your audience time to understand (a lot of them are non-native speakers, too),
- they can create a little or a lot of suspense and drama (interesting),
- they can replace any »ums« or »ahs« you might want to say.

Stress key words

Secondly, put stress on some of the key words. That's like giving the music of your text some rhythm – a bit of a beat.

Exercise

Stress the marked words and hear the difference – the above text could »look/sound« like this:

We are **sure** you must have seen sentences... that go on and on ... without any **full stops** or **commas** or **capital letters** ... and are so long that they are **difficult** to **understand** ... and **sometimes** even go over **three lines** or more ... and use a **lot** of difficult long **words** and **phrases** that are **not needed** ... and just go **on** and **on** and **on** and **on** and **on** ...

11.2.3 Advanced techniques

If you wish, you can make your presentation more interesting and have some fun with your voice at the same time. You don't need to be an actor nor sound like someone different. Stay yourself, but try »stretching« yourself, to gain more impact and get your message across to your international audience even better.

Put contrast in your voice

The problem is that same speed, same volume and same tone can be monotonous. A monotonous voice is usually boring and difficult to follow. Contrast is the key. It's not difficult. You can put contrast into your voice in these three areas:

- speed (fast vs. slow)
- volume (loud vs. quiet)
- pitch (deep vs. high)

Exercise

Try it out on this text for fun (or on your own presentation). Read the first line fast, the second slowly, the third fast, etc. Then read it again, the first line loudly, the second quietly, the third loudly, etc. And finally, again, the first line in a deep voice, the second high, the third deep, etc.:

We are sure you must have seen
sentences that go on and on
without any full stops or commas or capital letters
and are so long that they are difficult to understand
and sometimes even go over three lines or more
and use a lot of difficult long words and phrases that are not needed

A final point – if you find your time is limited and you have only 15 minutes to do your 45-minute presentation, talking faster won't work. You will not finish on time because you probably can't speak English as quickly as German. In addition, the audience will find it very difficult to follow, especially if they are non-native speakers. Decide quickly what percentage of 15 minutes each part of your presentation should take. Keep your eye on your watch and limit yourself to the key concept in each portion. Next time, be prepared. Think about what you'll keep in the presentation if your time is divided in half or if you are only given 5 minutes.

11.3 Making transitions

German speakers often use long, formal phrases to make links. You don't usually need them when presenting to an international audience. Fewer words often make more impact.

11.3.1 Between slides

Rhetorical questions are a simple method of linking, but don't overuse them. Alternatively, state the content of the slide with little or no introduction.

Useful phrases

- What's next? (*click to next slide*) The technical features.
- The technical features are next.
- The technical features are shown next.

- Next, we have the technical features.
- These are the technical features.
- Here are the technical features.
- The next slide shows the technical features.
- What options do we have? This is the first of three possibilities. (*click*)
- Why is A important? This is why. (*click*) What is the current A? Here it is. (*click*) What does the future A look like? This is it. (*click*)
- What is the current status? Here it is. (*click*) What are the figures? Here they are.
- Where are we now? Here we are. (*click*) What do the figures look like? Here they are. (*click*)
- What are the benefits? You can see them here. (*click*)
- What is the technical functionality? You can read the description here. (*click*)
- How did we solve the problem? This is how. (*click*)

11.3.2 Between sections

Making clear links between the introduction and main section and between sub-sections can help your international audience to follow your presentation more easily.

Useful phrases

- Let's get started.
- Are we ready to start? (*introduction*)
- Good. Next comes the ...
- Okay. So ...
- So. Our first point – the worldwide total sales last month ... So far, so good. Our second point is ...
- Let's go to the next section, the time schedule for the data migration.
- Let's move on to the service level agreement.
- Moving on to the qualifications needed ...
- Now, we'll look at the summer campaign.
- I'd like now to turn to the year-on-year analysis.
- Next, I'd like to look at the process steps.
- The new range of summer cosmetics is next.
- (*Show agenda slide*) Where are we? We have covered A and B in the last twenty minutes, now I'd like to look at C before the break.
- So, we have looked at A and B, now let's go on with C.
- After Europe, the Middle East and Africa, let's move on to the Americas.
- Now we have a detailed picture of the problem, let's look at the options on offer.

- We looked at the content of the migration and the suggested time schedule. Let's go on to look at the manpower and distribution of tasks.
- Okay. We outlined the hardware features and showed you the network system. Let's go on to service and maintenance now.
- Good. That was the old system and then the new system. Now, let's look at the advantages of the new system one-by-one.

11.3.3 Between breaks

Breaks of ten minutes or less are usually impossible for people to come back on time. Try fifteen or twenty minutes and allow for an extra five minutes on top to be sure. If you announce a clear time to continue, your chances of having everyone back are better.

Announcing breaks

- (*Show agenda slide*) We have covered A, B and C. Now let's have a break before we go on to D and E.
- That was the first half, now it's time for a break before the second half.
- Okay. We looked at the current figures for all 46 product lines and analysed them compared to last year's figures; now, I think we all need a coffee/ some refreshment.
- Good. That's all for now. A and B are covered; we'll look at C and D after lunch.
- Can we all be back here in twenty minutes? That's eleven-twenty by my watch.
- Let's start again at two-forty-five.
- I'd like to carry on at three-fifteen.

Giving information about refreshments, lunch, etc.

- Coffee, tea and cookies are at the back of the room.
- Refreshments are just outside the door.
- You can order a drink from the waiter/waitress.
- We can have a drink at the bar.
- Lunch is in the canteen in the next building. Please don't forget to take your visitor pass with you.
- For those (people) here for the first time, the canteen is on the second floor in the next building. Just follow the others.
- Lunch is booked in a Greek restaurant in the Schellingstraße. I suggest we form small groups to walk over there together.
- Who knows the way to the restaurant? Okay then, for those who don't know the way, just follow one of these people.

11.3.4 After the break

If people are missing, you can either start, wait a while or ask your contact or audience what to do. It depends on the situation. In China, France, Italy, Japan and Saudi Arabia, among others, it is usually necessary to wait for the most important person. This is, of course, also true in other countries. It normally doesn't make sense to start without the main decision maker. It is always important for you to keep your audience informed, so that everyone knows what is happening.

Useful phrases

- Okay, let's carry on with point C.
- Good, let's continue.
- I'd like to go on to the final section, now.
- So, what's next?
- It's now eleven-twenty. Not everybody is back yet, but I'd like to carry on anyway.
- Okay then, it's eleven-twenty and there are a few people still missing. Let's give them another five minutes and start again at eleven-twenty-five.
- It's eleven-twenty. Would you like to continue or wait for the others? I don't mind.

!

Important

US English »I don't care« means the same as UK English »I don't mind«. UK English »I don't care« is very negative – use »I don't mind« or »It's all the same to me« for international audiences.

11.4 Explaining slides and diagrammes

Don't compete with the slide. Your audience will always try to read whatever is in front of them, regardless of what you are saying. The next four steps can help you get your message across effectively – especially when your audience includes non-native speakers:

1. Announce your slide.
2. Show your slide.
3. Let people read it, before you start speaking. During this time, you should demonstrate what you want the audience to do – you should turn to your slide and read it silently yourself.
4. Speak about the most important point(s) of the slide and/or give details, examples and real-life stories about those main points.

11.4.1 Text slides

Be sure to state the main point first, before going into specific details – you can think of this as »big picture versus little picture«.

!

Examples

What's important here? The main point is that the figures are positive on the whole. We went over 36 of 54 product targets; we were just under 12 targets and missed 8 targets by between 5 and 13%. However, the total is positive.
Data availability is the most important of these six key strategy points for us here today. It's fundamental. If we don't have the data, then we can't negotiate better prices. For example, it's far easier for us to get better rates with an order volume worth € 300,000 than with an order volume worth € 30,000. It makes sense.
The main point here is that we are represented in 12 different countries worldwide. We have our headquarters in Austria, factories in the Czech Republic and Singapore, as well as branch offices in another 9 countries throughout Europe, the Americas and Asia.

!

Important

Do not read the slides word for word. This can be very dry and boring for your audience. Let them read themselves. You choose the main or most interesting point(s) and give details, an example or real-life story about only those point(s).

Useful phrases

- What's important here? The most important thing is …
- Why is this interesting to us? Well, it's interesting because …
- What's unusual here? It's unusual because …
- XYZ is the most important message here. Let me tell you why …
- XYZ is the most important point. When consumers make the decision to buy …
- The most important message is …
- The main point here is …
- The main difference between this system and the old one is …
- We have 12 points on this list – the most important two are …

11.4.2 Charts and diagrammes

A graph has an x and a y axis with lines or curves. If it has blocks then it's a graph or a chart. A diagramme is a more general word and can often be used for different types of graphs and charts. You don't need to know the name of your chart, diagramme, graph or table. You can just say »Take a look at this«

or »Have a look at this«, followed by »As you can see, here … and here …« US prefer »take«, UK prefer »have«.

As before, be sure to explain the »big picture« first, before going to the »little pictures«:

1. Main point
2. Explanation of layout
3. Highlight key points

!

Examples

Here are the total estimated savings in thousands of euros for this financial year. The black section shows savings already achieved and the grey section shows savings to be achieved by the end of the financial year.
Here we have sales by product line (*point to x axis*) in hundred thousand euros (*point to y axis*). The black line shows last year's sales for each product; the blue line shows current sales and the red line shows the target. So ... (*give your audience time to look*) ... we have 20 product lines here – two are not going very well, six are going alright, ten are going fine and two are going very well indeed. Let's look at the first two and the last two in more detail ...

Main point

- Here are the total sales shown in hundred thousand euros.
- This is what the XYZ should look like in the future.
- This is a summary of the XYZ data.
- This is all of the ABC put together.

Explanation of layout

- Up here/down here we have the ...
- On the right is/are the ...
- On the left is/are the ...
- In the middle is/are the ...
- Top right/middle right/bottom right
- Top left/middle left/bottom left
- This axis shows ABC along here (*point*) against DEF up here (*point*).
- This graph shows total sales, with … up on the left and … across the bottom.
- This chart shows FY2018 compared to FY2019, with … down on the left and … across the top.

Highlighting key points

- The three problem areas are highlighted in yellow.
- I highlighted the three problem areas.

- The top performer in each section is in bold.
- See the next chapter on how to interpret and explain connections between the data.

!

Important

The German word »Kurve« can mean a curve (the line showing the results) or a graph (the diagramme with an x and y axis). Be sure you use »graph« to talk about the whole diagramme and »curve« to talk about the line showing the results.

11.5 Business English terms

Business English is definitely not the same worldwide. Differences exist between American, British, Australian, South African English and many, many more. What does this mean for you when presenting internationally? You shouldn't learn any complicated expressions or local sayings – you risk making unnecessary mistakes or, even worse, saying the expression in the wrong tone of voice, and losing the meaning completely. Simple, well-used words are best.

11.5.1 Reasons behind events

!

Examples

The increase in revenue is a result of a great many factors. The main ones are first the products themselves – the current range is excellent, next is the fact that one of our competitors Company ABC went bankrupt and the final major factor is that the exchange rate is currently very favourable for exports.
The decrease in profitability is due to a number of different reasons. First, we had a raw material price increase of 5% in October, secondly, we opened the new warehouse in November and finally, we had to recall the XYZ product at the end of the year.
The rise in costs is mainly due to the raw material price increase.
The increase in amount of services on offer is because of the customer need for flexibility.
The product range diversification is partly a result of the customer survey findings.
The drop in revenue is largely due to the fact that the weather was so bad.
The fall in the number of new customers is because we have new competition.

Useful phrases

- This is due to + *noun*
- This is because of + *noun*
- This is a result of + *noun*

- This is due to the fact that + *sentence*
- This is because + *sentence*
- This is the result of the fact that + *sentence*

Useful vocabulary

current	aktuell/gegenwärtig
because of	infolge/wegen
due to	ist auf … zurückzuführen/wegen
a result of	ist ein Ergebnis von/der/des .../wegen
largely	im Wesentlichen/zum größten Teil
mainly	hauptsächlich/in erster Linie
partly	teilweise/zum Teil

11.5.2 Results

! **Examples**

So, we know what happened, and why – the question now is what next?
All of this means we will need to work even harder next quarter, to make sure we keep our existing customers.
As a result, we will need to revise the next quarter forecast.
This could lead to the need for a new system.
This may mean cutting down on the number of products next year.

Useful phrases

- All of this means …
- As a result we will …
- This could lead to …
- This may mean …
- This may result in …
- … will be a direct result.

11.5.3 Change and development

Examples !

What major changes were there compared to the last quarter? As you can see, there was a huge increase in sales, due to the good summer weather. We are 25% up on the previous three months and 5% over target, which is very good news indeed.
What are the most recent developments? Well, there are two points I'd like to highlight – first, ... and second, ...
What main differences can we see? From the user point of view, none really. From the IT point of view, the interfaces will change, with the Global Framework Platform becoming the single central data exchange point.
The number of on-time deliveries increased a little.
The figures improved at the start of the year.
The number of new customers decreased steadily.
The amount of claims rose substantially.
Return on investment (ROI) is not as high as last year.
Shareholder value is not as low as this time last year. In fact, it's 3% up.
There was a slight drop in the number of existing customers.
Profits fell slightly in the plastics division.
The quality level stayed steady.
Despite a great deal of fluctuation, the overall result was positive.
The figures fluctuated a lot, but the situation is stable now.

Important !

»What« is used when you have a non-limited choice – »what sort of food do you like?«; »Which« is used when the choice is limited – »which sort of food do you prefer, Italian or Chinese?«

Useful phrases

- There was a small increase over the last three months.
- … is 25% up on last quarter.
- I'd like to highlight three main points: first …, second … and third …
- There was a slight drop in the number of …/the amount of time spent … (*-ing*).
- The … will change and the … will become …
- The … is likely to cause the most challenges.
- The … increased/rose a little/a lot.
- The … improved at the start/in the middle/at the end of the year.
- The … decreased/fell steadily/slightly/substantially.
- The … is not as high/low as last year.
- The … stayed steady compared to last quarter.
- Despite/in spite of a/the …, the overall result was positive/neutral/negative.

- The ... fluctuated a lot, but the ... is stable now.
- The ... is quite unstable.

Useful vocabulary

a decrease/a drop/a fall	Abnahme/Rückgang
Fluctuation/to fluctuate	Schwankung/schwanken
large/substantial/a lot	reichlich/eine Menge
to raise	Anheben/erhöhen
a rise	Steigerung/Anstieg
to rise	ansteigen
small/slight/a little	klein/geringfügig/ein wenig
to stay steady to remain constant	gleich bleibend/unverändert konstant/ beständig/gleich bleiben

Please note:

- The words »rise« and »raise« often cause confusion: the noun »a rise« is used for a price rise, a rise in productivity, a sunrise and can also mean an increase in salary. The noun »a raise« usually means an increase in salary – »Gehaltserhöhung«.
- The irregular verb »to rise – rose – risen« is used to express that something happened: prices rose by 8%, productivity is rising. The regular verb »to raise – raised – raised« is used to say that something or someone made something happen: we raised the prices by 8% (**not:** we rose the prices by 8%); productivity was raised by cutting the number of process steps (**not:** productivity was risen by cutting the number of process steps).
- In German, »die Fluktuation« specifically means employee movement whereas »fluctuation« in English means any type of movement, more like »die Schwankung«.
- Adjectives describe a noun – a slight increase, a substantial drop. Adverbs describe a verb – the figures increased slightly; overhead costs dropped substantially. »-ly« is often added on to the end of an adjective to form the adverb. German speakers mostly add »-ly« too often – if you are not sure, leave it out.

11.5.4 Problems

Problems and bad news are often difficult to present, not only because first, you need to keep an international viewpoint in mind, and second, you need to think of the words of the English language, but also because of existing internal and external company politics and relationships that you are dealing with. Choose from the following examples and phrases, depending on your specific presentation situation.

International viewpoint

Use the cultural checklist »Checklist: preparation international viewpoint« (chapter »Preparation«) to decide on your strategy. Be careful. Talking openly about problems or admitting bad news could mean losing face in a lot of Asian countries. A presentation might not be the right thing – ask your cultural insiders – you might have to discuss bad news one-to-one and not in front of a group. Once you decide on your tactics, don't forget that a lot of the rest of the world is likely to be more indirect than a »typical« German speaker. However, although both British and North American speakers value politeness, North Americans are generally more straightforward and can appear impolite to the British!

English language points

When presenting problems, it's quite usual not to use the word »problem« at all, except perhaps in a positive sentence (»we fixed most of the problems«). Indeed, talking about »problems« can be seen as very negative, or even extremely direct and harsh from an international point of view. Look at the examples for different options.

- Use negative opposites such as: not good (*instead of* bad), not smooth (*instead of* rough), not simple (instead of complicated), not reach (*instead of* miss), not easy (*instead of* difficult).
- Use softeners such as: actually, in fact, well (at the beginning of your sentences, especially when answering questions. This will make you sound less abrupt).
- Use qualifiers such as: a few, a couple ..., a number of ..., quite a few, a bit, a little, very... (to sound more rounded and less staccato).

Examples !

Actually, we had a few minor setbacks at the beginning, nothing unpredictable, but a lot of people needed to do a lot of work in a short space of time to make sure that the system stayed up and running. The situation wasn't good for a number of days but then stabilised.

In fact, there were a number of challenges on the way which caused quite a few headaches. These included a lack of information, insufficient communication and unclear allocation of responsibilities.

Well, not everything went smoothly, but we were able to sort out most of the points in the first couple of days. We didn't have any major breakdowns, but a couple of short machine stoppages.

Some elements were not as simple as foreseen and needed a lot more manpower than planned.
Despite very thorough planning, we underestimated a bit the time needed for the commissioning phase. We fixed this by bringing in a second team of engineers, but had to bear the costs ourselves.
In spite of extremely careful planning, we overestimated the amount of materials needed and ended up with a surplus.
The target wasn't quite reached this month, but I'm sure we'll do better next month; the figures are looking much better this week already.

Useful phrases

- Actually .../In fact .../Well ...
- We had/There were a few minor setbacks.
- We had/There were a number of challenges.
- We didn't have/There weren't any major breakdowns.
- A lack of information
- Insufficient communication
- Unclear allocation of responsibilities
- ... to make sure that the system stayed up and running/didn't break down.
- ... we could fix/sort out most of the points.
- This was more difficult/complicated than foreseen.
- It was more expensive/time-consuming than planned.
- We underestimated the number of ... (*countable items*).
- We overestimated the amount of ... (*uncountable items*).

Useful vocabulary

allocation	Aufteilung/Verteilung
to bear costs	Kosten tragen
challenge	Herausforderung
to fix things (problems)	etwas in Ordnung bringen
to go smoothly	reibungslos über die Bühne gehen
to overestimate	überschätzen
setback	Rückschlag
to sort out problems	Probleme lösen
surplus	Überschuss
thorough	gründlich
to underestimate	unterschätzen
unpredictable	unvorhersehbar/unkalkulierbar

11.5.5 Making comparisons

When making comparisons in English, make sure you know the key words you need.

!

Examples

The first option is more economical than the second because it needs less maintenance. However, the initial costs would be higher.
Splitting the delivery would be uneconomical and relatively complicated. We think the best thing to do is to delay the total shipment.
This new development is extremely useful. It cuts the number of process steps by half, compared to the previous method. It's much simpler than before, as well as being more accurate, faster and more reliable.
Option A would be extremely time-consuming. Option B is the quickest, most effective and straightforward method. Even if it costs more, it will save money in the long term.

Useful phrases

- The first option is more economical than ...
- However, the initial costs would be higher.
- ... would be uneconomical ...
- We think/It seems the best thing to do is to ...
- This is more accurate/faster/more reliable compared to the previous method/system/product.
- Even if it seems to cost more/need longer planning/need more maintenance, it will save money/time/manpower in the long term/short term.

Useful vocabulary

to delay	(sich) verschieben
economical	wirtschaftlich
long-term	langfristig/längerfristig/auf lange Sicht
maintenance	Wartung/Instandhaltung
reliable/unreliable	verlässlich/unzuverlässig
short-term	kurzfristig/kurzzeitig
time-consuming	zeitintensiv/aufwändig
uneconomical	unwirtschaftlich

11.5.6 Plans and goals

!

Examples

This slide shows current progress, with the tasks listed on the left and the time along the bottom. As you can see, most of the building work is on schedule. The electricity lines and water pipes are actually a few days ahead, but some of the piling is two weeks behind schedule. The drawings were delayed and we had to postpone some of the work. We hope to catch up by the end of August.
Overall we expect to hit the total revenue target by the end of the financial year. We missed the target in the first quarter by just 20,000 euros; we' re below target again in the second quarter by 30,000 euros, but recovered in the third quarter and exceeded the target by more than 60,000 euros, which put us back on course for the end of the year.

Useful phrases

- The ... is ahead of/on/behind schedule.
- ... is a few days/weeks/months ahead/behind.
- The ... were delayed.
- The ... was postponed.
- We should catch up by the end of the week.
- The plan is to be back on course/target/schedule by the end of the month/year.
- We expect to hit target.
- Everything is on target.
- The ... target was missed by only 15 units.
- We were below the ... target by just 15 units.
- The ... recovered in the third quarter.

!

Important

You can pronounce »schedule«as »SKedule« or »SHedule« – both are correct.

11.5.7 Useful Vocabulary

ahead of/on/behind schedule	dem Zeitplan voraus/im Zeitplan/im Verzug
to bring forward	*hier:* vorverlegen
to cancel	absagen
to catch up (time)	Zeit aufholen
to delay	(sich) verschieben

to hit a target	ein Ziel erreichen
to miss a target	ein Ziel verfehlen
over/on/below target	über/im/unter Soll
to postpone	verschieben/zurückstellen
to recover	*hier:* einholen

11.6 Dealing with questions

Handling questions well requires a lot of different skills. As with presenting problems and bad news, a great deal depends on your situation and the balance of power – especially the question of whether to take questions throughout your presentation (mostly recommended) or save them until the end.

11.6.1 International viewpoint

The interaction between you and your audience could be very different and surprising to you. This is because of the following four main points:

- presenter vs. audience responsibility – who gives or obtains the information?
- structure – should questions be taken anytime or at the end?
- timing – do you need longer to allow for the foreign language?
- speech patterns (turn taking) – how can you interact best with international listeners?

Presenter vs. audience responsibility

Your responsibility as presenter changes in different parts of the world. In Germany the presenter is responsible for the audience receiving and understanding the information presented. This often means a lot of time, first, thinking about what exactly to present and second, preparing slides. These carefully prepared slides are often, in the presenter's opinion, never good enough. It also most often leads to a great deal of detail, background information and general content – slides packed full of writing – usually to ensure that nothing is left out. A lot of questions could mean that you didn't present the right information.

In other parts of the world, America or Britain, for example, it's the other way round. The audience is responsible for obtaining the information. It's their job to get what they want. This may mean that an American presenter will prepare a number of slides, but not worry too much about details because they will go with the flow – depending on what the audience needs, depending on which questions they ask – and will usually be quite happy to show slides from other presentations.

Your French, Italian and Spanish audiences may find your amount of content detail very »dry« and »uninteresting«, preferring to ask questions and have a discussion based on key points in slides. On the other hand, of course, presenters from other countries may appear »unprepared« to you – with little detail in their slides and not enough background information or analysis.

! **Examples**

When you present to North Americans or Europeans in general, don't be surprised by a lot of questions. This usually means a high degree of interest.
Presenting to a group of Japanese can be very different. The more important the people you are presenting to, the more people they are likely to have with them. They may be surprised if you are alone and wonder where the others are. It is not unusual for the audience to close their eyes while listening. You may not be asked any questions at all. Do not try to ask specific people if they understand or if they have any questions, this could be much too direct and very embarrassing, especially if they are not the most important people. It might be out of place for them to speak. The discussions and decision-making are unlikely to take place during the presentation, but more likely afterwards, between you and the most important people (as long as you are on the same hierarchy level as they are), possibly at a restaurant or in a bar in the evening.

Structure

If you request your audience to ask questions only at the end of the presentation, this could be very frustrating to polychronic cultures. When presenting to international audiences it is better to allow questions anytime.

Timing

Whether or not you choose to make a presentation with a lot of detail, you most likely need more time for questions than when presenting to fellow nationals. A good rule could be to plan 50% of the time for presenting and 50% of the time for questions. Longer presentations of one hour or more can be planned with the 50% rule for questions anytime, but with a back-up or additional section such as a case study, if needed. If you plan like this, the worst possible thing that could happen, is that you finish sooner than expected – this would probably be welcomed by your audience and not be a bad thing at all.

There are a number of possible reasons for needing more time, including:

- Some cultures such as French and Italian simply prefer discussion and talking together more than a presentation in which only one person speaks at a time,
- Many cultures, such as those from the Middle East, see time differently. There is always more of it and there is not the same need to keep one's comments short and to the point, as desired in Germany.

Speech patterns or »turn taking«

When taking questions, you need to be aware of speech patterns, also called turn taking.

The standard **German speech pattern** (in general, as always of course!) is as follows: person A speaks. When they finish, person B speaks. When they finish, A speaks again. There are usually no pauses between the speakers and they are not expected to overlap each other. Overlapping could be seen as impolite.

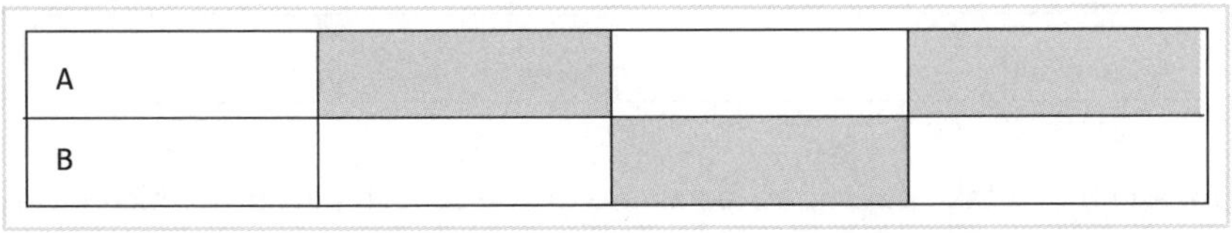

A			
B			

The standard **North American and British speech pattern** is as follows: person A speaks. When person B thinks they are coming to the end of their sentence because the tone of the voice changes and A makes eye contact with B, B starts to talk. When A thinks they are coming to the end of their sentence, A starts to talk. There are usually no pauses between the speakers and they overlap each other a little. A little overlap is expected.

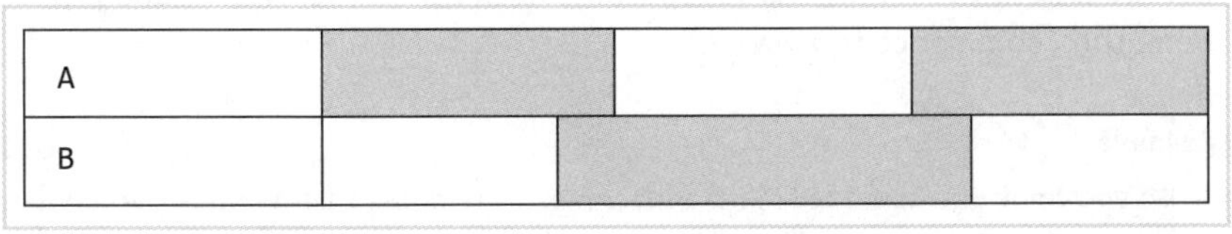

A			
B			

The **standard polychronic, mostly southern European (inc. French) and Middle Eastern speech pattern** is as follows: person A speaks. Person B agrees with them and speaks, too. A may make a pause and then continue speaking. C talks, too, continuing the same topic of conversation. There are usually no pauses between the speakers and they often overlap each other. Overlapping is expected. Indeed, no overlapping could be interpreted as lack of interest and enthusiasm, or understanding.

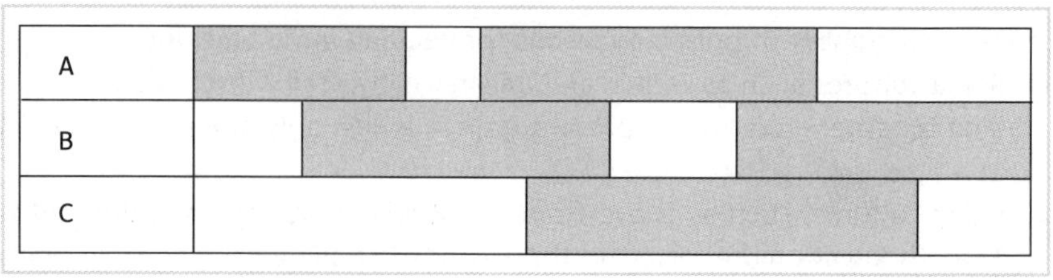

A

B

C

The **standard Japanese (and also a lot of Asian cultures) speech pattern** is as follows: person A speaks. When they finish, person B thinks about the words that were said, thinks about the words they want to say and then speaks. When they finish, A thinks about the words that were said, thinks about the words they want to say and then speaks. There are usually pauses between the speakers and they are definitely not expected to overlap each other. The pauses show respect, first, for the importance of the previous speaker's words and second, for the importance of thinking carefully before speaking.

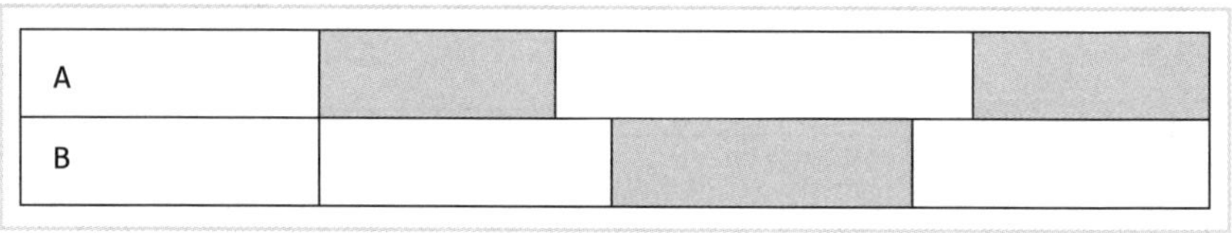

A

B

So, when you take questions, be aware of the speech patterns which influence when you should start your answer. With the first and the last speech patterns, you should normally wait for the speaker to come to the end of their question. With the second speech pattern, you should also wait for the speaker to finish, unless they continue at length.

If you find they speak at length, then you can use the technique for polychronic speakers. If you try to wait for polychronic speakers to come to the end of their question, you might wait a long time. Pick up on their words and repeat them, then commence to answer.

! **Example**

A: Do you think you could tell me exactly why we are doing this? What is the point of this change? The last new system was only introduced two months ago and we are still learning it. I mean, we always have new systems and new methods, (*) it's never-ending. I think the company just doesn't think about the impact that this change could have....

B: (*starts speaking around * slowly and softly at first, then normally*)... new systems and new methods, yes ... yes... well, the fact is that we need to stay ahead. None of us really likes change, especially the older we get, the more we like to stay in our routines. It's human nature. We need to change to keep up-to-date, to stay ahead.

If you are hoping for questions from the Japanese, you need to say nothing and wait for a while. If there is a longer silence, then you can continue.

Checklist: questions/international viewpoint

You should realise that taking questions at the end of the presentation may be your preferred way (if not, no problem!), but not necessarily that of others. You should
▪ not be surprised if there are lots of questions from North Americans and Europeans,
▪ not be surprised if there aren't any from Asians – the business will be done later,
▪ usually offer to take questions anytime,
▪ be prepared to answer questions anytime,
▪ allow a lot of time for questions, 50% for presentations less than one hour,
▪ be aware and react accordingly to speech patterns when taking questions.

11.6.2 English language points

If you cannot understand the questioner, ask again, ask the audience for help or suggest that you meet later to discuss the question together. Don't forget – always make sure that you assume the problem: »I don't understand.« or »That was too fast for me.«

Important !

In German, you usually say »bitte?« when asking someone to ask their question – directly translated into English as »Please?« is wrong! The word in English is usually »Yes?« often with an open hand raised in the speaker's direction. »Yes?« is usually sufficient, perhaps with the name of the person for small groups if you know them.

You may require some of the following phrases for larger audiences. Phrases for opening a discussion are to be found in »Ending components«.

Useful phrases
- The gentleman/lady at the back/in the middle/at the front.
- The gentleman/lady on the right/in the middle/on the left.
- I can see someone with a question at the back.

Delaying questions
Whenever you can, give a short answer to a question. If you feel you really must ask the speaker to wait until later, be very careful that your tone of

voice is friendly and that you don't sound like a schoolteacher. »Please can you wait until later?« is technically polite, but often sounds wrong with a group of adults in business. Make an »I-statement« (Ich-Botschaft) whenever possible.

Useful phrases

- Can you tell me why ...?
- I'd really like to cover that later and finish the analysis first, because it's quite complicated.
- Yes, but just briefly, why ...?
- Well, I don't have a short answer I'm afraid. If I can just go on for another few minutes, everything should become clear.
- I want to be sure you have the full picture.
- I'd like to be sure that we all have the necessary information.

!

Important

A lot of difficult questions or disturbances can be avoided by

1. not fighting and
2. concentrating on the »here and now« with
3. I-statements as necessary – »Yes, D, E, F are important, I agree, but right now, in this meeting, I want to concentrate on A, B, C.«

11.6.3 Preparation and procedure

You need to do just these three things – they really work:

1. **Question preparation**	Briefly write down all of the most difficult, unwanted questions you can think of and then practise the answers.
2. **Five-step technique**	Use the technique in the next section when answering.
3. **Attitude**	Stay calm. Don't fight. Not ever.

1 Question preparation

Briefly write down all of the most difficult, unwanted questions you can think of, each one on a separate card, then pick out cards at random and practise the answers. At the very least, write a list of keywords of difficult, unwanted questions and think through the best answers. Don't just hope that the questions won't come (that can be very stressful). Make sure you know what you will say if they do come.

Types of questions with possible answering strategies:

- **Nice questions** – these are questions that you would like to answer. Use the technique in the next section and be sure to answer clearly and to the point: »You're asking about the number of defective units produced per month – we have between 5 and 10 returns per month, which we replace with a new unit.«
- **»Don't know« questions** – these are questions that are relevant, but you don't know the answers offhand. Look around to your colleagues to see if they know; if not, offer to provide the information later. Don't just say »I can find out and tell you later«; you need to be specific to be credible: »You're asking about month-on-month figures for sector C. I don't have the figures with me, but if you would like to give me your business card at the end, I can send them to you next Monday when I'm back in the office.«
- **Hypothetical questions** – these are questions about what would happen if ... if ... if ... This is something you don't know, or cannot really say. You have two options. Option one: you say you don't know and focus on the present: »What would we do if ABC happened? I don't know – we would change our plans, for sure. At the moment we're concentrating on fulfilling the requirements of the plan we have now.«
  Option two: give an answer, but make it clear that it's just speculation: »What would we do if ABC happened? *If* that happened, then maybe we *would* start to produce a matrix machine, but that's just speculation on my part. It would require a whole decision-making process involving a lot of people. It wouldn't be just my decision.«
- **Multiple questions** – These are two or more questions from one person at the same time. Your reaction depends on who's asking. If it's someone very important, ask them to talk slowly while you take notes, then answer them one by one (it's extremely difficult to remember them off by heart). If you think the person is less important, then you can
  a. choose the question you would like to answer,
  b. answer the first question or
  c. answer the last question.
  If they don't forget the other questions, they will ask again. The responsibility lies with them to remember the other questions.
- **Internal political questions** – these are questions asked for a specific internal political reason. Pause and think before choosing to answer or not. You can
  a. answer the question carefully and as neutrally as possible,
  b. say that those decisions are not made by you (if it's true) or you're not the right person to talk about that or it's not the right time and place: »Yes, I know what you mean and we can talk about it together again over lunch today, if you want, but that's the way it is at the moment and I really

don't want to discuss it now. I'd like to concentrate on showing you the next steps for putting in the final three systems.«
c. just say you'd prefer not to talk about it and then come back to the present: »Well, I don't think I'm the right person to talk to about that, I don't make those decisions. What I *can* say is that we now have the system in place in 12 out of 15 locations, which is the job we were asked to do.«

- **Irrelevant questions** – these are questions that don't seem connected to your subject. Be sure to repeat the question – maybe you didn't understand it correctly. Then answer it politely and briefly if you can. If you can't, refer them to the person or department that can, or ask if you can talk about it at a later time together: »You'd like to know about ABC? Could we maybe discuss that together at the end because I'd like to concentrate on DEF for now.« (Your presentation is about DEF, you work on ABC, too, but that's another project.)
- **»Stupid« questions** – these are questions that seem stupid or pointless. Answer them concisely and move on. Again, never make your audience seem unimportant. The questioner has some reason for asking, even if you don't know what it is. You could ask after answering, if it is suitable or useful: »You're asking about switching off the machine. Yes, it really is off when it's switched off. The power supply is cut. Do you have a particular reason for asking?« Be careful your tone of voice is not sarcastic; this could be the person responsible for fire and safety, who is very interested in such details.
- **Confidential questions** – these are questions about confidential information. Explain politely but firmly that you cannot answer that question: »I'm afraid I can't answer that; it's confidential.« or »I'm sorry, but I can't disclose that sort of information.«
- **Forced answer questions** – these are negatively formulated questions. Take your time to think, there is no hurry. Always reformulate the question neutrally, then give an answer: »Is the product unreliable because of A or B?« You: »The reliability of the product. Our product is as reliable as current technology allows. We at Smithson Metals are leaders in research in this field. We have not reached 100% reliability with this product but are definitely working towards that. At the moment we're working on both A and B.«
- **Negative comments** – these are not always questions, but can be comments based on previous experience, or stories from elsewhere. Focus on the things you know. You don't need to comment about something you don't know: »... the same product launch in Shanghai was disastrous.« You: »Well, I'm afraid I can't comment on that – I'm not involved in it. What I do know is that our product launch is carefully planned for this market here, starting next month.«

- **»Obvious« questions** – these are questions about points that you talked about at least ten times in your presentation. Don't say something like »As I said before« or »As I mentioned in the first section« – you don't need to make your audience feel as if its questions were insignificant. For some reason, the questioner didn't get the message. Show any relevant slide again, answer concisely and move on: »The last quarter figures. (*Go back to relevant slide.*) Yes, they're here. The most important point is that they stayed constant when compared to the previous year.«
- **Questions already asked** – these are questions that someone has already asked. Don't point out that someone has already asked – never make your audience feel unimportant. For some reason, the questioner didn't hear or understand the answer. Maybe they were thinking about something else. Answer it concisely and move on. If the audience is annoyed with the person asking the same question, then they are annoyed with that person and not with you.

2 Five-step technique

1. Listen
2. Pause
3. Repeat (all or part)
4. Answer
5. Link (if suitable)

You can use this technique for all of the reasons described below.

- Listen – this shouldn't need to be said, but people so often just wait for the others to finish, instead of really listening. Listening can save a lot of time. Don't move around; this could look as if you are not listening. Stand still and just listen.
- Pause – take the time to think of what you want to say (including any important English words). Pausing can feel strange when you first do it, but it creates a very good effect as well as being useful.
- Repeat or reformulate all or part of the question – this is especially useful for two reasons:
  - to be sure you answer the question you were asked,
  - to make sure everyone has a chance to hear the question with larger audiences.

  You may not need this step if you are presenting to a small group when the question is clear and you know that everyone can hear.
- Answer – keep it short and to the point, as soon as you have finished, stop talking. People often continue answering, repeat themselves, go on and on (and on and on) well after the questioner has nodded to indicate that his question has been answered. Keep it short. If people want more

details, they will ask. If they want less information, there's not much they can do.

- Link to a main point – if suitable, link to one of your main points to help the audience remember what's important. This is especially useful when answering difficult questions (see previous section for more details). A good technique is to link to what is happening »here and now«.

3 Attitude

Your questioner excitedly asks a question, speaking fast and forcefully, almost aggressively. You answer in the same style: fast, forcefully, almost aggressively, too. The next questioner joins in (or the same one again) and is maybe a bit faster, a bit more forceful. Your answer matches the style: a bit faster and a bit more forceful and ... before you know it ... you're in a fight. You may not even be disagreeing with each other!

!

Important

If *you* stay calm and answer slowly, clearly but firmly, the situation should not escalate. It's difficult to »fight« with someone who doesn't »fight« back.

Alternatively, your questioner is calm, but asks a question you didn't want. You reply defensively – defending your decision, defending the reasons, instead of stating the reasons calmly and neutrally. The sentence »Yes, it was a difficult decision. At the time, it seemed like the right decision with the information we had then,« can sound like a defence or a neutral statement, depending on the speed and tone of voice. If you start to defend yourself, the questioner or other people are more likely to attack, just because you are defending. Again, if *you* stay calm and answer slowly, clearly and strongly, the situation should not escalate. It's not necessary to attack someone who isn't defending himself.

What about really difficult questions, e.g. if the questioner is right with his objection? You should already be prepared for the question, but if not, take the time to think. Is he right? Can you admit it? What *really* happened?

Useful answers

- You're asking why we didn't take option B? Well, back in March, under those conditions, we decided that option A was best. If we had the same situation again today and the same conditions, option A would still look best. Now, with the new information, we know that option B would be better. We couldn't have known that back in March.

- You'd like to know why we didn't do XYZ? Well, I would have liked to have done XYZ, for sure. There are a lot of things I would like to do in addition to what we do now. I think that could be true for a lot of people here today. We didn't do XYZ because we had to make a choice with the resources and manpower we had available, we chose to do RST and UVW.

Important !

Watch other people dealing with questions at work, on talk shows or on the news to see how situations can escalate or be de-escalated.

11.7 Handling interruptions and disturbances

Helicopters, emergency vehicles, people coming in, phone calls – the list of possible disturbances is endless. One rule is golden: Disturbances take priority. If something else is happening and distracting people's attention, it's difficult for them to listen to you at the same time, and you should act. However, you only need to act when something is really a disturbance – this means it is really distracting people's attention. In some cultures such as those of Italy, Kuwait and Saudi Arabia, it's completely normal to keep cell phones switched on the whole time and often to take the calls in the middle of a presentation, without leaving the room. If they are the customers, then you should accept it. If it's a disturbance to the others, then they will ask the person to leave the room.

As with technical problems, you should do what you want your audience to do – stay calm and focused. One of the simplest ways of handling interruptions and disturbances is to stop talking and see what happens. As always with your presentation, however, a lot depends on the setting and formality – size of the room, number of people and level of familiarity. A technique that is suitable for one hundred people is not necessarily suitable for a group of three.

If it is not a disturbance to others, then it may be alright to let people talk a bit in the background, now and again. Indeed, it's routine for many polychronic cultures such as the French, Italians and Spanish. Put yourself in the audience's shoes and ask yourself – do you really need total silence the whole time?

Be very careful not to act like a schoolteacher dealing with children. Remember these are adults, just like you, and sometimes there is a need to talk.

11.7.1 Getting attention at the beginning

Especially with larger groups of people who have come a long way, the amount of noise can be quite intense to start with and may take some time to stop. A louder voice than usual, repetition and stopping mid-sentence is a good way to get attention: »Good morning ladies and gentlemen (talking), good morning, (*short pause, talking continues*) … ladies and gentlemen, good morning … (*longer pause until talking stops*), ladies and gentlemen. We are here today to …«

Another option is silence – stand at the front, raise your hands and get eye contact with people who are talking, then bring your hands together and start.

11.7.2 Audience member working on laptop

People working on laptops can create a distraction. If you let them carry on, you might be sending the wrong message to your audience – namely, it's okay to do something else during my presentation. More forcefully expressed – it's alright if you don't listen to me. If it's standard procedure in your company, then a change of policy is necessary before anything can be done. If it's not standard procedure, you can try silence, moving closer to the person(s) or making a comment.

Useful comments

- It would be very helpful if we could all stop what we're doing, then we could get started. Okay … (*pause*) … I'd like to get started now (*move closer to the people working on their laptops*).
- I understand that everybody has a lot to do … (*pause, long if necessary, to get eye contact*), but I'd really like everybody to concentrate fully for the next twenty minutes, because we need to make an important decision based on the information in this presentation.

! **Important**

Don't use names to highlight the »naughty« people – use »we« or »it«.

If none of the above works you could either ignore them or try asking how long they need: »I see some people are busy with e-mails – how long do you need?«

11.7.3 Interruptions from people coming in

People coming in can be distracting in smaller groups (usually less distracting in larger groups). Either just stop talking until the person is settled, or make a short comment. Don't forget, even though you would prefer everyone to be on time, people coming late are absolutely normal. Your best policy is to make them feel welcome – use their name if you know it. If a lot of people come late and it's annoying, then leave it to the audience to make comments.

11.7.4 Useful comments

- (*Person comes in*) »Aha, good morning Giovanni. Come in – this seat is free here, or that one over there. You can hang your coat up in the corner and there's coffee over on the side ... (*wait until most of the noise has subsided*) ... let's just wait until you're settled ... okay, where were we?«
- (*Another person comes in*) »Aha, good morning Brian. This seat here is still free. You're not the only one who was late, don't worry. You can hang your coat up in the corner ... (*wait until most of the noise has subsided*) ... okay, let's carry on ...«

11.7.5 Audience member on a telephone call

A telephone call can also create a distraction. If necessary, state clearly but politely how telephone calls should be dealt with at the beginning of your presentation (see »Introduction components«). If you are in a small group and someone takes a call, just stop talking and get eye contact. The person will either finish the call quickly or leave the room. If you are in a larger group and someone taking a call causes a distraction, try the same, or walk up to them in a friendly manner. If it's someone important, either ignore it and continue with your presentation or wait for them to finish.

What to say and what not to say
You probably don't need to say anything, but if so, then be careful not to sound over-polite and sarcastic: »Can you take the call outside please?« is okay, but NOT »Could you possibly take the call outside please?« This can easily sound sarcastic.

11.7.6 Outside noise

Drilling and hammering, window cleaning, whatever – it's not unusual for presentations to take place in meeting rooms in hotels and then be disturbed by background noises or activities. Don't be afraid to take a short break and either telephone reception, go there yourself, or ask someone to go, and ask them to stop or do the work at the end of your meeting or in your lunch break. If the disturbance doesn't cease, name the problem, state the options, decide on the action and carry it out – keep your audience informed at all times.

Useful comments

- Let's wait for that to go by ... good, okay, where was I? Ah yes, one of the key advantages of this system is ...
- We seem to have some workmen nearby. We can either continue or I can go and see if they could stop ... (*Wait for the audience's reaction, if any, then make a clear decision.*) I'd prefer as little background noise as possible, so I'd like to take a two-minute break and just ask reception to tell us what's happening.

11.7.7 Audience members talking

As already mentioned at the beginning of this section, you only need to act if the talking really is a disturbance – so probably not in France, Italy and Spain and to a certain extent, America and Britain. Stopping to talk yourself is usually very effective, moving closer to the people if necessary and finally, if really necessary, making a comment:

Useful comments

- Is there anything unclear at the moment? (*referring to your presentation with your hand*)
- Is there something we should all be talking about?
- I can see you're talking about something important. Is it relevant right now or could you leave it until later please?

!

Important

Don't translate from German directly and say »Can we have only one discussion please?« This can sound extremely rude and aggressive.

11.7.8 Unwelcome interruptions from audience

If someone interrupts with something important but not urgent, just remember why you are all there and ask everyone to focus on »here and now«. Stay calm and fix when to do the other task(s).

Examples !

(*Other:*) We really need to set the time schedule for ABC and DEF. It would be a good time to do it now, because everybody's here.
(*You:*) Yes, everybody is here, but I'd really like to finish this report first. That's the main reason for this meeting today. Can we do it another time?
Or: (*You:*) Can we do it as soon as I'm finished? Just before lunch? (*Other:*) Well, no, not really, I have another appointment at lunchtime. (*You:*) Okay, how about finishing five minutes before lunch, if that's okay with everyone else?

11.7.9 Heating and light disturbances

If you see your audience yawning, it might not be due to dryness of content but lack of fresh air. Either turn down the heating or open or ask people to open windows as required. Alternatively, you can take a five-minute break and leave doors and windows open.

Useful phrases

- Hmm, I think we need some fresh air. Let's open the windows and take a five-minute break. Can we start again at 11.20 or so? Good.
- Can somebody help me to turn down/off the heating and open the windows?

If someone objects because they like the heat, then just say:

- Okay, then let's leave the heating on and air the room every now and again.

If you have problems with sunlight in people's faces:

- Could somebody lower the blinds a little?
- Could you pull that curtain so that we don't have direct sunlight?«

12 Ending your presentation

Whether short or long, informal or formal, your presentation needs to have a clear, well-structured and professional ending. This chapter includes information on: making a good finish, ending components, saying goodbye.

12.1 Making a good finish

»Well, okay, that's all we've got time for ... um ... thank you for ...um ... your attention and ... um ... thank you for listening and... um ... thank you and goodbye.«

This sort of weak ending is not unusual. Many people put a lot of effort into their presentation introductions and slides, but don't give much thought to the end. You need to end your presentation well because people most often remember your last words best. A good ending is important especially when your audience comes from all over the world and you don't meet very often. You want them to remember you and your message. A good ending is the reverse of a good introduction – opening, objective, overview and organisation – and has four main components as follows:

1. ending signal,
2. review: gives people a last chance to remember any remaining questions,
3. objective achieved: gives value to the time spent,
4. next steps (and closing): provides direction.

You have a lot of different alternatives at the end, depending on if you want (or have time for) any (more) questions. You can have a final discussion and/or question time – depending on the situation, how many questions you already had and the timing. You can review before or after the final discussion, or both, depending on the topic.

12.1.1 International viewpoint

The ending should not be the time to present new information, recommendations or conclusions. It is a very brief review of what has been covered and is likely to be much shorter than a typically correct German ending to a presentation. A typical ending would be only five or six sentences long, lasting a minute or so.

12.1.2 English language points

Be sure to formulate objective(s) achieved carefully – don't directly say »we all now understand.« but »I hope we all now have a good idea of what the process will look like«. This indirect formulation is more suitable for worldwide use.

! **Example**

So, we're at the end now. We looked at the new product features, the planned integration and potential challenges – does anybody have any more questions at all? (*People raise hands.*) Yes? ... (*More questions asked.*) Okay, we have time for one more question right now, but you can speak to me in the lunch break or contact me again anytime – so, the last question for now – the gentleman at the back ... Good. Well, I hope that everybody now has a clear picture of the product, how we plan to integrate it and overcome potential challenges. Our next product presentation will be in Madrid in June. If you need more information in the meantime, you know how you can reach me. Thank you very much everybody.

12.2 Ending components

Ending signals

- So, that brings us to the end.
- We're at the end now.
- Looking back ...

Review

- We('ve) looked at A, B and C.
- We('ve) covered A, B and C.

Opening discussion

- Does anybody have any (more) questions?
- Are there any (more) questions?

! **Important**

Don't say »Next question, please.« This can sound quite military and aggressive.

Closing discussion

No need to say anything like »We're running out of time« or put in the word »only« – »We only have time for one or two more questions« – these are negative comments.

- Okay, we have time for one more question right now ...
- We have time for one or two more questions here today, and then we have to finish ...
- ... but you can speak to me in the lunch break or contact me again anytime.
- ... but I'm here all day and reachable back in the office next week.

Objective(s) achieved

- So, I hope you now know how important A, B and C are for you in your job.
- Well, I hope you now have a clear picture of progress on this project.
- That's all for this morning – I hope you now know how technologically advanced, reliable and flexible our (product) is for you.
- Okay, so, I hope you can now see why we at Alpha Chemicals are the very best partner for you.
- Good. I hope you now have a clear overview of the figures.
- I hope you are now updated on our marketing campaign for the third quarter.

Next steps and contact details

- The next meeting on D, E and F will be organized by our team assistant.
- Our next progress meeting is in … (*place*) on … (*date*). The next step is to discuss any further requirements. We look forward to working together with you in the future.
- Our next financial update will be in … (*place*) on … (*date*). If you have any points to discuss in the meantime, you know how you can reach me.
- Should you have any further questions in the future, my e-mail is … (*slide*).
- You can find me in the company staff directory if you ever need any information; just call me or send me a mail.

Thanks and closing

A good strong ending is to say »thank you everybody« and then stop talking. People often say »thank you for …« then add »your attention and …« then have to say something else and find it hard to finish because they continue to say »and …«. Thanking people for their attention can sound like school or the army. A good, clear »thank you« is suitable for most occasions.

- Thanks a lot everybody.
- Thank you everybody.
- Ladies and gentlemen, thank you very much.

! **Important**

Don't say »thank you and goodbye« at the end of a presentation. This is completely wrong and can be misinterpreted as »thank you and go away«. »Goodbye« should only be said when people leave each other, physically go away and do not see each other for a time.

12.3 Saying goodbye

When you leave someone, at the company reception, the station, the airport, wherever, that is the right time to say goodbye (and not at the end of your presentation). Saying goodbye can often be unnatural and awkward. People want to be polite but don't know exactly what to say. Don't hurry – play »ping pong« by making return comments.

! **Examples**

A: Okay then, thanks a lot for coming and talk to you next week.
B: Yes, we'll be in touch.
A: Alright then, bye for now.
B: Bye for now.

A: I'd like to thank you for coming.
B: It was our pleasure.
A: It was good to meet you.
B: It was good to meet you, too.
A: We'll be in touch about the next steps.
B: Yes, we'll look forward to hearing from you.
A: I hope you have a safe journey.
B: Thank you very much.
A: Oh, please give my regards to Jonathan when you see him.
B: Yes, of course. And thanks once again for inviting us over.
A: It was a pleasure.
B: Okay then, goodbye for now.
A: Goodbye for now.

A: So, here we are.
B: Yes, on behalf of our company, we'd like to thank you very much for the invitation. It was an honour for us to come and visit you and your people and to see the products that you produce. We very much look forward to doing business with you in the future and we hope that we will have a long and fruitful business partnership.

A: Thank you very much. We were delighted that you could come to visit and very much enjoyed getting to know you. We also look forward to a long and fruitful business partnership. We wish you all a safe journey home and we will be in touch in the next few days.
B: Thank you, we look forward to hearing from you.
A: Then, we wish you a safe journey.
B: Thank you, goodbye.
A: Goodbye for now.
B: Goodbye.

12.3.1 International viewpoint

Length and formality of saying goodbye are the two main differing factors worldwide. British and American will tend to be briefer and less formal than Germans. Chinese, Japanese and other Asians will tend to be longer and more formal. It is, however, again very dependent on the situation. Watch people's body language and try to »see« how they feel – if they want to make quick goodbyes or are happy with more formal short speeches.

Useful phrases

- It was nice/good to meet you. *Answer:* It was nice/good to meet you, too.
- It was nice/good meeting you. *Answer:* It was nice/good meeting you, too.
- We'll be in touch. *Answer:* Yes, we'll look forward to hearing from you.
- We'll let you know. *Answer:* Yes, we'll wait to hear from you.)
- Talk to you next Monday, then. *Answer:* Yes, we'll talk next Monday.
- Talk to you soon. *Answer:* Yes, talk to you soon.

13 Useful examples

13.1 Basic outline – non-specific content

Good morning, I'm Benno Donauer from the electronic engineering department at Opus GmbH and it's good to be here in Rio with you on this sunny Friday morning.

By the end of this presentation, you should know why A, B and C are important for you.

First, we'll look at A, then move on to B and finish with C.

We have 40 minutes altogether.

If you have any questions at any time, do please ask.

Okay, let's start.

So, why is A important? This is why ... (*click to next slide*).

What is the current A? Here it is ...

What does the future A look like? This is it ... (*click to next slide*).

Next .../Now ...

This graph shows A, with A1 on the left and A2 on the right.

This chart shows A3 compared to A4.

So, that brings us to the end.

Are there any (more) questions?

So, we('ve) covered A, B and C.

I hope you now know how important A, B and C are for you.

The next meeting on D, E and F will be organized by our team assistant.

If you have any points to discuss in the meantime, you know how you can reach me.

Thank you everybody.

13.2 Product presentation

For those who don't already know me, my name's Bernd Niederhuber, I'm from the Electronics Assembly Systems Department at Drive Technologies AG in Berlin.

So, here we all are in Madrid, today, October 5th, 20XX and by the end of this presentation (*show title slide*) »Serrano Limitido and Drive Technologies«, I hope you will know how technologically advanced, reliable and flexible our machines can be for you, and be able to see why we at Drive Technologies are the very best partner for you.

We'll look at the X-machine technical functionality to start, then move on to possible adaptations for you, Serrano Limitido, and finish with our service offer – how we can work well together.

We have around three hours scheduled, with a break halfway through for coffee.

If you have any questions at any time, do please ask me.

Good.

Let's get started.

What are the main technical functions? Here they are ... (*click to next slide*).

Okay, we covered technical functions; now let's look at possible adaptations ...

So, finally, our service offer to you at Serrano Limitido.

We're at the end now. Does anybody have any more questions?

So we looked at the X-machine technical functionality, then possible adaptations for you, Serrano Limitido, and finally our service offer – how we can work well together.

I hope you now know how technologically advanced, reliable and flexible our machines are for you and that you can see why we at Drive Technologies are the very best partner for you.

We look forward to working together with you in the future.

Ladies and gentlemen, thank you very much.

Teil 4: Meetings in English

Autorinnen: Lisa Förster, Annette Pattinson

Wer Geschäftskontakte mit internationalen Partnern pflegt, nimmt früher oder später an Meetings auf Englisch teil. Sind Sie auch in dieser Situation oder wollen Sie sich schon einmal vorsorglich fit machen? Dann sind Sie mit dem Wissen aus diesem Kapitel auf der sicheren Seite. Denn Meetings und Verhandlungen können in Ihrer Muttersprache schon schwierig genug sein, umso mehr in der Fremdsprache.

Wir zeigen Ihnen, wie Sie in Meetings auf Englisch durch Kompetenz, Verlässlichkeit und Höflichkeit Vertrauen aufbauen und überzeugen – egal, ob Sie das Meeting selbst leiten oder nur daran teilnehmen. Für alle Situationen eines Meetings – von der Begrüßung über die eigentlichen Verhandlungen bis zum Protokoll – geben wir Ihnen die notwendigen sprachlichen Mittel an die Hand und zeigen Ihnen kulturelle Besonderheiten.

Wenn Sie weniger aktive Erfahrung mit der englischen Sprache haben, bekommen Sie Tipps für einen selbstbewussten Auftritt. Aber selbst Fortgeschrittene finden neue Ausdrücke und Wendungen, die ihren Sprachschatz sinnvoll ergänzen. Und um einen zusätzlichen Trainingseffekt zu erzielen, ist auch dieses Kapitel auf Englisch geschrieben. Wir wünschen Ihnen in Ihren künftigen Meetings viel Erfolg!

14 Preparing a meeting

In the run-up to a meeting there are a lot of things to bear in mind, especially when you are the one organising it. Booking a meeting room is only one task among many.

14.1 Inviting people to a meeting

In formal business relationships, you may wish to write a letter or email to a business associate to suggest an initial meeting. This correspondence can then be followed up with a telephone call or an email to confirm the meeting time and place.

14.1.1 Suggesting a meeting

In an established business relationship, a less formal style can be adopted for suggesting meetings by both telephone and email. Email is especially useful if a number of participants are involved. In a formal email, the style of language, salutation and complimentary close is the same as that used in a letter.

Example: formal UK-style letter/email !

Marketing proposal: initial meeting
Dear Mr Smith
Thank you for your telephone call of this morning. I am pleased to enclose [letter]/ attach [email] the information you requested and would welcome the opportunity to meet you in person to discuss the proposal and to answer any questions you may have.
I will contact you by telephone in the next few days to arrange a time that is convenient for you.
In the meantime, please do not hesitate to contact me if you require any further information.
Yours sincerely
David Braun
Business Development Manager

Important !

The correct way of writing salutations and endings
In **British English** letters and emails, the trend is to omit punctuation in the salutation, people's names (Mr, Mrs, Ms, Dr, etc) and in the complimentary close. Letters and emails end with »Yours sincerely«, when the person is addressed by name, or

»Yours faithfully«, when the letter begins »Dear Sir or Madam«. In **US English**, a period (🇬🇧: full stop) follows abbreviations and the salutation ends with a colon, as in »Dear Ms. Jones:«. Standard complimentary closes are »Sincerely yours,« and »Sincerely,« (note that both end with a comma).

Useful phrases

Less formal style

- I was wondering if we could meet in the near future to discuss ...?
- Perhaps it would speed things up if we met face to face to discuss this?
- Shall we meet next week to discuss the details in person?

14.1.2 Responding to a request for a meeting

Useful phrases

- I'm afraid my schedule is very full in the next few weeks. Would it be possible for us to discuss the matter by telephone instead?
- As we're both very busy, I would like to try to resolve the matter by telephone, if possible.
- I think it would be a good idea for us to meet.
- I agree that it would be beneficial for us to meet face to face.

Useful vocabulary

initial: erste(r, s)
complimentary close: Schlussformel
proposal: Vorschlag
to welcome an opportunity: eine Gelegenheit gern wahrnehmen
convenient: angenehm, bequem
schedule: Terminkalender
to resolve a matter: eine Sache klären

14.2 Making meeting arrangements

In an informal setting, once you have agreed with your business partner that you would like to meet, arrangements can be made by telephone or email. In both cases, the language used for organising the meeting is informal yet polite.

14.2.1 Who would like to meet when?

If you are organising a meeting with a larger number of participants and have to find out about their general availability on certain dates, »Doodle« can help. This is a clever tool you'll find online free of charge at www.doodle.com. You create your doodle by just entering the dates and/or times you would like to suggest. A link to this doodle is automatically sent to your email account. You can then forward the link to all the prospective participants, asking them to state when they would be available and when not. There is also a field for comments.

Lunch meetings

If you meet over lunch make sure you can still take notes on a small pad. Follow your host's lead with regard to drinking alcohol. In Great Britain drinking alcohol in moderation is generally acceptable over lunch or dinner with business colleagues. However, if your business partners are sticking to water and you want to keep a clear head, avoid alcohol altogether.

Useful phrases

When?

- Would 20 November suit you?
- What does your schedule look like on 3 December?
- I'm afraid I'm away on business for the whole of that week. How about 25 November?
- What would be a convenient time for you?
- What time would suit you best?

Where?

- Where shall we meet? I would be happy to come to your office if that's more convenient.
- I can recommend a quiet restaurant near the city centre that would be easy for us both to reach.

To be confirmed (TBC)

- I need to check back with my colleague about that. Could I get back to you on that this afternoon?
- Could I confirm that with you tomorrow when I've spoken to my colleague?

It's a date

- Yes, that's fine. I look forward to seeing you at 3.00 p.m. on 25 November at your office.
- That's perfect for me, I can make it then. So let's fix our meeting for 25 November.

! **Important**

Avoiding confusion with dates
When dates are written in figures in **British English**, the day comes before the month. For example, 9 March 2019 becomes 09/03/19. Note that, in **US English**, the same date is written March 9, 2019 and therefore becomes 03/09/19. Due to these different conventions, it is advisable to write dates out in full.

Useful grammar
The conditional tense, as in »would« and »could«, is used frequently in the above phrases. Conditional verbs make questions and suggestions sound open for discussion, rather than fixed and already decided, and therefore lend the suggestion a politer note.

Useful vocabulary
and yet: und doch
to suit: (gut) passen
prospective: künftig
to get back to sb: zurückrufen, sich melden

14.3 Rescheduling, cancelling or confirming a meeting

In the interest of informing meeting participants as quickly as possible, it is common to postpone or cancel meetings by telephone or email, especially if this is necessary at short notice. In either case, it is a good idea to give the reason for changing the arrangement if appropriate, and to suggest another time for the meeting to take place.

14.3.1 Rescheduling

! **Examples**

Example 1: calling to reschedule a meeting
A: Hello. This is Sarah from XYZ Com.
B: Oh, hi Sarah.
A: I'm calling regarding our meeting on 6 June at two o'clock. I'm afraid I have to ask if we could reschedule the meeting for the same time on 7 June? I'm very sorry to inconvenience you.
B: That's not a problem. Only, could we make it three o'clock on 7 June instead?
A: Yes, that's fine. Thank you for being so flexible. I look forward to seeing you at three o'clock on the 7th.

B: Okay, see you then. Bye bye!
A: Thanks again. Bye!

Example 2: postponing a meeting by email
Subject:postponement of project meeting of 20 December
Dear Steve
Unfortunately it is necessary for me to change the arrangement we made for next Monday due to the rail strike that has been announced for next week. Please let me know what alternative day and time would be convenient for you.
I apologise for changing our arrangement at such short notice and look forward to hearing from you with regard to an alternative date and time.
Best regards
Simon

Useful phrases

- I'm very sorry, but I'm afraid I have to postpone our meeting of next week, as I've been called to an urgent meeting at our head office. Would it be possible for us to meet the week after instead?
- I'm afraid I've been called away on urgent business next week, which unfortunately means that we have to reschedule the meeting we arranged for next Tuesday. Would any other days next week be convenient for you?
- I was wondering if it would be possible to bring the meeting forward by a week/postpone the meeting until the week after?

14.3.2 Cancellation

Useful phrases

- I'm very sorry, but I'm afraid it is necessary to cancel our meeting of next week until further notice.
- Due to unforeseen complications with the draft contract we are obliged to cancel next week's meeting.
- I very much regret to inform you that we have no other option but to cancel our meeting in Salzburg on Friday.

14.3.3 Confirming a meeting

It is a good idea to confirm an arrangement – especially one made by telephone – in writing. This also provides a good opportunity to give visitors travel directions if necessary.

When you write or email to confirm a meeting, it is recommended to send out travel directions and/or a map for reaching the meeting destination, so as to give your business partner plenty of time to make travel arrangements. See »Hands-on organisation« for tips on giving directions.

!

Examples

Example 1: confirming a meeting by email
Subject:marketing proposal meeting on 25 November
Dear Mr Smith
Following our telephone conversation of this afternoon, I am pleased to confirm our meeting at our offices on 25 November. The meeting is scheduled to take place from 3.00 p.m. to 4.30 p.m. Please find attached directions to our offices.
I very much look forward to meeting you on 25 November. Please do not hesitate to contact me if you require any further information in the meantime.
Yours sincerely
David Braun

Example 2: confirming a meeting (email to a colleague)
Subject:meeting of 25 March – Peter Smith ok
Wanda
Just to let you know that Peter Smith can make the meeting on 25 Nov after all. I made a reservation for the Arctic meeting room from 3 to 4.30. Hope you can still make it!
Best
David

Useful phrases

As a participant invited to a meeting, you can also confirm by phone:

- Hello. My name is Sarah Hughes and I'm calling from XYZ Com. I am due to attend a meeting at your company on 14 May and I would just like to
  - check the best way to reach your offices by car/public transport?
  - confirm the time of the meeting.
  - check whether there is an overhead projector in the meeting room?
  - find out if there any suitable hotels near to your offices?

Useful vocabulary

at short notice: kurzfristig
to bring it forward: vorverlegen
to decline: (von vornherein) ablehnen
to reschedule: verlegen, neu anberaumen
inconvenience: Unannehmlichkeit
directions: Wegbeschreibung
to postpone a meeting: (nach hinten) verschieben
to attend a meeting: dabei sein, teilnehmen
to make the meeting: schaffen

14.4 Making the agenda

All well-structured meetings should have an agenda, which is usually prepared by the chairperson. Depending on the type of meeting, agendas can be formal or informal, but all should start by stating the date, time and location of the meeting.

It is useful to include the name of the person who will be presenting a specific agenda item. You may also find it helpful to include a note of the time allocated to each point. Some more detailed agendas also state objectives for individual agenda items, for example: »Agree on product design«.

Formal agendas differ from informal agendas in that they start with routine items, which always appear in a specific order. In addition, each point on the agenda is clearly numbered. Nowadays, agendas for all but the most important company meetings (board meetings, annual general meetings) tend to use an informal style.

Important !

Catchwords and abbreviations

Note how both informal and formal agendas have a concise style and tend to be written in note-like form, often omitting articles before nouns and using abbreviations. For example, AOB stands for »any other business«, which refers to topics that are not covered by other agenda items or which have arisen after the agenda was distributed.

Examples !

Example 1: informal agenda (eg customer or team meetings)

Agenda for end-of-year sales meeting

5 January, 9.00–10.30 a.m., Meeting room 2A

- Presentation of last year's sales figures (Andreas) – 15 mins
- Forecasts and targets for the coming year (Sally) – 15 mins
- Analysis of last year's sales promotions (Peter) – 15 mins
- Proposals for and scheduling of promotions for the current year (all) – 45 mins

Example 2: formal agenda (eg board meetings)

Agenda: Quarterly board meeting

10 April, 10.00–11.30 a.m., Board room suite

1. Apologies
2. Minutes of the last meeting
3. Matters arising from the minutes
4. Presentation of first quarter results (CEO)
5. Departmental presentations (heads)
6. Motions
7. AOB

14.4.1 Compiling the agenda

Besides giving the meeting structure, the purpose of the agenda is to ensure that the time available is only used for discussing the items listed. Some people hold that topics that are important enough to be discussed should be included as items on the agenda, keeping AOB to a minimum. This can be done by asking participants to submit items for inclusion on the agenda. Email is a practical means of doing this, especially when a large group of people is involved. If the agenda is long, or in the case of a formal meeting, you may wish to circulate the draft agenda to participants as an email attachment, rather than including it in the body of an email.

!

Examples

Example 1: asking for contributions to the agenda
Subject:agenda for end-of-year sales meeting, 5 January
Dear all,
Thank you all for agreeing to attend the end-of-year sales meeting on 5 January, from 9.00–10.30 a.m. in meeting room 2A.
As usual, the items below will be included on the agenda. Please could you let me know by 20 December if you would like any further items to be added to the agenda. I will then circulate the finalised agenda before the Christmas break.

- Presentation of last year's sales figures (Andreas)
- Forecasts and targets for the coming year (Sally)
- Analysis of last year's sales promotions (Peter)
- Proposals for/scheduling of promotions for the current year (all)

Regards,
Simon

Example 2: circulating a draft agenda and asking for input
Subject:draft agenda for quarterly board meeting, 1 April
Dear all,
Thank you for making time for the quarterly board meeting on 1 April, from 10.00–11.30 a.m. in the boardroom suite.
Please find attached a draft agenda for the meeting.
I would be grateful to receive any further submissions for the agenda by 25 March at the latest. Many thanks in advance.
Kind regards,
Simon Webber

14.4.2 Submitting items for the agenda

If you wish to add an item to the agenda, make sure you submit it to the chair before the deadline for contributions. If this isn't possible – eg if an urgent issue has arisen after the deadline for submissions – let the chair know that you would like to include the item under »Any other business«. Start your proposal by thanking the chair for the draft agenda and say why you think the item is relevant and should be included.

Useful phrases

- I would like to propose the item »Potential overseas office« to follow item three, as this was discussed at the last managers' meeting and I think it is also relevant to the European sales team.
- I would like to insert the item »Introduction of monthly sales targets« after item two, as this may be the last opportunity to discuss this issue prior to the sales conference next month.
- I recently received important new information from the customer regarding product specifications. If it is not possible to add the item to the agenda at this late stage, I would like to propose including it under AOB.
- I recently came across some software that could be of interest to the team. Since the deadline for submissions to the agenda has passed, I would like to put this item forward for inclusion under AOB.

14.4.3 Circulating the agenda

After you have asked the participants for their contributions to the agenda, it is important to circulate the finalised agenda to them in good time. Email is an expedient way of doing this, but for important external meetings you may choose to send the agenda out by post instead, particularly if you have to enclose other important background documents with the original. This is also a good opportunity to ask participants what technical equipment they require for the meeting and if they have any special dietary requirements.

Example: circulating the agenda !

ABC GmbH
Altstr. 26
56710 Altstadt
Germany

Mr P Smith
Development Manager
EFG Co. Ltd
123 New Road
Newtown NEW 1IT
Great Britain

24 July 20XX
Agenda for project meeting of 25 August
Dear Mr Smith
Thank you for your contribution to the agenda for the forthcoming project meeting. Please find enclosed a copy of the finalised agenda.
I also enclose a copy of the service agreement, signed by us, to be discussed under item four on the agenda.
I would be grateful if you would let me know by 10 August what technical facilities you will require for your presentation, and also whether you have any special dietary requirements we should note when arranging refreshments and lunch.
We look forward to seeing you on 25 August. In the meantime, please do not hesitate to contact me if you have any questions or require any further information.
Yours sincerely
Simone Roth
Project Manager

Travel and weather tips

If you didn't send out travel directions and/or a map for reaching the meeting destination when you confirmed the meeting (»Confirming a meeting«), you have another opportunity to do so when circulating the agenda. If your visitors are travelling from countries with different climates, they may also appreciate some tips on the weather and appropriate clothing for the time of year. For example: »Please note that we are approaching the coldest time of year here in Scotland with frequent rainstorms and low temperatures. We recommend bringing warm and waterproof clothing for your visit.«

Useful vocabulary

chair (= chairperson): Vorsitzender, Leiter des Meetings
to allocate: zuweisen
motion: Antrag
to compile: zusammenstellen
to circulate: an alle Teilnehmer versenden
item: (Tagesordnungs-)Punkt
prior to: vor
extension of lease: Verlängerung des Pacht-/Mietvertrags

14.5 Hands-on organisation

Author Alan Barker *(How to manage meetings)* states: »Ninety per cent of an effective meeting happens before it takes place.« Therefore, when organising the practical aspects of a meeting, it is essential to book everything in good time. Think ahead to what the participants might need – technical equipment, refreshments – and ask attendees about their requirements in advance when you confirm the meeting or circulate the agenda.

14.5.1 Giving travel directions

Providing your visitors with clear travel directions can save them considerable time when they come to arrange their trip. A good time to do this is when confirming the meeting or circulating the agenda, to give visitors plenty of time to make their travel arrangements.

!

Example

You can reach our office/the meeting venue as follows:
By car:
Exit the M25 motorway at Junction 13
Follow the signs for Milton Keynes
At the first roundabout take the second exit to Little Dunbary (follow A25)
Go straight on at the second roundabout
Turn right at the T-junction
Continue straight on until you reach the turning for Little Dunbary Industrial Estate on your right (opposite the Fox & Hounds pub)
You will find us at Unit 98, Road B. Entrance on the left-hand side of the car park.

By public transport:
Nearest train station: Little Dunbary
Bus 42 to Little Dunbary Industrial Estate leaves the bus station in front of the railway station every 30 minutes (on the hour and half hour); journey takes 30 minutes.

From Birmingham airport:
Take the airport shuttle to Birmingham city centre bus station (shuttle leaves the bus stand in front of the airport every 10 minutes); journey takes 40 minutes
Bus 42 to Little Dunbary Industrial Estate (see above); journey takes 15 minutes
On arrival, please report to reception and we will show you to the meeting room.

14.5.2 Giving information on local accommodation

If visitors are travelling from far afield or from abroad, they may need to make an overnight stay close to the airport or to the meeting venue. You can save them much time and help them to arrange things by suggesting suitable places to stay in the area.

Useful phrases

- If you wish to make an overnight stay in the area, we can recommend
  - the Comfortable Inn, which offers reasonably priced accommodation and is located less than 500 metres from our office.
  - the Travellers' Guest House, which is within walking distance of/a short bus/taxi ride from the office.
  - the Luxus Hotel, which is a comfortable hotel located in the city centre and easily accessible from the office by taxi.
  - the Wings Hotel, which is situated in the immediate vicinity of the airport and accessible by shuttle bus.

14.5.3 Finding out about visitors' special dietary requirements

If people from different cultures are attending the meeting, don't forget to bear their dietary requirements in mind when organising meals or refreshments. Some visitors may have food allergies that must be taken into consideration, so prior to the meeting it is a good idea to ask them to inform you of any special requirements when confirming the meeting or circulating the agenda.

!

Examples

Example 1: asking about dietary requirements
Subject:project meeting of 25 August
Dear Mr Smith
Please find enclosed a copy of the agenda for the forthcoming project meeting.
As we will be organising lunch for the meeting attendees, I would be grateful if you would let me know by 10 August if you have any special dietary requirements we should note.
We look forward to seeing you on 25 August. In the meantime please do not hesitate to contact me if you have any questions or require any further information.
Yours sincerely
Simone Roth

Example 2: communicating dietary requirements
Subject:project meeting of 25 August
Dear Ms Roth
Thank you for your letter of 24 July enclosing the agenda for the forthcoming project meeting.
Your letter requested information on special dietary requirements. I am allergic to wheat products and would therefore be most grateful if you could make arrangements for gluten-free meals. Many thanks in advance.
I very much look forward to seeing you at the meeting on 25 August.
Yours sincerely
Peter Smith

Useful phrases

- I only eat halal meat/kosher food.
- I am a vegan/vegetarian.
- I don't consume any alcohol – even in cakes and sauces.
- Unfortunately, I'm allergic to gluten/wheat/dairy products/nuts/seafood.
- I have a wheat/dairy/nut/seafood allergy/lactose intolerance.
- I follow a gluten-free/wheat-free/dairy-free diet.
- I'm afraid I can't eat seafood.

14.5.4 Finding out about visitors' technical requirements

Many people bring laptop computers and other devices to meetings and there are a host of other types of equipment they might need you to supply. Don't forget to check in advance what the participants require. If you're responding to the organiser's request for information on technical equipment, make sure you reply before the deadline.

Useful phrases

- I would be grateful if you could let me know by 10 August what technical equipment you will need for the meeting/your presentation.
- Please let me know by 10 August if you require any technical equipment for the meeting/presentation.
- I would be most grateful if you could supply/provide an overhead projector and a local adapter for my laptop power cable.
- I will be bringing my laptop with me to the meeting. I would therefore be most grateful if you arrange for an extension lead to be provided.

14.5.5 Booking meeting facilities

Once you have gathered information on the participants' individual requirements and have a clear picture of what will be needed for the meeting, it's time to book the meeting room, necessary facilities and refreshments.

Examples !

Example 1: telephoning to book meeting facilities

A: Hello, I'd like to book a meeting room for the Sales Department from 10.00 to 12.30 on 10 January, please.

B: Sure. How many people will be attending the meeting?

A: There'll be 15 of us.

B: Okay, I'll just check what's available ... Conference Room A is free at that time.

A: That's great. Could you just let me know how many power points are in that room?
B: I'll just check for you ... Room A has six power points.
A: Okay, in that case we'll need two extension leads with five sockets each, as most of the attendees will be bringing laptops.
B: That's fine. I'll reserve two extension leads for you.
A: Thank you. Could I also book an overhead projector?
B: Sure, no problem.
A: And some people will be joining us remotely. Could I book conference call equipment and a technician to set it up for us as well?
B: Certainly.
A: Thanks very much.

Example 2: telephoning to arrange for refreshments
B: Will you be requiring refreshments for the meeting?
A: Yes, please. We'll be taking a break at 11.00 a.m. Please could you arrange for refreshments for 15 people?
B: Certainly. Any special requirements?
A: Oh, yes. One person has a dairy allergy and has requested soya milk.
B: No problem at all. Do you need anything else?
A: The meeting will finish at lunchtime. Could you lay on some sandwiches for around 12.30, please?
B: Certainly. Any particular preferences?
A: Yes. We have two vegetarians and someone who only eats kosher food. Could you make provision for that, please?
B: Absolutely. Do you need anything else?
A: I think that's everything, thank you. If you could perhaps let your colleagues on reception know that some visitors from Japan will be joining us and to show them the way to conference room A?
B: Of course, we'll see to that.

14.5.6 Intercultural considerations

Besides culture-related dietary requirements, other cultural aspects come into play when arranging a meeting involving participants from different parts of the world.

Times of the day and public holidays
Particularly if you are organising a teleconference involving participants in different countries, it is important to ensure that the meeting will take place at a time that is reasonable for all the participants, wherever they are located. Remember, too, to check for important public holidays in your colleagues' countries. The website www.timeanddate.com contains a world clock and

a meeting planner comparing times of the day in different countries. It also enables you to create calendars for different countries which display public holidays.

Important time zones		
abbreviation	**explanation**	**where? when?**
Europe		
GMT (UTC)	Greenwich Mean Time (= Coordinated Universal Time)	Stays the same all year round; used all year round in Iceland and during the winter in UK and Ireland
DST	Daylight Saving Time (= Summer Time)	Term used when time is advanced by one hour during the summer time
BST	British Summer Time	UK, summer
IST	Irish Summer Time	Ireland, summer
WET/WEST	Western European Time/Western European Summer Time	
CET/CEST	Central European Time/Central European Summer Time	
EET/EEST	Eastern European Time/Eastern European Summer Time	
Canada and USA		
AST/ADT	Atlantic Standard Time/Atlantic Daylight Time	»Daylight Time« is used in summer time
EST/EDT	Eastern Standard Time/Eastern Daylight Time	
CST/CDT	Central Standard Time/Central Daylight Time	
MST/MDT	Mountain Standard Time/Mountain Daylight Time	
PST/PDT	Pacific Standard Time/Pacific Daylight Time	
Asia-Pacific		
CST	China Standard Time	Whole of China, all year round
IST	India Standard Time	Whole of India, all year round
JST	Japan Standard Time	Whole of Japan, all year round

The abbreviations »a.m.« and »p.m.« are often used in English: »a.m.« stands for »ante meridiem« (= before noon/midday), »p.m.« stands for »post meridiem« (= after noon/midday). »Midday« (12.00 noon) is 12.00 p.m. (and therefore 13.00 = 1.00 p.m.) and »midnight« (12.00 at night) is 12.00 a.m. (01.00 therefore = 1.00 a.m.).

Where confusion could arise, it is a good idea to use the 24-hour clock system for specifying times of the day (in which case you no longer need »a.m.« or »p.m.«), or to say, for example, »seven o'clock in the morning« (meaning 7.00 a.m.) or »seven o'clock in the evening« (meaning 7.00 p.m.).

Hierarchies and seating arrangements

However, in some countries, hierarchies play a more important role in business culture, so keep this in mind when making seating arrangements.

In general, the seat with the back to the door is the worst, as you cannot see who enters and leaves without turning around. The seats on both sides of the chair signal closeness to the leader. Seating arrangements must be carefully made in meetings with Asians: the top-ranking person should sit as closely as possible to the centre of the table with his or her subordinates on either side, in descending order of responsibility. The hosts should also sit closer to the door to greet the guests.

Asians usually bow as a greeting, with younger people and lower-ranking employees bowing lower to show their respect. An American-style slap on the shoulder would not be the right way of greeting a Japanese business partner and neither would »la bise« (the French way of greeting familiar faces by a slight kiss on both cheeks).

! **Important**

No matter of age

In English-speaking cultures, it is not unusual for junior staff to participate in meetings and for managers higher up the hierarchy to ask their opinions where their particular areas of expertise are concerned. It is acceptable for people at all levels to contribute ideas or ask questions regarding aspects outside their specialist area to gain a clearer overall view of the problem.

Evening entertainment

Culture may also affect your choices of evening entertainment. Whereas dinner is universally accepted as the number one choice for the evening, the Japanese also take their business partners out to a Karaoke bar, and in England it is not unusual to attend a sporting event together or, in informal situations, to have a beer at the local pub.

Useful phrases

Inviting someone out

- Can I invite you to join us for a drink before dinner?
- How about Joe's Karaoke bar for tonight?
- Our company sponsors the local cricket club. Would you like to join us for Saturday's match?

Accepting an invitation

- What a brilliant idea! I'd love to join you.
- Absolutely! I've never been to a cricket match before, thank you!
- I'm afraid I'm tied up all Saturday with a family event.
- I'd rather stay in tonight. I am really tired from the long journey. I hope you understand.
- I'm afraid I'm not really into cricket.

Useful vocabulary

junction: Autobahnausfahrt
roundabout: Kreisverkehr
industrial estate: Industriegebiet
venue: Veranstaltungsort
on the hour: zur vollen Stunde
in good time: rechtzeitig
device: Gerät
overhead projector (= OHP), projector: Beamer [this is a German word, not an English one! In informal British English »beamer« means a BMW]
transparency (for the OHP), slide (PowerPoint): Folie
power point/power socket (for laptops, etc): Steckdose
adapter (for power cables, etc): Adapter
extension lead: Verlängerungskabel
to attend a meeting: besuchen, teilnehmen an
remote: nicht vor Ort, standortfern

15 Arriving at the meeting

The time before the meeting actually starts is valuable time for socialising and getting to know the other participants better. There is no second chance to make a first impression, as the saying goes, so this is why introducing yourself to others and making introductions for the attendees you know are very important. Last but not least, the physical surroundings and the technical equipment for the meeting also have to be in place and running.

15.1 Arriving in reception

When arriving at reception, start by giving your name and the name of the person you are here to see.

Useful phrases

- Good morning, I'm here to see Ms Smith. My name is Sylvia Ackermann. I'm a little early, actually.
- Hello, my name is Sylvia Ackermann. I'm here for a meeting with/to meet Hilary Smith.

Important !

Being on time

While punctuality is not always strictly observed internally at companies in English-speaking countries, punctuality for external meetings is considered very important. Lateness is seen as impolite, unless there are very good reasons for it. If you are going to be unavoidably late, phone ahead and let the person you are meeting know what is happening – people rarely mind if you have a good reason and keep them informed.

15.1.1 Receiving visitors on arrival

If you are responsible for welcoming visitors, the reception you give them will form their first impression of the company. So it helps to have some friendly phrases at the ready. If your visitors are visiting the company for the first time, they may well have planned in extra time for their journey and arrived a little early. If there will be a short wait while the person they have come to see finishes what they are doing, put them at ease with a little small talk.

Useful phrases

- Hello, Ms Ackermann. I'll let Hilary know you're here. Please take a seat for a moment.
- Good morning, Ms Ackermann. Welcome to ABC Ltd. Please take a seat. Ms Smith will be with you shortly.
- Ms Ackermann – Hilary knows you are here and her meeting is just coming to an end. She will be with you very shortly. Can I offer you something to drink while you wait?
- Ms Smith will be with you in just a moment. Can I bring you a tea or coffee in the meantime? Or some water?

15.1.2 Lift talk

Perhaps you've been asked to show the visitor in reception the way to the meeting room. On the way down the corridor or in the lift, it is customary for both parties to make some small talk to break the ice. In this situation, small talk is generally restricted to topics such as travel, or the weather.

!

Example: arriving at a meeting and making lift talk

A: Ms Burmeister? Good morning. I'm Rosi Forster, Dr Huber's assistant. Welcome to Hamburg!
B: Thank you, Ms Forster. Nice to meet you!
A: Nice to meet you, too. Did you have a good trip?
B: Yes, thank you.
A: The meeting is on the second floor. Shall we take the lift or would you like to walk?
B: Actually, stretching my legs wouldn't be a bad idea, after so many hours on a plane! But before we go, is there a restroom I could use?
A: Of course, over there behind the column, to your left.
[Five minutes later]
B: So, that's better. Ready to roll.
A: Fine. Let's take the stairs. Is this your first time in Hamburg?
B: Yes, it is. I hope I'll have a chance to do a little sightseeing. I expect the harbour must be especially worth a visit?
A: That's right. It's really interesting. What was the weather like in New York when you left?
B: It was awful, really, slush and snow, and grey skies.
A: It's unusually cold for the time of year here, too. Here we are, room Sao Paolo. Can I take your coat?
B: Thanks.
A: Would you like something to drink? Water? Coffee?
B: Just a sip of water would be nice, thanks.
A: Still or sparkling?
B: Sparkling, please. And would you have a few ice cubes?
A: Sure. I'll be back in a minute.

Useful phrases

- How was your journey here today?
- Did you travel by car? Was the traffic good today?
- Is this your first visit to the area/the company?
- Did you find us easily enough?
- How long will you be staying in Germany?
- I'm afraid you're a little unlucky with the weather. How is the weather in Florida at the moment?
- Well, it looks like we'll have some nice weather during your stay.

If you're the visitor, naturally your responses should be upbeat and cheerful and you should have some questions and phrases of your own up your sleeve.

- The journey was very good, thanks. Ms Smith's directions were very clear.
- Yes, it's my first time here. I'm hoping to see a little of the local area during my stay.
- Has the company been situated here long?
- The company seems to be very conveniently located. Does it take long to travel into the city from here?
- It's much warmer here than where I've travelled from. Is this weather usual for the time of year?
- At home, it's lovely and warm. It's spring-like!
- It's pouring/coming down in torrents/buckets.
- It's absolutely freezing/boiling.

Useful vocabulary

to arrive in reception: an der Rezeption ankommen
restroom (🇺🇸): Toilette
to stretch my legs: sich die Beine vertreten
to boil: kochen; sehr heiß sein
slush: Schneeregen
a sip: ein Schluck
to cheer up: aufklaren
to be worthwhile: sich lohnen

15.2 Introducing oneself and others

When you reach your destination, be sure to thank the person who has shown you the way before they go. The next step will be to introduce yourself to your host and the other meeting attendees. It is usual to shake hands as you do so.

15.2.1 »How do you do?« and »How are you?«

»How do you do?« is a standard phrase people use when meeting for the first time. It is very polite and more formal than »Pleased to meet you.« Although this sounds like a question, the required response is: »How do you do?« In the US, people meeting for the first time sometimes substitute »How do you do?« for »How are you?« (response: »How are you?«). This phrase is also becoming more widely used in UK business culture. The phrase »Nice to meet you« also exists and is a little less formal than the alternatives above. »Pleased to meet you« is more appropriate in a business setting. When people who have met on previous occasions ask »How are you?«, the usual response is: »Fine, thanks, and you?« or, more formally, »Very well, thank you, and you?«. Americans might also reply »Good«, which may sound a little informal for speakers of UK English.

Useful phrases

- How do you do? I'm Sylvia Ackermann.
- How do you do, Ms Ackermann? I'm Hilary Smith.
- Hello, I'm Sylvia Ackermann from DEF GmbH in Germany – pleased to meet you.
- Hilary Smith. I'm pleased to meet you, Ms Ackermann.

! **Important**

First name or last name?

It is usual to give both first and last names when introducing oneself or others. However, use of first names is very widespread in English-speaking countries, even between people at different levels of seniority and people who have never met face to face. If they call you by your first name, feel free to do the same. If you use the last name, the usual form of address is Miss (for an unmarried woman or if you are unsure whether she's married or not), Mrs (for a married woman) or Mr.

15.2.2 Introducing others

There are several ways to introduce other people to one another, depending on the formality of the situation. It is useful to follow the introduction with a line about the person you are introducing. The more formal types of introduction are at the top of the following list and the least formal towards the end.

Useful phrases

- Mr Stevenson, may I introduce Peter Korb? Mr Korb is Marketing Director at DEF GmbH in Munich.
- Mr Stevenson, I'd like to introduce Peter Korb. Mr Korb has come from Germany to join us for today's meeting.

- Michael, I'd like you to meet Peter Korb. Peter is Marketing Director at DEF GmbH.
- Michael, have you met Peter Korb from DEF GmbH?
- Michael, this is Peter Korb, Marketing Director at DEF in Germany.
- Michael Stevenson – Peter Korb.
- Michael – Peter. Peter – Michael.

15.3 Small talk

As is well known, it is customary for business partners in English-speaking countries to make some small talk before getting down to the business at hand. With someone you have just met for the first time, the aim of small talk is to break the ice and to find out a little about him or her from a business perspective. Generally speaking, the better you know a person, the more topics you can add to the list of small talk subjects. For people who know each other well, the weather tends to be further down the list of small talk topics.

!

Examples

Example 1: small talk with someone you know well

A: Peter, good to see you again!

B: Same here, Jack! How has life been treating you since we last met? And how is Susanne?

A: Thanks, Susanne is fine. We're going to have twins in July.

B: Congratulations, that's great news.

Example 2: small talk with someone new

A: So you also arrived from London, I heard?

B: Yes, that's right. I flew in from Stansted this morning. Awful traffic on the M11, just one big traffic jam after the other.

A: I know what you're talking about. I live in Cambridge and have to take the M11 every morning to go to work.

B: Poor you! Where exactly are you based?

A: At the Harlow office. Been there for about 18 months now.

B: Do you happen to know Peter Brooks? From accounts.

A: Peter, sure! We used to have adjacent offices. How do you know Peter?

Useful phrases

- Have you travelled far for today's meeting?
- Whereabouts are you/is your company based?
- So, how long have you been with the company?/Have you been at the company long?
- What is your role at the company?

When talking to someone you have met on previous occasions and with whose job and company you are already familiar, you might start by asking the person about how they are. Then look for common ground with regard to other business or work-related topics and industry developments.

- Hi, John. Good to see you. How are you?
- Hello, Mark. How are you settling in in your new role?
- I heard about your promotion to Sales Director. Congratulations!
- Did you attend the technology conference last week? What did you think of ... ?
- I saw your presentation at the annual convention last month – it was really interesting.
- Have you heard that CBC may be merging with Smith Technologies? How would that impact your business?
- Have you been affected by the recent increases in fuel costs at all?

!

Important

Handshaking

Handshaking is usual during first introductions but not necessarily at every subsequent meeting. While participants in important meetings are likely to shake hands when arriving at the meeting, in informal settings business partners who have met each other on previous occasions and feel relaxed in each other's company may not necessarily shake hands every time they meet.

15.3.1 How's business – and life?

A common phrase English-speakers use with people they have met before and with whom they are on informal terms is simply, »How's business?« This signals your interest in your conversation partner and their company without pushing for any specific information. This phrase leaves it open for your conversation partner to go into as much detail as they wish in their response. Business partners who know each other well may also graduate to small talk topics regarding their private lives.

Useful phrases

- How's the family? Please give/pass on my regards to [name of partner].
- So, how's life treating you?
- Have you been busy of late?
- So, how was your break in Spain?
- Have you managed to get away for a holiday yet?
- Last time we met you were off to the Bahamas. Did you have a good break?

Checklist: levels and topics of small talk

Situation	Example small talk topics
Escorting someone to a meeting	Journey; travel plans while staying in the area; weather
Post-introductions; meeting someone for the first time	Journey; person's role at their company/their work; information about their company/industry; travel plans while staying in the area; weather
Someone you have met before; waiting for the meeting to start	How are you? How's business?; journey; trade fairs/ conferences, etc; industry developments; events of shared interest: work or business-related; weather
Someone you know well	As level above, and also: family; holidays; news, sports, music events, etc

15.3.2 Effortless small talk

To make your small talk more fluent, you should bear some tactics in mind. They will make it easier for your partner to carry on with the small talk, and you will be perceived as a person who takes an interest in others and is open and friendly:

Checklist: tactics for effortless small talk

Tactic	Example
Give answers in full sentences.	Where in Germany are you from? I'm from Passau, that's in the south, close to the Austrian border.
Listen for indirect signals.	We had quite a storm on the lake yesterday and almost capsized. So you must be a good sailor?
Give some information about yourself.	I really need to leave the meeting on time. I've got my ballet class at seven.

Useful vocabulary
to merge, a merger: fusionieren, Fusion
to impact sth: sich auswirken auf
to be affected by sth: betroffen sein von
adjacent: nebeneinander liegend

15.4 Setting up the meeting room

Even if you reserved the necessary technical items, things don't always run smoothly on the day of the meeting itself. You may need help setting up the equipment – especially if you are using conference call equipment. Ask a technician to check if it is set up properly before the meeting starts.

Useful phrases

Asking for help

- I'm afraid this extension lead isn't quite long enough. Could I trouble you for a longer one?
- I'm having a little trouble with the projector. Please could you give me a hand to set it up?
- Is there anywhere I could plug my mobile phone in to charge during the meeting?
- Do you mind if I plug my laptop into this power socket?

Offering help

- Are you okay with that? Do you need any help at all?
- Can I give you a hand with setting that up?
- Do you need an extension lead for your laptop?
- Just a moment – I'll ask someone from technical support to come and give you a hand with that.

Useful vocabulary

to give/pass on regards to sb: Grüße ausrichten, grüßen lassen
to give/lend sb a hand: helfen

16 Conducting a meeting

Besides playing a key role in preparing the agenda, the chairperson gives structure to the meeting itself. He or she provides a framework for discussion of the agenda items by performing the formalities at the start, throughout and at the end of the meeting.

16.1 Opening the meeting

The main task of the chair is to make sure the meeting runs smoothly. He or she opens and closes the meeting, manages time, facilitates conversation, assigns tasks and summarises what was achieved during the meeting.

!

Example: the start of the meeting

Chair: Good afternoon, everyone. Before we start, Susanne Braun has asked me to pass on her apologies: unfortunately she can't make it today as she's attending the sales conference in Athens. I would also like to introduce David Barnes from ABC Europe who has flown in from Brussels to join us today. David, could I ask you to tell us briefly about your role in the project?
DB: Yes, thank you, Stephan. I'm heading up the project team in Brussels. We're a team of six and we're dealing with the logistics side of the product launch in Europe.
Chair: Great, thank you, David. For David's benefit, could we all introduce ourselves, going anti-clockwise around the table?
[Round of introductions]
Chair: As you all know from the agenda, today's objective is to agree on the packaging for the new product. Now, we do need to make sure we finish on time this afternoon so that David can make his evening flight back to Brussels. We've allowed 15 minutes for each item on the agenda and a further 20 minutes for questions at the end. So, shall we get straight on with item one?

Useful phrases

- Good morning, ladies and gentlemen. Thank you all for joining us today. Shall we make a start? [Formal]
- Good morning, everyone. Thanks for coming. Shall we get down to business/ get the ball rolling? [Informal]

16.1.1 Introductions and apologies

At external meetings where the participants do not yet know each other, the chair is likely to start by making formal introductions or asking the participants to introduce themselves.

Useful phrases

- Perhaps we could start by introducing ourselves, moving clockwise around the table?
- For those of you who haven't yet had the chance to meet, I would like to start by introducing ...
- Our presenter today is Sarah Hughes. Sarah is going to talk to us about ...
- On my left is ...
- Also joining us is ...
- I have received apologies from David Smith, who is unable to join us today, and Fred Burnes, who will be arriving a little late.
- Has anyone seen Martha? She's supposed to come, too.

How to say »I'm sorry«

Whether to use »apology« or »excuse« depends on the situation. In a meeting, you use »apologies from Paul«, meaning that Paul was unable to attend. An »excuse« can also be used in the sense of the German »Ausrede, Vorwand«. In formal English you would say, »I apologise for being late«, in informal English »I'm sorry I'm late«. In both cases, you would add the reason for being late, eg: »My plane was delayed«.

You use »excuse me« to catch someone's attention, eg: »Excuse me, could you pass me the coffee, please?« »I beg your pardon?« or »Pardon?« are formal ways of stating that you haven't understood what someone was saying. In informal situations you simply say »Sorry?«.

16.1.2 Introducing the agenda and the objectives of the meeting

Useful phrases

- As you know, we're here today to discuss ...
- The objective/purpose of today's meeting is to reach agreement on ...
- Does everyone have/does anyone need a copy of the agenda?
- We have approximately 15 minutes for each point on the agenda.
- So, moving onto the first item/point on the agenda, ...

16.1.3 Initiating the discussion

Useful phrases
- The first agenda item – renewal of company insurance – was put forward by Jill Baker. Jill, would you like to start us off?
- Simon, you put forward item three on the agenda. Perhaps you could fill us in on this point?
- Jürgen, could you bring us up to date on item four?
- Stephan, would you outline item five for us?
- Peter, could you fill us in on the background?

Useful vocabulary
to get down to business, to get/start the ball rolling: beginnen, anfangen
clockwise, anti-clockwise: im Uhrzeigersinn, gegen den Uhrzeigersinn
to fill sb in on sth: informieren

16.2 Guiding the discussion

It is the chair's responsibility to make sure all the participants have their say – by guiding the discussion, encouraging everyone to speak up and, if necessary, curtailing the flow of speech of individuals who are too vociferous.

Useful phrases
- Thank you, Stephan. Peter, do you have any thoughts on this?
- So, Peter agrees with Stephan regarding this item. Barbara, could I bring you in at this point?
- I'd also like to hear Julie's opinion at this point.
- Could you elaborate on that for us, please?
- Does anyone else have anything to add to this?

16.2.1 Dealing with dominant participants and interruptions

Useful phrases
- Thank you, Jim. Could I just stop you there for a moment, because I'd like to bring Phil in here.
- Jim, could I ask you to let Phil finish his point and then we can hear your view?
- I'm sorry, Jim – I'd just like to finish hearing what Phil has to say on this point and then we'll come back to you.
- I'm sorry, Tatjana, we don't have time to talk about that now, I'm afraid.

! **Important**

Tricks for the chair

Notice how the chair phrases requests as suggestions or questions. He addresses the participants by name to secure their attention and handles interruptions tactfully with »I'm sorry«, followed by an assurance that the person concerned will have their say afterwards.

16.2.2 Encouraging quiet participants to contribute

! **Example: facilitating a balanced discussion**

Chair: Item one is the font used on the outer packaging. Jo, could you outline the design department's view on this?
Jo: Sure. We've come to the conclusion that Option A is the best choice as it's the most legible against the blue background and consistent ...
David: Can I come in here? I think ...
Chair: Sorry, David, could we just let Jo finish her point and then we'll hear your view.
Jo: ... and it's consistent with the overall branding.
Chair: Thank you, Jo. Did you want to comment on that, David?
David: Yes – in Logistics we strongly prefer Option B. It's far more eye-catching.
Chair: So we have Option A for Design and Option B for Logistics. Sue, could you please tell us Manufacturing's perspective?

Useful phrases

- I'd like to ask Petra to tell us about the new development at this point, if I may.
- Mr Baker, what is your opinion here?
- Jim, it would be useful to hear your perspective on this.
- Pam, how would this affect the HR [Human Resources] department?
- Julie raised the point that our existing contract is about to expire. What's your take on this, Jan?
- Tara, you've been working with this client for some time now. What do you say to the point Helen raised?

16.2.3 Reminding participants to be brief

Useful phrases

- Before we move on to the next item, could you quickly give us your opinion on this, Maria?
- I'm afraid we have to move on to the next item. Could you bring your point to a close, please?

- I'm afraid I have to stop you there. Time is ticking away.
- Could I ask you to keep your comment brief, please?
- Can I remind you that we only have 15 minutes for each item?

16.2.4 Keeping to the agenda

!

Example: directing the discussion

David: ... and therefore we would be strongly in favour of B, because, as I've already said, we ...
Chair: Could I stop you there for a moment, David? I'm afraid time's running short. Jo, what do you think about item two?
Jo: Design would like to rethink the shape of the packaging. We'd like to make it a little taller, because ...
David: I totally agree. Some years ago we opted for square packaging for another product and it was a total flop. In fact, this particular product was ...
Chair: That's a valid point, David, but I'd like to bring the discussion back to this year's launch if possible ...

Useful phrases

- I think we risk moving away from the agenda here. Could we bring the discussion back to ...?
- We have a lot to cover this morning – I'm afraid we don't have time to go into that. Can we focus on ...?
- I'm afraid we're getting sidetracked. Let's return to ...
- That's an important point, but I think that's a discussion for another day. I'd like to go on with the sales figures.
- That's a valid point. May we come back to that later?

16.2.5 Summarising and concluding an item

Useful phrases

- So, we've established that the July deadline is too ambitious. What is a more realistic target?
- So, just in order to summarise/sum up/recap what we've said, ...
- So, to bring this point to a close, we can say that ...
- So, am I right in concluding that we'll ... ?
- I think we've agreed/we're all in agreement that ...

16.2.6 Moving on to the next agenda item

Useful phrases

- The next point/item two on today's agenda is ...
- I'd like to move on to item three now.
- Now, turning to item four, ...
- Anyway, about the new location …

Useful vocabulary

to raise a point: einen Punkt ansprechen
to expire: auslaufen
font: Schriftart
to focus on sth: sich konzentrieren auf
square: rechteckig
to elaborate: etwas ausführen
ambitious: ehrgeizig

16.3 Bringing about a decision

The purpose of most meetings is not only to exchange information, but also to reach decisions. If a decision does not come about naturally, the chair might have to »push« the participants to make up their minds. Sometimes it may also be necessary to postpone taking a decision.

16.3.1 How to reach consensus

Attendees need sufficient time to express their opinions. Nobody likes to be rushed into a decision. Minority views should receive ample attention so that their owners feel they were heard. A short break often helps to bring about a decision.

Summarising the general mood at the end of each item on the agenda contributes to a clear outcome. Every attendee is more aware of what the general views are. The chair can also help the participants reach a decision by phrasing questions carefully. If the chair has the feeling that there are more outspoken supporters in favour of an issue, they should ask: »Does anyone object?« rather than »Does everyone approve?«

Example: summarising and bringing about a conclusion !

Chair: So, to sum up item five, we've agreed that we're going to opt for silver packaging. The next item on the agenda is »Cardboard or plastic packaging«. We've already heard everyone's views on this topic, so could we move straight to a show of hands for cardboard? That's six. Thank you. For the minutes, that's a majority decision in favour of cardboard.

Useful phrases

- Could we make a yes or no decision on this item? Could all those in favour please raise their hands?
- Could we have a show of hands for going ahead with the measure, please?
- Am I right in saying that we've decided in favour of/against this move?
- So we have decided to commission Union Brozers with the catering for the event.
- Is it okay with everybody to bring the launch forward by two weeks?
- It would certainly be wrong to rush into a decision. Could we leave this until another time?

Useful vocabulary

to opt for: sich entscheiden für
majority decision: Mehrheitsentscheidung
show of hands: per Handzeichen

16.4 Closing the meeting

16.4.1 Initiating further action

Before the meeting closes, all the »to dos« should be allocated. In the closing remarks, the chairperson or participants may also wish to discuss the date and time for the next meeting, when the minutes will be available or the date by which a decision should be made.

Example: allocating follow-up tasks !

Chair: Jo has kindly offered to follow this up with the shipping department. Can you do this before next week's meeting, Jo?
Jo: Yes, no problem.
Chair: Great. Can somebody volunteer to contact the supplier before next week? David? Thank you. We're almost out of time, but does anyone have any last questions before we finish? No? Well, so we can finish the meeting. Thank you all for coming and for your input. I wish David a safe flight back to Brussels.

Useful phrases

- We need somebody to contact the supplier. Ian, could you do this for us?
- Tina has offered to file the application. How long do you think this process will take, Tina?
- Could you follow this up for us, please?
- Thanks for volunteering to do this, Marina. Do you think this will be possible in time for next week's meeting?
- Georg, when will you be able to email out today's minutes to everyone?
- Betty, do you think you could get back to us on that tomorrow by email?
- We'll meet again on the first of next month.
- I'll send out a group email with the minutes tomorrow.
- Can we fix the date for the next meeting, please?
- So, the next meeting will be on next Tuesday.
- What about the following Wednesday? How is that for everyone?

16.4.2 Bringing the meeting to a close

There are different reasons why a meeting comes to an end. Time may have run out or all of the items on the agenda may have been checked off. Some meetings will end earlier than expected and others will run late. Before the chair closes the meeting, he or she will let the participants know the meeting is drawing to a close.

Useful phrases

Formal meetings

- I am officially ending today's meeting. You will receive the minutes within two days.
- I declare the meeting closed.
- The meeting is adjourned until tomorrow, 8.00 a.m.

Informal meetings

- It looks like we've run out of time.
- Before we bring the meeting to a close, does anyone have any other business to discuss?
- Well, we're almost out of time for today. Are there any last questions before we finish?
- Is there any other business?
- I think we've covered everything on the agenda.
- As you can all see from the agenda, that was the last item. If no one has anything else to add, then I think we'll wrap this up.
- That brings us to the end of the meeting.

- Let's call it a day, then.
- The meeting is closed.

16.4.3 Thanking the attendees

Thanking the participants is usually one of the last remarks. However, even after closing the meeting the chairperson might realise they have forgotten something. There is almost always one last thing to say.

Useful phrases

- I'd like to thank you all for coming and I wish you a safe journey back.
- Thank you all for your participation.
- I'd especially like to thank Karl for coming over from Glasgow.
- Oh, before you leave, please make sure you have signed the attendance sheet.
- Could I have your attention again, please? I didn't mention that ...
- If you could all return your chairs to the room next door that would be much appreciated.

Useful vocabulary

to adjourn a meeting: vertagen
to call it a day: beenden, Schluss machen
to wrap sth up: abschließen
to follow sth up: an etwas dranbleiben

17 The meeting itself

There are different roles and goals in a meeting. The chair is in charge of smooth and efficient »housekeeping«. However, participating also has its pitfalls and requires particular types of language for achieving one's aims, above all when it comes to politeness and expressing oneself diplomatically.

17.1 Roles at a meeting

Whether your meeting is formal or informal, it will run more smoothly if one of the participants assumes the role of chair (»Conducting a meeting«).

Other important players at the meeting are the minute-taker and the participants. The minute-taker writes the minutes, i.e. he or she records the meeting and keeps track of what has been said. One could also say that the minute-taker is the administrator for the meeting.

The participants can take various roles, such as the role of the presenter, who provides information, or the role of a task owner, meaning that an individual is in charge of a certain topic. Participants are also thinking resources – they contribute ideas, help to solve problems and shed light on issues from different perspectives.

17.1.1 Assigning and accepting roles

For formal meetings, the above roles will usually be allocated before the meeting itself. At more informal meetings, one of the chair's first tasks during the meeting may be to assign these roles to other participants.

If this role has not been assigned yet – which usually happens in the run-up to the meeting, as the minute-taker should prepare in advance (writing equipment, preliminary information, etc) – perhaps the easiest way is to ask for volunteers.

Example: asking for a minute-taker
Chair: Do I have any volunteers for minute-taker today? Don't all jump at once! No volunteers? Okay. Peter, could I ask you to take the minutes today? Peter: I'm afraid I'm pretty tied up this week – I don't think I'd be able to turn them around in time for the next meeting.

!

Chair: No problem. How about Sarah?
Sarah: I'm sorry, but I'm on a training course in the Manchester office all next week.
Chair: I see. Jack, do you have time to do the minutes?
Jack: Yes, certainly.

In the above example, two participants use the following polite formulations to decline the chair's request: »I'm afraid«, »I'm sorry, but ...« Notice how the chair continues to ask around the group until this important role has been assigned.

Useful phrases

- Do I have any volunteers for taking the minutes today?
- Who would like to be our minute-taker this morning?
- Bill, could I ask you to be minute-taker today?
- Jane, would you be so kind as to take the minutes for us?

Useful vocabulary

minute-taker: Protokollführer
to assume (informal: to take on) the role of: Rolle übernehmen
to be tied up with sth: viel zu tun haben
to turn sth around: etwas fertig machen und zurücksenden

17.2 Active participation and asking for more information

While it is the chair's job to manage the meeting, meeting participants also have an active role to play to aid communication and make the meeting as effective as possible. Asking questions is an effective method of obtaining more in-depth information, while active listening shows the person you are talking to that you are paying attention and have understood what they are saying.

17.2.1 Interrupting politely

Sometimes you may need to interrupt a speaker in order to ask your question before they move on to another point. Perhaps the speaker has finished their point and there is a natural pause in which you can ask your question.

Important !

Sorry!
This is the easiest and fastest way of attracting attention politely and stopping the speaker. This »catchword« should, however, be backed up by saying what you actually want. If you just want to check back if you have correctly understood what the speaker said, you could say: »Sorry – how much did you say?« or, »Sorry, when did you say?«

Useful phrases

Formal meetings

- Sorry, I'd just like to ask a question, if I may?
- Sorry, could I interrupt you for a moment? I'd like to ask a question.
- Excuse me, Peter, I wonder if I could interrupt you for a second?
- Sorry, could I come in here with a question?

Informal meetings

- Sorry to interrupt, but I have a question.

If, on the other hand, you are the speaker, you can prevent an interruption by either just ignoring the person or by saying one of the following phrases:

- Sorry, John, can you hear me out, please?
- Just let me finish, please.
- No, Mary, please hear me out.

17.2.2 Asking for more information

Once you have politely gained the speaker's attention, move straight on to your question. Asking for a person's opinion when you ask them a question – for example, »What do you think will happen?« rather than »What will happen?« – helps »soften« the question and makes it less direct. Notice, too, how the questioner below uses »would« and »could« instead of the more direct »will« and »can«.

Example: asking for and receiving further information !

A: Moving into the spring, we need to reassess the product range. Then, in the summer, we'll turn our attention to ...
B: Sorry, could I interrupt you there for a second? A: Sure.
B: I have a question: you mentioned reassessing the product range in the spring. Could I ask you to expand on that?
A: No problem. Sales of C123 and C124 dropped dramatically last year, so we want to look at the reasons for this and perhaps make some adjustments to the range.

B: Do you mean introducing new products?
A: Actually, it's more likely that some products will be discontinued.
B: I see. What timescale do you have in mind for this process?
A: Well, we're planning to start the assessment in the first week of March and we anticipate that we'll be finished by mid-April.
B: Right. That's good to know – thank you.

Useful phrases

- You mentioned that [repeat the key point]. Could you expand on that for us?
- Could you elaborate/go into more detail on that for us?
- Could you explain that in a little more detail?
- I'm afraid I don't quite follow you there. Could you be a little more precise/specific?
- How do you think that will affect ...?
- What do you think would be the outcome of that?
- What do you consider to be the highest priority here?
- How do you envisage implementing ...?
- What is the timescale likely to be for that/what is the anticipated timescale for this?
- Do you foresee any problems/issues/difficulties there?
- What do you think would be the possible repercussions of that?

17.2.3 Active listening

If you don't want to interrupt the speaker's flow, active listening can simply take the form of single words or »polite noises«, such as »okay«, »aha«, »oh«, »mmm«. Body language, such as nodding and smiling from time to time, should of course accompany all your polite utterings to show that you are listening. Use the handy phrases below if you want to signal to the person speaking that you understand.

Useful phrases

- I see.
- I understand.
- Right.
- That's interesting.
- Oh, really?
- That makes sense.
- Okay, thank you for explaining that.

17.2.4 Responding to questions

If you need a couple of seconds to think before answering a question, one trick is to repeat the asker's question and clarify what they want to know while you gather your thoughts. When a speaker needs more time to think, they may also try to ask a question back. Maybe they don't have a good answer up their sleeve right away. In this case, they can simply acknowledge the question and play for time before giving a real answer. English-speakers frequently also introduce their answers by starting with, »Well ...«.

Example: buying time to think and respond
A: So, how do you see this measure taking shape? B: How do we see the measure taking shape? Well, first of all, we plan to ...

!

Useful phrases

- I'm not quite sure what you mean by that. Could you explain?
- It all depends on what you mean by the »extra costs« you mentioned.
- That's a very good question.
- I'm glad you asked that.
- It's hard to say.

Or, perhaps you've been caught on the back foot by an awkward question you weren't quite expecting and need to politely decline to answer.

- I'm afraid I'm not in a position to/able to comment on that/answer that question just now.
- Well, it's rather difficult to say at present.
- I don't have enough information at my disposal to consider all the implications at the moment.
- Maybe we could leave the legal issues aside for a moment, the real challenge for ACME is on the European level.

Useful vocabulary

timescale: Zeitrahmen
to envisage: voraussehen, ins Auge fassen
to anticipate: voraussehen, rechnen mit
specific: besondere, speziell, präzise
at sb's disposal: zur Verfügung haben
outcome: Ausgang
to foresee: vorhersehen, absehen
repercussion: Auswirkung

17.3 Expressing agreement and disagreement

In English-speaking cultures, politeness and tact are key elements when expressing approval and disapproval of other people's suggestions and ideas. When expressing disagreement – the more sensitive of the two areas – many English-speakers, and particularly the British, tend towards understatement and often use diplomacy so as not to sound impolite.

17.3.1 Agreeing with an opinion

! **Example: expressing agreement**

A: So, I really think we should wait until next year to launch the campaign.
B: I couldn't agree more. I can't see how launching a new model this late in the season will benefit the range.
C: You're quite right – we could put the remainder of this year's budget to far better use.
A: Well, I'm glad we're all agreed on that.

! **Important**

Cultural differences between the US and Britain
Although politeness is important in both the US and British cultures, North Americans tend to be more forthcoming and direct than their British counterparts when expressing their agreement, and especially their disagreement.

Useful phrases

Total agreement

- I couldn't agree with you more.
- You're absolutely right (there).
- I totally/completely/fully/absolutely agree (with you on that point).
- I'm in total agreement with that.

Neutral agreement

- I agree.
- I would agree with that.
- I'm with you on that.
- I think you're right.
- That's a fair point.
- That's true.

Mild agreement

- I tend to agree.
- Maybe you're right.
- I suppose so.
- Possibly.
- Could be.

17.3.2 Diplomatic disagreement

In English-speaking cultures, disagreeing without putting forward an alternative solution is generally viewed as unhelpful. Therefore, the emphasis is on what is known as constructive criticism, which essentially involves coupling disagreement with an alternative suggestion and backing it up with good reasons. So, people often handle disagreement by highlighting an element of an idea they find positive before moving on to tactfully express disagreement with another aspect.

Example: disagreeing diplomatically !

A: I hear what you're saying about that but I do have some reservations about the timing.
B: I see. Could you be more specific?
A: Well, we have the international sales conference coming up in September. Surely we should aim to finish the proposal by then so that we can discuss it at the conference.
B: That's a good point, but I think rushing the proposal to finish it before the conference could be counterproductive.
A: I'm just a little concerned that the French sales team will be left out of the discussion completely if the issue isn't addressed at the conference.
B: I take your point, but I think we'll struggle to compile all the data we need by September.
A: Oh, I see. In that case, what about putting together an overview of the proposal in time for the conference and then scheduling a meeting to discuss it in full at a later date?
B: Yes, that would work.

Useful phrases

- I like what you said about the book launch, but I feel we might need to rethink some aspects of it.
- I think the concept is good overall, but I'm not entirely convinced about the marketing element.

- I'm concerned that advertising in this way won't achieve our objective, because ... Have you thought about the possibility of ...?
- My only concern with that is that we could run out of time. Have you considered trying ...?

When »yes« means »no«

The German culture is what is known as a low-context culture. In such cultures, it is considered most effective to formulate statements in an unambiguous and direct way. Americans are also known for their no-nonsense, straight-to-the-point approach. In high-context cultures, such as in Britain, non-verbal communication, including body language, plays a more important role. High-context culture speakers are often reluctant to say »no« in a straightforward way, so be sensitive to »yes, but« statements that really mean »no«:

- Yes, I take your point, but ...
- Yes, I agree with you, but ...
- Yes, I see what you're saying/what you mean, but ...

When you want to answer in the affirmative way, there are many possibilities besides a simple »yes«. The same applies to »no« and »maybe«, as you can see from the following table.

Alternatives to the words »yes«, »maybe« and »no«	
Yes	Sure
	certainly
	of course
	right
	hmm
	yeah
	okay
	fine
	I am/I was/I did
	I think so
	absolutely
Maybe	Perhaps
	could be
	I don't know
	it's hard to say
	I'm not sure

Alternatives to the words »yes«, »maybe« and »no«	
No	Not really
	I don't think so
	not just now/not at the moment
	I'm not/I wasn't/I didn't
	not completely

Degrees of disagreement

Bear in mind that, out of politeness, particularly British speakers tend towards understatement in their expression of disagreement. Therefore, phrases that express mild disagreement often conceal opinions that are stronger than they sound. If you're the speaker, remember that toning down your statements a touch will still have the required effect.

!

Example: various grades of disagreement

A: Yes, I agree, but that target is fairly unrealistic based on last year's figures.
B: I'm not sure I agree there. As we said, last year's turnover was down due to external factors beyond our control.
A: Yes, but that's not to say that the targets weren't too high in the first place.
B: I beg to differ. We were on track to hit our targets before the general downturn in the industry.
A: I see what you're saying, but surely our targets should have allowed some leeway for that possibility.
C: I totally disagree. Sales have increased year on year for the past five years ...

Checklist: disagreement

- Politeness and diplomacy are key.
- Bear understatement in mind, both when interpreting other people's statements of disagreement and formulating your own. Making your statements milder will still get your point across in the English-speaking world.
- If possible, highlight any items you agree with before being specific about the aspects you disagree with.
- Use constructive criticism: always try to put forward alternative solutions to problems.
- Back up disagreement with good reasons.
- »Yes, but« statements are a tactful way to say »no«.

Useful phrases

Mild disagreement

- I'm not sure about that.
- I'm not sure I agree.
- I'm not totally convinced about that.
- I hesitate to agree with you there, because ...

Neutral disagreement

- I'm sorry, but I can't agree on that point.
- I'm afraid I don't agree.
- I tend to disagree.
- I beg to differ.

Strong disagreement

If a speaker strongly disagrees with a standpoint, »softeners«, such as »I'm afraid«, »I'm sorry, but« tend to fall away:

- I totally disagree.
- I don't agree at all.
- I'm in complete disagreement with you.
- To the contrary, I think ...

17.3.3 Expressing criticism

As with disagreement, diplomacy is called for when it comes to expressing criticism in the English-speaking world. English-speakers often tone down criticism by using a positive word in the negative, rather than a negative word:

- not very good: bad
- not up to standard: below standard
- not very encouraging: disappointing.

!

Important

Try to soften criticism

Criticism is usually received best if it is expressed diplomatically. To soften a statement in English, try using:
»not quite/not really« + a positive word (eg »adequate«) or
»a little/somewhat« + a negative word (eg »disappointing«).

Criticism: can you read between the lines?	
What is said	**What is meant**
This isn't quite what we were expecting. This falls a little below our expectations.	This doesn't meet our expectations at all.
The design isn't quite what we were hoping for. The design is not exactly what we were looking for.	We don't like it at all.
Their performance isn't really up to scratch. Their performance is a little under par.	Their performance is not acceptable.

17.3.4 Straight talking

Despite your best efforts to put your point across tactfully, sometimes there are situations which call for a more direct approach. In English, unpleasant news is often preceded by short phrases which brace the listener for what is to come.

!

Example: let's face facts

A: I accept that sales were a little lower than expected.
B: Let's not beat around the bush: they were very disappointing.
A: Frankly, I think that's overstating it a little. Those kinds of figures are to be expected in the current business climate.
B: Look, I think we should face facts: the product is just not performing as we planned. To be honest, I think it's time we pulled the plug ...

Useful phrases

- Let's not beat around the bush ...
- Let's face facts ...
- Let's be honest ...
- Let's get one thing straight ...
- To be honest, I ...
- Frankly, I ...
- I don't want to rock the boat/upset the applecart, but ...
- I don't want to paint too black a picture, but ...

Useful vocabulary

remainder: Rest
range: Produktpalette
to conceal: verstecken
to brace: wappnen
to beat about/around the bush: um den heißen Brei herumreden
current: aktuell
to rock the boat/upset the applecart: die Pferde scheu machen

17.4 Making suggestions and having your say

!

Example: making suggestions

A: I would advise the Board to slash the budget for tobacco advertising. That way, we are on the safe side.
B: Why do you think that?
A: The new EU directive poses an immediate threat to our market share.
B: In my view this prospective danger is still in the stars. What I think is that we should deal with the problems at hand, rather than musing about what might happen in ten years' time!
A: I'm not dodging the issue of teenage smoking, if this is what you mean. On the contrary! We'll have to face the music sooner or later. I assure you that I do care about the issue.

Informal formulations and questions for making suggestions are also suitable for meetings. A more tentative way of making a suggestion includes »would«, »could« or »might/may«.

Useful phrases

- Why don't we try ...?
- Let's take a novel approach in this matter.
- Shall we ...?
- May/might I suggest we stick to our initial plan?
- Wouldn't it be worth trying to give a new supplier a chance?
- Could there be another way forward?

17.4.1 Expressing your opinion

Of course, you can simply state your opinion by plainly saying what you mean. You would usually use an introductory phrase like »I suggest« or »I would advise that...«

In a discussion, your tone of voice and intonation would of course also influence the way your opinions come across. Quite naturally, the point you want to make should be pronounced more emphatically than the rest of the sentence. Another way of emphasising and adding stress is to use auxiliaries that you would not need for grammatical reasons.

Useful phrases

Neutral expression of an opinion

- I suggest that we reconsider our standpoint.
- My proposal is to start negotiations as fast as we can.

Strong expression of an opinion

- I strongly recommend investing in commodities.
- It is high time we became active in this field.
- I advise all of you to reconsider your views.
- There's no alternative to buying new machines.
- It's not a rumour, our competitors are launching the new storage system, that's a fact.
- I do think it's important to meet before the 17th!

However, the best phrases won't make an impact unless your entire performance radiates confidence. Here are some tips.

Checklist: how to have your say

- Try to avoid a thin voice, hurrying or stuttering – there's no need to be afraid.
- There's no need to hesitate if you know your point is valid. If you are not sure yourself, say that you are not sure.
- Look at the group: make eye contact with everyone in the group, don't avoid it by looking at the ceiling, the flipchart, the walls ...
- Play with your voice: emphasise important points, breathe deeply to make your voice stronger, make your voice more interesting by modulating your pitch.
- Express yourself accurately: no generalisations, avoid words like »never«, »always«, »everyone«.
- Keep your hands and feet still – no fiddling or fidgeting.

Useful grammar

Don't forget that question tags may also be used to make a statement more palatable to your counterpart and to urge him or her to react. Note that a negative tag asks for agreement, whereas a positive tag shows that you are looking to your counterpart to share your disagreement.

- I think April is a good month for team trainings, don't you?
- Mr Meyer isn't the right person for the job, is he?

Useful vocabulary

to slash: radikal kürzen
to pose a threat to: eine Gefahr darstellen für
directive: Richtlinie
to fiddle: herumfummeln
to fidget: auf dem Stuhl herumrutschen
to face the music: die Suppe auslöffeln
emphatically: betont

17.5 Enquiring and resolving misunderstandings

Remember, it is always better to resolve a misunderstanding immediately so that it cannot lead to problems later or cause the meeting to drift off in a completely different direction. One way to check the facts is to ask for them again.

17.5.1 Asking for repetition

!

Example: sorry?

A: So, overall, the figures for ... [sound of loud drilling outside]
B: I'm sorry, it's terribly noisy with the window open. I didn't hear your last point. Could you run through it again, please?
A: [speaks very quickly] I was just saying that until we look at the figures we just aren't in a position to know if it actually made a difference to the bottom line and it would be premature to move onto A3 without taking this step. We really should hold fire on this for a while.
B: Okay, so just to clarify, by A3 you're referring to the summer promotion?
A: That's right.
B: I'm not sure I fully understand the point you were making about A3.
A: In a nutshell, we need to gauge the success of the previous promotion before launching the new one.
B: I see – and yes, I totally agree.

A good way to ask your counterpart for repetition or clarification of what they said is to use the following question words:

- *What* did you say?
- *Who* did you say?
- *When* did you say?
- *Why* did you say?
- *How many/much* did you say?

Useful phrases

- I'm sorry, I didn't quite catch that/the last thing you said.
- I'm sorry, it's a little noisy outside. I didn't hear what you just said.
- I'm sorry, could you speak a little louder, please?
- I'm sorry, would you mind repeating that last point, please?
- I'm sorry, could you repeat your first point for me, please?
- Sorry, could you explain that again, please?
- I'm afraid I'm not quite clear what you mean.
- Sorry, I don't quite follow you.
- Sorry, I'm not sure I understood. Would you mind going over that again?

17.5.2 Summarising for clarification

Another good way to check your understanding is to reformulate the speaker's point in your own words.

Useful phrases

- Are you saying that you can't deliver next week?
- Correct me if I'm wrong, but …
- Did I get it right that …?
- Have I understood you right? Do you mean …?
- So, just to check I understand you correctly, do you mean ...?
- Just to clarify, do you mean ...?
- So, just to make sure we're all singing from the same hymn sheet, you're saying that ...
- To quickly summarise, your point is that ...
- Just to recap, are you saying that ...?

Important !

Asking double questions
In natural English, speakers often double up a question to check what somebody said or to find out what they meant, for example:
Warranty? What exactly do you mean by warranty?
Whereabouts is Kemer? I mean, how far is it to the nearest airport?

17.5.3 Recapping and confirming

If you're the speaker, you may feel it is important to clarify your point or to check that the other participants have understood.

Useful phrases

- What I meant was ...
- What I mean to say is that ...
- The point I'm making is ...
- Are you with me so far?
- Are you following me?
- Does that make sense?
- Do you understand what I mean?
- I'm afraid that isn't quite what I meant.
- There seems to have been a slight misunderstanding.
- Maybe I didn't make myself clear.

- The point I'm making is that we are wasting a lot of manpower with the old equipment.
- Actually, I am not talking about renting, I am talking about profitability.

Useful grammar

There are specific verbs in the English language that must be followed by a gerund (-ing form). »To mind« is such a verb. Other verbs and fixed expressions of that kind which are useful for meetings are as follows:

- This would *involve bringing* in an external consultant.
- Shall we *consider expanding* into China?
- I *suggest planning* two years ahead.
- You cannot *avoid taking* risks altogether.
- This *risks spinning* out of control.
- I'm *looking forward to seeing* you.
- I *apologise for being* late.
- We *are thinking about investing* in oil shares.

Useful vocabulary

to run through it: noch einmal durchgehen
premature: voreilig
in a nutshell: kurz und bündig
to gauge [geidʒ] the success: Erfolg beurteilen, bewerten

17.6 Diplomacy and politeness

17.6.1 It's bad news, I'm afraid ...

Diplomacy and politeness are not only important elements when it comes to expressing agreement and disagreement in English-speaking meetings. They also come to the fore when English-speakers are about to deliver bad news or present information that they know may not be well received by the listener.

!

Example: using language to persuade

A: Right, we've got some broad agreement on the way forward, but let's now focus on some practical details. Karl, do you think I could ask your team to do the figures for the presentation?
B: Well, in principle, yes, but this comes as a bit of a surprise.
A: I see. What do you think would be a reasonable deadline?
B: I'm afraid I can't promise anything right now. Shall we say by the day after tomorrow, around noon?

A: That could be cutting it a bit fine – ideally we need the figures tomorrow at 5.00 p.m. at the latest.
B: Let me think. I was wondering if we could speed up the process by outsourcing some of the graphics. Wouldn't it be faster if the charts were done by our colleagues in Prague? You know, we're all pretty busy with the Wang project, which is already slightly behind schedule.
A: Okay, fair enough. Could you get on to them right away?

Useful phrases

- I'm afraid it's not good news.
- As (I'm sure) you appreciate, this is a difficult situation.
- I'm sorry to say that ...
- Regrettably, we ...
- Unfortunately ...

17.6.2 Polite questions

However, there is more to diplomatic language than just lists of readymade phrases: expressing the matter in a different way, i.e. using little twists with language can help. If you ask a question, eg, instead of making a statement, your request will sound more sophisticated and less dogmatic; »would« and »could« also sound far more polite than »can« and »will«.

For example, compare, »Wouldn't it be a good idea to deliver in two weeks?« with bluntly stating: »We will deliver in two weeks.« And the longer a sentence is, the more politely it is perceived to be by the listener; eg »How old is the car?« sounds much better if it is preceded by an introductory phrase:

- I was wondering how old the car is?
- Do you happen to know how old the car is?
- Do you think you could tell me how old the car is?
- Would you be able to tell me how old the car is?

The following table summarises what you can say to sound more polite:

Checklist: sounding more polite

What you want to say/do	What you say
Win time, make your counterpart curious about what you are going to say or prepare them for disagreement	Well
	actually
	right
	in fact
	to be honest
Give a negative statement	I'm afraid
Use a question instead of a statement to make it sound like a mere suggestion;	Is Monday next week okay for you?
a negative question sounds even more negotiable	Isn't Monday next week good for you?
Sound softer when refusing: »would« instead of »will«	That would be a problem.
Soften criticism – use words (qualifiers) such as »very«, »slight«, »some«, »little«, »a bit«, »some«	This sounds like a slight problem.
	There are some reservations about the concept.
Make counter-suggestions using comparisons or negative questions	It may be more convenient to … Wouldn't Friday be better?
Use your voice for stress	Of course we *can* do this.
	This is quite a *large* sum.
Sound less pushy by using the continuous form	As I was telling you …
Avoid negative adjectives, even if they are linguistically correct	The idea doesn't seem to be very helpful.
	I'm not very happy with that.

17.6.3 A diplomatic game of give and take

Discussion partners in English-speaking cultures are often more open to acknowledging their own mistakes if the other party is also willing to admit their share of responsibility for an error. The pattern that often emerges is an acknowledgement of responsibility followed by a polite request for one's discussion partner to do the same.

!

Example: a little diplomacy goes a long way

A: As Rob said, we're unhappy with the quality of the goods you supplied and will be looking for you to make some kind of price reduction. I'm sure you can appreciate that we haven't been able to charge our customers full price for the goods.
B: I'm afraid that will be quite difficult for us at this late stage. We're prepared to take on board that some quality issues arose at the production stage. However, having carried out an internal investigation, we do feel that some of the features you point to were not adequately defined in the specifications you supplied to us. Would you be willing to concede that these points were not made clear to us from start?
A: With the benefit of hindsight, we can see that the specifications were not as clearly formulated as they should have been. But this doesn't change the fact that our tools division incurred substantial losses last year due to the substandard quality of the products you supplied.
B: Your business is very important to us, but unfortunately we just aren't in a position to offer a price reduction now that you have taken ownership of the goods. Could you perhaps see your way to considering a discount on your next order with us in lieu of a reduction?
A: That sounds like a workable solution. I'm sure it would go a long way towards soothing our Finance Director's headache.
B: Good. I'm very pleased to hear that.

Useful phrases

Acknowledging faults

- We readily accept that some of the errors were due to a fault in our system ...
- I'm very sorry to say that we made a mistake with the order.
- As we've established, we need to address some serious issues in our production.

Asking for an acknowledgement

- Could you perhaps see your way to accepting that there's also some room for improvement at your end?
- Would you be willing to accept/concede that there were also some issues at your end with regard to ...?

Useful vocabulary

to come to the fore: ins Blickfeld geraten
cutting it fine: sich wenig zeitlichen Spielraum lassen
curious: neugierig
stress: Betonung
reservation: Vorbehalt
to incur losses: Verluste erleiden

with hindsight: im Nachhinein
in lieu of: anstelle von
to soothe: beruhigen
to stand sb's ground: sich behaupten

17.7 What to do in case of language problems

There is far greater potential for misunderstandings when you are attending a meeting that is taking place in a foreign language. Perhaps you just didn't hear what a person said or their accent is difficult to understand. Or maybe differences in the ways people from other cultures express themselves can lead to confusion. It may also happen that your counterpart uses a word or expression you have never heard in your life.

!

Example: asking for repetition

A: We are talking about one billion consumers in China.
B: Sorry, how many did you say? One million?
A: Oh, no. One billion, of course.

In any case, you should not hesitate to ask your counterpart for repetition and clarification – there's no shame in doing so. Just use the methods and phrases given above under »Enquiring and resolving misunderstandings«, namely

- asking for repetition,
- summarising for clarification,
- recapping and confirming.

17.8 Voting

Sometimes attendees cannot agree on an outcome. It may then be necessary to take a vote, which is usually done at formal meetings. However, voting should be seen as a last resort, as it will leave a number of attendees dissatisfied with the outcome. If a vote is necessary, the chair should keep strictly to the formal procedures.

A vote can either be done by secret ballot or by a show of hands. Before that, the subject of the voting has to be made clear. A suggestion or an idea that is to be put to a vote is called a »motion«. Before a vote can be taken, a motion needs to be »seconded«, i.e. supported, by another person. When a motion is put to the vote and agreed on, you say that it is »carried«. When there is no agreement, it is »failed«. Usually, majority votes are taken. In case of a tie vote, the chairperson often has the deciding vote.

Of course, the outcome of the vote has to be recorded in the minutes, eg: »Motion to allow for flexitime, moved by Peter« or »Motion to allow for flexitime, seconded by Jane.«

Useful phrases

- Can I ask for a show of hands, please?
- All in favour?/All opposed?
- Those for/against the motion, please?
- Aye! [say »aye« or raise your hand to show you agree]
- Any abstentions?
- The motion was carried unanimously.
- The motion has been rejected by four votes to two.

Useful vocabulary

flexitime: flexible Arbeitszeit
to make/second a motion: Antrag stellen, unterstützen
to table/introduce/present a motion: Antrag einbringen
to carry a motion: Antrag annehmen
a motion fails: Antrag fällt durch
majority vote: Mehrheitsabstimmung
tie: Stimmengleichheit
aye!: ja

18 After the meeting

After the meeting is before the next meeting – to put it simply. Most meetings are followed up with a written record of what was discussed and agreed: the minutes. These then need to be passed on to the attendees.

18.1 Making the minutes

The minutes have to be accurate and clear, summarising what was said. Lengthy sections can be boiled down to their essence. The minutes are usually circulated to all participants within a few days of the meeting and after approval by the chair. Remember that it is not necessary to include every word that is spoken, only important points and any votes and results. Indicating who said what is also necessary, which is why the minute-taker should make sure they know the names of the attendees. It is also recommendable to type out the minutes immediately after the meeting – this way you can make sure that you don't forget what was said.

Examples !

Example 1: short form for minutes

Minutes of the Steering Committee Meeting

Date: 1 February 20XX, 7.00–8.40 p.m.
Venue: San Siro Meeting Room
Present: John Snyder, Bill Meyers, Lisa Förster, Annette Joyce, Britta Pocklington
Apologised: Anita Ferrarotti

1. New company brochure

There was positive feedback on the first revamped edition. There were 5,000 copies printed, more are needed next time. More photographs would enhance the overall appearance. Bill to contact PR for further action.

2. Decision-making process

In Greg's opinion, decisions taken by the steering committee were not valid unless the Project Leader and Management both agreed with the decisions. The other project members see this differently.
John pointed out that in all other departments the Project Leader was simply a project member with an allotted task.
Lisa suggested the matter be clarified by a member of the board. The committee decided by four votes to one to have Dr Meyers clarify the issue. Britta asked Greg what he was going to do about his position. He said he would think it over and submit his reply in writing.

3. AOB

Interest was shown in a new approach in marketing as briefly explained by John. To be followed up in the course of the next meetings. Thanks expressed to Britta for doing an excellent job during the last trade fair in Berlin.
Next meeting: To be announced.

Example 2: action minutes
Minutes of the Steering Committee Meeting
Date: 1 February 20XX, 7.00–8.40 p.m.
Venue: San Siro Meeting Room
Present: John Snyder, Bill Meyers, Lisa Förster, Annette Joyce, Britta Pocklington
Apologised: Anita Ferrarotti

1. Newsletter
BM reported that our newsletter was in high demand. However, he felt that it lacked conciseness and that a more modern look would be appreciated by the readers. The discussion ended with the general decision to look into the costs for a revamp.
Action: BM by 19 Feb.

2. Digital cameras
JS suggested our staff's mobile phones should be equipped with cameras to allow for faster transmission of on-site findings.
The committee members were not sure if this was necessary.
Action: All – decide by 20 Feb.

3. Floor plan – hot seating
LF proposed changing the seating arrangements, as not all staff are present in the office Mon–Fri.
AJ added that the new home office day would also make for more desk space.
Suggestion welcomed by committee members.
Action: LF design new floor plan by 19 Feb.

4. AOB
JS reported on his trip to Brazil. He made substantial progress with the authorities and will present the outcome at the next meeting.
Action: JS presentation 20 Feb.
BP reminded all to come up with ideas regarding give-aways for the trade fair in Zurich in May.
Action: All by 20 Feb.
Meeting adjourned at 8.40 p.m.
Next meeting: February 20, 20XX
Venue: San Siro

18.1.1 Tips for minute-taking

Getting prepared

If you work on a laptop computer, prepare a file containing the names of the participants and the items on the agenda. Then either take the laptop with you to fill in the key words during the discussion (to be formulated in full later on), or write them down on a sheet of paper and complete the minutes after the meeting.

Very often, initials are used to refer to participants who made a contribution or who are to carry out an action point. If you generally find it hard to remember people's names, make a habit of taking a brief note of their seating position during the introductions at the beginning of the meeting. It is best to write the names on a piece of scrap paper in the seating order. Use the attendance list to check if all the names are spelled correctly.

Writing style
As a rule, the style is impersonal and concise. There are two ways of writing the minutes: one follows the chronological sequence of what was discussed, the other sticks to the written agenda (see examples above).

It is a good idea to stick to the format, style and content of the minutes which were written for previous meetings. Every organisation has its own conventions.

Important !

Variations for the word »say«
A repetition of »he said« sounds boring after reading it for the third time, so try some variation using the following verbs: mentioned, explained, confirmed, agreed, suggested, proposed, asked, introduced, discussed, reported, reminded, read out, indicated, pointed out.

Checklist: the minutes

In general, the minutes contain
▪ place and date of the meeting,
▪ names of participants: present (also when they left, if they leave early) and absent,
▪ subject of the meeting,
▪ approval of the last minutes,
▪ items on the agenda: discussions, outcomes, action items, who they are assigned to, deadlines,
▪ any other business (AOB),
▪ date, time and place of the next meeting.

Useful grammar
The minutes are generally written in the past tense. If reference is made to the future (»will« or »going to«) or the present, these tenses may also be used.

Another convention is to use the passive:

- No extra expense to be incurred without prior consent by the board.
- Session to be coordinated by John.

However, it is modern style to substitute as many unnecessary passives as possible with an active sentence structure. »It was mentioned by John that ...« sounds better if it is changed into an active sentence: »John mentioned that ...«

Useful vocabulary
approach: Ansatz
tangible: greifbar
shorthand: Stenografie
allotted: zugeteilt, zugewiesen
to stick to sth: sich halten an
revamp: neue Aufmachung
costs are incurred: Kosten entstehen

18.2 Following up the meeting

After the meeting, each role has its own duty to fulfil.

- The minute-taker has to get back to the attendees with the minutes in order to communicate the allotted tasks to the persons concerned.
- The chair has to follow up to ensure that all the agreed action items are carried out.
- The owners of action items should
  - complete them asap,
  - report back as agreed,
  - liaise with others, if necessary.

!

Example: email with attachment

Subject:Minutes of the Steering Committee Meeting
Dear all,
I am writing to thank you all again for the fruitful meeting last Tuesday. Please find attached the minutes as well as the updated contact list.
Could you please get back to me asap regarding the time and date for the next meeting? John suggested the 20th at around 7.30 p.m. Please let me know if this is convenient.
I look forward to seeing you again soon.
Best regards,
Lisa

Useful vocabulary
scrap paper: Schmierpapier
asap (= as soon as possible): so bald wie möglich
to liaise: Kontakt aufnehmen

19 Special types of meetings

With the advent of new technologies, new types of meetings, such as videoconferencing, became possible and more widespread. Project management, too, has given rise to new categories of meetings, as have creative techniques. Negotiations and customer meetings have become more global in terms of attendance, requiring greater cultural awareness and thought than meetings with your fellow nationals.

19.1 Meetings with customers

19.1.1 Getting in touch

Whether you meet the customer at their offices or at yours, make sure you make an appointment well in advance. Be prepared to offer several alternatives to suggest a meeting time that is really convenient for your (prospective) customer. Moreover, try to use the channel of communication that seems to be most appreciated by the other party: some people hardly ever check their emails, while others hate being disturbed by phone calls. But, first of all, you have to get in touch with them. When doing so, try to point out the specific issue that connects your company with them.

Useful phrases

- We used to have a branch office in Hamburg, close to your headquarters in the city centre.
- I learned from your website that you also work with H&Z. We've been their preferred suppliers for eight years now.
- We did a similar project for ABC, Inc. three years ago.

19.1.2 Identifying your client's needs

Once you have managed to get an appointment for a meeting, what counts is responding to a client's needs. First you need to know what these needs are by finding out how your products or services meet the customer's requirements. If they don't meet them yet, think about how you could bring this about. Find examples among your references to show that you have already met similar needs in the past.

Useful phrases

- So you said you needed a new training partner for internet applications?
- When will you open the new plant in Hong Kong?

19.1.3 Explaining your proposal in detail

Another crucial point is to create rapport with your customer, especially if this is a newly acquired customer. Apart from making small talk, you should establish common ground by telling them why your two companies fit together.

Useful phrases

- Did you see that our connector uses wireless technology?
- Can I draw your attention to the fact that fuel consumption is only three litres for this model?
- If you look at the illustration, you can see that this is where our product can be switched to 110 Volt. We use our own patent.

19.1.4 Anticipating objections

Any potential new customer will check out very carefully if you are the right person or company to meet its needs. Anticipate any concerns they may raise and address them by using positive statements.

Useful phrases

- We do have certificates according to DIN ISO for the product.
- An export certificate is not required for shipments to Bali.
- You don't need to worry about different sockets, we build in the British version as standard.

19.1.5 Ending the visit

It is highly recommended that you save some time at the end of the meeting to address any questions. Even if you cannot give an answer off the cuff, you can make a list of action items to follow up by email or letter. And of course, don't forget to use friendly parting phrases to end on a positive note.

Useful phrases

- Are there any questions I could help you with?

- Could we perhaps discuss delivery periods next time? And then there is still the issue of transportation costs.
- Would next week suit you for another meeting?
- I'll email you the documents as soon as I can.
- It was a pleasure meeting you.
- Thank you for coming. It's been a fruitful meeting.
- Have a safe trip home!
- I'm looking forward to meeting you again next month.

19.1.6 Attentive hosts

Being an attentive host is most important in a customer meeting. Apart from small talk (see the same-titled paragraph in chapter »Arriving at the meeting«), this involves watchfulness and attention, eg by providing ice cubes for your American guests. Preparing an agenda for the meeting and making it available to the client beforehand will be appreciated and show that you really care about this sales contact, just as much as a thank-you letter after the visit, accompanied by the meeting minutes.

Useful vocabulary
crucial: wichtig
fuel consumption: Kraftstoffverbrauch
off the cuff: auswendig, ohne nachzuschlagen

19.2 Negotiations

Everybody negotiates. On a day-to-day level, just as when the stakes are high in an international merger, wage negotiations or for a customer-supplier contract. Apart from the principle of win-win, all sorts of tactics are employed deliberately. The most important thing, however, is to know what you want to walk away with. In general, the following tips apply to all types of negotiation:

Checklist: negotiations

- Ask a lot of questions and listen, listen, listen. The more you find out, the better (»Active listening«).
- Use diplomatic language whenever possible.
- Make sure you are understood correctly.
- Make it clear that you understand what the stakes are.

! **Example: price negotiation**

A: So, Will, how much do you have in mind, let's say per unit?
B: Well, it all depends on how many units you would like to sign up for on a regular basis.
A: Sure, but I would really need to hear a basic price from you first: I need to see if we are thinking along the same lines.
B: Okay, as you may remember from our written proposal we were thinking about 350 dollars per shipping unit.
A: 350 dollars! Are you kidding? I could get each pineapple wrapped in gold foil from the Ivory Coast at that price! And they would arrive in Europe much earlier, too!
B: But you know how the market is at the moment. Supply is at a premium.
We have reserved 300 units for you because you are one of our long-standing customers. Otherwise we could have sold them already, and for a much higher price than that.
A: Okay, well, I will have to contact head office about that.
B: Certainly, there's no hurry, but don't forget our quality and reliability when it comes to delivery. Our fruit has always been good value for money.
A: I know, Will, I know. But what if the fruit goes bad during transit or if a container gets damaged? We would require insurance covering such events.
B: Of course we would grant you compensation, no question about that. The sum of the actual damage would have to be determined by an independent expert, however, at your expense.
A: If you don't mind, we'd better discuss this point next time. We can't move on this right now. And I feel quite tired after the long flight. I guess we should call it a day.
B: You're right. I want to see you in good shape tomorrow for the tour of the plantation.
A: So, before we meet next time, I'll find out about order quantities and you look into the point about shipping.
B: Right, and the insurance matter and the other outstanding issues as well.
A: Fine, so that's it then. Where are we going for dinner, Will?

! **Important**

Right contact and enough time
On an international level, it is important to invite or to send the right person to a negotiation. In Japan, a young manager might not be accepted, even if he or she has decision-making powers. Also bear in mind that other cultures need more time for decision-making and attach more importance to establishing a good relationship first. Some will also only do business with a person they trust.

19.2.1 Useful phrases

Establishing common ground and reformulating

- You know, the plot of land is worth a million right now.
- The track record of your module is really impressive.
- Let me check if I understood you correctly. You said you were looking for a long-term supplier?

Exploring positions

- Could I ask you how much you had in mind?
- When exactly do you need the material?
- Can you tell us what your standard terms are?

Making suggestions

- If you place an order for more than 5,000 units by the end of the month, we will ship them free of charge.
- We may agree to your terms, provided that you'll give us more leeway with regard to delivery times.
- It depends on how much you would be prepared to pay for our service.
- I'm afraid we can't accept that unless you offer us a three-year warranty.
- How about 50 pieces?
- Well, actually, 55 would be better.
- Why don't we try a more middle-of-the-road approach?
- Alternatively, we could offer you a discount.
- Let's think about preferred supplier status first.
- What if we offered you five per cent?

That might/may/would/could/can be an option!

Modal verbs are indispensable in negotiations. You can use them to vary the degree of certainty of your statements, i.e. you make what you say more or less probable.

- We *can* guarantee you delivery in five days. [Fact]
- We *could* deliver next week. [Real possibility]
- We *would* guarantee delivery ex works. [Possible, but under certain conditions]
- We *may* guarantee delivery to Bremen. [Maybe]
- We *might* deliver to the Arab Emirates. [Faint possibility]

Softening disagreement

- I'm afraid we really can't agree to five per cent.
- Unfortunately, that's not really the way we see it.

Pushing for a decision

Soft-sell approach

- We would need to see some movement on price.

Hard-sell approach

- Take it or leave it!
- This is our final offer!
- We'll have to call the whole deal off/take our business elsewhere.

Refusing

Soft-sell approach

- I'm afraid that's not quite what we had in mind.
- I'm afraid this is as far as we can go.
- I am very sorry, but your offer still does not convince us.
- We feel that this is a bit much.
- I'm afraid I'm not in a position to grant you that.

Hard-sell approach

- No way! You know what the market is like right now.
- That's completely out of the question.

Asking for more time and looking ahead

- I'll have to think it over.
- I'll have to talk to my line manager about that.
- We can't give you a definite answer just now.
- As a next step we should look at …
- If you don't mind, I'd like to come back to that later.
- Let's not rush things.
- I don't think we should make a decision just yet.

Agreeing

- That sounds/seems reasonable.
- That sounds like a sensible suggestion.
- In fact, that suits me fine.
- It's a deal!

Summarising what was agreed

- Can we run through what we've agreed?
- So, I'll summarise the important points of your offer.
- I'd like to check/confirm what we've said.

Next steps

- We need to meet again soon.
- So, the next step is to draft a formal contract.
- Before the next meeting we'll check the order quantities

Important !

Follow-up

A written follow-up summarises what was agreed and obliges the other party to act. It also shows that your intentions were serious. Sometimes a formal »letter of intent« is sent before any contracts are signed.

19.2.2 Useful grammar

How to express a must

Don't forget that »must« has no negative form and exists only in the present tense. »Must not« means »not allowed to« and, as it can only be used in the present tense, for all other tenses you have to resort to »have to do sth« in its respective tenses:

- We *must* meet again to discuss the details.
- We *mustn't* forget to send the draft today.
- We *had to* organise the TC differently.

If-clauses

An essential tool for bargaining are if-clauses. Particularly type I and II prove to be useful.

- Type I if-clause: The if-part of the sentence is in the present tense, the second part is formed by »will« + infinitive. It is used to talk about real possibilities: »If you agree on that, we will offer you a discount.«
- Type II if-clause: Type II is used to express a hypothetical possibility. The if-part of the sentence has to be in the past tense, with »would« + infinitive in the second part: »If you agreed on that, we would offer you a discount.«

All if-clauses can also be turned around, so that the if-clause forms the second part of the sentence, eg: »We *will offer* you a discount, if you *agree* on that.«

Useful vocabulary

what the stakes are: was auf dem Spiel steht
plot of land: Grundstück
leeway: Spielraum
on-site maintenance: Wartung vor Ort

line manager: unmittelbarer Vorgesetzter
at your expense: auf Ihre Kosten

19.3 Briefing and brainstorming

What these two types of meetings have in common is that they require a subtle and careful facilitation style. In brainstorming sessions the chair should give the participants the opportunity to have their say and interrupt as little as possible; in briefings he or she should make sure all the information comes across.

19.3.1 Briefings

As the name suggests, a briefing should be kept short by definition. It should not take longer than 30 minutes. In a briefing the information has centre of attention. The idea is to share and spread knowledge. It is a one-way transfer of information from the organiser to the attendees. There is no exchange of ideas, nor are decisions taken. Questions may be asked by the persons being briefed.

!

Example: briefing meeting for a facilitator

A: Thanks for coming in, Jane. Have you received the guidelines for the first group?
B: Yes, I have. In fact, I've read through them and I'd like to ask you some questions. As always, the devil is in the detail!
A: That's excellent, but first let me show you how the device works. Then I'd like to tell you what our main focus is.
B: Good, please go ahead. How do you switch it on?
A: The buttons are on the back panel, all of them.
B: I see. And what shall I say if people ask me who the sponsor of the study is?
A: Just tell them you don't know yourself, and that it is one of the major players in the market.

Useful phrases

- This is what we want to achieve: increased timeliness and accuracy.
- Just show your customers this list.
- There's no need to feel uneasy.
- Are these figures understandable?
- Do you understand what I am getting at?

19.3.2 Brainstorming sessions

Brainstorming is a creative technique aiming at the maximum number of ideas to address a certain area of interest or to solve a problem. In the first step, the value or feasibility of the ideas generated is not an issue – all ideas are welcome. In general, brainstorming makes most sense for group sizes of 4 to about 20. Superiors or managers should only be invited if their subordinates will not feel inhibited by their presence. There should either be a time set for collecting ideas or a maximum number of ideas (50 to 100) fixed in advance. After that time, the ideas are categorised and sorted. But first of all, the topic of the brainstorming session has to be set out clearly. Furthermore, it is important that all participants make an active contribution. As a rule, criticising ideas is not allowed, as this might hinder inventiveness and spontaneity. It may sometimes be necessary for the chair or the facilitator to remind participants of these basic rules.

After the time set for collecting ideas is over or when there are no more ideas coming from the participants, the suggestions are sorted and categorised and any unfeasible ideas are deleted from the list. This can be done either as a group or by asking each person to pick out the five ideas he or she likes best.

Useful phrases

- So, how can we achieve better customer service?
- What aspects can enhance the overall customer experience?
- Can we agree not to interrupt each other?
- Can I ask you to save your comments for later, please?
- Let me remind you of the basic rules of brainstorming ...
- Can you please let Peter finish what he was saying?
- The following phrases may come in handy when taking notes on a flip-chart during brainstorming.
- What was that again?
- Sorry, could you repeat/spell that for me, please?
- I think we have a double entry here.
- I see two main directions here, would you all agree?
- Can we filter out all the pros and cons, please?
- Shall we organise these ideas into two or three columns for a better overview?
- Can each of you now select the five ideas you think are the best?

Useful vocabulary

sponsor: Auftraggeber
feasibility, feasible: Machbarkeit, machbar
inhibited: gehemmt

19.4 Jours fixes and kick-offs

19.4.1 Jours fixes

The term »jour fixe« is derived from project management. The same day of the week and time is reserved for an internal meeting with the same people, eg the first Wednesday of a month or a week. The aim is to facilitate the exchange of information and to update all project members so they are at the same knowledge level.

!

Example: jour fixe team meeting

A: ... to put you all in the picture and bring you up to date with the latest developments.
B: Thank you, Brian. Are there any other points to be discussed?
C: Well, yes, actually, but it's a rather delicate issue.
B: Go ahead, Valerie, we're all curious.
C: Erm, right. It's about our colleague, George. He always passes the buck. He calls in sick every time a deadline is due.
A: I must say that I also find him very rude. [All the team nods]
B: I see, I see, so we seem to have an issue with George ...
C: An issue! Are you kidding? I'm fed up with being on the same team, let alone in the same room with this guy.
B: Val, just try to take it a little easier on him.
C: Why are you defending him like that?
B: Well, I'm not supposed to tell you this, but George isn't too well at the moment. He was diagnosed with a serious illness and is currently undergoing treatment. This is why he is often away from work.
C: Oh, I'm so sorry, I had no idea!
A: That's a different story. Poor George!

Regular team meetings increase commitment and prevent misunderstandings and rumours. Apart from conveying information, it is important to foster the feeling of being appreciated among the team. This is why the participation of all team members should be encouraged. They should always be addressed by name, including when giving positive feedback: »Thank you, Damian, for bringing this point up.«

!

Important

How to prevent boredom
Variety can be added by altering the style in which the meeting is held, as well as the activities that take place. Try to encourage all participants to become actively involved rather than just listening passively.

19.4.2 Kick-off meetings

Kick-off meetings are extremely important for the success of a new project. Their purpose is to signal to all team members and stakeholders that the project has now begun. They give the team orientation and direction and ensure that everyone understands what their roles are. As far as language is concerned, kick-off meetings contain the following features:

- introducing people (which is an important feature of a kick-off meeting, in particular when project owners and stakeholders have never worked together before),
- giving information (on the purpose of the project, its major deliverables, its risks and assumptions, as well as its milestones),
- getting agreement (on suggested project management procedures from all stakeholders),
- asking and answering questions.

Useful vocabulary
to facilitate: moderieren
to pull one's weight: seinen Beitrag leisten, sich ins Zeug legen
to pass the buck: den schwarzen Peter zuschieben
rude: unhöflich, barsch
stakeholder: Prozessbeteiligter (eigentlich: Aktionär)

19.5 Telephone conferences

Telephone conferences (TCs) are increasingly widely used. Important factors for the success of a TC are a clear agenda, as well as the discipline of the participants and unambiguous communication. The agenda should contain the timing for individual points and the allocation of roles, such as the chair, timekeeper, secretary and the call facilitator, who takes care of the technical aspects.

19.5.1 Agenda

Example: subject of a telephone conference !

Agenda: outsourcing event organisation
Date: 5 May 20XX, time: 11.00-12.00 CET
Participants: Dörte Gluchowski (chair), Peter Pan (call facilitator), Annette Joyce (timekeeper), Lisa Förster (secretary), Bridget Mayer, Marén Volkers, Tanya Feldman

Item		Presented by	Time
1.	Apologies	DG	5
2.	Minutes of the previous call	LF	5
3.	Approval of agenda	DG	5
4.	Report on Hamburg trade fair	MV	10
5.	Outsourcing proposal – discussion	AJ/all	25
6.	Date for next conference call	DG	5
7.	Feedback – discussion	DG	5

For a larger number of participants, it pays to prepare the agenda carefully and to circulate it in good time. The agenda should contain the timing for each point. When calculating the timing, you should bear in mind that each person's active contribution will take about three to five minutes per item. In our sample agenda, we have seven participants and 25 minutes allocated to the main discussion item. On the whole, the agenda should be kept as short as possible in order to limit the length of the meeting, as a TC is far more demanding in terms of concentration than a face-to-face meeting. If the TC is only held between a limited number of people and on a routine basis, an agenda is sometimes just made ad hoc, that is, at the beginning of the call.

Useful phrases

- Can we just quickly make a list of the items we need to talk about today?
- Does anyone have an agenda or do we need to jot a few items down so that we don't forget anything important?

19.5.2 Starting a conference call

Before the serious part of the conference call, participants are encouraged to make small talk, just as if they were meeting face to face. On the one hand, this will create better rapport between them, just as if they were in a real meeting. On the other hand, they can all tune in to each other's voices and accents – especially important for non-native speakers of English. Then, the chair starts the TC by welcoming the participants, doing a roll call, reviewing the agenda and summarising the aim of the TC.

Useful phrases

- Hi, this is Dörte. I'll be the chair in today's conference call.
- Can we go round the table and hear who has logged on already? Can you just say »yes« when I call out your names?
- Before we start the ball rolling there are a few technical issues to clarify. Have you all received the agenda?
- Are there any other items we need to talk about today? Or any suggestions regarding the agenda?
- As you know, the main focus will be on the outsourcing business. It's important that we establish common ground on further procedure.

The chair should also clarify if participants need to leave the call early:

- Does anybody have to leave the call early?
- Yes, I do, actually. That's Pauline.
- Pauline, when do you have to log out?
- Around twelve at the latest.

By the same token, participants should announce if they are taking a break and let the others know when they are back in the TC:

- Sorry. It's Lisa. I need to print out the agenda again. I'll be back in a minute.
- Annette here. I'm back in the call.

Important !

A memorable self-introduction

If the participants do not know each other, they should introduce themselves so that the others know who the new person is and why they are joining the TC. They should say their names and what they would like to be called, what their job involves plus a past achievement and something personal, as well as a »memory hook« so that the others will remember them better.

19.5.3 Controlling the meeting

The chair has to involve all participants and ensure that they take turns. On the other hand, it is sometimes necessary to cut a speaker short. In any case, the role of timekeeper is vital for sticking to the agreed timings. He or she should remind everybody to keep it short. In longer TCs it sometimes makes sense to interrupt the call for a few minutes to give everybody a chance to collect their thoughts, to find some more information or simply to stretch their legs.

! **Important**

Creating rapport

If you want to stress the group feeling and convey an atmosphere of cooperation, you should use the we-form. It includes everybody in the group and helps create rapport with the participants. That's why you should say »*We* think this is a viable suggestion« instead of »*I* think this is a viable suggestion«.

! **Example: directing a TC**

A: Bridget, would you kick us off, please?

B: Well, this is a great way to cut a lot of unnecessary spending. My figures show that we can save a lot of money.

C: Can I just come in here? That reminds me – we can't ask Marketing to organise the event again. It's unfair.

A: Sorry, Tanya, but I think this is a bit of a sidetrack. Let's try and keep to the agenda, okay?

C: Of course.

B: As I was saying, outsourcing the event organisation can really save a lot of money. It's obvious, if you ask me.

A: What do the others think? Is there anything else we should consider? Nothing? Okay. We seem to have dealt with the outsourcing issue. Let's move on to the website. We've budgeted 6,500 dollars to redesign it. Peter, what do you think?

D: Well, obviously we need to make cuts and this would be less painful than many of the others. But we really have to prioritise PR because this is the bread and butter of our business. Perhaps we can consider a limited redesign?

C: I agree.

B: I do, too. You know, Peter, speaking of the website, you should really consider using a different designer this time. I don't think the last one did a good job at all.

Useful phrases

- Bridget, what do you think?
- Perhaps Maria could make a start with her opinion on item six?
- I need to hear your opinions about the new structure. Can we go round the group quickly? Franz?
- Thank you, Elke – Mark?
- Marty, I think Bridget wanted to add something? Go ahead, Bridget!
- Sorry, Toni, but I don't think this is really our topic today. Can I ask you to come back to the issue at hand?
- Sorry, Lisa, but we said five minutes only for the review of the minutes.
- You've only got three minutes left, Marén. Could you speed your report up a little, please?
- Dörte, sorry to interrupt, just to remind you that we only have ten minutes left to wrap up the call.
- How about taking a ten-minute break here? Shall we reconvene at 12.45?

Documents are usually distributed by email before the TC. If you need to refer to them, you can use the following phrases:

- Could you all turn to page three, please?
- Have you all got a copy of the contract to hand?
- You'll find the total sum at the bottom of the page, on the right/in the bottom right-hand corner.

19.5.4 Ending a telephone conference

Wrapping up a TC involves the same elements as a normal meeting: summarising results, allocating action items and defining the next steps, including a time for the next meeting (see paragraph »Closing the meeting« in chapter »Conducting a meeting«).

Useful phrases

- Let me sum up the arguments for and against outsourcing.
- If I understood right, most people were in favour of Bangalore as the location for our new subsidiary.

19.5.5 Feedback on the TC

If telephone conferences are held on a regular basis, it is useful to ask the participants for their feedback on how the TC worked for them. The results can then be discussed at the beginning of the subsequent meeting or beforehand by email. Improving how TCs are run will ensure their ongoing success. The feedback should cover the following questions:

- Did the technical equipment work well?
- Were the timings adhered to?
- What could be done better?
- What should we continue to do and what should we stop doing?
- What should be avoided?

Checklist: TC dos and don'ts

- Introduce yourself the first time you speak: »Hello, everyone. My name is ... and I work in the ... department.«
- Make small talk to give the other participants a chance to »tune in« to your voice and way of speaking: »How is the weather over in California? It's rainy here in Munich.«
- When introducing yourself, mention something personal plus a memory hook so that the others will remember you better.
- Speak slowly, clearly and concisely. Use your voice actively, as people cannot see your facial expression.
- Use your name every time: »This is John speaking ...«
- Describe your body language, for example: »I'm shaking/nodding my head here.«
- Announce that you are leaving or returning after a break, for example: »This is John speaking, I am about to leave the call for five minutes./This is John, I'm now back in the call.«
- Keep in mind that all paper rustling, sipping or clicking pens will be heard by everybody.
- If you ask somebody for their input, address them with their name, repeating the question if necessary.
- Learn how to work the equipment properly, especially the mute button: remember others might hear the hold music while it is pressed.
- Don't sit on a leather chair! The sounds it makes when you move around will be quite startling to yourself and others. A fabric-covered chair is much safer.

19.6 Literature

»How to manage meetings« von Alan Barker, Kogan Page, London, 2002

»The language of meetings« von Malcolm Goodale, LTP, Hove, 1987

»Fifty ways to improve your Telephoning and Teleconferencing Skills« von Ken Taylor, Summertown Publishing, Oxford, 2008

Teil 5: Negotiations in English

Autoren: Sander Schroevers, Ian R. Lewis

Unsere Welt wird kleiner und geschäftliche Kontakte beschränken sich immer weniger auf den heimischen Markt. Deshalb ist die Kompetenz gefragt, Verhandlungen auf Englisch führen zu können. Effektives Verhandeln, basiert auf zwei Dingen: Verhandlungs- und Sprachkompetenz einerseits, interkultureller Kompetenz andererseits. Denn nur wer versteht, warum und wie der kulturelle Hintergrund den Stil und die Strategie von Verhandlungspartnern beeinflusst, wird international Erfolg haben. Der letzte Faktor ist nicht zu unterschätzen.

Deshalb gibt Ihnen dieses Kapitel zum einen die sprachlichen Bausteine einer erfolgreichen Verhandlungsführung an die Hand. Zum anderen zeigt es Ihnen, wie Sie die entscheidenden kulturellen Unterschiede bei Ihrer persönlichen Verhandlungsführung berücksichtigen. So können Sie Vertrauen aufbauen und gewinnbringende Vereinbarungen treffen – in vielfältigen Interaktionen und Situationen, von der Preisverhandlung bis zum Small Talk. Der Inhalt wird so zum ständigen, wertvollen Begleiter bei Ihren Verhandlungen auf Englisch. Wir wünschen Ihnen viel Erfolg dabei!

20 Negotiating skills

This chapter explores a variety of contexts for negotiations, and gives you practical examples of appropriate negotiating behaviour.

20.1 Preparation and planning

In the first century, Cicero, the Roman philosopher and lawyer, wrote: »Ex praeparato, nil desperandum« – preparation reduces trouble. And his adage is still relevant today, because the more thoroughly a negotiation is prepared beforehand, the more likely it is possible to anticipate trouble that might influence a successful outcome.

Experienced negotiators prepare by setting realistic objectives, and thinking about flexible scenarios toward different solutions. We used the word scenario because a negotiation is never a script, where the parties always know exactly what to say and when.

- **Script:** one fixed conversation line
- **Scenario:** an imagined, projected or suggested sequence of events

A scenario will be based around particular key items. Try to be as specific as possible, because unfortunately general objectives tend to render general results. Writing in English in advance will help you to prepare even better. The checklist below may prove a useful tool for developing your ideas for a scenario.

Checklist: preparation

- **Reason**: why are we negotiating?
- **Issues**: which (more detailed) issues will be involved?
- **Settlement objectives**: what do we want, what do they want, what don't we want, and what's our least acceptable result? What is a good alternative to the deal?
- **Priority of issues**: value each issue (high, medium, low importance) and do this for both parties.
- **People**: who is on our team and who is on their team, and what authority do members have? Do all members know their role as part of the team? Do we need a native speaker in our team?

- **Information**: what information do we have? What questions should we ask? What questions will they ask? How should we answer? Which information should be kept? What do we need to verify beforehand? Is there need for calculations, figures or any support materials? Who prepares statistical data and visuals?
- **Offer(s)**: what are our entry and exit offers, what could be theirs and what concessions should we have available?
- **Tactics**: who says what to whom? Who will take notes? Who will listen and observe? What if it doesn't work?

It can be helpful to brainstorm by yourself or with different team members using this checklist. Also realise that despite the fact a team is well prepared, unexpected issues may come up during a negotiation. Sometimes it is necessary to be flexible, or even make alterations to the prepared plans in order to reach an agreement.

!

Important

Anticipate 75% of the other party's questions, and prepare suitable answers, preferably already in English.

The above checklist can also help you to evaluate after the negotiation. For instance, to measure to what extent you were prepared for different factors? Or by afterwards measuring how well you anticipated their questions. In so-called negotiation debriefs or reviews, people evaluate what happened during a negotiation. Bear in mind that the objective of such a negotiation debrief is learning, not problem fixing or blaming others. The results of a debrief can be documented for future use, by the same team or by a wider audience. In the words of lawyer and NBA chairman David Stern: »The secret of effective negotiation is dealing from strength, and strength comes from preparation.«

Useful vocabulary

call a meeting: eine Sitzung einberufen
attend a meeting: an einer Sitzung teilnehmen
hold a meeting: eine Sitzung abhalten
schedule a meeting: eine Sitzung einberufen
attendee/participant: Teilnehmer
alteration: Änderung
objective: Ziel
debrief: Rückschau

20.1.1 BATNA: Best Alternative To a Negotiated Agreement

The BATNA strategy was introduced by the authors Fisher and Ury in their book »Getting to Yes«. BATNA is an acronym for »Best Alternative To a Negotiated Agreement«. It is a common tactic used in the English-speaking world. The central idea of this strategy is to think in advance about having alternative options available in order to leave the negotiation comfortably. This empowers you with the confidence to either reach a mutually satisfactory agreement, or walk away to an alternative supplier/buyer or keep things as they are. BATNA comes from planning, brainstorming and preparation with the key players in your organisation. It is a twofold process, as you first need to determine what alternatives are available, and secondly, you need to realistically estimate your counterpart's alternatives. Having a strong alternative strengthens your negotiating powers during the negotiation. If this is weak or you have no alternative, then you feel pressured to close a deal.

Example: BATNA !

Horst's company asks him to move to Hamburg; he now earns 70.000 €. He thinks about his alternatives: if he rejects the offer it might influence his position, resulting in a lower paid job within the company, therefore his BATNA is the salary of 60.000 €. He informs on the job market and discovers that he could realistically earn between 80.000 € and 65.000 €; therefore his BATNA is estimated at 75.000 €. By identifying another alternative, Horst has increased his BATNA from 60.000 € to 75.000 €, and thus his bargaining power. Horst also has to estimate the costs of moving to Hamburg, which he believes to be around 5000 €. His BATNA has grown to 80.000 €. Finally Horst will need to realistically estimate his company's alternatives or BATNA. If they have an alternative of moving Horst at a lower price than 80.000 €, a deal will not be easily made. But if Horst believes his skills and his direct usability for the company are to its advantage, he has increased his bargaining power by a total of 10.000 €. For Horst it was not only critical to calculate his own BATNA, but also to make an estimate of the other's BATNA.

The example shows us that both parties have their BATNA. Negotiating is the task of arriving at a reasonable outcome, given each party's next best alternatives. Negotiating is about trying to divide up the surplus, but in such a way that each party benefits. This demands preparation and correct judgement.

Checklist: BATNA

- Brainstorm about your best alternatives if you cannot make this particular deal.
- Elaborate on the most promising alternatives. The best alternative is your BATNA.

- Compare your own BATNA to all offers and proposals.
- When an offer is better than your BATNA, you are in a position to negotiate an agreement.
- When an offer is worse than your BATNA, try to improve on the offer from the other party.
- If the other party does not (or cannot) improve its offer, opt for your BATNA.

20.1.2 Parameters

Parameters are vital for your negotiations. What are the highest/lowest, best/worst, maximum/minimum requirements that are acceptable? These are often referred to as the ideal and fall back (bottom line). Using these parameters wisely helps to clarify what other information is relevant.

- The maximum: lay down what is the very best you hope to achieve. If you aim for a point that remains in a range that is believably possible, you allow yourself the potential of achieving it, having more room for concessions, and giving a stronger chance of reaching a satisfactory outcome. This is often referred to as the ideal.
- The minimum: the acceptable minimum gives you warning signs, when this is being breached and allows you ways to manoeuvre away from this point. This is often referred to as the fall back or bottom line.

Useful vocabulary
agree: zustimmen
disagree: nicht zustimmen
empower: befugen, bevollmächtigen
limits: Grenzen
meet halfway: auf halbem Weg entgegenkommen
mutually: gegenseitig
require: verlangen, voraussetzen

20.1.3 A negotiation agenda

During a negotiation it may be difficult to decide which topics are important to discuss and which are irrelevant. Establishing a negotiation agenda can render a discussion much more efficient for both sides. An agenda can be compared to the track a train runs on, as you travel through the negotiation. A negotiation agenda, unlike a meeting agenda, has specific content and an order that drives the negotiation forward.

Items of an agenda

An agenda includes the following items:

- Date, time and location of the meeting
- Names and titles of team members
- A general timescale for the period of negotiation
- The main issues to be addressed
- The proposed order

!

Example: Preliminary agenda

Meeting between IBL GmbH and TMA Inc.
At HES café, from 2 pm until 4 pm
Proposed new material for courses
Friday, 16 January 2011
Introductions by participants.
Agree on the meeting agenda.
Issues:
Who will use which material?
Which programme will pay the costs?
Who will be responsible during the trial runs?
How are the assessments done?
Refreshment break (HES café).
Who will present the outcomes?
What about digital aspects?
Summary of agreement.

Making an agenda will not only offer some structure to a negotiation, but it will also help you to identify your own priorities and goals and to compare these to those of you opponent. It will prevent an endless debate. The items on an agenda are usually called the »Heads of agenda«. Drafting an agenda may contribute to a positive atmosphere, as it shows that you are looking for progress in the negotiation. It may also be seen as a first small agreement between parties.

!

Important

Be careful not to reveal key aspects of your priorities, your preferences or your intended strategy in the agenda.

In more hostile relationships between negotiators, it helps to use less specific agenda headings (e.g.: »prices« instead of »price increases«), or perhaps even to only agree on an agenda as such, but to disagree on the order of the items. Especially when negotiating with international parties, it is wise to be flexible with the negotiation agenda.

Time limits

Negotiating can be an exhausting experience. Prepare to take proper breaks for coffee, lunch, dinner, sleep. Over and above these natural requirements, breaks or adjournments in the negotiation are very useful. Be aware that the other side may have a different perspective of time. »Time is money« is a common thought in North American minds, but time spent on socialising may influence others more.

Useful phrases

- I've drawn up an agenda.
- I hereby send you a copy of the revised agenda.
- Does the agenda meet your expectations? There are four items on the revised agenda.
- Are there any points you wish to add?
- We believe some points are missing.
- Is including point ... OK with you?
- Shall we include ... on the agenda after point 4?

Useful vocabulary

item on the agenda/agenda item: TOP (Tagesordnungspunkt)
agenda headings: Verhandlungsgegenstand, TOP
to be on the agenda: auf der Tagesordnung stehen
to delete from the agenda: von der Tagesordnung entfernen
circulate the agenda: die Agenda verteilen
chairman: Vorsitzender
AOB (any other business): »Sonstiges« als TOP
closure: Schließung
confine: eingrenzen
minutes: Protokoll
proceeding: fortführen
priority: Priorität, Vorrang
settled: entschieden
TBA (to be announced): wird angekündigt
timescale: Zeitplan, zeitlicher Rahmen
venue: Handlungsort

20.1.4 Promoting the climate

Being comfortable while negotiating is important. Sitting in a stuffy office without regular breaks or suffering from jet lag is detrimental to decision-making. One should be aware of creating a positive environment and working climate for the negotiations. If you are the host, make sure that you have comfortable rooms available. It's important to have space where parties can take a separate break to discuss privately.

The following aspects should be taken into account:
- A large comfortable room,
- A large table,
- Enough space to walk about,
- Material for presenting at hand,
- Discreet staff that prevent disturbances,
- Regular cleaning and serving of refreshments,
- Direct, secure telephones, internet access,
- Access to any equipment required, e.g. photocopiers, faxes, data projectors (beamers),
- Secure recess rooms for each team.

Ensure that you or someone else is in place to meet guests and make introductions. Doing this correctly is important in all cultures. People react better when they feel respected and looked after. Getting this right is not so easy. Many Europeans, for example, will become suspicious if they feel you are over-doing things, while many Asians will feel uneasy if they feel you are under-doing things.

20.1.5 Knowing the participants

It is important to find out exactly who you will be meeting with. What is that person's position in the company, and his/her decision-making powers? These matters may also influence the choice of venue, hotel bookings and even seating arrangements at the meeting itself. If it is possible to ask about the participants' preferences, this could be leading in, for instance, choosing refreshments or hotel bookings. An often overlooked issue is that national holidays differ substantially, which may influence the other party's travel arrangements.

20.2 Getting acquainted

The way people are welcomed, can influence the atmosphere substantially, as is illustrated in the following example;

!

Example: Wrong beginning

Delegates from Bangalore, India and Shenzhen, China arrive at Frankfurt airport, and are unpleasantly surprised by the fact that they weren't welcomed personally, but only received detailed (perfectly) written information. Such misunderstandings can influence the atmosphere negatively.

Greeting

First impressions are important. Research shows that during the first seconds of meeting individuals interpret the other person's character, mood, and even manner in how they are going to negotiate. We therefore need to give some thought as to how best present ourselves. This is also relevant when you have met the person or persons previously. The way you greet someone is a form of respect. Each culture has developed its own norms of greeting. Some are better than others at learning about another's greeting norms and being prepared for them. In most cultures of the world, seniority and hierarchy are important in whom to greet first.

Handshakes

Any face-to-face contact requires some handling. The English verb to handle is related to the word hand, and in most countries a handshake is the preferred way of greeting. In some countries a handshake is not acceptable, particularly between male and female, and in others, a bow is more appropriate.

!

Example: Handshakes with women

Handshakes with Iranian women aren't appreciated, whereas a lady from the Saudi delegation, for example, might shake your hand.

Additionally, there are subtle differences in how long a hand-shake should last. These may be mere seconds, as between European countries, but can last much longer further afield. A short handshake in some cultures means you're not to be trusted.

Welcoming words

In addition to a handshake, some welcoming words need to be said. Please note that the question »How do you do?« is best answered with »How do you do?« or »I'm fine, thank you. How are you?« A commonly made mistake by non-English speakers is to take such phrases seriously and reply in detail.

!

Example: Welcoming words

A: On behalf of Muster GmbH, I am very glad to welcome you to our Berlin office.
B: Joey, how are you?
A: Good to see you again, Horst. How are you?
B: Fine thanks. Have you met Anke?
C: Hello, I am Anke Laffort, responsible for international marketing at our Fraijlemaburg branch.
A: Nice to meet you Anke. How was your flight?

Below are some sample phrases for welcoming international guests.

Useful phrases

- Well, I'm delighted to welcome you all to our offices here in Düsseldorf.
- Thank you for coming, everyone.
- Welcome to Munich!
- I'm chairing ...
- On behalf of Muster GmbH, I am very glad to welcome you to our head office.
- It really is a pleasure for us to meet you all.
- How do you do?
- How are you?
- Nice to meet you.
- Hello ... Good to see you again.
- It is a pleasure to meet you, I'm ...

20.2.1 Introducing oneself and others

Having the greeting, handshake or bow, and welcoming words in place, how do we best introduce ourselves?

Names and titles

The easiest approach throughout the world when introducing yourself in English is to use your first name (or the name you generally use as your first name) and surname: »I'm John Smith, pleased to meet you.« Listen to how the other party introduces itself. For example, in Britain, Ireland, the US and Australia they may only give you their first name: »Hi, I'm John, glad you could join us today.« Some professions may continue to prefer the more formal surname: »Good afternoon, I'm Mr. Smith, partner solicitor in this firm.« Certain professions such as doctors or professors continue to use their title: »Hello, I'm Dr. John Smith, from the orthopaedic department.« If you have received correspondence in advance, letters or emails, they may give a clue as to how they would like to be addressed.

Useful phrases

- Let me introduce you to Mert Doğan. Mert's our key Account Manager.
- My name's Mert Doğan. I'm in charge of Corporate Affairs here in Estonia.
- Let me introduce you to Deshtan, who looks after our offices in Austria.
- Hello. I'm Ulrik Bisgaard, in charge of Marketing.
- I don't think you have met …
- John, this is Marie Müller, Marketing Director at Sanflower in Munich.
- Nice to meet you. This is ... She's in charge of...
- Jürgen, would you like to introduce your team?
- Let me introduce you to Dr. Hans-Peter Uhl.

Job positions

Stating your job position in the company differs from country to country. For example, in the UK, people may be shy about indicating their job title. John's title is General Manager of Sales Department but he is more likely to introduce himself as: »I'm John from Hounslow Engineering.« In the US, job titles are very important so they will usually specify: »I'm Joe, vice president of Sales, Houston Engineering.« In China or Japan people may give you their company name, followed by department, job title and finally their name.

- I'm from Donghua Daxui, the International Department.
- I'm the vice Dean, and my name is Frances Liu.

More specific job titles or positions may be:

- I'm the exclusive representative for….
- I'm one of the many local sales teams.
- My company is in the field of ...
- I'm commissioned by ...
- I have been given the power of attorney for...

20.2.2 Business cards

A lot has been written on how to receive a business card. For example, that it is important to study them respectfully instead of simply sticking someone's card into your pocket, or that in Asian cultures, people give and receive cards with both hands. Very little, however, has been written on what information is written on cards and their actual appearance.

!

Example: Business cards

In a country like South Korea someone's job description is considered very important, or in France people may add extra information.

In many cultures a card is simply something practical, containing contact information, but there are also cultures where much more attention is given to the quality of the material or the printing technique. It is logical that when visiting such countries you want to pay some attention to such details. Finally, it is advisable to have your business card translated on the reverse of your card in cultures where English is less commonly spoken. For example, if travelling to South Korea, have a Korean translation on the reverse. It is advisable to have your business card translated into English on the reverse when travelling to English-speaking countries, unless it is clear to non-German speakers. Being confronted with a business card in another language makes many English speakers uneasy.

Important !

Take enough time to have the translations and proofs double-checked by native speakers from the target country itself. Too many companies have made silly bloopers without knowing it.

20.2.3 Addressing others

For many English-speaking cultures, first names have become the usual way of introduction. It feels very formal and pompous to give your full name such as Mr. Smith unless in a specific job such as Dr. Smith. Thus, when doing business with Americans, Australians, New Zealanders, Canadians, British, South Africans or Irish, it may surprise you, how quickly they can switch to using first names. Many East Asian countries (China, Japan, South Korea) reverse the order so the surname comes first. This is a difficult hurdle for any cultural group to overcome, so we tend to find ourselves being called Mr Stefan instead of Mr Aust and we refer to them as Mr Jintao instead of Mr Hu. East Asians prefer to be more formal initially, particularly when older people are concerned. They are uncomfortable using first names and also nicknames.

People from cultures that use family names in combination with Mr and Mrs may feel a bit uneasy. Nevertheless, it is important to think about the social consequences of not being on first-name terms with people. It may seem too distant or even unfriendly. Therefore, simply follow the approach of your conversation partner. And note that it may sound somewhat strange to suggest »dozen«, as this option does not exist in English between »Du« and »Sie«; both mean »you«.

Many Americans or other English-speaking people commonly use nicknames in their business contacts. The English lan-guage often shortens first names.

! **Example: Common nicknames**

Examples of common nicknames are: Harry (Harold), Tony (Anthony), Bob (Robert), Gene (Eugene), Jack (John), Bill (William), Frank (Francis) and Ted (Edward).

To address business partners with their full first name could look somewhat strange. Some people will even mention their nickname on their business card (in quotation marks), for example: Robert »Chip« Loeffler. Their first name will naturally appear in full on most judicial documents. It is not uncommon for people to be known by another name other than their first in the British Isles. For example, Francis Gordon Lacey is known to everyone as Gordon except on official documents.

20.2.4 Socialising and small talk

For the majority of cultures, socialising in the work environment plays an important, sometimes vital role. Getting to know the person you are doing business with is as important as the actual business itself. In most of the Arab cultures it is practically impossible to do business without knowing the person very well. Leaving room for getting to know people is an important element in any negotiation.

Small talk is used both to get to know other people, as well as help put people at ease. Some cultures place more emphasis on this than others, but it's important at all times. Always begin with small talk even if late for a meeting. Never begin with business. If you arrive in the middle of a meeting, apologise even if it's not your fault for being late before you make your business points. If you start immediately with business, you are in danger of being thought of as anything between nervous to rude to downright dangerous.

Small-talk items

What is discussed during small talk is generally not business-related. This comes naturally to many people, but can be an issue for others. Items such as the weather, your journey to the meeting and sports are often the only topics mentioned, as they are usually non-controversial. Americans are happy to talk about their families in detail but other English-speaking cultures tend to keep family private. Talking about family is vital to cultures that need to build a relationship, such as certain Asian, Middle Eastern, African and South American countries as they need to have an overview of your family and your role in the family group. However, you do not have to go into great detail.

Politics, cultural differences, sex and religion are best avoided unless you already know they can be discussed. If these come up at any time during negotiations then it's best to be curious and open, rather than state opinions. Health is a subject most English-speaking cultures talk freely about. It is important to show sympathy with any illnesses mentioned, even if you may think they're purely psychological.

Important

!

»Let's get down to business« is a signal many use as the reference moment when enough small talk has taken place. It is best to try to feel the atmosphere before proceeding too quickly. You want to avoid making the other side feel uncomfortable.

How it works

Small talk is used in English speaking cultures to influence conversations in a positive way. Small talk is functional to introduce or end a conversation with a few phrases about friendly and risk-free topics. It helps to create a polite and friendly atmosphere. Try to use open questions (see section on Asking questions). It is also possible to answer a question with another question if you don't want to respond to the question asked.

Useful phrases

- How was your journey?
- How was the flight over?
- Is your hotel comfortable?
- Is everything all right with the hotel?
- Is this your first visit to Germany?
- Would you like anything to drink?
- You must be jet-lagged after such a long flight.
- Would you like me to order some coffee?
- How's the weather in France at the moment?
- How was your break in France?
- How's business in your sector?

20.3 Opening phase

All negotiations have an established procedural structure, regardless of the various partners or topics. The phases of negotiating we distinguish in this book are:

- Preparation and planning phase
- Opening phase

- Main phase
- Agreement phase

Although these phases are distinct, they do not necessarily have to follow the described sequence.

!

Example: Phases of negotiating

An offer sent by way of an email campaign, would already start in phase three: the main phase, whereas an interested recipient of the mail might want to look into the details of the product (i.e. the preparation and planning phase).

This implies that the main reason for identifying the four negotiation phases isn't that they are consecutive, but the fact that they ask for different skills. And whether we are aware or ignorant of these different phases: they all require specific behaviour. And that's something that comes of course with its own specific language requirements. The important elements of the preparation and planning phase have already been discussed in the previous chapter; we therefore concentrate here on what happens during the actual negotiation.

Once the socialising and small talk has taken place, the negotiation can begin. For smooth negotiations, the following steps are useful in the beginning:

- State the purpose of the negotiation.
- Agree on the agenda.
- State your interests.
- Listen to the other party's interests.
- Clarify anything unclear or incorrect.

20.3.1 Stating the purpose

Why are you negotiating? This may seem obvious, but it's surprising how often parties discover during a negotiation they are not discussing the same purpose. Stating clearly the purpose of the negotiation provides the basic framework for everyone. One of the most important moments in a negotiation is explaining your interests and what you hope to achieve. It is better to lay down what you want from the beginning. The first information discussed has a great influence in determining the outcome.

Example: Stating the purpose

!

We are here to discuss the acquiring of land for the purpose of constructing a petrol station and shop. Our desire is to be able to agree today on a satisfactory price for all concerned and achieve a timetable for planning operations with all the relevant stakeholders.

Objective criteria are the accepted standards between the parties, as to how all parties can fairly judge the outcome of the agreement. This could be market price, government regulation, precedent, local trading conditions, fairness or anything which all parties can accept. There may be more than one criterion. It is important that all the parties agree because without an agreed objective criterion there is no basis for an agreement.

Example: Objective criteria

!

The petrol station and shop are to be built between a motorway and an office building. The building regulations for foundations, distance from other buildings and from the road are strict. There is no point for the owner to sell the land to a buyer if he cannot meet such regulations. The objective criteria could thus be based on both price as well as the specific regulations.

Useful phrases

Below are some useful phrases a chairperson can use.

- Could I have your attention, please?
- OK, everyone, sorry to interrupt, but we are short of time, so let's get started.
- Ladies and gentlemen, we have a rather full agenda, so perhaps we had better get down to business.
- Shall we just go round the table, making sure we all know each other?
- OK, we've called this meeting in order to ...
- We're here today to try and reach an agreement about two items: payment terms and the penalty clause.
- As you know, we're here today to discuss ...
- The prime objective of our meeting today should be to agree ... .

Useful vocabulary

framework: Rahmen
acquire: erwerben
stakeholders: Hauptinteressenten
criterion: Kriterium, Maßstab
to get down to business: beginnen, anfangen
the objectives of the meeting: Ziele der Verhandlung
to fill somebody in on something: informieren

20.3.2 The agenda

The phrases below can be functional in getting participants to agree on a prepared agenda.

Useful phrases

- Firstly, can I suggest we start by taking a look at the agenda we have sent you?
- Today we will discuss some difficult points; therefore I'd like to suggest we try and stick to a meeting procedure.
- We have drawn up an agenda which covers the main areas for negotiation today. Are you happy about all this?
- Did everyone receive a copy of the agenda from Ms Bakridi?
- Let me inform you of the sequence of negotiation topics.
- On the agenda today we have ..., are there any comments on this?
- There are six items on the agenda. First ..., second ..., third ..., lastly .... Does your party agree that we take these points in this order?
- Your agenda allocates five minutes for this item, but we believe ...
- Diederik, could you bring us up to date on item three on the agenda?

Useful vocabulary

to delete from the agenda: von der Tagesordnung nehmen
to be on the agenda: auf der Tagesordnung stehen

20.4 Main phase

Now that the preliminaries are out of the way and the opening points have been stated, the train has left the station and the negotiation is moving along at its own speed. All the elements of negotiation planning, experience, and tactics come to life here. We take you through some of the most relevant aspects and give some suggestions on how to approach using appropriate English. Since asking questions, listening and dealing with people are so important we have placed them in separate sections.

20.4.1 Bargaining

Bargaining means to negotiate, argue, or barter about the terms of a business transaction, usually focussing on the purchase or selling price of a product or service. It therefore requires a party that has something to offer as an exchange. English speakers are very familiar with the terms »hard« and »soft«

approach. Usually they add the term sell or bargaining as in »hard sell« or »hard bargaining«. They might believe they're going to »drive a hard bargain« or make it seem like a »soft sell«. All of these force the negotiation towards a win-lose outcome despite everyone stating they want a win-win situation. Parties need each other; otherwise they would not be negotiating. Acknowledging this allows you to focus on the solution of what is on the table. Give and take, making concessions is required. Without these, stalemate can ensue which means nothing further happens. Making a concession can break the stalemate and move the discussions further towards an agreement, a win-win.

Price discussions

Bargaining predominates in one-time negotiations and often revolves around a single issue, usually the price. In lots of business cultures people are used to a higher degree of bargaining than in northern Europe. In such cultures the first offer is usually substantially higher or lower than the final offer in a negotiation.

Example: Price discussions

!

A: What discount could you give us on a larger order?
B: That depends, how many units you were thinking of?
A: We would like to buy something in the ballpark of fifteen units.
B: Okay. Well, if you were to order twenty units, I'd be willing to give you nine percent off the list price.
A: I understand, and what kind of a discount can we get on fifteen units?
B: Not that much, probably around four percent.
A: That means with the three percent for prompt payment, we are talking about seven percent off your list price. I'm afraid that's a bit of a stretch, I could agree to an offer of nine percent.
B: That seems high to me, Horst. Can you go a little lower?
A: Your changing the price by nine percent would enable us to seriously consider the deal.
B: You drive a hard bargain; I'd like to consult head office before committing.

Zone of possible agreement

In order to achieve agreement at a certain stage, you will need to have an idea of the other party's area or zone of agreement. The image below shows us that the buyer is willing to pay between 1,000 € (minimum) and 3,500 € (maximum), and the seller is asking for a minimum of 3,000 € and a maximum of 5,000 € in their respective settlement areas. The buyer and seller and agree on a price somewhere between 3,000 € and 3,500 €. This is known as the zone of possible agreement (ZOPA). Until parties are negotiating in ZOPA, they will be unable to come to an agreement.

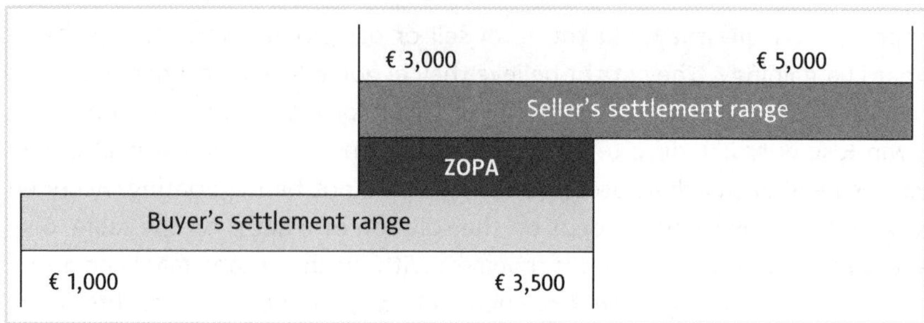

Useful phrases

- Can we talk about the price?
- Is this price negotiable?
- Is there a possibility you could move closer to our quoted price?
- Is that your best offer?
- What room for manoeuvre do you have here?
- We could offer you a slight reduction on certain conditions of course.
- We could reduce the prices in exchange for a guarantee on quantity.
- What would you say if we offered you …?
- I'm afraid we will have to look elsewhere, unless …
- We will increase our offer by ...
- We could alter the payment terms, would that do?
- We will cover the rate of interest, okay?
- If you pay in ten days, we will abate the payment terms.
- If you sign the contract now, we'll improve the payback period as you suggested.
- Could I ask you how much you had in mind?

Price reductions

Price reductions or discounts mean that you pay less than the regular or list price. If orders are incomplete or incorrect, negotiators can also ask for discounts. It might take some creative preparation; therefore the overview below lists a selection of reasons for asking for price deductions.

- Early payment
- Advance payment
- Payment of a deposit
- Purchase of several items
- Use of name in supplier advertising
- Order of large volumes
- End of stock purchase
- First of stock purchase
- Recommendation to other customers
- Loyalty to supplier over the years

- First-time use of supplier
- Placing all business with the supplier
- Delivery at unusual times
- Instant or delayed delivery
- Collecting ex-works (with own transport)

Useful vocabulary
price proposal: Preisvorschlag
high/low-priced: hoch/niedrigpreisig
to undercut somebody's prices: jemanden unterbieten
pricing factors: preisbestimmende Faktoren
to limit a price: Preislimit setzen
asked or asking price: geforderter Preis
authority to negotiate: die Befugnis zu verhandeln
something in the ballpark of: ungefähr
prompt payment: prompte, termingerechte Zahlung
drive a hard bargain: hart verhandeln
proposal for amendment: Änderungsvorschlag
settlement: Einigungsvorschlag
to submit proposals: Vorschläge unterbreiten
to carry on negotiations for a settlement: Vergleichsverhandlungen fortführen
counterproposal: Gegenvorschlag
open to negotiations: verhandlungsbereit
to take up negotiations: Verhandlungen aufnehmen
to refer back: verweisen auf

Having looked at the preliminary and exploration phase of negotiating, the next paragraphs will concentrate on some practical negotiation skills, such as how to mark transitions, or how to summarise the other party's propositions, and the how and why of adjourning during a negotiation.

20.4.2 Marking transitions

There are many ways to indicate a transition in an argumentative talk, for instance by gestures or changes in tone or volume, but because this may differ from culture to culture, it is often advised to mark transitions in words when negotiating internationally. The phrases below offer some examples for this:

Useful phrases
- I'd like to expand on that a little before we move on.
- Let me point out here that ...

- Now here's one more fact about ...
- What I'd like to focus on here is ...
- Let's look more closely at ...
- After this general look, let's now turn to specific issues.
- That was an overview; now let's look at some details.
- Let me first give you a brief overview.

20.4.3 Linking words

Linking words help to connect ideas and sentences, so that people can follow what is said more easily. Your advantage of using specific linking words or expressions is that they can give the people sitting at the conference table a better idea of the structure of your line of reasoning. The overview below offers some alternatives.

Making conditions

Use one of the following expressions to insist on something:

- If
- Unless
- Until
- Provided

Reiterating propositions

Use one of the following expressions for repeating:

- To reiterate
- In short
- All in all
- On the whole
- Altogether
- To reconsider
- In particular
- To recount

Additional arguments

When you want to add an extra argument or reason, it sounds nicer not only to use words like »and« or »also« but to vary a bit. The table below offers some alternatives:

- Furthermore, ...
- Moreover, ...
- In addition, ...
- Besides, ...
- Additionally, ...
- ...as well as ...
- What is more, ...
- On another point, ...

Overview

When you want to give an overview of the points mentioned, you can indicate this by using the following expressions:

- To conclude, …
- Summarising, …
- In other words, …
- All in all, …
- Finally, …
- To sum it up, …
- To recap it briefly, …
- In brief, …
- Most important, …
- In conclusion, …

Emphasising statements

Use one of the following linking words to accentuate things:

- Certainly
- Of course
- In fact
- Indeed

Providing an example

Use one of the following expressions to illustrate something:

- For instance
- To put it another way
- For example
- More specifically
- To illustrate
- In other words
- As an example
- To be exact

Linking conflicting facts

Use one of the words below to combine conflicting facts:

- On the other hand
- However
- In reality
- Nonetheless
- On the contrary
- In contrast

20.4.4 Interrupting

Getting your point across or interrupting the other person or people speaking can be delicate. Latin Americans and southern Europeans tend to be comfortable with talking over each other. Avoid beginning too directly, but use softening words instead such as those listed here.

Useful phrases

- Excuse me for interrupting, but …
- I'd like to comment on that.
- Sorry to interrupt, but perhaps the members of the board would like to know more about our … ?
- Could I just say one thing?
- I'm glad you brought that up, Bill.

- Could I just come in here?
- In my opinion this counter-offer is ...
- It's also worth noting that ...
- Mister, Madam Chairman?

20.4.5 Rephrasing

Rephrasing is an important tool for negotiators, as it allows them to express ideas in different, perhaps more acceptable ways. It can also prevent misunderstandings during negotiations with non-native speakers of English.

Useful phrases

- So, let's just recap on that.
- Sorry, what we actually meant (to explain) is this ...
- Basically, what our side is saying is this ...
- Earlier on I wasn't clear about our counter-offer.
- What my colleague is saying is that ... .
- My client would like to recap on the main points.
- I'd like to digress here for a moment and mention that ...
- Sorry, perhaps I didn't make the additional demand clear.
- I'm afraid I'm not quite clear what you mean.
- Sorry, I'm not sure I understood. Would you mind going over that again?
- Correct me if I'm wrong, but ...
- Did I get it right that ...?
- The point I'm making is that ...

Useful vocabulary

contradiction: Widerspruch, Gegensatz
dissent: Unstimmigkeit, Meinungsverschiedenheit
opposites: Gegensätze
by mutual agreement: im gegenseitigen Einvernehmen
counter-offer: Gegenangebot
to recap: kurz zusammenfassen
to digress: abschweifen von

20.4.6 Referring back

Use one of the following phrases to refer back to earlier mentioned discussion points.

Useful phrases

- To refer back to an earlier point, …
- Let's go back to what you were offering earlier.
- Let me go back to the cost break down of …
- Taking into consideration what Mrs Porath-Funk said …
- I'd like to return to what you were proposing earlier.
- Let's go back to the question of possible alternatives.
- To go back to what you said earlier …
- Let's look back for a moment.

20.4.7 Making your point clear

You will want to get your points across to the other side; otherwise coming to an agreement will be hard to achieve. Phrasing the sentence in reference to yourself takes any offence, discomfort, or loss of face away from the other parties. You take ownership for the opinion or information this way.

Useful phrases

- I really think it would be better to ...
- The way I see things …
- From my perspective …
- Well, in our opinion, ...
- In my (professional) opinion …
- In my experience …
- Past experience has taught me that …
- If you look at it from our point of view, then …
- What you're saying is that you …
- That's not exactly how I look at it.
- I think this proves the point that …
- Well, personally, I think the best solution is ...
- I feel that ...
- I suggest that we should …
- Therefore, it is clear that …
- I think it's obvious that …

20.4.8 Summarising

Summarising is a vital negotiating technique when so much has been said and interruptions have occurred. A summary can refocus attention on the issues at hand, particularly when not negotiating in your mother tongue. Summaries are of necessity in certain cultures.

!

Example: Summaries and different cultures

The Japanese will take it particularly seriously. English-speaking cultures tend to rush through this part, often referring to it as recapping, e.g. »Shall we recap before shaking hands?«

In general, you can say that summaries should be concise and neutral, and refer to one or more of the following elements:

- The different points covered,
- The proposals of each side,
- The discrepancies agreed between parties,
- What has been excluded,
- What is agreed upon.

Useful phrases

Use one of the following phrases to summarise points:

- To summarise, ...
- Let me quickly summarise the principal results.
- Let's summarise what is on the table.
- I'd like to go over the main points now.
- Let me briefly recap your suggested options.
- The pros and cons were as follows ...
- In addition to that, outstanding issues are ...
- There is still the question of ... to resolve.
- To sum up, we have made progress with the ...
- Parties have agreed the following ...
- Is there anything you wish to add?
- Is this an accurate summary?

Useful vocabulary

to give a summary: eine Zusammenfassung geben
recapitulation: Zusammenfassung
to recap: rekapitulieren
a concise explanation: präzise Darlegung
divergence of opinion: Meinungsverschiedenheit

20.4.9 Adjourning

To adjourn means to suspend proceedings to another time or place. Depending on the circumstances, adjournments can be for a few minutes, a couple of hours or even a few weeks. In certain negotiations, it may be constructive to take a break or adjourn a meeting. Usually this is the case in one of the circumstances mentioned below:

- To digest new important information received,
- To consult or obtain instructions from decision makers,
- To regroup a negotiation team,
- To diffuse tension,
- To counteract pressure from the other side that is pushing for a decision,
- When coming close to the least acceptable position,
- When being close to a deal,
- Or simply because people are getting tired.

Example: Adjourning

!

Chairman: »We have summarised the benefits for you of accepting the offer on the table. I propose that we adjourn, while each party consults its advisers. Can we then reconvene at 4 pm., to indicate acceptance or otherwise?«

Useful phrases

- If there are no further comments, we will adjourn the meeting here.
- I just have a few closing remarks and then you will all be free to go for lunch.
- It is getting too personal. Can I suggest we take a break?
- We propose adjourning and reconvening at two o'clock.
- Before we adjourn this meeting, let me just summarise the main items.
- Shall I go over the main points?
- Let's bring things to a close for this part of the negotiation.
- I'm afraid we're going to have to cut this meeting short.
- I think we'll wrap up this last point, and take a break.
- Well, we have even finished ahead of schedule.
- If no one has anything else to add, then I guess that will be all for today.

Useful vocabulary

to adjourn sine die: sich auf unbestimmte Zeit vertagen (»sine die« = lat. für »ohne Tag«)
closing: Schließung
concession: Zugeständnis
stalemate situation: Pattsituation
to come to a deadlock: ergebnislos verlaufen, stecken bleiben

20.5 Agreement phase

Research shows that in the last ten percent of the meeting time, approximately ninety percent of negotiations get settled. Sometimes negotiating parties miss the moment of agreement, simply because they do not pay attention to the atmosphere at the table. The right moment for agreement has come when:

- The differences between parties have become small,
- One party really stops making concessions,
- You have reached your prepared targets,
- You start reaching your own deadline.

20.5.1 Reaching an agreement

Now the train is pulling into the station and you want to step off with a successful result. Before making an agreement (closing a deal), think over the situation carefully.

- Will it achieve your goal; does it cover all your interests?
- Is it within you parameters?
- Is it better than your alternative (BATNA, see chapter »Preparation and planing«)?

Once you are happy to agree on a final offer and close the deal, you want to be sure this is actually happening. Double check to be sure everyone is in agreement. Think about how the other parties may perceive the outcome.

!

Example: Reaching an agreement

The Scandinavians, Czechs and Dutch will be more in line with your own thinking about the long-term elements. The British will have a more flexible approach to future issues, the Americans prefer all important elements to be covered in the contract, and those cultures that are relationship-based, will focus on how everyone is reacting to the issues being agreed.

Whether the follow-up of an agreement will be called a contract or not, a good agreement represents the result of what has been negotiated, in a mutually acceptable form. English-speaking countries do not distinguish the type of agreement. Whether it's a simple or very complicated agreement it is classed in the same manner. Some sectors have their own specific agreement formats or legal requirements.

- A draft agreement would mean you have not reached a final agreement and it is temporary.

- A preliminary agreement is the basis for a more extensive final agreement and although it is not 100% confirmation, it does provides comfort that a final agreement will be made.
- A non-disclosure agreement means that one or more parties to the agreement must not divulge the information (or part of) to anyone else.

Useful phrases
- I believe both parties can agree to these terms.
- Can we agree to what we have proposed jointly?
- I propose that we leave it this way for the moment.
- Can we set about implementing our agreement as it now stands?
- We've been brainstorming back and forth over this issue for some minutes now, but it really sounds like we've found some common ground here.
- Can you agree to the adaptation of the written proposal?
- We would need to see some movement on price.
- Can we agree to what we have proposed jointly, and set about implementing our agreement as it now stands?
- This is our final offer.
- Can your client agree to the second proposal?

20.5.2 Ensuring agreement

Some useful sentences are provided here to help with ensuring that you are in agreement:
- Well, I think we've both agreed on the terms. Can we shake on it?
- I think we should get this in writing.
- We can certainly agree to this new counter-proposal.
- We agree on this particular clause in the contract.
- We agree with you, as far as this is concerned.
- By mutual agreement we have decided that ....
- We feel exactly the same way.
- We agree with you, as far as this is concerned.
- We can accept that.
- That's right/correct/possible.
- I certainly agree to that.
- We feel exactly the same way.
- We agree on this matter.
- I couldn't agree with you more.
- I agree with you entirely.
- That sounds like a very good idea to me.

Useful vocabulary:
to agree on: sich einigen über
as agreed upon: wie vereinbart
unless otherwise agreed: soweit nichts anderes vereinbart ist
agreed price fixing: Preisabsprache
to come to an agreement: eine Einigung erzielen
to reach an agreement on the price: sich über den Preis einigen
to decide upon concerted action: sich zu einem gemeinsamen Vorgehen entschließen

20.5.3 Disagreeing

You may find that you cannot agree with the proposals and need to find a suitable way to let this be known. Directness is not to be used. Asian and Latin Americans may lose face. The British will be uncomfortable at the least. Saying no doesn't work in some cultures. Even saying yes does not necessarily mean you agree. Yes from a Japanese means: »Yes, I hear you.« not: »Yes, I agree«. Therefore some softening of the information by using extra apologetic wording is required. The sentences below are listed in the order of least confrontational to most confrontational to English speakers:

Useful phrases

- We're afraid we'd have to disagree about that.
- We're not sure we agree with that.
- This isn't quite what we were expecting.
- We may have to disagree.
- That's probably not possible for us.
- This is missing some details.
- I'm afraid my management cannot accept the proposed explanation in this form.
- I tend to disagree because....
- I'm sorry, but I can`t agree because.....
- I beg to differ.
- I'm afraid we cannot accept your statement because....
- We don't agree on that because... .
- That's all very well but....
- With all due respect, I disagree on....
- Please do not misunderstand me but.....
- I don't wish to be rude but....

Useful vocabulary:
in the event of disagreement: falls keine Einigung zustande kommt
to contradict: widersprechen
to express disapproval: Missbilligung aussprechen

20.5.4 We agree, but...

Just about the moment you think agreement has been reached, you hear something like: »Your offer is acceptable, but there is just this small detail«. When you have met their points to reach an agreement, another small detail appears again. What strategies can you implement to deal with this? Try techniques like the two examples below:

!

Example: Strategies

1: Are there any other issues you still have, if I may ask? Then I suggest that we first try to consider them together in a package.
2: We cannot really accept any changes on this small detail; however, if you were to adjust point ..., we can consider the change you suggested.

20.5.5 No subdivided agreement

In most cases, there are many rounds of negotiations. The preliminary round may uncover the major issues, while subsequent rounds may be needed to resolve them. Many issues will have been raised and either agreed upon or set aside for one or another reason. It is advisable not to agree to finalised parts of the negotiation separately. Always try instead to include all issues in one final agreement. This way, you will keep more space to manoeuvre. This can be best said as follows: »I agree to the proposal subject to the final agreement«.

20.5.6 Closing remarks and next steps

It is necessary to indicate to the participants that negotiations have come to a close. Having come to an agreement, it is time to finalise. Depending on the importance of the agreement it may be a handshake, a signing ceremony and/or celebratory drinks. It is unwise to depart as soon as the agreement is reached. Most cultures require some form of recognition. For simpler agreements, a lot of handshaking and smiling should be enough. Americans, Australians and Latin Americans may even slap you on the back.

Useful phrases

- Our meeting today has been very productive.
- I think we have made excellent progress today.
- Our meeting today has given us a lot to think about.
- I suggest that we address the matter of clarifying the contingency sum again in our next meeting.
- Shall we meet again once we have had some time to consider the options?
- Can we set the date for the next meeting, please?
- We'll meet again on the twenty-seventh of next month, same time.
- We'll draft a detailed summary before the next meeting.
- I'll send out an email with the minutes in two days.
- The next step is to draft a formal contract.
- If anyone has any questions about what we agreed today, feel free to send me an email.
- It simply remains for me to thank you all for attending.
- I declare the meeting closed.
- We will send you the missing documents/deeds.
- We will take care of the formulating of the contract.
- Thank you all for your participation.

Useful vocabulary

successful conclusion of negotiations: erfolgreicher Abschluss einer Verhandlung
to contract for: sich vertraglich verpflichten
contracting party: Vertragspartei
to award the contract: den Auftrag vergeben
to receive the contract: den Zuschlag erhalten
contract in writing: schriftlicher Vertrag
to conclude a contract: einen Vertrag schließen
set the date: einen Termin festlegen
for your comments: zur Stellungnahme
to call it a day: Schluss machen, beenden

20.6 Asking questions

Asking questions to confirm what has been said or to clarify the information given can be extremely useful, as it helps to avoid misunderstandings. This is particularly important if the information is complicated, or when the parties do not know each other well, especially during cross-cultural negotiations, or when one or more of those attending are not native English speakers.

20.6.1 Clarifying

This section looks at how to clarify and evaluate positions when asking questions during a negotiation. It is important to achieve mutual understanding while trying to bring about an agreement. This is accomplished by making both your own team's position clear, as well as by understanding the other side's point of view concerning the offers or positions at hand. Try to avoid wording questions that are a direct challenge to the other person's position. It is clever to avoid questions like »If you want … how can you also expect … ?« or »Did you not say that … ?«

Confirming questions

- Am I right in thinking that … ?
- Could I just go over your main points again?
- In other words, you're interested in developing ... ?
- Did I understand correctly that what your board of management is saying concerns … ?
- If I understand you correctly, you are asking ...
- Am I right in thinking that your …
- Correct me if I'm wrong. What I understand here is that you are asking … ?
- From your point of view, you consider the only way to resolve the packaging is to ….
- You state that you will write 64 pages, but can you confirm this will actually be possible given the timescale?
- Is this a good summary of your position?

Asking for clarification

- I'm afraid I didn't quite catch that.
- I'm sorry, could you simplify/rephrase your point?
- If I understood you correctly, you would like to ask … ?
- I'm sorry. I don't quite understand the meaning of ….
- I'm afraid I don't see the connection here.
- Sorry, I'm not really sure what you mean.
- Could you go over that again?
- Do you mind me asking ... ?

20.6.2 Question categories

In order to understand the other party's interests, it is important to obtain as much information as possible. The best method is to ask lots of questions. Using various types of questions helps to bring about a more complete view of the other party and draws them further into the negotiation. These help to increase your knowledge in order to enhance your strategy and find synergies and mutual gain.

Emotional questions

- How do you feel about ... ?
- What are your thoughts about ... ?
- Why is that so important to you?

Open questions

- When can we expect ... ?
- How can we deal with that problem ... ?
- Where does your information come from?
- How much would you be willing to offer?

Particular questions

- Why are you interested in our product specifically?
- Which other suppliers are you dealing with?
- Why is that particular deadline so important for you?

Ensuring questions

- Sorry to interrupt, but I would like to know more about ...
- Excuse me, may I ask how you arrived at these results?
- One question. How do you plan to ... ?
- You mentioned ..., can you expand on that?
- Could you clarify what you said about ... ?
- Could I go back to the point you made about ... ?
- I want to take you up on what you said earlier about ...
- My client is interested in your opinion about ...
- Do you want us to draft that before our next meeting?
- Could I have that in writing, please?

!

Example: Ensuring questions

A: I'd like to talk you through the various points, if that's OK?
B: Sure, go ahead.
A: Well, to start with, we think that the payment terms need adaptation to the prevailing Swiss conditions.
B: Just a minute, Horst. Could you clarify something for me?
A: Of course.
B: What exactly do you mean by »the Swiss conditions«?
C: Look, sorry to digress, but what we'd particularly like to ask you about are the payment terms.

A: Oh, right, OK. Well, what is it in particular that you want to know about the payment terms?

What-if questions

Using »what if« questions can be very helpful during negotia-tions because they elucidate potential negotiable issues. What-if questions can be used for exploring possible settlements in a conflict or deadlock situation. Their advantage is that they also avoid laying responsibility on any party as they are considered a suggestion rather than a proposal.

Example: What-if questions !

A: Well, to start with, we think that the payment terms need adaptation to the prevailing Swiss conditions.
C: Look, sorry to digress, but what we'd particularly like to ask you about, are the payment terms.
A: WHAT IF we were to consider delaying the payment deadlines, would that serve your interests?

- If you ..., what would it be?
- What if ... ?

20.6.3 Question the facts

A proven method to create negotiating opportunities is to ask questions about how the other party arrived at their proposal. Why did they make certain assumptions, based on which facts, how relevant were the applied criteria, how reliable were the sources used, etc.. By forcing your negotiation counterpart to explain the build-up of their proposal, you are sure to find material to strengthen your own position. Think of questions like:

- What data did they use to calculate these figures?
- Excuse me, may I ask how you arrived at this result?
- On which facts is this proposal based, if I may ask?
- Can I ask you: what forms the basis of the claim in paragraph three of the proposal?
- How did you calculate option C on page four, if I may be so bold as to ask?
- Could I ask what source this information comes from exactly?
- Aren't these figures possibly setting too high a valuation on it?

20.6.4 Avoiding asking questions

Recent research has shown that German negotiators have some of the lowest scores with respect to asking questions during negotiations compared to other cultures. On the other hand, they have a very high level of self-disclosure. Brazilian, French or Spanish business people tend to negotiate quite self-assertively or forcefully, using a high percentage of threats, warnings and even commands. Naturally, there is the danger of stereotyping people, but then again the described cultural differences are worthwhile considering when preparing for any negotiations in an international context.

20.7 The art of listening

Listening to the other party is one of the more important tools in understanding its requirements and obtaining a mutual agreement. Experienced negotiation teams appoint an extra team member, solely for observing the other party members. Having asked a question it is important to understand the re-sponse. Listening is not as easy as it seems. People often just listen to themselves or their colleagues, not the others involved. Especially when under the pressure of negotiating, listening gets harder since stress inhibits people from listening properly.

!

Important

Avoid searching for responses to what is being said, but rather try to understand the other party as it sees itself.

It is sometimes explained in a simple way: »People have two ears and one mouth; they should try and use them proportionally«. Listening involves concentrating on what the person is actually saying and assessing his/her body language. Many people are not sure of what they actually want. Confirming and clarifying questions therefore helps to understand their perceptions, emotions and constraints. It is advisable to make these questions positive from the other party's point of view. In other words avoid saying anything that makes the other party defensive. On the other hand, it is not necessary to agree, because understanding is not the same as agreeing. Misunderstandings are a frequent source of the reasons for poor negotiations or failure of negotiations. A foreign language can be especially problematic. Body language is also more important to be aware of than in your own culture. Confirming and clarifying can help to overcome such issues.

Benefits of listening

- It improves what you have to say and offer,
- It allows you to find mutual solutions,
- It helps overcome language misunderstandings,
- It allows the other person to feel they have been taken seriously.

People have a need to be heard. A successful negotiation only occurs when all parties feel their interests have been listened to.

Useful phrases

The following phrases show that you are listening:

- Hm, I understand.
- That's very interesting.
- Right.
- Okay, thank you.

20.8 When things get tough

It is difficult enough to resolve tensions and conflicts, but it is particularly challenging when a foreign language is involved.

20.8.1 Reducing tension

Naturally participants in negotiations can be somewhat tense, especially when they are operating outside their own environment. Here are some ways to contribute to a positive atmosphere. Before the start of the meeting it helps to walk around a bit, and have some informal contact or small talk. Another technique is to use a more careful choice of words.

Choice of words

The examples below show you the difference between direct and indirect wording:

Direct	Indirect
impossible	difficult
never done	not normally done
contrary to company policy	without precedent
no way	not under the current circumstances
not very encouraging	disappointing

Other Techniques

Besides a careful choice of words, some other techniques can contribute to a positive atmosphere. For example:

- Help build up a positive climate,
- Listen to the reasoning of others,
- Respond to remarks,
- Have a sense of humour,
- Relate to common interests,
- Avoid a tense or too formal attitude.

Reading between the lines

Cultures that use indirect speech, which includes most of the English-speaking world, use wording that requires reading between the lines. This means searching for the important words in sentences spoken. The highlighted words in the following sentences show where the important information is:

- As I'm sure you appreciate, this is a **difficult situation**.
  Means: this is very serious.
- This sounds like a slight **problem**.
  Means: we have a problem.
- I'm **not** very **happy** with that.
  Means: they're very unhappy.
- I like the idea, **but** we should look at ...
  Means: they don't like the idea.
- That's **not** quite what I **meant**
  Means: that's not correct.

Useful phrases

- We should look at the benefits from both sides.
- It's in all our interests to resolve the problem.
- We're here to try and find answers for all parties.
- Let's try to focus on the positive aspects.

20.8.2 Anger management

People identify themselves with the negotiation and particularly the outcome. When things are not going well, they may start to display irrational behaviour. Sometimes people start shouting or banging the table. Some cultures find this more acceptable than others. These may be tactics to put you under pressure, but more often people are becoming upset because they feel their interests are slipping away from them. In order to successfully control emotions, the suppression of your own thoughts, perceptions and emotions is advisable. This is not easy. It helps to hold your emotions in check by focussing on the issue and not on yourself or the others involved. The authors Fisher and Ury use the term: »Separate the people from the problem«.

!

Example: Separate the people from the problem

If someone blames you for something, do not respond negatively. Depending on what it's about, you may be able to accept what they say or disagree.

This allows the issue to stand on its own and the negotiations to move on.

Useful phrases

- Your point is interesting, can you tell us more?
- If you are opposed, what is it that you object to?
- We need you to fully understand our priorities.
- We were slightly annoyed by ..., do you feel the same way?
- We feel pressured on our side, and this seems to influence our trust in these negotiations. I believe we should do something about this.
- Perhaps we are misunderstanding the situation.

20.8.3 Dealing with impasses

One of the best ways of finding a route around an impasse is reviewing the situation from the other side's perspective. What would you need or want, if you were the other party? You may then be able to find some common ground to propose a suggestion for moving forward. Within your strategy you should have options available that could now be used, or you may take another route if you have thought out an alternative position. Throwing a new idea into the ring will have a ripple effect and a good chance of producing a breakthrough.

!

Important

Writing up the items of the agenda can sometimes unblock stalled negotiations. This entails making a short list of areas to discuss. They do not need to be in a set order and shouldn't be presented as proposals.

Useful phrases

- How can we find a compromise for this?
- May I just explain our point of view?
- Your position is a different approach; can you tell us more?
- I think I see what you're getting at. Can I suggest a break; I would like to talk this through with my team.

20.9 Tables, graphs or charts

People in today's business community are so accustomed to the use of computerised visual aids that this can also be relevant for negotiations. The paragraphs hereunder give you an overview of the necessary key phrases. Having facts and figures at hand in a negotiation may strengthen one's position. There are many graphs or charts available in spreadsheet programs such as Excel and they all have their own specific use. The table below lists an overview of their names and German translations:

German	English
Baumdiagramm	tree diagram
Bilddiagramm	pictogram
Diagramm	diagram
Flussdiagramm	flowchart
gestrichelte Linie	a broken line
grünes Dreieck	green triangle
Histogramm	histogram
Säulendiagramm	bar chart *
Kreisdiagramm	pie chart
Kurve, Graph	graph
durchgezogene Linie	a solid line
Punktlinie	a dotted line
Schaubild	chart
schraffiertes Rechteck	shaded box
Tabelle	table
X-Achse, Y-Achse	x-axis, y-axis

* Note that (bar) graphs in American English are mostly called (bar) charts in British English.

Useful phrases

- I'd like to illustrate this by showing you …
- The horizontal axis represents ...
- Each line on this second graph features ...
- The red shaded box here shows ...
- The blue dotted line gives us ...

Explaining graphs

Tables, graphs or charts can clarify situations, developments and processes, which would otherwise take a long time to explain in words. Visuals reduce the talking you have to do, which is of course easier when you need to negotiate in a foreign language.

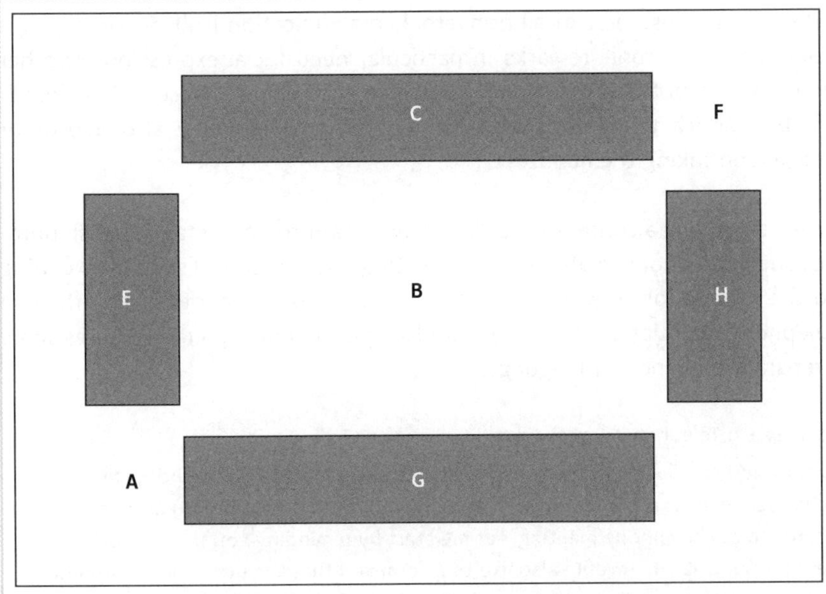

A. In the bottom left-hand corner or: Down the left side of the chart
B. In the centre
C. Across the top
E. On the left
F. In the upper right-hand corner
G. Across the bottom
H. On the right

Useful phrases

- What you can see across the top is ...
- In the right-hand corner you will see ...
- Let us look at the upper half of the chart.
- But our chart shows a significant rise/dramatic increase in the number of ...
- Last year the number of ... went up sharply.
- Can you explain this trough in your graph?
- But your graph falls gradually after July.
- There has been a significant decrease in the number of ...
- We can see that the number of returns has stabilised/has reached a plateau/ has levelled out.

20.10 Telephone negotiating

It is not always possible to meet face-to-face, but with the improvement of technical possibilities many companies nowadays prefer conference calls or video conferencing over long flights and hotel stays. There are still some points that make taking part in a telephone negotiation different from an ordinary meeting. First of all nonverbal communication isn't possible over a telephone, and ironic remarks in particular need facial expression. Another point is that not everybody will recognise each other's voices. Therefore it can be practical to mention one's name before talking. This is also helpful for the person taking the minutes.

When attending a conference call, it is important to understand English phrases and expressions related to such meetings. Also practical skills like keeping to the agenda, or knowing how to refocus, are components of an effective telephone negotiation. This may sound simple in German, but it requires some preparation in another language.

! **Example 1: Telephone negotiating**

Thank you for dialling in today and welcome. My name is Wil Hazelhoff, I'm the chairperson of this conference call and I would like to welcome you all as participants to our telephone meeting. Let me start by reminding you that our call ends around 12 am. I would also like to inform you that the necessary conference documentation is called »ibl.doc«. I will now quickly introduce you to all the other participants. May I ask you to greet the other members after your name is mentioned? This allows us to check that everyone is connected properly and that the technology is working smoothly. Thank you.
Then I would like to welcome Mr. Erik Borst from Freiburg, Germany. He will update us on the latest ICT Service bulletins and will be available for questions afterwards. May I then ...

Useful phrases

Beginning a telephone negotiation

- Let me inform you of the sequence of discussion topics.
- There are four items on the agenda. First ..., second ..., third ..., lastly ... Shall we take these points in this order?
- If you have a comment, please introduce yourself by name.
- Could you please indicate when you need to leave the phone for a short time, and mention your name?
- We have to end this conference call before the end of the hour.

During a telephone negotiation

- I know most of you, but there are a few unfamiliar voices.
- As chair, I'd like to take a moment to introduce Claudia.
- Let's quickly go through the minutes from the previous meeting. Claudia, can I put you in charge of reviewing the minutes from the last meeting for us?
- We cannot speak all at once, please.

Ending a telephone negotiation

- I think we've covered everything on the agenda.
- Shall we summarise the points of agreement?
- I will send the proposal to you for your comments.
- Before we close this meeting, let me just summarise the main items.
- Again, thank you all for taking time out of your busy schedules to be present.

Useful vocabulary

conference call: Telefonkonferenz, Sammelgespräch
audio recording: Tonaufnahme
summary: Zusammenfassung
connected: angeschlossen
bottom line: Fazit, letztes Angebot

Example 2: Telephone negotiating !

A: Well, hello, everyone. My name is Bert, I am the Director at the Amsterdam office and I'm chairing today's meeting. We've organised this conference call to collectively decide by vote on Frankfurt's proposition. I hope you've all had a chance to look at Nasma's report. I suggest we go in the same order as our last meeting and each say what we think, and afterwards we will vote. Wil, what is your opinion on the proposal?
B: Wil speaking. Thank you. Personally, I think the best solution is to simply wait, despite Paul's analyses.
C: André here; I'd like to comment on that. I'm not sure I agree with that, because as time passes the value decreases.
B: Well, in my opinion, that loss is not decreasing proportionately.
C: I really think it would be better to act now, Bert.
A: We've been arguing back and forth for some minutes now, and we're running short on time. However, we'll have to come to a consensus here, so I suggest we put it up for a vote now. Those of you in favour of the proposition please push the star key; all those opposed: please push the pound key. Thank you.
A: Ladies, gentlemen: on the screen I can now see the outcome of the vote, and the proposal has been adopted. It looks like we've run out of time, so I guess we'll have to adjourn our conference call here.

21 Cross-cultural negotiations

This chapter is intended to raise your level of awareness of the many factors to consider when approaching an international negotiation. From experience, we advise you to develop a flexible personal negotiation style which will allow you to accommodate a variety of cultures. Before you make reservations to go to another country, invest some time acquainting yourself with the differences and similarities between you and the people on the other side of the conference table.

21.1 Relation orientation

Before engaging in negotiations, it may be helpful to look at the relevance of the focus of the negotiating partners. People, for instance, can be deal-focussed or relationship-focussed, and such a basic difference in focus can influence any negotiation. Additionally, age, gender, personality, or culture can also play a role. Some societies are more relationship-focussed. This means they prefer to build a relationship with the person, not the company or organisation. Trust is built up and any problems arising later can then be resolved personally. These societies rely less on written agreements, and you may expect lengthy, rapport-building preliminary small talk, before actually negotiating. Below is an overview of countries.

Deal-focussed	Moderately deal-focussed	Relationship-focussed
Germany	France	India
United States	Hungary	China
United Kingdom	Spain	Brazil
Sweden	Portugal	Emirates
Denmark	Italy	Japan
Australia	Hong Kong	Latin America
Switzerland	Singapore	Arab world
Netherlands	Poland	most of Asia
South Africa	Romania	most of Africa

Deal-focussed societies like the United States or Germany concentrate on the contract or written agreement and not so much on the relationship. When problems are encountered they return to the paperwork to clarify. The gap between such approaches is normally narrowed by a combination of relationship and deal-focussed orientation, but where the parties are both strictly adhering to their own approach, any deals reached are likely to unravel later. In the specific country chapters later on in this book, you will learn to deal with such differences in detail. This generally is necessary because contrasting values often cause conflict at the conference table.

21.2 Sociolinguistic influences

Interpreters at the European institutions in Brussels are only too aware of this: translating is also cultural enciphering. A word by word translation hardly represents the original intention of a text, because of the interlaced sociolinguistic influences. Is this of any consequence for negotiators? The answer is, that this is indeed plausible, looking at the examples of British English below.

Well-mannered

In Anglophone cultures, people are taught from childhood to use polite and indirect signals in their communication. And despite the different images that may exist about the British, Americans or say Australians, linguistic research has shown that all Anglo-Saxon cultures put strong emphasis on verbal politeness. German people don't interweave their phrases with the same number of »thank you's« and »please's«, which is imperative for native English speakers. Therefore, just being able to translate German vocabulary into English, simply isn't enough. If the phrases below were translated into German literally, they might even be judged as too submissive:

- I was wondering if you could possibly reduce your initial offer to ...
- Excuse me, I was wondering whether I could copy your report?
- Do you think you could help me with that PowerPoint presentation?

English can be a rather formal language, which reflects its subtle sense of hierarchy. An easy memory aid for trying to be more polite is to simply use longer sentences. The three sample phrases above illustrate such different levels of indirectness also in phrase length.

Unspoken codes

There are various ways to express differences. Many of these are unspoken codes, or subtle distinctions that can be hard to distinguish for foreigners. The point is that in our upbringing we are often taught certain values. Cultural groups, for instance, the Germans, Swiss, Scandinavians or Dutch tend to be quite direct in their communication, and usually express exactly what they mean. Scientific research has shown that the way Germans express their thoughts can be quite to-the-point. The problem is that other cultures may sometimes perceive this to the point as just »blunt«. Native English speakers tend to opt for highly scripted, requesting behaviour. The majority of the requests take the form of:

- Could you,
- Would you,
- Would you mind ~ing ...

Therefore try to be aware that the specific levels of directness appropriate for given situations might differ cross-culturally. And remember that a language like German tends to use more direct-level requests than British English. The table below shows a selection of cultures and their levels of directness in communication. The ranking of the United Kingdom explains the differences described above.

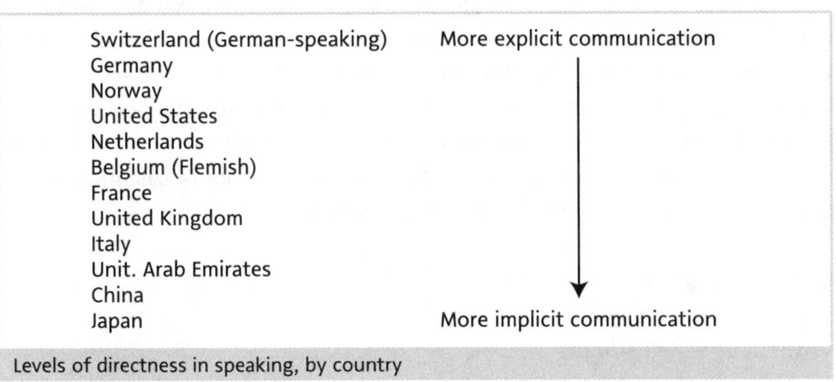

Switzerland (German-speaking)	More explicit communication
Germany	↓
Norway	
United States	
Netherlands	
Belgium (Flemish)	
France	
United Kingdom	
Italy	
Unit. Arab Emirates	
China	
Japan	More implicit communication

Levels of directness in speaking, by country

The table also makes clear why Americans generally use more direct and explicit communition. Indeed, British English can seem vague at times, but there's a very simple reason for that: vagueness is used to maintain politeness or avoid confrontation. The same applies to friendly small talk, humour and understatements, which are normally used to soften the style. Humour comes in many varieties in Britain, and can be used for all sorts of different situations: humour, self-mockery, criticism, paying a compliment, awkward moments, etc.

Non-verbal communication

International differences exist in the way people understand certain information. This may involve elements you don't always think of, like certain gestures you are used to making. A well known example is the OK sign (thumbs-up) and the perfect sign (thumb to forefinger, making a circle) because these can have offensive or insulting meanings in other cultures. The thumbs-up is comparable to raising the middle finger in large areas of Asia Minor, and the circle sign means »zéro« in France, money in Japan and the posterior opening of the alimentary canal in Brazil. Such unexpected differences can therefore cause misunderstandings. Like the typical Greek example of nodding which may be understood as a »Yes« where in fact it means »No«. This is comparable in countries like Bulgaria, parts of Turkey, Iran and, for example, India. When doing business with someone from a different cultural background, it is worth researching this often forgotten element of communication beforehand.

Humour and jokes

Naturally cultural differences are reflected in our way of holding a meeting. In talks we will probably use some of the same strategies we are used to in face-to-face contact to ask or convince someone. The point is of course, that when we use a certain meeting style, this will influence the reaction of attendees at a meeting. This applies for the use of humour and jokes in a meeting. Anglophone negotiators make more and easier use of humour than for example German or Scandinavian speakers. A French or Russian speaker will probably prefer not to make any jokes, as that damages the desired image. Finding the correct type of humour is somewhat tricky, as humour doesn't always travel well. In Asian countries, types of humour like sarcasm, satire and parody aren't always understood or appreciated.

Useful vocabulary

submissive: unterwürfig
self-mockery: Selbstspott
posterior: Hintern
attendee: Anwesende

Using interpreters

It is of the highest importance to prepare interpreters and/or translators beforehand. This is done by means of small pre-talk and sending lists of jargon, key terms, common abbreviations and brand names. When negotiating with an interpreter, try to maintain eye contact with your negotiating counterpart, not with the interpreter. An interesting anecdote of how a senior Russian negotiator obtained an advantage in his negotiations with an American was his use of the interpreter. Despite the fact that the Russian spoke English adequately, he made use of an interpreter for an entirely different reason: while the interpreter was translating, the Russian could study the American's nonverbal expressions without hindrance. And when the American spoke, the Russian had twice the response time, because of the translation time required.

21.3 Negotiating internationally

Globalisation, not to mention the European single market, has been extending its influence on the way we work. As a consequence, we find ourselves having to communicate more and more with professionals from other countries. Recent research shows that international managers spend approximately twenty percent of their time on some sort of negotiation activity. Because negotiating is communicating to a large extent, it seems only logical that there will be local differences.

This book started by explaining many aspects of the English language but language constitutes only about thirty percent of overall communication. For that reason this section will now focus on other communication elements that play an essential role in international negotiating. Unfortunately, most books on international negotiating seem to revolve around the idea that there is one universal way of negotiating. This chapter tries to give you examples of how adapting elements of your usual negotiating tactics to particular cross-cultural differences will substantially improve your negotiation results.

Potential pitfalls

Techniques that work well at home, may fail in another country because the expectations of a negotiation party may simply be very different. The usual focus on win-win or win-lose cannot solve expectations in the fields of:

- Normal bargaining techniques,
- Terms for making convincing arguments,
- Expectations in regard to seniority,
- Ideas about hierarchy or decision-making authority,
- Habits in eye contact, interruption, intonation etc.
- Use of time.

A European study (Elucidate) clearly showed that around forty percent of the international negotiations in a European programme failed because of such cross-cultural conflicts. The problem is that most people who need to negotiate internationally haven't been schooled in this area. Usually only governments or large multinational corporations have specialists in that field. For most companies, negotiations abroad are carried out by those in middle management positions or technical specialists. So probably they will need to improvise, which in terms of risk management, can be problematic.

Different goals

Scientists interviewed negotiating teams from, amongst others, Japan, Brazil and the United States about their expectations for a specific negotiation. The analyses showed that culture does influence the expectation of a negotiation. The Japanese, for instance, were much more focussed on the long-term relations, whilst the Americans were mainly concerned about the short-term deal. The principal goal of the different negotiators also showed significant differences; where the Brazilian chief negotiator was concerned about achieving a respectable negotiation outcome, the Japanese negotiator was mainly focussed on market share, and the American on a short-term high profit. It is fair to say that some knowledge of specific Asian, Latin or western expectations will lead to better results.

Timing differs

What is the right moment to start the negotiating process? Do all cultures follow the same timing pattern as here in Germany? The answer is: absolutely not. People in neighbouring countries like France or Poland have different ideas on this. What, for instance, would be the right moment, to make an offer in France during a business lunch (dînatoire)? The answer is: probably close to the time dessert is being served. It is often felt that starting business any earlier could be too blunt. The overview below shows us which selected trade cultures open talks directly, and which cultures use more small talk, because they consider it less well-mannered starting straight away:

Country	Early	Half	Late
Germany	✓		
China			✓
Emirates			✓
Finland	✓		
France			✓
Italy			✓
Japan			✓
Netherlands	✓		
Poland		✓	
Portugal			✓
Spain			✓
Sweden	✓		
United Kingdom		✓	
United States	✓		

21.4 Local negotiation techniques

Scientists have studied negotiation techniques in Japan, Brazil and the United States in combined research of universities from the same countries. They interviewed various participants and analysed many hours of video recordings. The results showed some remarkable differences.

Behaviour tactics	Japan	US	Brazil
Silent Periods (number of silent periods longer than 10 seconds, per 30 minutes)	5.5	2.5	0
Overlaps (number per 10 min)	12.6	10.3	28.6
Facial Looking (minutes of gazing per 10 min)	1.3	3.3	5.2
Touching (per 30 min/not including handshaking)	0	0	4.7

The Japanese, for instance, can maintain several seconds of total silence. When a negotiator isn't aware of this, he or she may be influenced by a silence that means something other than expected. In Mediterranean cultures on the contrary, people can overlap in their conversation, meaning that people talk simultaneously. The same applies for interrupting people. This is considered rude in north-western European cultures, but in more southern cultures it is quite normal, and as such, thought of as a form of active listening. The table above also shows us that Brazilian negotiators touch their counterparts much more. The so-called comfort zone between people in Brazil is also much smaller than, for instance, in Germany. Latin people feel, especially when talking about confidential matters, that they want to stand closer to each other. Northern people, however, usually feel uncomfortable and try to create some space, often by stepping back a bit. It can sometimes lead to amusing movement patterns of participants at international summits.

Compromises

Making a compromise is considered positive in certain cultures and in other cultures not. For instance, the Dutch, Belgians or Swedes have learned to compromise from a young age on, whereas Russians, Spaniards or French have developed skills in another direction. A Spaniard, for example, generally believes that a compromise might damage his honour (pundonor). Knowledge of such cultural differences can help in preparing appropriately, and should assist in negotiating more successfully.

Look me in the eyes

As the table above shows, the time spent looking directly into each other eyes makes up only thirteen percent of the time in a country like Japan. Indeed in Asian cultures direct eye contact is generally seen as assertive or emphatic. Many people in the West wouldn't trust someone who avoids eye contact of one form or another, and people in the Middle-East use much stronger eye contact in negotiations than Europeans.

Listening habits

The way you prepare for a negotiation should take into account which opponent you are addressing. Research shows that the way specific cultures talk and listen differs to a great extent. An example: German, Swedish, Dutch and Finnish business cultures put great emphasis on factual information and they know how to listen well. Spaniards, French or Italians, according to their expectations, prefer imaginative topics. They prefer using eloquent phrases and knowing how to present themselves. They would much rather hear things presented with flair or grandeur than dry facts or technical details. The same applies for the listening span, which can be relatively short.

21.5 Strategic negotiating framework

Stephen Weiss examined cultural aspects of the international negotiating process. He concluded after studying many negotiation cases, that for successful outcomes it mattered that negotiators reflect on their own cultural negotiation script, as well as on that of the other parties involved. By choosing strategies accordingly better results were achieved. Depending on how much knowledge each party had of the culture of the other party, a choice for a negotiation sequence or script could be made. Depending on the scale of such awareness one of four possible scripts can be elected for a maximal international negotiating outcome.

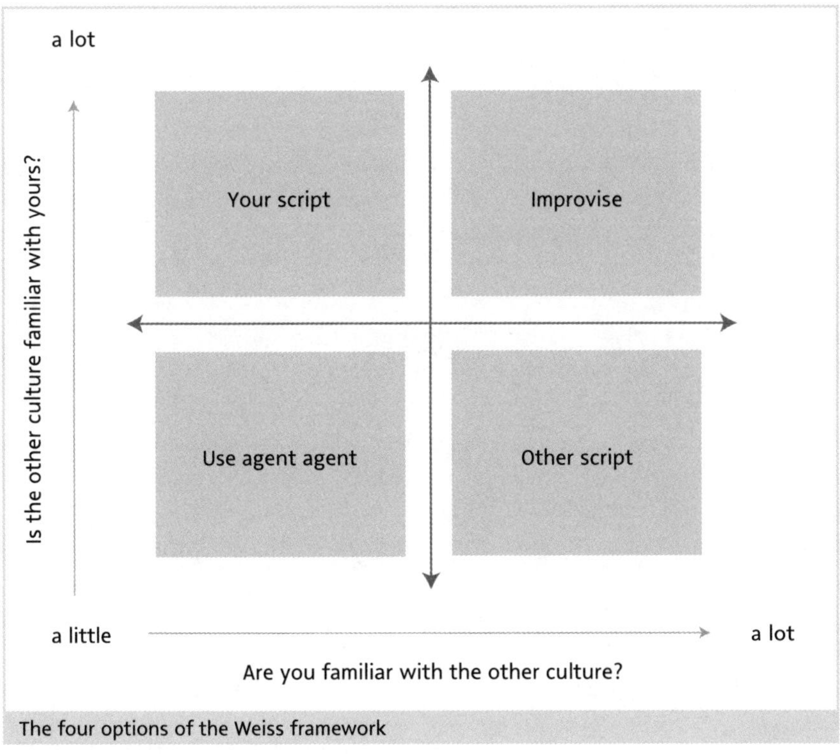

The four options of the Weiss framework

22 Country-specific negotiating

National culture is one of the factors that influence behaviour at the negotiation table, just like personality, gender or organisational culture. But recent scientific research has shown that there are considerable differences in approach, and perhaps that explains why forty percent of international negotiations seem to fail. In this chapter you will gain insight for selected trade cultures into the following aspects of negotiating:

- Country typical meeting behaviour,
- Relevant local value systems.

22.1 Introduction

This part of the book is dedicated to specific communication habits and local value differences per country. And as the world seems to be getting smaller and smaller, the chances of negotiating with partners from less familiar cultures are augmenting strongly. Such negotiations often take place in English, but because language only counts for some thirty percent of communication, it is helpful to have some insight into the other elements that influence the way people communicate in a particular country. Since the eighties of the last century more and more research has been published on comparing national negotiation styles. Trainers, consultants, as well as Chambers of Commerce offer all sorts of seminars to help businessmen prepare for negotiating with foreign opponents. It seems there is a practical need. And since negotiating relies so strongly on communication, a fair amount of it will relate to cross-cultural awareness.

With the use of internet technology nowadays there are some very useful tools available in order to compare the average values or rankings of countries. Partly based on world wide surveys, partly based on statistics, such information may help to predict behaviour. Even as a generalisation (as no human being can be put on a list), this predictability is helpful for developing a negotiations strategy for a foreign country. The next pages introduce such country-specific behaviour for the (weighted) main trade partners of Germany.

22.2 China

Despite the fact that the word »foreigner« translates as »yang guizi« (foreign devil) in Mandarin, China is Germany's eighth export market, and its second biggest import partner (after the Netherlands). Looking at the economic forecasts, the export of goods will increase substantially in all likelihood. When dealing with Chinese take the following aspects into account.

Meeting

Preliminary meetings mainly serve to get to know each other better, business therefore isn't really discussed. The Chinese speak less, and use longer periods of total silence (in China silence is also eloquence). The Chinese language also knows many different wording possibilities depending on the status of someone. This calls for skilled interpreters or translators. Individual expression of thought is less common in China, as it may harm consensus. Creative brainstorming during a meeting will not produce many results; it will be more effective to adjourn, allowing your Chinese opponent room for thinking. There are usually (hard working) note takers present at meetings to produce detailed minutes. Chinese feel less ruled by their agenda.

Negotiations

It is interesting to see how Chinese make deals, as they tend to think much more about the consequences of a deal for their relationship networks. Preparation therefore usually includes collecting data on people and the involved relations (guanxi). Important business decisions tend to take a long time, due to the desire for consensus. Foreign parties negotiating mainly need patience, and that's something the Chinese have plenty of. Government approval is indispensable (national, local, as well as provincial) for any major project. This influences both planning as well as profits sometimes. Contracts are considered less binding than in western trade cultures.

Relevant values

Confucian values still influence the Chinese society to a large extent. As common in collectivist cultures, the stronger party is generally expected to accommodate the weaker party. This underlying value also applies to negotiations sometimes. Protocol and hierarchy are omnipotent. Chinese schools, for instance, are used to very strict discipline. Corruption is not uncommon. Statistics show that Germans are three times more individual than the Chinese, and only half as hierarchically orientated. For a complete overview of all variable scores and rankings, please refer to the tables at the end of this chapter (»Countries: Statistics and value facts«). Some influential values or patterns are described below:

- It's not what you know, but who you know (»guanxi«),
- Seniority and connections cancel out achievements,
- Behave harmoniously and show respect to authority,
- It's impolite to say »no« or openly criticise (loss of face),
- Only do so in private with close ones (»naixin«),
- Do not directly display negative emotions.

22.3 Czech Republic

The Czech Republic represents the westernmost presence of Slavic culture in Europe. It is a stable environment for foreign trade and business investment opportunities, given the fact that nowadays foreign-owned companies account for seventy percent of its exports. The chances of having to negotiate with a Czech opponent are considerable, as thirty percent of all foreign trade is conducted with Germany. When dealing with Czech counterparts take the following aspects into account.

Meeting

As is the case in German business life, Czechs prefer to plan meetings in advance. Points on an agenda are to be followed; people are good listeners and do not really interrupt each other. During meetings, the Czech shows calmness and self-control. A display of emotions is less likely than in neighbouring countries such as Poland or Hungary. As a result the (measured) tone of voice is usually softer. Discussions proceed in an orderly fashion and decision-making is usually methodical.

Negotiations

Just like Germans, the Czechs are task-oriented, meaning that very little time is spent on small talk at the beginning of negotiations. Besides, the Czechs are known for a very direct communication style, again like in Germany. The only difference is that they can be less straightforward when saying »No«, and might feel less comfortable giving negative answers. Argumentation is best done with empirical evidence and facts supporting the proposals. Step-by-step consensus seeking techniques give better results than aggressive negotiation tactics. Czechs aren't very fond of arguing or haggling; therefore it is advisable to keep the difference between the starting price and the final price within a logical margin. Business meals play less of a role, as Czechs separate business and social circles.

Relevant values

The Czechs have a tradition of avoiding conflict and confrontation, as the Czech national history proves. Take, for instance, the »Velvet Revolution« of 1989 which took place without violence as did the »Velvet Divorce« of 1993, when Czechoslovakia peacefully split into the Czech and the Slovak Republic. The values scores aren't very different, except for the hierarchical acceptance, which is almost double that of the German score. Other significant differences are the amount of bureaucracy and the relatively higher corruption perception index. For a complete overview of all variable scores and rankings, please refer to the tables at the end of this chapter (»Countries: Statistics and value facts«).

! **Important**

Command of languages in the Czech Republic:
German: 28%, English: 24%, Russian: 20%.

Useful vocabulary
task-oriented: aufgabenorientiert
straightforward: geradeheraus, unkompliziert
haggle: herunterhandeln, feilschen

22.4 France

France has been Germany's number one export partner for many years now, and those who have dealt professionally with »la douce France« know how different business communication can be. Some relevant differences are described below.

Meeting
The French are trained in both debating skills as well as analysis from an early age. It is generally considered important to prove a point by way of logical argumentation. The simple notion that the facts are different is not always accepted, if not backed up by lengthy rhetorical argumentation. Meetings are not always grounds for discussion, but are often used to inform about what has been decided. Business lunches may last two hours. Don't let business be a topic of conversation too early, and therefore prepare something else to talk about.

Negotiations
The French can be persistent at times when a strategy has been chosen. Compromise isn't considered a very positive thing by everyone. A direct »No« is (unlike in Germany) generally avoided. The French prefer to say something like: »Oui mais« (yes, but), »Oui-non, nous verrons« (yes-no, we'll see) or even »Si vous voulez« (if you like). It is a mistake not to understand such remarks as a »Non«. Whatever is being proposed or agreed upon during negotiations, will only be a sure thing when approved afterwards by the PDG (Président Directeur Général).

Relevant values
Most value scores are comparable to the German ones. However, hierarchical acceptance is twice as strong as in Germany, as is the corruption perception. For a complete overview of all variable scores and rankings, please refer to the tables at the end of this chapter (»Countries: Statistics and value facts«).

- In France some forty percent of higher functions are occupied by women,
- Using beautiful language combined with semi-philosophical logic seems to be a goal in itself,
- Etiquette is a French word, and knowledge thereof may give some self-assurance,
- Being refined or special is an important quality that is reflected in the choice of negotiation venue, restaurant, wines, as well as clothing.

Important !

Command of languages in France:
English: 36%, Spanish: 13%, German: 8%.

Useful vocabulary
obstinately: stur
self-assurance: Selbstbewusstsein
venue: Handlungsort
command of languages: Sprachkenntnisse

22.5 India

The second most populated country of the world is at present Germany's twenty-fifth trade partner. In the near future, however, India will play a more prominent role in global economics. First of all the population is growing faster than China's and the GDP is also increasing rapidly. Today India has about three hundred million middle class consumers, but the country adds a North Rhine-Westphalia every single year (...).

Meeting
Indians have a preference for eloquent respectful speakers. Too many dry facts don't work well. Meetings will contain a semi-euphoric atmosphere with sympathetic verbose talks in Victorian English. Despite the fact that certain Hindi words have become part of (financial) Indian English, it is advisable to study the most common of these beforehand. Many meetings will not follow an agenda, will have plenty of interruptions, and may possibly go over time. Therefore, don't make too many appointments on one day, and take the dense traffic into consideration as well.

Negotiations
Negotiations normally start in a sympathetic atmosphere, whilst the negotiation part can be serious with long haggling. Expect negotiations to be long,

but usually changes will be proposed in a polite way to find agreement. The ease of doing business ranking, as well as legal contract enforcing possibilities is low compared to European standards. Insert mediation and arbitration clauses in all legal contracts. Be careful that Indians cannot directly say »No«, and will therefore normally revert to expressions like: »maybe«, »we'll try« and so forth. Vice versa, Germans should be careful with saying »No« too directly. Decisions need to be ratified by the higher levels; therefore check already during negotiations which parts have been firmly agreed and which not. Socialising can be a pleasant part of business in India, and Indian hospitality has a lot to offer visitors. On the other hand, I know that Indians visiting North-West Europe can be surprised or disappointed with the treatment given.

Relevant values

India is a contact instead of a contract culture, where relationships are more important than a deal at hand. Companies are strictly hierarchical and empowerment is hardly seen, although a younger generation is getting a taste of it at universities now.

- Getting frustrated will neither help, nor win friends,
- Value is placed on empathy and consensus,
- Dinners start late and last long.

Useful vocabulary

verbosity: Wortschwall
dense: zusammengedrängt
mediation: Vermittlung
revert to: zurückgreifen auf

22.6 Italy

Italian culture has had a demonstrable influence: the Roman Empire, the Renaissance or the weight of the Vatican. As a country, Germany is Italy's main trading partner, both in import and export. Most of the Italian businesses are SMEs (KMU), almost three-quarters of the Italian economy in fact. Moreover, quite a few of these are family run businesses. It is plausible that this might affect negotiations in some way.

Meeting

Initial meetings in Italy are usually intended to get people acquainted, not to do straight business. Meetings themselves often seem noisy and unstructured compared to German standards. There is a considerably longer time frame reserved for small talk, and mobile phone calls are often acceptable during a meeting. Improvisation is valued, just as interruptions, and indeed many Italians think that following the agenda strictly could interfere with the quality of a discussion. Italians also prefer to present an argument in an articulate way, partly because »feeling« is recognised as a factor in decision making.

Important !

Command of languages in Italy:
English: 29%, French: 14%.

Negotiations

Negotiating in Italy can sometimes be a lengthy process, where patience works much better than irritation, because business and social life can be so intermingled. Personal alliances are often influential in Italy. It's not »what« you know, but »who« you know, and people are also judged on their ability to cultivate relationships. Smaller companies tend to have a rather hierarchical structure, often with an autocratic style of management. In Germany, the facts are much more separated from the person; Italians tend to take direct rejections more personally. They also may feel that Germans are overly concerned with facts and procedures and like to explore a contextual background. Perhaps they feel that the over-pragmatic Northerners lack a sense of deeper thinking.

Relevant values

Jokes and private remarks are exchanged much more than in Germany, and are judged as functional in a business environment. Italians have difficulty saying »No« directly.

- Successful business relations invest in socialising,
- Pay attention to dress and style, as often someone is judged on that,
- »La bella figura« refers to more than just fashion; charm, formal elegance, tact and confidence also play an important role in Italy,
- Italian contracts can be written in a labyrinthine way and contain complicated terminology,

Useful vocabulary

SME (small and medium enterprises, USA: SMB): KMU (kleine und mittlere Unternehmen)
interfere with: beeinträchtigen

22.7 Japan

Although its economy has stagnated recently, Japan is still one of the world's richest societies – with one and a half times as many inhabitants as Germany, and Greater Tokyo as the largest metropolitan area in the world, with over 30 million residents.

Meeting

Initial meetings in Japan are intended to get people acquainted, and reinforce a consensus that may already have been established. They do not serve to do straight business. The atmosphere in Japanese meetings tends to be highly formal (in contrast to the business entertaining afterwards). Japanese negotiators generally like to be well informed about the focus of a meeting and who will be attending, so they can prepare a well-matched team. Be clear about the status of the members in the organisation (also on business cards). Some communication distinctions influence Japanese business meetings compared to elsewhere. This primarily has to do with:

- Difficulties due to English language abilities,
- The particular importance of inexplicit and polite conversational style, (never interrupt, apologize non-stop),
- The long silences in between phrases.

Negotiations

Negotiating in Japan can be a lengthy process, where patience is a necessary commodity. This is because teams never make decisions at the meeting. The main reason is that a consensus has to be reached within the own company departments, as well as with other existing relationships. Japanese negotiation teams give the least information compared to other cultures, whereas German negotiation teams score highest. On the other hand, the Japanese are willing to make the most concessions, while the Germans are the toughest negotiators. In Japan, the customer and supplier relationship shows a very different power balance than is customary in Germany, where the customer does not play as strong a role. The Japanese value long-term relationships.

Relevant values

Japanese businesses prefer to first establish the right relationships before business can be conducted. After this, people work in a quite task-oriented manner and with self-effacing dedication. The Japanese expect people to show self-knowledge of their position and behave accordingly; therefore, what is not said can also be very important.

- The Japanese tend to be inconceivably conscious of detail,
- »Saving face« is essential in interpersonal contact,

- Japan's corruption index is comparable to Germany's,
- The Japanese have one of the highest scores on status.

Useful vocabulary
commodity: Handelsartikel
self-effacing: zurückhaltend
inconceivably: unfassbar

22.8 Netherlands

This small neighbouring country has the highest density in Europe (one fifth of the German population, living on one tenth of its area). And it may come as a surprise that the Netherlands have become Germany's number one trade partner. .On the other hand, the Dutch focus has been on Germany for many years, with more than two-thirds of its population speaking (some) German.

Meeting
Dutch meetings are pragmatic and quickly focus on results and responsibilities with clear action plans. During meetings, everybody may contribute and voice an opinion, whether it is positive or negative. The goal of meetings is consensus-building and planning. The Dutch are used to freedom and assertiveness starting from a young age and they communicate accordingly. They are quicker on first-name terms and seem less driven by protocol. The Dutch value experiment, and don't mind making tentative suggestions during meetings.

Important !

Command of languages in the Netherlands:
English: 87%, German: 70%, French: 29%, Spanish: 11%.

Negotiations
Negotiators tend to get right down to business, with little time for small talk or getting acquainted. Dutch can be direct in asking what they are looking for. Despite well-defined divisions of tasks, the Dutch are used to speaking up openly in negotiations. And although time efficiency is usually a leitmotif, the decision-making process may take time because of the need for in-company consensus.

Relevant values
The Dutch society is characterized by open-mindedness and tolerance. It is also remarkably egalitarian, with flat and transparent management structures. The biggest value differences between the Netherlands and Germany is

the lower Dutch score on achievement orientation, and the stronger position of women in society.

- Dutch can be more pragmatic and as such, deviate from fixed procedures,
- To discuss business details during lunch or dinner is quite normal,
- Socialising mainly happens after a good working relationship has been established between parties,
- Too open displays of wealth are generally distrusted, partly due to their (mainly) Calvinistic background,
- Dutch are allowed to make jokes, while being serious.

Useful vocabulary
density: Dichte
assertiveness: Durchsetzungsfähigkeit
accordingly: dementsprechend
division of tasks: Aufgabenverteilung
deviate from: abweichen von

22.9 Poland

Poland constitutes the largest market in Central Europe; from the Polish perspective Germany is the largest trade partner.

Meeting
Meetings in Poland start and finish relatively on time and few interruptions occur. Poles do not always prepare for meetings, since they also have a social function. Poles prefer a face-to-face meeting over an e-mail. This proves that despite the fact every culture uses the same means of communication, the difference often occurs in how and when the media are deployed. Initial meetings in Poland, for instance, are often just opportunities for establishing relationships, not making business decisions. Socialising after work is very common and a necessary aspect of gaining trust. Meetings can start earlier, due to the Polish daily schedule, which starts and finishes earlier.

! **Important**
Command of languages in Poland:
English: 29%, Russian: 26%, German: 19%.

Negotiations
The fact that the Poles use the word »rozmowy« (conversation) more than the word »negocjacje« (negotiation), indicates the importance of enough

warming-up time in developing business relationships. In German business life, people are used to strict planning, detailed discussions and a separation between their private and professional lives – three things that are quite different when doing business in Poland. Poles value improvising skills more; therefore general task descriptions or milestones have proven to be more acceptable. In addition, negotiations may take more time; therefore only the patient managers manage in Poland.

Relevant values

Generally speaking, Polish business culture has been characterised as one with a hands-on mentality mixed with emotional decision-making. Foreign managers initially seem unaware of the patience and understanding required for the local differences. If we look at the style of communication, Poles tend to express themselves in a formal but more indirect way than Germans, and prefer expressive capacity and anecdotes or metaphors over literal messages. On the other hand, people can ask explicitly for information or when making requests. But generally they don't like to say »No« (»nie«) directly, and likewise, they also don't like to be told »No«.

- Leadership uses hierarchy to a large extent,
- The Catholic religion is a powerful value in Poland,
- The level and influence of bureaucracy are still apparent, although not always transparent.

Useful vocabulary

constitute: darstellen
deploy: einsetzen
hands-on: praktisch
apparent: wahrnehmbar

22.10 Russia

Russia is the world's largest country in size, and about fifty times as big as Germany. The Russian economy is connecting more and more with the European Union and hence the number of professional contacts is also increasing. Visiting negotiators find that the Russian business culture has its own characteristics, as described below:

Meeting

Russians tend to care less for punctuality, as meetings do not only start later, but also run longer than anticipated. Interruptions and conversations on the side are frequent, and the agenda is not always adhered to. Russians are generally well educated and like ornamental metaphors or story-telling in business. Therefore an exposé full of facts will not challenge their minds. Meetings in Russia are not always result-focused, while much time may be devoted to discussing and understanding a problem. This may challenge the minds of German managers. In Russia, meetings might end with the signing of a protocol, which is simply a report of what was said but has no legal implication.

Negotiations

As in many countries, a senior negotiation team will receive more respect, regardless of the decision-making authority. Russians in general negotiate to win, not to find a consensus. It is wise to slot in enough room for negotiations or trade offs. Just as in chess games, negotiators will think several moves ahead. Vodka toasting is a symbolic element in Russian business entertainment, and may happen directly after an agreement. A contract is often considered less binding than it is here, and in many companies unanimity is prescribed for essential choices.

Relevant values

Russians have a strong sense of national pride for »Motherland« (родин, rodina). Unlike in Germany, planning is not seen as omnipotent, and work and private life will be quite mixed. Just as in Asia, the so-called »loss of face« is an important value. It is important to use the word »No« carefully, or give direct criticism or complaints. Business can still be rather bureaucratic, and to obtain faster results in Russia, the use of personal networks (блат, blat) can be indispensable.

- Power is very centralised and often concentrated,
- Status is an important aspect of Russian society,
- A person who only concentrates on business, might come across as less trustful,
- Instead of dry facts, intellectual and philosophical debate is higher valued,
- The working day may start quite early.

Useful vocabulary

to adhere: erfüllen, einhalten
trade off: Austausch
indispensable: unentbehrlich
exposé: Bericht
omnipotent: allmächtig

22.11 Spain

The country Spain is about one and a half times the size of Germany, and more than half of the German population. Business in Spain is usually acquired through personal relationships; therefore business entertaining is an essential process of any professional contact. The substantial differences in conducting meetings and negotiations are explained below:

Meeting
Initial meetings in Spain are usually just meant for becoming acquainted, not to do straight business. Meetings are different compared to German standards, as they often don't follow an agenda order, and people frequently interrupt each other (which isn't judged negatively). Agendas play a lesser role, because meetings serve more to exchange ideas and to invest in the personal relationships, than actually reaching decisions. Meetings also often run over time. On the other hand, a Spaniard doesn't say that »time flies«, but that »time walks«. And indeed the word »mañana« can refer to a moment in time, not necessarily being tomorrow. The siesta interruption was abolished by the Spanish government in 2005, although certain companies might have a separate morning or (late) afternoon staff.

Negotiations
Hierarchical acceptance in Spain is double that of what it is in Germany, and indeed Spanish leadership is characterised by both its charismatic and autocratic aspects. In order to successfully negotiate with Spaniards, it is also essential to realise that the need for facts and planning isn't supported in the same way in Spain. Spanish negotiations often follow the win-lose concept. Therefore preparations should focus on negotiable points and parrying bargaining. Spaniards are also articulate and meandering speakers, connecting to the larger picture, perhaps even philosophical concepts. As they are relationship and not task-orientated, a fair amount of socialising will probably take place after negotiation rounds.

Relevant values

- Face-to-face contact is preferred over e-mail or phone.
- Wait long enough before talking business at business lunches, or let your Spanish counterpart lead.
- To openly damage someone's pride is a cardinal sin.
- There are very strong regional sentiments, with their own language and identity.
- Most people speak »castellano« as the term »español« usually denotes federal things.
- Spain has an enormous number of public holidays.

Useful vocabulary
abolish: abschaffen
parry: parieren, abwehren
meandering: mäandern, abschweifen

22.12 United Kingdom

The United Kingdom comprises Great Britain and Northern Ireland. And although described as incurably insular and different, Britons are nevertheless Germany's fifth trading partner. Those who conduct meetings and negotiations with British people often describe them as different from those on the continent. The following paragraph takes a closer look:

Meeting
Meetings in Britain typically begin and end with small talk. Meetings will be structured, but perhaps less so than one is used to at home. During the course of the meeting it is acceptable for people to take calls, or join later (or walk out earlier). In addition, people will not always have spent a lot of time preparing for a meeting. Discussion is an essential part of meetings, as is debating, but the British don't appreciate open verbal conflict. Their communication style uses politeness as a courtesy. Not only do British managers use their sense of humour in business meetings, they also have a great many varieties: irony, sarcasm, self-mockery etc., and these are generally called for with professional purposes in mind.

Negotiations
When preparing negotiations, it is useful to know that British managers prefer target-driven proposals that yield short-term benefits. A non-disclosure agreement is quite common, and shouldn't really be seen as distrust. Negotiators are often empowered to make decisions and get things done; most British firms nowadays have an increasingly flat hierarchical structure. After the initial meeting, first names are quickly used; academic credentials don't play much of role. After-work drinking is quite a common thing. British negotiators can be rather vague when declining an idea or proposal. This indirectness is referred to as »coded speech«. An example is when someone doesn't agree and she/he will say: »hmm, that's an interesting idea«. It might help to study facial expressions closely or the tone of voice for that matter. Command of foreign languages is limited in the populated south part of Britain.

Relevant values

British managers look for a leadership style in which they will seem reasonable and righteous. Although British value scores hardly differ from German ones, British culture has a higher degree of individualism. In fact, it is the only language which capitalises the word »I«.

- One should never make a scene,
- The British typically have a sense of fair play,
- The class system is still evident in Britain.

Useful vocabulary

insular: insular, inselartig
take a call: einen Anruf entgegennehmen
self-mockery: Selbstspott
decline: ablehnen
tone of voice: Tonfall
righteous: rechtschaffen

22.13 United States

Knowing the United States through popular culture (for instance cinema), isn't the same as doing business with Americans. The following paragraphs inform you in brief about the cultural business norms of the United States of America, a country spanning six times zones.

Meeting

Meetings generally are seen as a platform to make decisions and drive action by the end of the meeting. Most Americans tend to have a preference for incomplex empirical information, adhering to the KISS axiom (keep it short and simple). They are quick to use first names or even nicknames, and do not care for academic credentials. As most professionals are very busy, meetings can take place over business breakfasts or after work. The focus on time management is very strong in the United States.

Negotiations

Negotiating in the States is often characterised by so-called »hard sell«. American negotiators prefer to secure a favourable deal or short-term commercial results. They do so in an informal way, using a direct assertive communication style and logical reasoning for the most part. Self-promotion is judged positively, because a confident strong pitch creates trust. Americans negotiators expect decisions to be taken during a negotiation, and are usually empowered to agree, without approval of senior leadership. In wanting to secure an agreement, some negotiators may »take no for an answer«. Americans generally prefer target-driven proposals that yield short-term benefits. Convincing arguments will focus primarily on speed, cost and efficiency. Although information is shared openly between partners, information may be released in negotiations only after signing a non-disclosure agreement. Contracts and legal documents tend to be very lengthy in the US.

Relevant values

The cultural value scores aren't that different from the German ones, expect that Americans are highly individualistic; in fact English is the only language which capitalises the word »I«.

- America is a can-do, achievement-focused culture,
- Americans might prepare less than Germans in advance,
- There is a high tolerance for failure in the US.

Useful vocabulary

axiom: Grundsatz
credential: Diplom
pitch: Verkaufsmasche
non-disclosure agreement: Vertraulichkeitsvereinbarung

22.14 Cross-cultural differences

The table on the following pages quantifies the relevant cross-cultural differences in the field of international negotiating for the selected countries. The following seven indicators have been used:

1. Population/area (compared to Germany),
2. German trade rank (weighted export/import),
3. Ease of doing business,
4. Enforcing contracts,
5. Corruption perception,
6. Achievement orientation,
7. Hierarchical orientation,
8. Individualism.

Figures under number one show how many times a country and its population is smaller or bigger than Germany. The values of the numbers two to four are ranking indicators, of which the »Ease of doing business« and the »Enforcing contracts« come from the yearly country ranking of the World Bank (183 countries in total). The first indicator is based on the study of laws and regulations which influence doing business in a country. Thus, if a country has a low ranking, it is logical to expect influences on the time line of a negotiation, and a delay doesn't necessarily have to mean tactics of the negotiating partner. The indicator »Corruption perception« is a yearly index of transparency.org (180 countries). These three mentioned rankings are weighted in order to offer you a more long-term view. Where possible or applicable, future forecasts of the Economist Intelligence Unit have been used for rounding off an amount to the nearest decimal.

The indicator numbers six to eight are at a country level and unchangeable. The three indices used are: »Achievement orientation«, »Hierarchical acceptance«, and »Individualism«. They refer to the country scores of the cultural dimensions research by Geert Hofstede. In his (original) study, scores from 1 to 100 were possible. For example, the German 35 score for hierarchical acceptance (originally called: PDI or power distance index) is much lower than the Chinese score of 80, but more than double the Austrian score of 14. We can also see that the average German score is much higher than the Chinese score as far as individualism is concerned. Such statistics may help to predict behaviour and think of a strategy when preparing for negotiations. For example, in the case of China, the power of a decision of a negotiating partner may be limited by hierarchical approval, whereas a German export manager may have more possibilities to make decisions on the spot. This means that negotiations might take longer, which in turn has an influence on the planning of a business trip and the number of possible appointments.

Another interesting aspect is that research shows that in countries with a high hierarchical acceptance score, the value of written contracts is considered lower than the opinion of the highest management.

In short: although this table presents a great many combinations of dry numbers, it does in fact offer the reader a chance to forecast negotiating positions driven by culture.

Countries: Statistics and value facts

Country	Population/ area (in times Germany)	German trade rank export/ import	Ease of doing business	Enforcing contracts
Germany			25	7
China	16,3 27	8 2	89	18

Country	Population/ area (in times Germany)	German trade rank export/ import	Ease of doing business	Enforcing contracts
Czech Republic	0,1 0,2	12 10	74	82
France	0,8 0,8	1 1	31	6
India	14,4 9	12 10	133	182
Italy	0,7 0,8	5 5	78	156
Japan	1,6 1,1	18 14	15	20
Netherlands	0,2 0,2	2 2	30	30
Poland	0,5 0,5	10 10	72	75
Russia	1,7 1,7	13 13	120	19
Spain	0,6 0,6	11 11	62	52
UK	0,8 0,7	4 6	5	23
USA	3,8 27	3 4	4	8

Country	Corruption perception	Achievement orientation	Hierarchy orientation	Individualism
Germany	14	66	35	67
China	80	66	80	20
Czech Republic	52	57	57	58
France	24	43	68	71
India	84	56	77	48
Italy	63	70	50	76
Japan	17	95	54	46
Netherlands	6	14	38	80

Country	Corruption perception	Achievement orientation	Hierarchy orientation	Individualism
Poland	51	64	68	60
Russia	149	36	93	39
Spain	33	42	57	51
UK	18	66	35	89
USA	19	62	40	91

22.15 Practical reference

22.15.1 Financial numbers

When writing numbers or amounts of money, the English language observes a few other conventions compared to German. The most important difference probably is the reverse use of commas and full stops (periods). Australian texts may use a space instead of a comma, and Swiss texts often use an apostrophe to separate the thousands. The position of the currency can be placed before or behind the amount, depending on the local linguistic convention. There is no space between the British pound sign and the amount in English, unlike the German habit.

Important !

Is this important in negotiations? An answer to that question may be best given by the mistake of aeronautics company Lockheed Martin. as they lost seventy million dollars, when they agreed to an equation for adjusting the sales price for changes to the inflation rate. The reason: because of the difference between periods and commas...

Decimal points

The examples below show you how to pronounce numbers with decimal points in them, as well as amounts of money and temperatures:

Number	Pronouncing
3.50	three point five oh
45	forty-five
550	five hundred and fifty

Number	Pronouncing
6 500	six thousand five hundred, or: sixty-five hundred
75 000	seventy-five thousand
850 000	eight hundred and fifty thousand
9 500 000	nine million five hundred thousand, or: nine and a half million
-5.9	minus five point nine
-20 000	minus twenty thousand
10 °C	ten degrees Celsius, or: ten degrees centigrade

Indicating larger numbers

For describing larger amounts or numbers in the English language you may come across the following abbreviations:

- thousand: K
- million: m
- billion (in German: Milliarde): bn
- trillion (in German: Billion): T
- quadrillon (in German: Billiarde)

A billion is a thousand million, a trillion a thousand billion, a quadrillion a thousand trillion. Monetary units, such as dollars or pound sterling, are often abbreviated with their own currency symbols. Note that in the United Kingdom a middle dot is often used as the decimal point on price stickers (e.g.: £ 6·95). Besides the currency symbols, you may also wish to use the international monetary abbreviations as stated in the list of currencies from the International Organization for Standardization (ISO 4217: Currency names and code elements). Then the word »euro« is written in small letters in English. EU legislation prescribes the use of the words »euro« and »cent« in both singular and plural. But in the rest of the English-speaking world it is common to use the natural plural in -s. Most financial media in the UK also prefer »euros« and »cents« in the plural form.

Fractions

Generally fractions are used for rough figures (e.g.: a hectare is 21/2acres) and decimals for more exact figures (although in reality fractions are more precise than decimals). Do note the hyphen between the elements of a fraction, for instance: three-quarters. Further, the preposition »of« is used when describing fractions. For example: two-fifths of our clients. Just less than two-thirds of our customers.

Symbol	Word
1/2	a half, half, one-half
1/3	a third, one-third
2/3	two-thirds
1/4	one-quarter
3/4	three-quarters three fourths (us)
1/5	one-fifth
5/6	five-sixths
1/8	one-eighth
3/8	three-eighths
10/10	ten out of ten

22.15.2 Language transfer

Language transfer means that a speaker applies elements from his native language to a foreign language. This could be grammar influences, but the most common form of language transfer is known as »false friends«. It is interesting that psychologists have reported that when people speak English as a second language, the tendency is to use the English word but retain its primary language's meaning for that word. The table below contains pairs of words that look similar, but differ in meaning in two languages. Because false friends are a problem for second-language speakers, the table below compiles both German-English as well as English-German false friends.

English	German	False friend	Translation
to get	bekommen	to become	werden
management	Direktion	direction	Richtung
competition	Konkurrenz	concurrence	Übereinkunft
draft, plan	Konzept	concept	Begriff, Idee
corporate	Konzern	concern	Belang
CEO	Manager	manager	Filialleiter
brand	Marke	mark	Note

English	German	False friend	Translation
fair; mass	Messe	mess	Unordnung
personnel	Personal	personal	persönlich
entrepreneur	Unternehmer	undertaker	Leichenbestatter
if	wenn	when	wann

Identical words too abstract

The English language knows some words that are identical to German words. The problem is that we tend to use such words a lot, as they are frequently used in German, but that they can sound rather abstract in English. To avoid such stylistic pitfalls it is sometimes better to use other alternatives. The table below gives an overview.

English	German	Alternative
initiative	Initiative	proposal
integral	integral	entire, total
optimal	optimal	ideal
philosophy	Philosophie	approach
realise	realisieren	achieve
vision	Vision	view
perspective	Perspektive	expectation

22.15.3 British and American English

There are some differences in spelling or vocabulary, although not many words cause misunderstandings. A relevant example for negotiations is the expression »to table a motion«. Which in the UK means: »to place it on the agenda«, while in the US this means exactly the opposite: »to remove it from consideration«. No idea how this is dealt with in bilateral negotiations... George Bernard Shaw once wrote: »Britain and America are two countries divided by a common language«. That probably sounds a bit tall; nevertheless, really different words are sometimes used. Some of the more common ones are mentioned in the table below (listed by German translation, for convenience):

British English	American English	German
at cost price	at cost	Selbstkostenpreis
autumn	fall	Herbst
banking account	bank account	Bankkonto
banknote	bill	Banknote
bill	check	Rechnung
booking	reservation	Reservierung
company	corporation	Betrieb
enquiry	inquiry	Erkundigung
expiry date	expiration date	Verfallsdatum
inland revenue	duty income tax	Steuereinnahmen
let	hire	vermieten
solicitor/barrister	attorney	Rechtsanwalt
transport	transportation	Transport

Teil 6: False Friends in Business English

Autorin: Stephanie Shellabear

Ein »falscher Freund« (engl. false friend) ist ein Wort in einer Fremdsprache, das genauso oder ähnlich klingt oder geschrieben wird wie ein Wort in Ihrer Muttersprache, aber eine andere Bedeutung hat. Deshalb ist ein false friend nicht der korrekte fremdsprachliche Begriff. Wenn Sie false friends im Gespräch oder im Schriftverkehr benutzen, kann dies unterschiedliche Folgen haben: Muttersprachler mit guten Deutschkenntnissen werden in der Regel wissen, was Sie eigentlich sagen oder schreiben wollten. Sie werden Sie aber nur korrigieren, um Missverständnissen vorzubeugen oder Sie davor zu bewahren, sich lächerlich zu machen. Häufig sprechen Ihre Geschäftspartner jedoch kein Deutsch – und werden durch false friends in der Regel ziemlich verwirrt sein.

Und Vorsicht: Es gibt sehr viele false friends! Dieses Kapitel zeigt Ihnen die wichtigsten, zunächst anhand zahlreicher typischer Business-Situationen – von der Bewerbung über den Small Talk bis zur Verhandlung. Auf diese Weise können Sie sich die korrekten englischen Begriffe besser einprägen. Eine umfangreiche Liste der false friends dient Ihnen als ständiger Begleiter zum schnellen Nachschlagen.

23 False friends for beginners

When it comes to doing business, you always need to be prepared. If you are doing business in English, but your mother tongue is German, then you need to be prepared for the traps that the English language holds for you.

This part of the book has been written in British English. In the explanations of the false friends there are references to American English terms if they vary from their English counterparts.

23.1 Different types of false friends

Same or similar word but different meaning

Take the German word *Mappe*. ›Map‹ exists in English but, while you are talking about something to put papers in, your English-speaking business contact thinks you mean a large piece of paper with roads and towns on it (*Landkarte*). The correct English word for *Mappe* – in this particular case – is ›folder‹. Other examples are Gift/gift, Kredit/credit, Fabrik/fabric. You will find a list of the more frequently heard false friends in the latter half of this book.

Same or similar word and similar meaning

These are words that generally mean the same, but it depends on the context. Here is a standard example: *extra* and *Extra-*. If you say in German *Ich habe es extra so hingestellt, damit du es sofort siehst*, you would need to say in English ›I put it there deliberately so that you would see it‹. If you are in a restaurant, though, and order *eine Extra-Portion Gemüse* you can say in English ›an extra portion of vegetables‹. There is one verb which deserves special mention here, because it is probably the most frequently made mistake, namely: *machen/make*. We make mistakes, we make coffee, we make a fuss, but we do sports, we do courses and we do the accounts.

Via direct translation

You probably already know not to describe an *Unternehmer* as an undertaker, unless of course that particular entrepreneur or business owner really is an undertaker (*Leichenbestatter*). Similarly, it is widely known that a *Hochschule* is not the same thing as a high school.

Pseudo-anglicisms

These are English words that have found their way into everyday German usage but mean something completely different to the original English word, such as *Handy, Peeling* and *Body*. Others, such as *Neckholder*, do not even exist in English; and some can shock your audience or perhaps make them laugh although you meant to be serious: take *public viewing*, for instance, which until now meant solely *öffentliche Aufbahrung (einer Leiche)*! It is better to talk about a ›live transmission on a big screen‹. Who knows, perhaps these terms will gradually find their way into everyday English.

Non-existent English words

One particular type of false friend is a phenomenon which occurs with just a few German words. They are often translated by German speakers into words that do not exist in English. Three examples of this type are *reservieren, präsentieren and bestätigen*. The speaker knows the correct English nouns (›reservation‹, ›presenation‹, ›confirmation‹) but not the correct verb form, so we often hear what he or she assumes to be correct: ›reservate‹, ›presentate‹, ›confirmate‹, none of which are English.

Only a false friend in certain contexts

Take the German word *isoliert*: if the context is a location that is far away from anywhere else, then the translation is indeed ›isolated‹. However, this is a false friend if we are talking about buildings and stopping the heat escaping from them; in this context you need to speak of something being ›insulated‹.

23.2 Degrees of confusion

How disappointed or confused (or perhaps shocked!) will your conversation partner or email recipient feel if you use a false friend? The answer is: it depends. It depends on the word itself, and on how tolerant your opposite number is of hearing mistakes. It also depends on whether the person you speak or write to has any knowledge of German. The less German they know, the more potential there is for misunderstandings.

The cringe factor

Below is a simple scale to show you how other speakers of English, but especially native speakers, may feel when they hear mistakes made by (other) non-native speakers. These signs will help you to see how critical the use of a false friend can be, and it will hopefully help you to recognize which things you need to pay particular attention to:

↓	small error; it can cause some confusion,
↓↓	more critical; potential for big misunderstandings,
↓↓↓	don't say this: it may cause shock or embarrassment!

23.3 Applying for a job

There is no denying it: English is everywhere. If you are searching for a new job, it is likely that you will see under the list of requirements for the position: *gute* (or perhaps *hervorragende*, maybe *verhandlungssichere*) *Englischkenntnisse*. What sort of things should you be aware of when you apply?

Example 1: letter of application containing false friends !

I am applying for the job of photograph which you advertised in the Daily Times on Friday 3 September 2010.
Enclosed is my CV. You will see that I started to study to become an advocate, but I discovered a love of cameras and decided to become an undertaker instead and started up my own photo studio ...

What needs improving?

- The German word is *Fotograf* and the English for this is **›photographer‹**. This applicant has just described himself as a photo. ↓
- An advocate is someone who supports, for example, an idea, e.g. ›he is a strong advocate of renewable energy‹. It is not the same as *Advokat*, which in English is **›lawyer‹** or **›attorney‹**. ↓↓
- If only the English for *Unternehmer* were undertaker – life would be so easy! An undertaker is, as already mentioned, *Bestatter*, and the word the applicant should have used is **›entrepreneur‹** or **›business owner‹**. ↓↓↓

Example 2: letter of application with some false friends !

Dear Sir/Madam
I have been following the developments of your company for a while now with great interest. It is my wish to work for a globally successful company and so I am sending you my CV in case you actually have a vacancy for someone with my qualifications.
I was an executive assistant in the direction of a medium-sized German company for three years and am a very engaged team worker. My former chief was very satisfied with me and I am enclosing the reference that he wrote ...

What needs correcting?

- The German adverb *aktuell* and the English ›actually‹ are very similar but they mean different things. *Aktuell* translates as **›currently‹**. The English adverb ›actually‹ means *eigentlich*. ↓
- The applicant says she worked ›in the direction‹, which means *in der Richtung* ... What she should have written was, for example, **›in the office of the board of directors‹** or **›at head office‹**. ↓↓

- Last but not least we have the classic false friend *Chef*. Although there are titles such as ›Chief Accountant‹ (*Hauptbuchhalter*) and ›Chief of Staff‹ (*Generalstabschef*), ›chief‹ also means Indianerhäuptling! The correct translation for mein Chef is **›my boss‹** or **›my manager‹**. ↓

! **Example 3**

Dear Ms Terry
With regard to your announcement in the Good Thinking magazine on 15th January I would like to apply for the job of Sales Assistant.
I enclose my CV which shows that I have worked in the sales resorts of several companies. I read about your fusion with Alex plc and I am sure that a fresh and competent face in your sales department will bring your company many benefits ...

What's not right?

- Announcement. *Annonce* is so similar to this. However, ›announcement‹ means *Ankündigung*. The correct thing to say in the case above is **›advertisement‹**. ↓
- We speak of ›holiday resorts‹ in English (*Ferien-/Urlaubsort*) but not of sales resorts or personnel resorts. The right word for this is **›department‹**. ↓↓
- The applicant mentions a ›fusion‹ of Alex plc and the company she is writing to. Does she know that she has used the translation of *Verschmelzung*? The word that describes the joining together of two companies is **›merger‹**. ↓

Useful vocabulary

catch on	Schule machen; sich durchsetzen
recipient	Empfänger
opposite number	Gegenspieler; Verhandlungspartner
cringe	schaudern

23.4 Your CV

This is an interesting challenge: trying to fit the details of a large part of your life on just one or two pages. That is why it pays to get it right first time. There is not much you can do wrong with your personal details, but things like your education and work experience need a little care.

!

Example 1: CV containing false friends

Education

1992 – 1994	Promotion in Business Administration, University of Bayreuth
1987 – 1991	Diploma in Business Administration, University of Bayreuth
1979 – 1986	Unting Gymnasium

Be careful!

- When you talk or write about the achievements in your educational history, do find the correct translation. The English word ›promotion‹ means *Beförderung* in German. The qualification you gained was in fact a **›doctorate‹** or **›PhD‹**. ↓↓
- ›Diploma‹ is a universal word. It can be used for all kinds of qualifications after various lengths of study and/or work experience. If you studied for several years at a university, though, it is safe to call your final qualification a **›degree‹**. ↓
- Do not say you went to school at the ›gymnasium‹. That is the hall in which you do sports activities and exercise (*Sporthalle*). You can choose between **›secondary school‹** and **›high school‹** to refer to *Gymnasium*. ↓↓↓

!

Important

Did you know that ›bachelor‹ also means *Junggeselle*? Say ›He's got a bachelor in Chemistry‹ or ›He did his bachelor's in architecture two years ago‹. If you say ›He's a bachelor‹, you might need to explain whether you mean he has this qualification, or that he is unmarried.

!

Example 2: CV containing false friends

Employment

01/2009 – date	Expanded company into Austria – overtook **WeWillDesign**. Now Managing Director of three companies
12/2008	Built second company **Olidesign**, specializing in floors
01/2005	Grounded and led own decorating company **Außen.Innen** with German state's existence grounding money
01/2003 – 12/2005	Apprenticeship as decorator

Is s/he or isn't s/he?

The information in this CV is **confusing** (*irritierend*) not: ›irritating‹).

- Let us start with the oldest piece of information: ›decorator‹. Does this person mean ›decorator‹ as in *Maler/Tapezierer* or perhaps **›interior designer‹** (*Dekorateur*)? ↓
- The next thing we see is that this person **founded** (not ›grounded‹ – *aus dem Verkehr ziehen*) his own company. ↓
- *Leiten* is sometimes ›to lead‹ but in this context it is better to write **›managed (my) own company‹**. ↓
- The *Existenzgründer* support is better explained as a state grant given to people to set up their own businesses. *Existenz* in this case is not ›existence‹ but **›one's own company‹**. ↓↓
- *Bilden* is a verb you see often, but it is better translated as **›to form‹**. You can build a **factory** (*Fabrik*) but you **form** (or **found**) a company. ↓
- Does the company Olidesign specialize in floors (*Böden*) or **hallways** (*Flure*)? ↓
- Lastly, ›to overtake‹ means *überholen*. It is better to say **›took over** WeWillDesign‹, or better still: **›acquired‹**. ↓↓

!

Important

If you really want to get the job you are applying for, ask someone with excellent English – someone who knows you well – to check your CV before you send it. As the English saying goes: better safe than sorry (*Vorsicht ist besser als Nachsicht*).

23.5 The interview

Has an interviewer ever tested your English during a German interview? Or have you attended an interview that was held entirely in English? Some people love to demonstrate their knowledge of a foreign language and have no trouble speaking with confidence. Nevertheless, look out for false friends!

23.5.1 Some typical questions

Here are just a few of the types of question you will be confronted with in interviews. What is wrong with the answers?

- Even before I absolved my study I wanted to work in the financial branch. ↓
- Your concern has such a great reputation all over the world and that is why I am so interested. ↓↓
- The marketing ideas that you create are genial and I want to be a part of that. Yours is a very representative company. ↓↓

What experience could you contribute to this job?

- First and foremost my experience in great, successful companies: I am calm even when there is a lot of hectic in the office. I can stay focused under pressure. ↓
- My biggest hobby is cars. I've spent my whole life with them and I have several old-timers at home. You won't find anyone as passionate about them as me – and I can use this momentum to achieve a lot at work. ↓↓↓
- Because we have a family business, I have always spent weekends and holidays working there. Over the years I have learned a lot about loan accounting, sales, advertising and personal. ↓↓

What do you do in your spare time?

- I am doing a part-time study in translation. The next exam is in two weeks, so I am spending most of my evenings learning at the moment. ↓
- I enjoy reading in my free time. I like all kinds of different lecture. ↓
- I make a lot of sport. In the winter I go skiing, and in the summer I like wandering in the mountains. ↓↓

23.5.2 What's wrong?

Did you work out which statements are not correct? Here they are, one after the other. Notice the differences and try to memorize them for future use.

This was said:	But this was meant:
absolve	passed; got
freisprechen	*absolvieren*
study	studies; degree
Arbeitszimmer	*Studium*
concern	corporation, enterprise
Sorge	*Konzern*
genial	brilliant
gesellig	*genial*
representative	prestigious
repräsentativ für etwas	*repräsentativ*
great	large
großartig	*groß*

This was said:	**But this was meant:**
hectic	a lot of activity
hektisch	*Hektik*
old-timer	antique car; vintage car
alter Hase	*Oldtimer*
loan	salary; payroll
Kredit	Lohn
personal	personnel, human resources
persönlich	*Personal*
learning	revising (for a test or exam)
lernen	*lernen*
lecture	reading material; books
Vortrag	*Lektüre*
make sport	do sports
Sport schaffen	*Sport machen*
wandering	hiking
umherwandern	*Wandern*

24 False friends in business communication

If you are going to talk to someone on the telephone, write an e-mail or a letter, participate in a meeting, present to a group of people, or handle negotiations of some kind, it is a good idea to watch out for the language pitfalls illustrated in this chapter.

24.1 On the telephone

Telephone conversations with English-speaking business contacts can be a challenge. You cannot see those tell-tale facial expressions (rolling of eyes, frowns of confusion, or smiles of amusement) that would normally indicate whether you have said the right thing in English.

!

Example

Joachim calls his colleague John who is located in his company's British subsidiary.
Joachim: Hi John, it's Joachim here. Am I calling at a good time?
John: Hi Joachim, how are you doing? I've got a couple of minutes before my next meeting. What's it about?
Joachim: Nothing serious! I wanted to ask you if you're coming to the trade fair in London in two weeks. Can we have a date?
John: Pardon? ↓↓↓ *(John wonders if he should warn Joachim that he has just told him he wants a romantic rendezvous with him).* Do you mean can we arrange to meet up? Yes, I'll be free all day on the Wednesday. How are the preparations going?
Joachim: As usual everything is last minute. We are still waiting for the prospects to arrive. You can't go to a trade fair without prospects to give to people.
John: But the prospects are what you are going there to collect, aren't they? ↓↓ *(John does not realize that Joachim is talking about brochures. Prospects are potential customers that companies go to trade fairs to impress.)*
Joachim: I don't understand what you mean, but anyway, we will be ready on time. I hope you will be able to spend a few hours with us at the booth. There will be a special feature: a tour of one of our fabrics using virtual reality. The visitors won't need to use their fantasy because the experience will feel completely real.
John: Yes, I can imagine. It sounds interesting. Tell you what, as soon as I get to the exhibition centre, I'll come and find you and we can arrange a time to go off and have a chat. *(John is a little confused now because Joachim has talked about walking round a fabric – Stoff – and using one›s fantasy – einen Traum. Joachim should have said ›factory‹ and ›imagination‹.)* ↓↓
Joachim: OK. Bye John!

What is the cringe factor of this conversation? It could be rated as an overall ↓↓.

!

Important

Whatever you do, avoid using ›date‹ unless talking about a private, romantic type of meeting or, of course, a specific day. Everything else is an **appointment**.

24.2 In e-mails

Email is a means of communication with extra risks. It can be hard to get across in just a few words what you mean. If your email is going to be sent to everyone in your company – or even to external contacts or customers, your false friends could make a poor impact, at least on native English speakers.

24.2.1 Find the false friends

!

Example: email containing false friends

From: M. Prohl
To: All employees
Sent: 30 May 20XX
Subject: Summer feast
Dear colleagues,
we heartily invite you to our summer feast 20XX!
You all know the company tradition of a summer feast and many of you have already attended it over the years. This time, we have a special occasion to celebrate – the 10th birthday of our company. So the celebration will be a little bit different and certainly more special.
Please registrate yourself using the following link if you can attend and later you will become an armband in the internal mail which you will need to enter the event.
We will send you more information soon. Until then, the device is »let's have some fun!«
Many greetings,
Melinda

This email contains an array of entertaining false friends: entertaining for native speakers, that is, if they know a lot of German. Let us start at the top and take each one of these false friends in turn.

What's wrong?

- The first incorrect term is ›heartily‹. You should not translate this directly. Instead, use the phrase ›You are **cordially** invited to ...‹. ↓↓
- Next comes ›summer feast‹, clearly originating from *Sommerfest*. Feast means *Festmahl* in German: a focus on eating (lots!); but what we are looking at here is a **summer party**. ↓↓

- Have you ever said ›registrate yourself‹ or perhaps ›reservate (a table)‹? If you ask English teachers whether they have heard their pupils – native German speakers – say this, many of them will say yes. The words ›registrate‹ and ›reservate‹ do not in fact exist, though you would be forgiven for thinking they did. Say **›register‹** (it is not reflexive) and **›reserve‹**. ↓
- Bekommen/become. They are practically the same, but so very different in meaning. We often hear ›I became a present‹, *ich bin ein Geschenk geworden*. This mistake has the potential to be embarrassing, so remember to use **›receive‹**. ↓↓↓
- So, after registering to attend the summer party you will receive an armband: *einen Schwimmflügel* (in British English)! It also means one of those wide fabric bands that a soccer team captain wears around the upper part of his/her arm during a match. This type of entrance ticket to big events and parties is better described as a **›wristband‹**. ↓↓
- If you want to say *die Devise ist ...*, don't say the ›device is ...‹ (*das Gerät ist ...*), use **›the motto is‹** instead. ↓↓↓
- ›Many greetings‹ is not the English form of *viele Grüße*. Write ›Best regards‹ or ›Kind regards‹ instead. ↓

Tips for emails

- Just as in letters, the first line after the greeting should start with a capital letter.
- Use a spell-check function before you press send.
- If your email is important and intended for an international list of recipients or for customers, ask a native speaker to proof-read and correct it first.

24.3 In letters

We tend to communicate mostly by email, text message and telephone these days. However, letters are not yet extinct.

Example: letter containing false friends !

Dear Mr Todd
Thank you for your letter dated 10 February 20XX.
We want to say a hearty thank-you to you for the allowance to display your painting in our house during our 10th anniversary celebration. The painting represents very strongly the engagement of our staff and it is thanks to them that our company is so successful.
I enclose opera cards for you and your wife to enjoy an evening out together, as a token of our thanks.
With best regards ...

What needs correcting?

This was written:	But this was meant:
a hearty thank-you	many thanks; a warm thank-you
ein deftiges Dankeschön	*ein herzliches Dankeschön*
allowance	permission
Taschengeld	*Erlaubnis*
in our house	at our premises
in unserem Haus	*in unserem Hause*
the engagement of our staff	our staff's commitment
die Verlobung unseres Personals	*das Engagement unseres Personals*
opera cards	opera tickets
Opernspielkarten	*Opernkarten*

24.4 In meetings

Do you tend to spend the majority of your time in meetings? It may help to learn a few phrases off by heart and avoid false friends that way. Can you spot any mistakes in the phrases below? Not all of them contain errors, by the way.

24.4.1 Typical phrases in meetings – with false friends

- Hello everyone.
- Shall we start?
- Can I ask you to write the protocol?
- The meeting will end at 5pm. We'll have a short pause at 3.30 for coffee and cakes.
- Have you all got a copy of the agenda?
- Can anyone let me have a sheet of paper? I've left my block in my bureau.
- The first item on the agenda is ...
- So that's the situation. What is your meaning?
- Barbara, do you want to begin?
- Does everyone share that opinion? If not, what is the ground?
- Are there any disagreements?
- I don't completely agree. We all have different arguments.

- Could I just say something? I'm sure we can arrange ourselves.
- I'd like to just point out that eventually ...
- Sorry to interrupt but I need to mention here that ...
- Can I just finish what I was saying?
- Shall we return to the main issue?
- Let me summarize what we've just agreed upon punctually.
- I'll make a notice that the deadline is ...
- The date for the next meeting is ...

Important !

The sentence above contains the word ›date‹. In this case it is completely correct because this time it is about *Datum* and not *Termin*.

What is the correct term?

Don't say this:	Say:
write the protocol	write/take the minutes
die Benimmregeln schreiben	*das Protokoll schreiben*
a pause	a break
eine Atempause	*eine Pause*
cakes	biscuits/cookies
Kuchen	*Kekse*
block	notepad
Klotz	*Block*
bureau	office
Amt	*Büro*
What is your meaning?	What is your opinion?
Was ist Ihre Bedeutung?	*Was ist Ihre Meinung?*
What is the ground?	What is the reason?
Was ist der Boden?	*Was ist der Grund?*
arguments	points of view
Streitigkeiten	*Argumente*
arrange ourselves	come to an arrangement
sich ordnen	*sich arrangieren*
eventually	perhaps

Don't say this:	Say:
schließlich	*eventuell*
punctually	point by point
pünktlich	*punktuell*
a notice	a note
ein Aushang	*ein Notiz*

Do you keep your meeting agendas, papers, notes, and perhaps business cards, a notepad, and a pen in a medium-sized, flat object that you normally carry under your arm or in your hand? What would you call it in English? Many German speakers are tempted to call it a ›map‹, because of the German term *Mappe*. If you ask an English speaker ›Is it ok if I put my map down here?‹, he or she will think you want to put on the table a very large piece of folded paper showing towns and roads: *eine Landkarte*. The word you need is **›folder‹**, or **›file‹**, or if it is made of leather: **›briefcase‹**.

24.5 Making presentations

For natural performers, this is a chance to shine. But for the less confident among us – especially where English is concerned – this can be a daunting situation. See what effect these typical false friends have.

Better phrases for presentations

Avoid saying this:	Say this instead:
Good morning everyone. I want to say how lucky I am to be here today.	Good morning everyone. I'd just like to say how great it is to be here to talk to you today.
... was ich für ein Glück habe, heute hier zu sein.) ↓↓	*... wie glücklich ich bin, heute hier zu sein.*
The theme of my presentation is ...	The subject of my presentation is ...
Die Titelmelodie/Das Motiv meiner Präsentation ist ... ↓	*Das Thema meiner Präsentation ist ...*
First, I will talk about ...; next I will tell you about ...; and last I will give you some stuff to think about.	Firstly, I'd like to talk about ...; then I'll go on to tell you about ...; and finally I'd like to provide you with some food for thought.

Avoid saying this:	Say this instead:
Zuerst will ich über ... sprechen und als nächstes will ich Ihnen über .... erzählen. Zum Schluss will ich Ihnen etwas Zeug zum Nachdenken geben. ↓↓	(*Ich will* and ›I will‹ are often used as if they were identical, but of course they are not. ›I'd like to‹ has a better ring to it – it shows that you are taking your audience into consideration.)
Can we move the beamer a little? It blends in this position.	Could we move the projector a little? It's shining right in my eyes at this angle.
Können wir den BMW ein wenig umpositionieren? So wie er steht, mixt er. ↓↓↓	*Können wir den Beamer ein wenig umpositionieren? So wie er steht, blendet er mich.*

Important !

If you are showing an unfinished presentation to your colleagues with information that you plan to change soon, do not write on it ›To be overworked‹. It could be that you were overworked when you wrote the presentation (*Sie waren überarbeitet*) but the correct text is ›To be updated‹ (or ›revised‹ or ›amended‹).

24.6 Negotiating

Negotiating is all about two sides reaching an agreement. Watch out for false friends and make sure that your wishes are understood.

Example: Negotiation containing false friends !

Holly: Hello, Pia. Come in and have a seat.
Pia: Thanks.
Holly: So, what did you want to talk to me about?
Pia: I know we normally talk about these things in the yearly evaluations, but they are not for another six months.
Holly: Go ahead.
Pia: Because the theme is important to me, I wanted to talk to you sooner about becoming a salary raise. I have been in the department for five years and my pay is still the same. This is relatively low for our branch when you think of the work that I do and my engagement.
Holly: I can understand your situation. However, business was bad the last two years and we are now only just beginning to increase turnover again. We aren't quite out of the woods yet.
Pia: Yes, I understand about the conjuncture. But I would like to see my performance paid at the market price. Inflation has increased in the last five years, too, also I am earning less than at the start, though I work harder.
Holly: My hands are tied where money is concerned. I can't allocate any more for salaries until the evaluation round. What I can do at present, though, is offer you other concessions ...

Which false friends were used?

- Pia spoke about a ›theme‹ that was important to her. As already mentioned, in this context it is better to say **›subject‹** or **›topic‹**. ↓
- Pia wants ›to become a salary raise‹ (*sie will eine Gehaltserhöhung werden*). This mistake happens a lot and can be forgiven, but it certainly confuses English speakers with no knowledge of German. Use **›to have‹** or **›to receive‹**. ↓↓↓
- Another common error is using ›branch‹ as a translation of *Branche*. You can talk about the Frankfurt branch of a German company (*die Frankfurter Filiale*) but otherwise say **›sector‹** or **›industry‹**. ↓↓
- ›Engagement‹ was also mentioned earlier. It is not Pia's *Verlobung* that she should be emphasizing, but her **commitment**. ↓↓↓
- Also/*also*? Be careful here. ›... also I am earning less ...‹ should be ›... **so** (or **therefore**) I am earning less ...‹, because Pia is pointing out a consequence. ↓

Tips for negotiations

- Write down on paper the things you want to talk about, your point of view and the reason(s) for it. Check it before your meeting.
- If you are not used to conducting negotiations in English, look up the vocabulary you are not sure about beforehand – online dictionaries are a good resource if they provide example sentences to show the correct use of words that have various meanings.

Useful vocabulary

in turn	der Reihe nach
pitfall	Falle
tell-tale	verräterisch
an array of	eine Vielzahl
text message	SMS
extinct	ausgestorben
off by heart	auswendig
daunting	beängstigend
out of the woods	aus dem Gröbsten raus

25 False friends on a business trip

Do you travel often? Here are some of the situations you are most likely to encounter on a business trip. Maybe there are a few things in this section that you will have the opportunity to try out right away.

25.1 At the airport

The check-in staff at international airports can usually speak at least one other foreign language, so checking-in is normally easy, especially now it is more automated. Still, watch out for false friends, whether you are an airport employee or a business traveller.

!

Example

Lisa has arrived safely in Manchester, but her luggage has not.
Lisa: Hello, my coffer hasn't arrived. Is there someone who can help me?
Baggage claim attendant: Coffer? *(The man smiles. He knows ›a coffer‹ as a wooden box full of treasure that pirates normally search for.)* What does it look like?
Lisa: It's big, blue, and it has rolls.
Baggage claim attendant: *(understands: groß, blau und hat Brötchen! Looks at the empty baggage carousel.)* No, it doesn't seem to be here. Do you see that office over there? The lady in there can help you.
Lisa (in the office): Hello, my coffer has not arrived. Do you know where it is? Here is my pass, and here is my boarding pass from the machine I came in.
Employee: *(Wonders what type of machine Lisa travelled with – normally air passengers travel by plane.)* Aha, I see. I'll look in the computer and perhaps we can locate your luggage. I see it was just one suitcase, am I right?
Lisa: Yes, that's correct. I knew something would go wrong. We started an hour late and ... this is really a problem.
Employee: I'm afraid the database has no record yet of the whereabouts of your suitcase, but I expect it will be updated any moment. When it arrives, we can have it delivered to you. Could you tell me where you are staying?
Lisa: But what will I do until my suitcase arrives? All my things are in it ...
Employee: I can give you a voucher so that you can buy the essentials, and I am certain you will have your case by this evening.
Lisa: I see I have no choice. I will give you the address of my hotel and my handy number.
Employee: *(understands: nützliche Telefonnummer)* Thank you; that would be great.

What needs to be corrected?

Don't say this:	Say:
coffer	suitcase
Truhe	*Koffer*
rolls	wheels
Brötchen	*Rollen*
pass	passport
Bergpass; Eintrittsschein	*Pass*
machine	plane; flight
Maschine/Gerät	*Maschine*
start	take off
beginnen	*Start*
handy	mobile/cell phone
handlich	*Handy*

25.2 At a restaurant

There are some clear winners among the false friends that show up in restaurant talk. At some time or other you will be eating together with English-speaking colleagues or customers, be it lunch, an evening meal or even a business breakfast. Look at the phrases below and see if you can work out the mistakes.

25.2.1 Typical phrases in restaurants – with false friends

- Hello. I reservated a table for four people under my name: Gold.
- Could you bring us the cards, please?
- What is the menu of the day?
- We'd like two bottles of water – one with gas and one without gas.
- Excuse me, I have become the wrong beer – I ordered alcohol-free.
- Is the Thai curry very sharp? Can I have it with crabs?
- I would like my steak English, please.
- Could you bring some more sauce for the beef, please?
- I would like the ›warm apple strudel‹ for dessert. Does it come with vanilla sauce?
- (And last but not least when paying the bill) Where do I underwrite?

What's not right?

- German speakers very often say ›reservate‹ for *reservieren*. ›Reservate‹ was mentioned earlier and does not exist: it is a strange type of false friend that is said automatically by German speakers of English. You need to say **›reserve‹**. ↓
- ›Card‹ has several different uses, but if you mean *Speisekarte*, say **›menu‹**. ↓↓
- That takes us to *Menü*, which is known as **›daily special‹** or **›dish of the day‹**. ↓↓
- ›With/without gas‹ is understood easily in most countries when you order in English. If you want to sound less like you are asking for water with or without *Erdgas*, ask for **›sparkling‹** or ›**still water**‹. ↓
- ›I have become the wrong beer‹ – *ich bin das falsche Bier geworden*. This has the potential to make your waiter or waitress grin widely because it sounds so funny. Could this be the number one false friend? Remember: *bekommen* is **›to receive‹** or **›to get‹**. ↓↓↓
- *Krabben* are called **›prawns‹**. Crabs are those large, pink crustaceans with dangerous claws. ↓↓
- ›Sharp‹ is good for describing things like knives, people's intellect and lemons. If you are talking about curry, you should say **›spicy‹** or **›hot‹**. ↓↓
- ›Sauce‹ is too unspecific in English when it comes to food. If you mean *Fleisch-* or *Bratensoße*, say **›gravy‹**. *Warme Vanillesoße* is called **›(hot) custard‹**.
- And now to the bill/check: ›underwriting‹ is the job of insurers; when you receive the credit card printout in a restaurant, you **sign** it.

Tips for visits to restaurants

- Often, it is not so much what you say in a restaurant that is important but how you say it. Although it is accepted in German restaurants to motion to the waiter and discreetly say ›We'd like to pay‹, in English it is more polite to say ›We'd like the bill/check now, please›.
- Although this is not really a false friend, *Garderobe* is translated by some as ›wardrobe‹ (*Kleiderschrank*). The correct word for the place you leave your coat is the ›cloakroom‹, or a ›coat stand‹ or ›coat rack‹.

25.3 When shopping

If you have reached your destination but your luggage has not, perhaps you need to buy a few essentials. Or maybe you have a day or two free in between meetings and have a shopping trip on your to-do list. Read on and take note of potential false friends.

25.3.1 Better phrases for shopping

Clothing is a subject in which there are many false friends. Several terms started to appear in German not so long ago that really do not mean the same thing in English. However, as mentioned at the start of this book, some things have been accepted into English now, even though they did not exist before. If, in the past, you had said in a clothes shop ›I'm looking for a red body to go with my outfit‹, the sales assistant's face would have been a picture! *Ich suche einen roten Körper, der zu meinem Outfit passt.* This piece of underwear used to be called a **›teddy‹** – and it still is, but nowadays the term **›body‹** is indeed used.

›Overall‹ is a good false friend: if you say this in English it will be understood as *Schutzanzug* or *Blaumann*. The correct name for this, if it is a piece of fashionable clothing that you are talking about, is **›jumpsuit‹**.

The word *neckholder* does not exist. You need to use the term **›halterneck‹** instead.

An amusing case of direct translation has to be ›hand-shoes‹. You need to say **›gloves‹** (*Handschuhe*).

!

Important

Please note that if you ever need to talk about the following things, be careful. There is potential here for a high cringe factor! In British English, ›slip‹ means *Unterrock*, and ›vest‹ means *Unterhemd*. If you need to talk about *Unterhosen* – one never knows! – women's are called ›pants‹ or ›panties‹ and men's are called ›underpants‹. In American English, ›pants‹ are *Hosen*, so simply use the term ›underwear‹ if it's something you wear *drunter*.

With clothing, avoid:	Say this instead:
I am going to a prize event this evening and I need a smoking.	I am going to a prize-giving event this evening and I need a dinner jacket (UK) / tuxedo (US).
Heute Abend gehe ich zu einer Preisverleihung und brauche dafür ein Rauchen. ↓↓	*… und ich brauche dafür einen Smoking.*
Is there a vest with this jacket too?	Is there a matching waistcoat (UK) /vest (US) for this jacket?
Der Brite versteht: *Gibt es dazu ein Unterhemd?* ↓↓	*Gibt es zu diesem Sakko/ dieser Jacke eine passende Weste?*

With clothing, avoid:	**Say this instead:**
Excuse me, I want to buy a jeans-jacket. Do you sell these?	… I'd like to buy a denim jacket. Do you sell them?
Entschuldigen Sie, ich will eine Jacke aus Jeans kaufen. Haben Sie so was? ↓↓	*... ich möchte eine Jeansjacke kaufen.*
Hello, I need some help. I'm looking for some slippers.	... I'm looking for some casual shoes/ loafers.
Guten Tag, ich suche Pantoffeln. ↓↓	*Guten Tag, ich möchte ein Paar Slipper.*

Other things to avoid:	**Say this instead:**
Excuse me, where is the next warehouse?	Excuse me, could you tell me where the nearest department store is?
Entschuldigen Sie bitte, wo ist die nächste Lagerhalle? ↓↓	*Entschuldigen Sie bitte, wo ist das nächste Warenhaus?*
I want to buy a liquor to take home as a gift. Can you show me something typical or traditional for here?	I would like to buy a liqueur ... (You need to pronounce this as lik-ior. Liquor is pronounced likker.)
Ich will eine Spirituose/ Alkohol als Geschenk für zu Hause kaufen. ... ↓↓	*Ich möchte einen Likör als Geschenk kaufen.*
Marmalade is always a good present. What sorts do you have?	Jam is always a good present. Which types do you have?
Orangen- oder Zitronenmarmelade ist immer ein gutes Geschenk. Welche Sorten haben Sie? ↓	*Marmelade ist immer ein gutes Geschenk. ....*
Excuse me, where's the cash? I want to pay for these things now.	Excuse me, where will I find the till/ the check-out counter? I would like to pay for these things now.
Wo finde ich das Bargeld, bitte? Ich will diese Sachen bezahlen. ↓↓	*Wo finde ich die Kasse? ...*
This cup is a gift for my mother. Please could you pack it in a carton because I'm taking it back to Germany in my suitcase.	This is for my mother. Please could you pack it in a box because I'm taking it back to Germany in my suitcase (and I don't want it to break).
Diese Tasse ist ein Geschenk für meine Mutter. Könnten Sie sie bitte in eine Tüte tun, weil ich sie nach Deutschland zurücknehme? ↓	*Diese Tasse ist ein Geschenk für meine Mutter. Könnten Sie sie bitte in einen Karton tun, ...*

25.4 Small talk

Is small talk the big, bad wolf of business English? Many non-native speakers are certainly afraid of it. Small talk is important for creating long-lasting business relations and for making a good impression in social circles. If you do not practise, you cannot improve, but before you dive right in, do take note of some more of those typical false friends.

25.4.1 Phrases for business situations

It's relatively easy to say hello to someone and ask how he or she is doing. Here are some less obvious phrases that are useful to know in business situations.

!

Example 1

Birgit has just arrived at her company's office in the UK.
Birgit: Hello, I have a meeting with Mr Johnson at 14 hours. I am sorry I am late. I went to the wrong stock: 32 instead of 23.
Receptionist: *(Understands the mistake ›stock‹ because Birgit mentioned the floor numbers).* It's ok. I will call him and tell him you're here. Please have a seat while you're waiting.
Birgit: Thank you. There was a little hectic today because my machine from Hamburg fell out and I had to fly one hour later.
Receptionist: *(Confused about what it means when a machine falls out.)* Here's Mr Johnson now.
Birgit: Mr Johnson, hello!
Bill Johnson: Hello! Please, call me Bill. It's Birgit isn't it?
Birgit: Yes. It's nice to see you. I have some blooms for you because I heard it is your birthday today. Congratulations!
Bill Johnson: *(Hears the small mistakes, but understands and does not correct Birgit.)* Thank you very much, what a nice surprise!

How do we really say it?

- ›Stock‹ means *Lagerware*. The correct word for the numbered levels in a building is **›floor‹**. ↓↓
- You can say **›things were a little hectic‹** but not ›there was a little hectic‹, because this word is an adjective in English, not a noun as in German. ↓
- Birgit's ›machine fell out‹. Non-German speakers will be scratching their heads over this. The correct phrase is **›my flight was cancelled‹**. ↓↓↓
- Taking a gift to someone who has a birthday is a kind gesture, but ›blooms‹ are better described as **›flowers‹**. ›Blooms‹ are *Blüten*. ↓

- The correct greeting for someone with a birthday is ›**happy birthday**‹. ›Congratulations‹ sounds almost ironic – almost like ›it's great that you made it through another year‹! ↓↓↓

Important !

Although it is usual to say the afternoon and evening times in German using 13, 14, 15 etc, it is not said like this in normal everyday English. Any time after 12.59 in the afternoon should be expressed as ›1pm, 2pm, 3pm‹ and so on.

Example 2 !

Birgit is back at reception at the end of her day in the UK.
Birgit: We've finished our meeting now. Could you help me find a taxi?
Receptionist: Oh I can call you one. It will only take 10 minutes for it to arrive.
Birgit: Great. I need it to bring me to my pension. Oh dear, look at my costume! I spilled sauce on myself at lunchtime. That's typical of me.
Receptionist: *(Is smiling politely, but is getting distracted by the strange English she's hearing)*. It doesn't look bad. I am sure the mark will come out easily.
Birgit: I have a free day tomorrow. Can you recommend anywhere to visit? I'm not a city person – I like to be in the nature, but I have heard there is a beautiful dome near here.
Receptionist: That's right. I have a brochure here if you're interested. There is a concert taking place there tomorrow evening. My husband is playing in the orchestra.
Birgit: That sounds good. I love classic music.

What can be improved?

- Birgit wants a taxi to bring her to her pension – *ein Taxi, das sie zu Ihrer Rente bringt*. She needed to say ›**to take me to the guesthouse I'm staying at**‹. ↓↓↓
- She spilled sauce on her costume – *verschüttete Soße auf Ihre Verkleidung*. It is no wonder that the receptionist was beginning to get confused. To be precise, she **spilled gravy on her suit**. ↓↓↓
- She likes to be ›in the nature‹ (›**outdoors**‹ or ›**in the countryside**‹) and wants to visit a ›dome‹ (*Kuppel*) – though she clearly meant a ›**cathedral**‹. ↓↓
- Last but not least, Birgit loves classic music – *Klassiker* – though she no doubt means ›**classical**‹ music. ↓

Useful vocabularv

whereabouts	Verbleib
voucher	Gutschein
essentials	Lebensnotwendige
grin	grinsen

underwrite	garantieren
motion to sb.	jemandem ein Zeichen geben
matching	passend
denim	Jeansstoff
to mingle	ein Bad in der Menge nehmen

26 False friends in different departments

So far you have been seeing some situational examples of false friends used in English. This chapter takes a different perspective and deals with the functionally relevant false friends: those that crop up in some of the different departments of a company.

26.1 Human resources

One of the responsibilities of the HR department is to collaborate with other departments in the preparation and writing of job descriptions.

!

Example

An HR assistant has received some information about a vacant position from a colleague and has translated it into English for the job description.

Job description	Examples
Job title:	Leader of IT
Reports to:	Company direction
Start date:	As soon as possible.
Advertising of vacancy:	Internally and announcement in national newspaper.
Stand-in:	Colleagues
Objectives of this function:	Development of department according to company's actual goals. ...
Responsibilities:	Controlling the department's processes and implementing methods of improvement. Cooperating with leaders of other departments to optimize IT's services. ...
Professional requirements:	IT study at university. Five years experience in a similar position. Great and sovereign knowledge of standard office IT systems. ...
Personal requirements:	Excellent analytical skills. Excellent communicator. Because of different nationalities in teams must be sensible to different cultures. ...

What needs to be corrected?

This was written:	But this is meant:
leader	head (Head of IT)
Führer	*Leiter*
company direction	company management
Firmenrichtung	*Direktion*
announcement	advert
Ankündigung	*Annonce*
actual goals	current goals
tatsächlichen Ziele	*aktuelle Ziele*
controlling processes	examining processes
Prozesse steuernd	*Controlling-Prozesse*
IT study at university	university degree in IT
Studieren der IT an der Uni	*IT-Studium an der Uni*
great and sovereign knowledge	wide-ranging, expert knowledge
großartige und adlige Kenntnisse	*große und souveräne Kenntnisse*
sensible	sensitive
vernünftig	*sensibel*

You may already have seen some of these false friends in this chapter. The alphabetical list of false friends at the end of this chapter contains many more examples which relate to a range of different business and personal areas.

26.2 Logistics

If your goods and/or services are supplied physically to the customer, then the main purpose of logistics is to deliver those goods and services to their destination without delay.

Effective communication is therefore of paramount importance.

!

Example: email containing false friends

Jürgen is still waiting for a consignment of office furniture that he ordered for his company two months ago.

From: Jürgen Mann
To: Jeff Jones
Sent: 25.11.20XX
Subject: Reclamation – Order Number 5789614

Dear Mr Jones,
This is about our order of ten desks and ten office chairs on 20 September 20XX. Last Monday I spoke on the phone with your lager. I told them that the furnitures had not arrived yet. They controlled all our order dates and said they knew what had happened. They told me that the furnitures were on the way to our city by train but a wagon was defect.
They said I should become everything yesterday but nothing has arrived.
Please could you find out where our furnitures are and call me with informations as soon as possible, because my colleagues do not want to work on the floor!
Thank you.
Regards,
Jürgen Mann

What's not right?

This was written:	But this is meant:
reclamation	complaint
Rückgewinnung	*Reklamation*
lager	warehouse
helles Bier	*Lager*
control	check
steuern	*Kontrolle*
order dates	order data
Bestelltermine	*Bestelldaten*
become	receive
werden	*receive*

!

Important

It is incorrect to say ›furnitures‹ and ›informations‹ in English. Neither of these terms has an s at the end. The plural forms are simply **›furniture‹** and **›information‹**.

26.3 Finance and accounting

If you work in the finance department of a large, international company, perhaps you have a lot of contact with colleagues in offices in different parts of the world, and no doubt English is your company language for all communication with these colleagues.

!

Example: phone conversation containing false friends

Julio is Spanish and works in accounting in the London office of a global company. Kirsten is a German colleague working in the company's Frankfurt office.
Kirsten: Hello Julio, it's Kirsten from the Frankfurt office. How are you?
Julio: Hello Kirsten, fine thanks. How are you?
Kirsten: A bit stressed. I'm calling to ask about a booking on one of our cost centres that was done in the London office. We are making an internal revision at the moment and the controller wants to know more details about the post.
Julio: (*Wonders what is being changed internally. In addition, he is accustomed to hearing the term ›Controller‹, though in Britain, people in these jobs are called ›management accountants‹.*) So it's about some post? Was it a courier delivery? We normally only charge big amounts to projects if they are higher than 100 pounds, otherwise the amount goes straight to general administration costs.
Kirsten: No I don't mean post like sending letters; I mean the booking that was made on the cost centre. It is for 2000 pounds.
Julio: A booking? Do you mean a reservation? Perhaps it's to do with an event then. Can you tell me the cost centre code and the month and I will look at it in the system.Kirsten: It's ACY24.60 and it was July. But it isn't a reservation, it's a real booking.
Julio: Do you mean a charge that was entered?
Kirsten: Yes, that's right.
Julio: Oh, now I understand. You know what? If you email me a pdf of the report showing the charge, I will call you back as soon as I have the information you need.
Kirsten: That would be fine. Thank you Julio.

What caused the confusion?

- Strictly speaking, ›a booking‹ is something you make when you want hotel rooms, concert tickets or tables in restaurants. Also, footballers can receive bookings from the referee, meaning they are shown the yellow or red card for fouling other players during a match. When talking in German about a *Buchung* in an accounting system, in English it is more specific if you can say **›an entry has been made**‹ or **›a debit has been charged to‹** or on the positive side: **›an amount has been credited to‹**. ↓↓
- An ›internal revision‹ sounds like changes being made within the company, whereas in this case an **internal audit** is taking place. ↓↓
- The correct accounting term for *Posten* is not ›post‹ but **›item‹**. ↓↓

!

Important

One of the terms that can often confuse native English speakers is the German speaker's use of the term ›controller‹ and ›to control‹. It gives a sense of *die Macht haben über etwas/jemanden*, but in the financial context it is usual to say **›management accountant‹ for** *Controller* and **›to monitor/to check‹** for *kontrollieren*.

26.4 Sales and marketing

Not so long ago, German companies such as car companies, perfume sellers and cosmetics manufacturers began marketing their products and filming adverts (*Spots*) with English slogans. With time, some of them have realized that the non-English speaking population often do not understand the message; so they have reverted to using German slogans.

The most amusing situations – for native speakers of English, that is – arise from German companies using pseudo-anglicisms to name their products. Here are some examples:

Product name in German:	What the English speaker understands:
Shirty (a type of nightdress)	›Shirty‹ is used to describe a person and means *aufgebracht*.
Shorty (pyjamas with short trousers)	›Shorty‹ is a nickname often given to people who are not very tall: *Kleine(r)*.
Body (name given to one-piece underwear: one type worn by women and a type also made for babies)	›Body‹ means *Körper*. The kind worn by women is typically known as a ›teddy‹ but, as mentioned earlier, it is also now called a ›body‹ in stores in Britain. The type worn by babies is called a ›babygrow‹ 🇬🇧 or a ›onesie‹ 🇺🇸.
Bodybag (a rucksack with a single strap that lies diagonally across the front of the body)	Bodybag means *Leichensack*. This is not a good choice for your product name!
Neckholder (a piece of clothing with straps which are tied behind the neck)	›Neckholder‹ (*Nackenhalter?*) does not exist. The correct English expression is ›halterneck‹, e.g. halterneck dress, halterneck top.

This is not simply a recommendation: it is a necessity. If you wish to use English words to name, describe or advertise your products and/or services, it is crucial that you have them checked for their meaning in all of the English-speaking countries in which you hope to sell them.

26.5 Production

This is the division (*Ressort*) that manufactures products; it is the place where your ideas, in the form of designs, are turned into reality. In this context it is acceptable to speak of your concepts being ›realized‹ (*realisiert*).

!

Example: a meeting dialogue containing false friends

At a product team meeting, three colleagues of different nationalities are updating each other on the status of the production of a plastic kitchen utensil. They are Hannes from the *Konstruktionsteam*, Melinda from *Materialentwicklung* and Sam, a native English-speaking product manager.

Sam: ».... as I was saying, we're having one main issue with the product and I was hoping we could start analyzing it by going back to the source. Hannes, the main difficulty we are having is with this section of the product *(Sam points to a diagram)*. As an engineer, perhaps you can see immediately what we need to improve.«

Hannes: »You know I am not an engineer really, but I see the problem and I think that the construction needs to be improved at this place here ...«

Sam: »OK, I see – but so that we all understand this correctly, we're talking about the design, right? The construction is the building of the product.«

Hannes: »Oh, you're right, yes, the design. We need to make a change to this part of the product, make it thinner.«

Melinda: »But I am not sure if the material will still be as strong as before. If you make this part thinner, the product could break more easily and that would mean a lot of reclamations.«

Sam: »Reclamations? What do you mean exactly?«

Melinda: »When customers are angry about the product breaking and want their money back.«

Sam: »I see. You mean complaints.«

!

Important

In Germany, only people who have an engineering degree are permitted to call themselves engineers. Native English speakers use the term less strictly: the people who come to repair your washing machine, your TV, your fridge or your freezer can all be called an **›engineer‹** or a **›technician‹**.

Tip

It is normally very rare for native speakers to correct other people's English, because they do not want to create any embarrassment or cause you to feel insulted. If it does happen, then it is probably because the situation is very important and it is necessary to make certain that there is absolutely no confusion. In cases such as these you should make a note to remind yourself of your mistake.

Useful vocabulary

to crop up	auftauchen
of paramount importance	von größter Wichtigkeit
consignment	Lieferung

27 Useful false friends to know

If you mean...	say this:
This...	**means:**

* Words which are separated by a semi-colon have different meanings.
** Words separated by a slash have similar meanings and can be used as synonyms for each other.

absolvieren	to pass; to complete* He passed his exams with flying colours. They have all satisfactorily completed the software course.
absolve	*freisprechen*
Advokat	solicitor 🇬🇧 /lawyer** She has just qualified as a lawyer.
advocate	*Verfechter; Befürworter*
Aktion	campaign It was a very successful advertising campaign.
action	*Handlung; Bewegung*
aktualisieren	to update The statistics have now been updated.
actualize	*verwirklichen*
aktuell	current What is the current situation in banking?
actual	*tatsächlich; Ist-*
alarmieren	to alert Please alert the police in the event of theft.
alarm	*in Angst versetzen; erschrecken*
also	well/so Well, if you really want my opinion ...
also	*auch*
Ambulanz	outpatients' (department) She's waiting in the outpatients' department to have her arm x-rayed.
ambulance	*Krankenwagen*
amüsieren, sich ~	to enjoy oneself We really enjoyed ourselves at the theatre.
amuse	*belustigen; amüsieren*

If you mean...	say this:
This...	**means:**
Angina	tonsillitis He's off sick with tonsillitis.
angina	*Herzschmerzen*
annoncieren	to advertise The vacancy is advertised in this week's newspaper.
announce	*ankündigen; verkünden*
apart	elegant/stylish That's a very elegant suit you're wearing!
apart	*abseits, entfernt*
Argument	point I'm not sure I understand your point. But: The arguments for and against a change.
argument	*Streit; Auseinandersetzung*
arrangieren, sich ~	to come to an arrangement They've finally come to an arrangement about who will take over the job.
arrange	*ordnen; sortieren*
Arrest, unter ~ sein	to be detained He's being detained and I don't know why.
arrest	*verhaften; festnehmen*
Art	type/kind/sort; nature This type of product sells extremely well. It's not in his nature to complain.
art	*Kunst*
Artist	performer She's an excellent performer.
artist	*Künstler/in*
ausfallen	to be cancelled My meeting was cancelled this morning.
fall out	*herausfallen*
ausmachen	to represent These statistics fully represent our clients' opinions.
make out	*ausstellen; dahinter kommen; darauf kommen*

If you mean...	**say this:**
This...	**means:**
Band	volume; recording; ribbon This is the 3rd volume in the series. We have a recording of the whole conversation. I'd like a ribbon tied around the gift, please.
band	*Kapelle; Gruppe; Streifen*
Bank	bench; riverbank We waited outside on a bench. The spectators watched the boat race from the riverbank.
bank	*Bank (Geldinstitut); (Fluss-)Ufer*
Basis, (~-)	grass-roots; basis We need a grass-roots approach to this issue. But: We used the statistics as a basis for our decisions.
basis	*Fundament; Ausgangspunkt*
Beamer	(multi-media) projector I need a projector to show my presentation.
beamer	*BMW*
bekommen	to receive/to get I received a letter today from the tax authorities.
become	*werden*
beliebt	popular This type of advertising is very popular.
beloved	*(heiß)geliebt*
bilden	to form Have you formed a plan yet?
build	*bauen*
Billion	thousand million /trillion How many trillion dollars have they lost?
billion	*Milliarde*
Biskuit	sponge cake This dessert consists of sponge cake and cream.
biscuit	*Keks*
blamieren	to make a fool of oneself/to embarrass oneself She made a complete fool of herself.
blame	*beschuldigen*

If you mean...	say this:
This...	**means:**
blank	shiny/bright Whose shiny, new company car is that? But: Never give anyone a blank cheque!
blank	*unbeschriftet; Blanko~*
blenden	to dazzle/to blind The light is blinding me. I need to move.
blend	*mischen; vermengen*
blinken	to indicate You need to indicate before you turn left!
blink	*blinzeln*
Blinker	indicator Do you know your indicator is still on?
blinker	*Scheuklappe*
Blitz	lightning That plane was hit by lightning in 1998.
blitz	*Blitzkrieg*
Block	notepad/writing pad Could you pass me a notepad, please?
block	*Klotz*
Blume	flower Those flowers are beautiful! Is it your birthday?
bloom	*Blüte*
Box	loudspeaker We need bigger loudspeakers in here.
box	*Kiste; Karton*
Branche	sector/industry I work in the insurance sector.
branch	*Filiale; Ast*
brav	well-behaved/good I agree; their children are very well-behaved.
brave	*tapfer*
Brief	letter All the information you need is in this letter.
brief	*Kurzdarstellung; Kurzanweisung*

If you mean...	say this:
This...	**means:**
Brillant	cut diamond His company trades in cut diamonds.
brilliant	*glänzend; großartig*
bringen	to take; to bring Shall I take this parcel to the post office now? I'll bring the report when I see you tomorrow.
bring	*bringen*
Büro	office She won't be in the office until this afternoon.
bureau	*Amt; Unterabteilung*
Buchung	debit/credit entry There's a debit entry on my cost centre that I don't agree with.
booking	*Reservierung; Verwarnung (Fußball)*
checken	to realize I didn't realize that she was the boss!
check	*kontrollieren; überprüfen*
Chef	boss I'll introduce you to my boss. But: Who is the current US Chief of Staff?
chef/chief	*(Chef-)Koch; Häuptling*
City	town Shall we travel into town together?
City	*Londoner Finanzdistrikt*
Controller	management accountant; cost controller You need to be a qualified management accountant to apply for this position.
controller	*Lotse; Kontrolleur; Steuergerät*
Controlling	cost control I work in cost control.
controlling	*Steuern; Überwachen*
Daten	data; dates Here are the final data from our survey.
dates	*Verabredungen; Kalenderdaten*

If you mean...	say this:
This...	**means:**
Datum	date What's the date today?
date	*Rendezvous; Tagesangabe*
defekt	out of order/not working The photocopier is out of order.
defect	*überlaufen; Störung*
definitiv	definitely We are definitely going to attend the event.
definitive	*endgültig*
Dekorateur	interior designer; interior decorator He's an interior decorator. She's studying to become an interior designer.
decorator	*Maler*
delikat	sensitive; subtle This is a sensitive subject. This dish has a very subtle lemon flavour.
delicate	*zerbrechlich; zart*
Delikatesse	delicacy Which dishes are considered a delicacy in China?
delicatessen	*Feinkostgeschäft*
dementiert	denied The boss has denied all knowledge of this matter.
demented	*verrückt/wahnsinnig*
demolieren	to vandalize The shop was vandalized during the night.
demolish	*abreißen; vernichten*
desinteressiert	indifferent You seem very indifferent about this subject.
disinterested	*unparteiisch; unvoreingenommen*
Devise	motto I think our motto is clear.
devise/device	*ausdenken/Gerät*

If you mean...	say this:
This...	**means:**
dezent	subtle The message we're sending is very subtle.
decent	*anständig; ordentlich*
dick	fat/overweight More and more people are overweight.
thick	*dumm; dick (für alles außer Menschen)*
Direktion	head office/headquarters; company management He works at head office. She works directly for the company management.
direction	*Richtung*
Dissertation	thesis I wrote a thesis about bilingualism in children. But: What is your dissertation all about?
dissertation	*Doktorarbeit; dissertation*
Dom	cathedral Have you ever visited Salisbury Cathedral?
dome	*Kuppel*
Dusche	shower The shower in my room is not working.
douche	*Intimdusche*
einschlafen	to fall asleep I fell asleep on the train to Hamburg.
sleep in	*ausschlafen*
energisch	forceful He's always quite forceful in his opinions.
energetic	*energiegeladen; aktiv*
engagiert	committed My team is fully committed to achieving our company's goals.
engaged	*verlobt*
Erlaubnis	permission First you need to get your boss's permission.
allowance	*finanzielle Unterstützung/Taschengeld; Rücksicht*

If you mean…	say this:
This…	**means:**
Etikett	label Could you remove the label for me, please?
etiquette	*Etikette; Benimmregeln*
eventuell	perhaps/maybe/possibly It would perhaps be a good idea to sell it now.
eventually	*schließlich/im Endeffekt*
Evergreen	(golden) oldie They're using a golden oldie in their TV ads.
evergreen	*immergrüne Pflanze*
Exemplar	copy Could you send me a copy of the newsletter please so that I can check it?
example	*Beispiel*
Existenz	livelihood His whole livelihood depends on the success of his company.
existence	*Bestehen; Dasein*
extra; Extra-	especially; on purpose/deliberately I brought along this English newspaper especially for you. We dropped the price deliberately to see if it would increase demand. But: Please could you bring us an extra portion of fries?
extra	*zusätzlich; besonders*
Fabrik	factory We are going to build a new factory in Bavaria.
fabric	*Stoff; Gewebe*
Falte	wrinkle; crease We are going to start producing a new anti-wrinkle cream. My shirt is all creased from the long flight.
fold	*Falte (Papier~); falten*
familiär	domestic/family He has resigned for family reasons.
familiar	*vertraut; bekannt*
Fantasie	imagination She doesn't have a very active imagination, unfortunately.
fantasy	*Fantasiebild*

If you mean...	say this:
This...	**means:**
faul	lazy I've been very lazy this week. But: Where is that foul smell coming from?
foul	*widerlich; übelriechend*
fehlen	to be missing/absent; to be lacking Three colleagues are absent today due to illness. Our ideas are lacking something, but I'm not sure what exactly. But: Words fail me. I don't know what to say.
fail	*durchfallen*
Fehler	mistake/error There's an error in that formula. Let's check it.
failure	*Misserfolg*
Fest	party We are throwing a big party to help Chris celebrate his retirement!
feast	*Festmahl*
fixieren	to stare; to locate Everyone was staring at me; I don't know why. I couldn't locate which part of the machine the noise was coming from.
fix	*reparieren*
flattern	to be in/get into a flap He really got into a flap about that email.
flatter	*schmeicheln*
Fleisch	meat What do we call the meat from deer? But: Don't worry; it's just a flesh wound.
flesh	*Fleisch*
Flirt	flirtation It was just a brief flirtation, nothing more.
flirt	*flirten; Flirt (d. h. Person)*
Flocke	flake The snowflakes were enormous.
flock	*Herde*
Flur	hallway Please leave your coat in the hallway.
floor	*Boden; Stockwerk*

If you mean...	say this:
This...	**means:**
Folie	film; transparency/slide We are developing a new type of coated film that can be removed without leaving marks. You can see our sales figures on this slide.
foil	*Metallfolie*
Form	shape Our machines can produce any shape you want.
form	*Formular*
Format	dimensions; stature Is it possible to manufacture the same product according to different dimensions? He is a man of stature. But: Can you print this in the same format?
format	*Format*
Formular	form Please could you fill in this form? Thank you.
formula	*Formel*
Fotograf	photographer She's a photographer by trade.
photograph	*Foto*
Fraktion	parliamentary group; faction It's a parliamentary group for animal welfare. They belong to a very liberal faction of the party.
fraction	*Bruchteil*
Fusion	merger
	After the merger they changed the firm's name.
fusion	*Verschmelzung; Zusammenschluss*
Gasthaus	restaurant; inn Have you tried the small Italian restaurant next door yet? Let's go to that little inn on the outskirts of town.
guesthouse	*Pension; Gästehaus*
genial	brilliant That's a brilliant suggestion!
genial	*freundlich; gesellig*

If you mean...	say this:
This...	**means:**
Genie	genius You're a genius – that's a great idea!
genie	*Dschinn/Flaschengeist*
Gift	poison You sell rat poison? Oh!
gift	*Geschenk*
glücklich	happy I'm very happy to be here today.
lucky, to be ~	*Glück haben*
Grad	extent; degree (°C, °F) We can only service the equipment for free to the extent of our warrantee. The temperature in Athens today is 30°C.
grade	*Note; Qualität, (Schul-)Klasse*
Gratulation	Congratulations! Congratulations on your promotion! But on birthdays: Happy birthday!
congratulations	*Gratulation!; Herzlichen Glückwunsch!*
groß	large/big I work for a large company in France.
great/gross	*großartig/ekelhaft*
größte/r/s	largest/biggest Our company is the largest in the world.
greatest	*beste; großartigste*
Grund	reason That's the reason why I cannot attend today.
ground	*Boden; Erde*
gründen	to found He founded the company 20 years ago.
ground	*Hausarrest erteilen; aus dem Verkehr ziehen*
gültig	valid My passport is only valid for two more months.
guilty	*schuldig*

If you mean...	say this:
This...	**means:**
Grüße	wishes Best wishes, Marla/Warm wishes, Megan But: Greetings from Munich! Simon
greetings	*Grüße*
Gurke	cucumber I'd like my salad without cucumber, please.
gherkin	*Gewürzgurke*
Gymnasium	secondary school; high school
gymnasium	*Sport-/Turnhalle*
halten	to keep Please keep the information confidential.
hold	*(fest-)halten*
handeln	to deal; to act What's the best way to deal with this problem? We have to act now if we want to see results. But: How do you want to handle this matter?
handle	*handhaben/behandeln*
Handy	mobile phone/cell phone My mobile phone has been stolen!
handy	*handlich*
Haus	office I'm sorry; he is not in the office today. But: I invited them to my house for dinner.
house	*Haus*
Hektik	rush You always seem to be in a rush. Take it easy!
hectic	*hektisch*
Helm	helmet You need to wear a safety helmet in the factory.
helm	*Steuer/Ruder*
herzlich	cordial; warm You are cordially invited to join us in celebrating ... With warm regards, ...
heart(il)y	*zünftig; tiefempfunden*

If you mean...	say this:
This...	**means:**
Hochschule	university; college I went to university in Birmingham, England.
high school	*Sekundarschule: Gymnasium, Realschule, usw.*
honorieren	to reward; to pay We would like to reward all the hard work you have done for us. How much are they prepared to pay for the work?
honour	*ehren; auszeichnen*
Hose	trousers The waiter spilled red wine on my trousers.
hose	*Gartenschlauch; Strumpfhose*
human	humane They are demonstrating for humane working conditions!
human	*Mensch; menschlich*
Hymne	anthem Can you sing your national anthem off by heart?
hymn	*Kirchenlied*
imprägnieren	to coat with/to spray with If you spray your shoes with this substance, it will protect the leather.
impregnate	*schwängern; imprägnieren*
irritieren	to confuse I was confused by my colleague's statement. But: I was a little irritated by his criticism.
irritate	*ärgern; reizen*
Jubiläum	anniversary The club will be celebrating its 20th anniversary this year. But: Do you remember the Queen's Silver Jubilee?
jubilee	*Jubiläum*
Kalender	diary; time-planner I'm not sure if I have time on Wednesday. Let me just check my diary. But: There's a calendar over there on the wall. Can you see what day of the week the 30th falls on?
calendar	*Kalender*

If you mean...	say this:
This...	**means:**
Kamerad	mate/pal Can I introduce you to Simon? He's an old mate of mine from my schooldays.
comrade	*Genosse*
Kanal	channel We don't receive channel TV where I live. We are too remote. But: Goods used to be transported around the country on the canals and waterways.
canal	*Kanal/Wasserstraße*
Kanne	pot; jug Could you pass me the coffee pot, please?
can	*Konservendose*
Karte	ticket I have tickets for a gospel concert on Saturday. Would you like to come along?
card	*Karton; Visitenkarte; Grußkarte; Ansichtskarte*
Karton	box? Where will I find a box to put my files in?
carton	*Tüte; Schachtel*
Kasse	till; check-out Can you show me where the check-out is, please?
cash	*Bargeld*
Kaution	deposit; bail If you wish to take this apartment, you'll have to pay a deposit of three months' rent. The actor was allowed out of prison on bail.
caution	*Warnung*
Kissen, Kopf~	pillow Ask the flight attendant for a pillow and blanket. It'll help you to sleep. But: Our waiting area is not very comfortable. Let's buy some cushions for the seats.
cushion	*Sitzkissen*
klassisch	classical I enjoy listening to classical music.
classic	*Klassiker; klassisch*

If you mean...	say this:
This...	**means:**
kochen	to boil Water boils at 100°C. I'll make some coffee. But: My husband only cooks at the weekends.
cook	*kochen*
Konfession	religious denomination This section of the form is where you need to tick the religious denomination you belong to.
confession	*Beichte*
Konjunktiv	subjunctive I always had problems at school understanding the subjunctive. You too?
conjunctive	*verbindend*
Konjunktur	economy The economy has suffered a lot lately but it finally appears to be recovering.
conjuncture	*Sachlage; Zusammentreffen*
konsequent	consistent It is important to maintain a consistent strategy.
consequent	*daraus folgend*
konstruieren	to design We have succeeded in designing a model which can be manufactured in one piece.
construct	*bauen*
Konstruktion	design This is an award-winning design.
construction	*Bau*
kontrollieren	to check It's my job to check the travel expense claims.
control	*steuern*
kosten	to taste You must taste this dish; it's superb.
cost	*Kosten*

If you mean...	say this:
This...	**means:**
Kostüm	ladies' suit You should wear a suit for your interview, Evelyn.
costume	*Kostüm; Verkleidung*
Kraft	strength/energy I eat lots of fruit because it gives me energy.
craft	*Kunsthandwerk; Gewerbe*
Kredit	loan The bank has agreed to give us a short-term loan.
credit	*Guthaben*
Kritik	criticism; critique If you have any constructive criticism, we'd be happy to hear it. Try not to read a critique of the show you are about to see; it might spoil the experience.
critic	*Kritiker*
Lager	stockroom/storeroom; warehouse I will just check the stockroom for your size. Our warehouse is located a few streets away.
lager	*helles Bier/Lagerbier*
Land	country; state; countryside He's from another country, but I'm not sure which. Our headquarters is in the state of North Rhine-Westphalia. We have a cottage in the Welsh countryside. But: They've bought some land from a local farmer.
land	*Grund und Boden*
Landschaft	countryside; scenery Have you ever travelled by train through the English countryside? The scenery is breathtaking in certain regions. But: This part of the country is characterized by its agricultural landscape.
landscape	*Landschaft; quer*
Leiter	Head We have created a completely new position: Head of Quality Management. But: He is a very respected team leader.
leader	*Führer; Anführer*

If you mean...	say this:
This...	**means:**
Lektüre	reading matter; read I've picked up a lot of reading matter on this subject. I'll summarize it for you on Friday.This novel is an excellent read. I can highly recommend it.
lecture	*Vortrag*
lernen	to revise Sorry, I can't come out with you all. My accounting exam is in ten days' time and I need to revise for it. But: I would love to learn Japanese some day.
learn	*lernen*
Likör	liqueur This is a special Finnish liqueur; it is very sweet and has a strong liquorice flavour.
liquor	*Spirituosen; alkoholisches Getränk*
liquid(e)	(financially) solvent Her company is no longer solvent. They might have to declare themselves bankrupt.
liquid	*flüssig*
Lohn	wages/pay Their pay is supplemented by set amounts for overtime and work at weekends and on public holidays.
loan	*Darlehen*
Lust (haben auf)	to fancy Where do you fancy going for lunch today?
lust (to ~ after sth/sb)	*Begierde; etw./jdn. begehren*
Mann	husband I sometimes accompany my husband on his business trips. But: He's a very demanding man; he will keep you on your toes, believe me.
man	*Mann*
Mappe	folder I have all the documents we need in this folder here.
map	*Landkarte*

If you mean...	say this:
This...	**means:**
Marmelade	jam/jelly (US) I think I will buy some jam from Harrods as a present for my sister.
marmalade	*Citrusmarmelade*
Maschine	plane; flight Our plane landed early. That doesn't happen very often. I missed the flight and had to take the later one. But: We will be presenting our new machine at the trade fair in two weeks.
machine	*Maschine*
massiv	solid All of the furniture we produce is made of solid wood.
massive	*riesig*
meinen	to think What do you think about our new financial strategy? But: No, that's not what I mean. Let me explain it a different way.
mean	*bedeuten*
Meinung	opinion We've heard everyone's opinions now. Shall we put it to the vote?
meaning	*Bedeutung*
Menü	set meal; daily special We've ordered a set meal for the evening event. But there will be a vegetarian alternative.
menu	*Speisekarte*
Mimik	facial expression Your facial expression tells me you aren't satisfied with my proposal.
mimic	*Imitator*
mobben	to bully We are having problems with bullying in the workplace.
mob	*umlagern*
Moderator	presenter/host; facilitator He's a TV presenter. His show is on at 8pm every Thursday. We have asked Harry to act as facilitator at today's meeting.
moderator	*Moderator; Bremssubstanz*

If you mean...	say this:
This...	**means:**
Montage	assembly My team is responsible for the machines' assembly and — installation.
montage	*Bildmontage*
Moral	morale; ethics How do we effectively boost morale within the company? Team ethics will play a very important role in this particular project.
moral	*Moral*
Motor	engine He can fix anything with an engine: generators, ship's engines, car engines, you name it.
motor	*Motor; Auto*
nächste/r/s	nearest Hi, can you tell me where the nearest petrol station is? But: Who is presenting next? We're ready for them now.
next	nächste/r/s
Natur	outdoors; countryside There's nothing more relaxing than being outdoors, away from suburbia. But: I have a question of a private nature.
nature	*Natur*
neulich	recently I saw a documentary on the TV recently that was all about the effects on consumers of precisely this type of marketing.
newly	*neu(-)*
nobel	posh/fancy; classy I am not a fan of posh restaurants. I prefer something more down-to-earth. It's a very classy place. It'll be perfect for this year's Christmas party.
noble	*adelig; großzügig*
Note	grade/mark I never got good marks at school in maths. I was always bottom of the class.
note	*Notiz*

If you mean...	say this:
This...	**means:**
Notiz	note I'll make a note of that and check it when I am back at my desk.
notice	*Mitteilung; Anzeige*
Objekt	property We are currently looking for a new property to develop into office suites for small companies.
object	*Gegenstand*
Objektiv	lens The photographer is here somewhere. I think he went to look for a spare lens for his camera.
objective	*objektiv*
Oldtimer	antique car/vintage car We had a brilliant team event: a vintage car rally during the day and a cocktail party to round off the day.
old timer	*alter Hase*
ordinär	vulgar His uses very vulgar language. I will have to speak to him about it.
ordinary	*alltäglich; unauffällig*
Paar	couple Here's some office gossip for you: those two have been a couple since the summer party. But: I need a pair of brown shoes to match my suit.
pair	*Paar*
Paket	parcel/package Hello, Peter? Can you come to reception, please? There is a parcel here for you.
packet	*Packung/Schachtel*
Paragraf	section We would like to draw your attention to section C of the contract where we stipulate our terms and conditions.
paragraph	*Absatz; Paragraph*
Pass	passport May I see your passport?
pass	*Passierschein; Eintrittskarte*

If you mean...	say this:
This...	**means:**
pathetisch	emotional The managing director gave an emotional speech.
pathetic	*jämmerlich/miserabel; herzergreifend*
Pause	break OK, let's take a 15-minute break and then go on to point 3.
pause	*Pause*
Pension	guesthouse I decided to stay at a little guesthouse near the client's this time. I wasn't satisfied with the service at my last hotel.
pension	*Ruhestandsgeld*
per	by I sent the invoice last week in the post. Haven't you received it yet?
per	*pro*
Perlen	beads Are these real Murano glass beads? They're beautiful. But: I inherited these pearls from my grandmother.
pearls	*Perlen*
Personal	staff/personnel; human resources I have a meeting with my staff this afternoon. I'll give them the news then.
	He's head of human resources.
personal	*persönlich*
Plastik	sculpture In this exhibition you will see various sculptures from the German Renaissance era. But: All of these machines process plastic materials, whereas the other machines work with metal materials.
plastic	*Kunststoff*
Platz	square; seat I'll meet you on the main square in the town centre. Please have a seat.
place	*Ort; Stelle*

If you mean...	say this:
This...	**means:**
Pointe	punchline I was listening to him tell a joke, but there was an interruption so I completely missed the punchline.
point	*Punkt*
Police	policy Shall we discuss the insurance policy now?
police	*Polizei*
Posten	item; position I've checked the accounts and I need some explanation of the following items. He's been offered a new position within the department. But: He has resigned from his post as ecturer.
post	*Post; Pfosten; Stelle*
prägnant	concise I'd like a concise summary of the meeting.
pregnant	*schwanger*
Präservativ	condom In order to prevent the spread of HIV we recommend the use of condoms.
preservative	*Konservierungsmittel*
Preis	prize; price This year's winner of the architecture prize goes to ... The price of gold has increased tremendously.
price; prize	*Preis*
Probe	test; sample My son has an English test at school today. Would you like a free sample of our new perfume?
	Sonde; Erforschung
Programm	channel; schedule Our company will be featuring in a documentary on Channel 3 this evening at 9pm. Can we keep to the schedule, please? But: I bought a programme when I was at the theatre yesterday. Would you like to borrow it?
program(me)	*Programm*

If you mean...	say this:
This...	**means:**
Promotion	doctorate/PhD He's writing a thesis on laser interferometry for his PhD.
promotion	*Beförderung; Werbeaktion*
proper	Neat/tidy Do you always keep your workspace this tidy? Mine looks like a bomb has hit it.
proper	*anständig; angemessen*
Prospekt	brochure Can I give you one of our brochures? There is a price list at the back.
prospect	*Aussicht; potentieller Kunde*
Protokoll	minutes (of a meeting) Who's taking the minutes today?
protocol	*Verhaltensprotokoll; Plan*
Provision	commission We get paid on a commission basis: 10% of all sales.
provision	*Bereitstellung; Rücklage*
Prozess	trial The public were not allowed to spectate at the trial. But: We must improve our working processes if we are to become more competitive.
process	*Prozess*
prüfen	to examine/to test When we interview the candidates today we need to test their English on the spot.
prove	*beweisen*
Publikum	audience Our audience seems very attentive today, don't you think?
public	*Öffentlichkeit*
Pudding	custard/blancmange (UK) We often used to have blancmange at school for lunch. I hated it because it was always lumpy.
pudding	*Nachspeise*

If you mean...	say this:
This...	**means:**
punktuell	point by point Let me give you a point-by-point summary of the negotiation.
punctual	*pünktlich*
Quote	quota/share Our exports are unfortunately limited. If we exceed our quota, we can be fined.
quote	*Zitat*
raffiniert	sophisticated/ingenious This is an incredibly sophisticated piece of machinery. But: We don't use refined sugar; only raw cane.
refined	*veredelt; raffiniert*
rasch	rapid/swift I had to make a swift decision.
rash	*vorschnell*
Rasse	breed You have three dogs? Wow! What breed are they? But: We welcome people of all races, beliefs and abilities.
race	*Rasse; Rennen*
Rate	instalment We have agreed to allow this customer to pay in instalments. But: The current rate of inflation is quite worrying.
rate	*Kurs; Preis*
raten	to guess; to advise Can you guess what the next graph is going to show? I would advise you not to say anything just yet.
rate	*bewerten*
Ratio	rationale I want to know the rationale behind this decision.
ratio	*Verhältnis*
rationell	efficient(ly) This equipment enables the operator to clean all surfaces quickly and efficiently.
rational(ly)	*vernünftig*
reell	reasonable Is there a reasonable chance of our sales increasing this year?
real	*wirklich; echt*

If you mean...	say this:
This...	**means:**
Reklamation	complaint This department deals with customer complaints.
reclamation	*Rückgewinnung*
Rektor/in	head teacher/principal (US) I need to leave the meeting early to go to my daughter's school for an appointment with the head teacher.
rector	*Pfarrer*
rentabel	viable/financially worthwhile We aren't sure if such an investment would be truly viable for our company.
rentable	*(ver)mietbar*
Rente	pension; annuity Have you thought about opening a savings account? You will need something to supplement the state pension. An annuity is a yearly payment of an allowance or income.
rent	*Miete*
repräsentativ	prestigious The consulting company has moved into some very prestigious new premises. But: These figures are not representative of the real situation.
representative	*charakteristisch*
Ressort	department He's in charge of the marketing department.
resort	*Ferienort; Ausweg*
Revision	audit; appeal I'm responsible for the internal audit. He's going to appeal against his court sentence.
revision	*Überarbeitung; Wiederholung (Lehrstoff)*
Rezept	recipe; prescription I know this amazing recipe for salmon lasagne. The doctor has given me a prescription for sleeping tablets.
receipt	*Quittung*
Rollen	wheels No, that's not my suitcase. Mine has wheels.
rolls	*Brötchen*

If you mean...	say this:
This...	**means:**
Roller	scooter My son has asked for a scooter with larger wheels for Christmas.
roller	*Lockenwickler*
Roman	novel I read two whole novels on the plane. It was a long flight!
roman	*Römer*
Rückseite	back/reverse. You will find the instructions on the back of this card.
backside	*Hintern*
Salat	lettuce I love all kinds of lettuce but my favourites are romaine and iceberg. But: I only eat salad for lunch. I have to watch my waistline!
salad	*Salat*
sauer	angry Have you any idea why the boss is so angry? But: This cocktail is rather sour. I don't think I can finish it.
sour	*sauer*
scharf	spicy/hot How spicy would you like your curry? But: Be careful with those scissors; they are really sharp.
sharp	*scharf; scharfsinnig*
Schatten	shade It's 35 degrees in here. Is the air conditioning not working? But: The murderer was hiding in the shadows.
shadow	*Schatten*
Schema	pattern All of our marketing ideas seem to have followed the same pattern. Let's try something new this time.
scheme	*Programm; Plan; Intrige*
schreien	to shout I came to see who was shouting. What's the problem?
cry	*weinen*

If you mean...	say this:
This...	**means:**
schwimmen	to float The advantage of this material is that it floats on water. But: I always go for an early morning swim in the hotel pool when I'm on a business trip.
swim	*schwimmen*
See	lake The boss has invited us to go fishing with him on a nearby lake at the weekend.
sea	*Meer*
selbstbewusst	confident She's a confident person. She'll go far.
self-conscious	*gehemmt*
senden	to broadcast; to despatch A recorded interview with the president will be broadcast on all channels this evening. We'll despatch the goods to you immediately.
send	*schicken; versenden*
Sender	radio station; TV channel; transmitter All of the radio stations and TV channels are interested in reporting about our new product. There may be some public opposition to the location of this transmitter.
sender	*Absender*
sensibel	sensitive Be careful when voicing your opinions to Charles; he's very sensitive.
sensible	*vernünftig*
seriös	legitimate Can you confirm that you received a legitimate offer for this car?
serious	*ernst(haft)*
skrupellos	unscrupulous We will not do business with any unscrupulous partners. Everything must be above board.
scrupulous	*peinlich genau*

If you mean...	say this:
This...	**means:**
skurril	quirky/bizarre I agree; he's quite a bizarre character. He does an excellent job though.
scurrilous	*gemein; ordinär*
Slip	briefs (men and women); underpants (men); panties (women) My luggage hasn't arrived. I need to know the nearest place where I can buy briefs and shaving things.
slip	*Unterrock; Zettel*
Slipper	loafers/casual shoes Have you seen my loafers? I need to pack a pair for the time off in between meetings.
slipper	*Hauschuh/Pantoffel*
Smoking	dinner jacket (UK) /tuxedo (US) Do I need to wear a dinner jacket this evening?
smoking	*Rauchen*
Soße	gravy Could we please have some more gravy for the beef? But: What type of sauce would you like with your burger – sweet and sour or hot chilli?
sauce	*Soße*
souverän	confident I have to say I was impressed by how confident you were when you gave your presentation today.
sovereign	*hoheitlich*
sparen	to save We can save at least 5% if we change suppliers now. But: Please, spare me the details. I get the idea.
spare	*verschonen*
spenden	to donate We have decided not to send Christmas cards this year. We will be donating money to charity instead.
spend	*ausgeben*
spendieren	to treat sb. to sth. Congratulations everybody, we've won the contract! Let's go the pub so I can treat you all to a drink.
spend	*ausgeben*

If you mean...	say this:
This...	**means:**
Spot	TV commercial/advert We've managed to get a local celebrity to appear in our commercial.
spot	*Pickel; Fleck; Ort/Stelle*
Sprecher	spokesperson A former colleague of mine has just become spokesperson for one of the major energy supply companies. But: We have invited a speaker today who is an expert in this field. I'd like you to give a big welcome to ...
speaker	*Redner; Sprecher*
springen	to jump; to run I would say that's a good reason to jump for joy, wouldn't you? I have to run over to the canteen again; I forgot to pick up my mobile when we left.
spring, to ~ sb.	*jdn. (z. B. aus dem Gefängnis) rausholen*
Stadium	stage/phase The product is still at the development stage.
stadium	*Stadion*
stark	strong I need someone strong to help me carry these boxes.
stark	*krass/schier*
starten	to take off; to launch We are sorry for the delay in taking off this morning. The rocket was launched punctually at 5am local time.
start	*beginnen*
Station	ward; stop She'll be staying in the maternity ward until Saturday. All exit the train! This is the final stop.
station	*Bahnhof; Stelle*
stationär	in hospital He's being treated in hospital for exhaustion. But: All traffic is stationary due to an accident.
stationary	*stehend; stationär*
stickig	stuffy Can we open some windows? It's so stuffy in here.
sticky	*klebrig*

If you mean...	say this:
This...	**means:**
Stock	floor; stick/cane Our offices are on the 25th floor. Since he broke his leg he's needed to use a stick to walk.
stock	*Inventar/Lagerbestand; Aktien*
Stoff	fabric; substance; topic We manufacture high-quality upholstery fabric. Our machines process a special type of material. This topic will provide plenty of discussion.
stuff	*Zeug*
streng	strict We have to follow very strict accounting procedures.
strong	*stark*
Studium	course (degree ~; at university/college)
study	*Untersuchung; Arbeitszimmer*
sympathisch	likeable She's a very likeable member of our team.
sympathetic	*mitfühlend*
Tablett	tray Do you know where we can find a tray to put all these champagne glasses on?
tablet	*Tablette*
Takt	interval; rhythm The train service runs in 30-minute intervals. I can't keep up with this rhythm. It's too fast! But: You need to show more tact when giving feedback.
tact	*Taktgefühl*
Tarif	charge/fee; Do you know what the fee is for translations of this type? We allocate pay increases to employees on the basis of the scales agreed with the trade unions.
tariff	*Zolltarif; Gebührenordnung*
Technik	technology Can you describe your company's technology to us in more detail? But: There is a special technique for doing this. Let me demonstrate it to you.
technique	*Methode/Vorgehensweise; Technik*

If you mean...	say this:
This...	**means:**
temperamentvoll	feisty/vivacious She's the most vivacious press agent we have ever had; she's so full of energy!
temperamental	*launisch; unzuverlässig*
terminieren	to schedule Can we schedule these meetings to take place every four weeks?
terminate	*beenden*
Thema	subject The subject of my presentation today is work-life balance. But: The theme surrounding the exhibition is ›light‹.
theme	*Motiv; Titelsong*
These	theory Our managers support the theory that employee motivation cannot be increased only by offering more money.
thesis	*Dissertation; Doktorarbeit*
Tick	quirk He talks to himself while he's working. It's just one of his little quirks.
tick	*Zecke; Häkchen*
Tipp	bet It's a safe bet that we will get the contract. But: Have you got a tip for me on how to avoid spam?
tip	*Ratschlag; Trinkgeld; Tipp*
tippen	to type I'll come over to you as soon as I've finished typing this report.
tip	*ein Trinkgeld geben; kippen*
Transparent	banner I thought we could put up a few banners on our stand at the trade fair. They will draw more attention to us.
transparent	*durchsichtig; transparent*
treu	loyal They are a loyal customer. Please deal with their request without delay.
true	*wahr/echt*

If you mean...	say this:
This...	**means:**
Trubel	confusion; hubbub This decision is causing a lot of confusion among my colleagues. Why is there such a hubbub around here today? What's happened?
trouble	*Ärger; Unannehmlichkeiten*
überarbeiten	update/revise/amend These statistics are from last week. I will update them before we present to the board.
overwork	*sich überarbeiten*
überhören	to miss (hearing); to ignore (a remark) I'm sorry but I missed that. Could you repeat it? I will ignore what you just said.
overhear	*zufällig hören*
übernehmen	to take over; to take on We are speculating that this company will take over at least one of its main competitors within the next year. Joanne will be taking on Silvia's responsibilities while she is on maternity leave.
overtake	*überholen*
übersehen	to miss (seeing) Oh, I'm sorry. I completely missed that part. I will finish translating it immediately.
oversee	*beaufsichtigen; überwachen*
Übersicht	overview Can you give us a short overview of the project?
oversight	*Versehen*
untergehen	to go down They failed to develop a good strategy. They're going to go down, mark my words.
undergo	*erfahren; sich unterziehen*
Unternehmer	entrepreneur/business owner
undertaker	*Leichenbestatter*
unterschreiben	to sign As soon as the contract is signed we can proceed.
underwrite	*garantieren*

If you mean...	say this:
This...	**means:**
Ventilator	fan This office is too hot in summer. I need to get a fan for my desk.
ventilator	*Belüfter; Beatmungsgerät*
Visite	rounds The doctor will talk to you when he does his rounds later this morning.
visit	*Besuch*
Vokal	vowel The vowels are a, e, i, o and u.
vocal	*Sänger; Gesang*
vorsehen	to budget; to set aside We have budgeted for a certain amount of bad debt. This money has been set aside for emergencies.
foresee	*vorhersehen*
wandern	to hike How about we take the whole department for a hike one weekend to boost morale?
wander	*umherwandern*
Warenhaus	department store If you need a souvenir, try looking in the department store in the main square.
warehouse	*Warenlager*
weil	because I want to go to the Budapest office because a face-to-face conversation will clear this problem up more effectively.
while	*während*
Werk	Plant/works I'm going to the Manchester works this week, but I'll be back in London next Monday.
work	*Arbeit*
Weste	waistcoat (UK) /vest (US)
vest	*Unterhemd* (UK); *Weste* (US)
will	want I want to show you how this will work.
will	*werde/wirst/wird/werden/werdet*

If you mean...	say this:
This...	**means:**
winken	to wave Can you wave the waiter over if you catch his eye?
wink	*zwinkern*
Wunder	miracle It's a miracle that we managed to survive the economic problems. But: Can you name all seven wonders of the world?
wonder	*etw. verwunderliches*
wundern	to be surprised I'm surprised that you don't have jetlag. Do you never suffer from it?
wonder	*sich fragen*
Zensur	grade; censorship I got a satisfactory grade in the interim exam. The film has caused some criticism and is currently undergoing the censorship process.
censure	*Kritik*
Zylinder	top hat Do all men wear top hats at English weddings? But: The gas is stored in cylinders.
cylinder	*Zylinder*

27.1 Internet resources

You can increase your knowledge of false friends by confronting yourself with them often. Here are some websites on which you will find more information about false friends:

www.business-english.de/false_friends_quiz.html
provides you with a test of your knowledge of general false friends.

www.business-english.de/quiz/false_friend_contr/
contains questions specifically for business English.

http://en.wikipedia.org/wiki/False_friend

has much more background information about the subject of false friends and deals with other foreign languages, not just German.

www.englisch-hilfen.de/words/false_friends.htm
offers a comprehensive, tabular list of false friends.

www.bbc.co.uk/languages/yoursay/false_friends/german/mist_common_false_friends_in_german_englishgerman.shtml
This BBC webpage has some amusing contributions from its readers.

The above-mentioned Internet addresses were correct at the time of going to press. The author is not responsible for the content or availability of these sites.

Teil 7: Appendix

28 Practical Reference

28.1 Linguistic Characteristics

28.1.1 The proper use of capital letters

In English the rules for using capitals are different from German rules.

Capital letters

In the following cases you do need to begin with capital letters:

- The pronoun ›I‹
- Proper names
- Names of
  - the days of the week,
  - the months of the year,
  - holidays
  - historical periods
  - buildings
  - positions or titles of people
  - organisations
  - languages
  - nationalities or ethnic groups
- Words expressing a connection with geographical places
- Significant religious terms
- Roman numerals
- The first word of direct quotations, sentences or fragments

Small letters

Other elements are always written with small letters, such as:

- Names of directions (e.g.: south etc.)
- Names of seasons
- Articles in proper names (e.g.: the Emir of Kuwait)

The title or name of a book, a film or a magazine usually has capital letters for every significant word, but words *like the, of, and or in* aren't capitalized, unless they are the first word. Like in: *Yesterday we saw The Silence of the Lambs on TV.*

In British English the first word after a colon (double-point) generally is not written in capital letters. American usage on the other hand often prefers a capital after a colon. As mentioned above: with direct quotations both language varieties use a capital to start the quotation.

Vocabulary:
pronoun: (Personal)pronomen
numeral: Zahlwort
quotation: Zitat
proper name: Eigenname

28.1.2 Using apostrophes

The apostrophe (') is a troublesome punctuation mark in English, and incorrect use of apostrophes will make someone's writing quickly look poor. Still there is a lot of confusion about using apostrophes.

Contractions
The apostrophe is used in writing contractions, that is shortened forms of words from which one or more letters have been omitted. The omitted letter is replaced by an apostrophe. Examples are: *it's* (*it is* or *it has*), *can't* (*cannot*), *aren't* (*are not*). When the word *not* is part of the contracted phrase, the apostrophe is always placed between the ›n‹ and the ›t‹. Traditionally contractions were considered as speaking language, and had no place whatsoever in formal business correspondence. Although using contractions in formal writing nowadays isn't considered wrong anymore, it's better to try to use them sparingly.

Full form	Contraction
cannot	can't
do not	don't
have not	haven't
he has (she)	he's, she's
he is (she)	he's, she's
I am	I'm
I have (we, you)	I've, we've, you've
I will/shall	I'll
is not	isn't
it has	it's
it is	it's
shall not	shan't
they are (we, you)	they're, we're, you're
will not	won't

Possessive forms

An apostrophe is also used in a possessive form like: *Hermann's report*. The basic rule is simple: a possessive form is spelled with 's' at the end. This also applies when the last letter is an ›s', for instance like: *Klaus's proposal*. But there is an exception: plural nouns which already end in an ›s‹, do not have a second ›s‹. They only have an apostrophe at the end as in: *four weeks' work*. When pluralising dates, there is a difference between British and American usage because the latter uses an apostrophe:

This model was designed in the 1990s.

This model was designed in the 1990's.

28.1.3 Using the spelling check

Especially in writing e-mails, spelling doesn't always seem to be a priority. Most errors can be simply prevented by using the spell check of your software. Below are some tips to make optimal use of this function. Always make sure that you turn on the function, and that you select the correct variety: for instance *English (United Kingdom)* or *English (United States)*. Besides local particular spelling conventions the second major difference is the vocabulary of each variety. The spell check takes this into account.

Homophones

One of the problems that German native speakers might have is that certain English words sound the same, but mean very different things, and they also don't have the same spelling. The little poem below gives no indication whatsoever of a spell check, but is of course absolute nonsense.

Important !

Finally eye used the English spelling chequer on my pea see,
This marked four my revue, the miss steaks I could knot sea,
So each time my chequer tolled me; eye quickly stroke the quay.

In linguistics these words are called homophones, i.e. words that have the same sound but a different spelling and meaning. Below is a selection of some relevant business homophones:

aisle	isle
buy	by

cell	sell
cent	scent
complement	compliment
fair	fare
hole	whole
hour	our
know	no
meat	meet
principal	principle
profit	prophet
right	write
sight	site
some	sum
stationary	stationery

28.2 Linguistic Differences: UK-USA

George Bernard Shaw once wrote that ›Britain and America are two countries divided by a common language‹. But although there are some differences in spelling conventions or vocabulary, only a few words really cause misunderstandings. An example of this is the expression *to table a motion*. In the UK this means to place it on the agenda, while in the US it means exactly the opposite (to remove it from consideration). No idea how this is solved in bilateral meetings...

Spelling differences

If we take a closer look at the spelling differences between British and American English, the examples in the table below show you some typical spelling conventions. Many nouns and adjectives are turned into verbs by adding -ize (standardize) in the US, and -ise in Britain. If in doubt, you can simply adjust the spell check on your computer.

UK	US
authorise	authorize
litre, theatre, kilometre	liter, theater, kilometer
colour	color
catalogue	catalog
cheque	(bank) check
defence, offence	defense, offense
programme (except computer program)	program
-our (labour, colour)	-or (labor, color)
-ogue (catalogue)	-og (catalog)
-ll (dialled, traveller)	-l (dialed, traveler)

But there are exceptions, for example: enrolment (UK), enrollment (US).

Different words

Besides the differences in spelling mentioned above, different words are simply used sometimes. Some of the more common ones are listed in the table below (listed by German translation for convenience):

Translation	UK	US
Bankkonto	banking account	bank account
Banknote	banknote	bill
Benzin	petrol	gas(oline)
Betrieb	company	corporation
Buchung	booking	reservation
Erkundigung	enquiry	inquiry
Führerschein	driving licence	driver's license
Herbst	autumn	fall
Lebenslauf	curriculum vitae	résumé, school transcript
Rechnung	bill	check
Rechtsanwalt	solicitor/barrister	attorney
Reservierung	booking	reservation
Rückfahrkarte	return ticket	round trip ticket

Translation	UK	US
Selbstkostenpreis	at cost price	at cost
Steuereinnahmen	inland revenue	duty income tax
Transport	transport	transportation
U-Bahn	underground	subway
Unterführung	subway	underpass
Verfallsdatum	expiry date	expiration date
vermieten	let	hire
vierzehn Tage	fortnight	two weeks
Wohnung	flat	apartment

Grammar differences

Some grammar differences are consistent between American and British:

UK	US
look out of the window	look out the window
last Monday week	a week ago last Monday
talk to, meet	talk with, meet with
I have (already) eaten	I (already) ate
River Thames, River Avon	Hudson River, Mississippi River
to be in a team	to be on a team
I've gone	I went

Apart from American and British, other well-known varieties of English are Canadian, Australian and South African. Countries such as India, Nigeria and the Philippines also have many English speakers.

Important

!

Contractions in British English are generally written without a full stop (e.g. Mr, Mrs and Ms). American English however usually uses a full stop (called period in North America): Mr., Mrs. and Ms.
Mr – British
Mr. – American

Vocabulary:
contraction: Zusammenziehung
full stop /period : Punkt

28.3 English around the world

Here are some useful general differences between British English and American English to note:

- British English allows the use of ›s‹ and ›z‹ in the spelling of some words, such as ›organise‹ or ›organize‹. American English uses only ›z‹.
- When you are writing any kind of correspondence on your computer, you can set the regional and language options in your word processing software to British English, American English, Indian English, Canadian English, or whatever you need at the time.
- Spelling- and grammar-checking extras also offer you the choice of using different versions of English.
- When communicating verbally in English to native speakers, you cannot expect to be corrected by your conversation partner. Even if you ask him or her to correct you, they will probably not do so, either out of politeness, or because they do not want to interrupt the flow of conversation. Watch their faces carefully for signs that they have not understood you, and if in doubt, ask.
- Learning false friends is the same as learning new vocabulary, but with the added importance of avoiding bigger misunderstandings.

Here are some practical tips for helping you to memorize new words and phrases:

If you see standard phrases in e-mails from other people that you want to use in your own correspondence, copy the sentences and paste them into a list. When you need them, you can copy them and paste them into your own emails or other documents.

Write new words and phrases onto sticky notes and put them on your bathroom mirror, your fridge, or a place that you look at frequently – perhaps your car dashboard, as long as it does not obstruct your concentration while driving! You will see the vocabulary again and again when you brush your teeth, are standing at your favourite place in the kitchen or driving to and from work.

28.4 Tables and Overviews

28.4.1 Types of companies

In many e-mail signatures businesses will write a company name with suffixes like AG, GmbH etc. This paragraph gives an overview of the different abbreviations that are in use in the Anglophone world. Although the judicial systems are very different, it is still sometimes very handy to have some kind of comparison. Therefore a German equivalent has been added, if applicable.

Abbr.	Country	Legal entity	Equivalent
Assocs.	USA	Associates	
(Edms.) Bpk.	RSA	Proprietary Limited (Afrikaans: Beperk)	GmbH
CC/BK	RSA	Close Corporation (Afrikaans: Beslote Korporasie)	
	UK	Company Limited by Guarantee	
	UK	Sole proprietorship, one-man business	EU
	UK	Unlimited Company	GmbH
Co.	USA	Company	
Corp.	USA	Corporation (see: Incorporated)	AG
Cpt	Irl	Cuideachta phoiblé theoranta (Public Limited Company)	AG
d/b/a	USA	Doing Business As.	EU

Abbr.	Country	Legal entity	Equivalent
ELP	Bah	Exempted Limited Partnership.	
IBC	Bah	International Business Company	offshore
Inc.	Can	Incorporated. Limited Liability	
Inc.	Aus	Incorporated Association	
Inc.	USA	Incorporated	AG
L.P.	USA	Limited Partnership	
LLC	USA	Limited Liability Company	
LLP	USA	Limited Liability Partnership	
LTD	Aus, India	Limited	GmbH
Ltd.	Can	Limited (Quebec: Limitée, Ltée)	GmbH
Ltd.	NZ, RSA	Limited	GmbH
Ltd.	UK	Private Limited Company	GmbH
(Pty.) Ltd.	RSA	Proprietary Limited	GmbH
N.A.	USA	National Association	für Banken
NT	Can	Intermediary	
P.C.	USA	Professional Corporation	
P/L or Pty. Ltd.	Aus	Proprietary Limited Company.	GmbH
PC Ltd	Aus	Public Company Limited by Shares	
PLC	Irl	Public Limited Company	AG
PLC	UK	Public Limited Company	AG
PrC	Irl	Private Company Limited by Shares	GmbH
Pty.Ltd. Pte. Ltd.	Various	Proprietary Limited company	GmbH
Pvt. Ltd.	India	Private Limited Company	GmbH
Teo	Irl	Teoranta	GmbH

Country abbreviations

Aus: Australia; Bah: Bahamas; Can: Canada; Irl: Irland; NZ: New Zealand; RSA: South Africa; UK: Großbritannien; USA: Vereinigte Staaten.

German abbreviations
AG: Aktiengesellschaft; GmbH: Gesellschaft mit beschränkter Haftung; EU: Einzelunternehmen.

Which abbreviation is from where?

Abbreviation	Country
Co	United States, Taiwan.
Co Ltd	Ireland, Gibraltar, Hong Kong, other Asian countries.
Corp	United States, Asian countries.
LLC	United States.
LLP	United States.
Ltd	United Kingdom, Canada, Gibraltar, Hong Kong, Ireland, Malta, New Zealand, Singapore, United States (occasionally).
PC Ltd	Australia.
PLC, Plc, plc	United Kingdom, Cyprus, Ireland.
Pty Ltd	Australia, Hong Kong, South Africa.
Co	United States, Taiwan.

28.4.2 Official holidays and translations

Finding the right translation for a national holiday during a conversation can be difficult. How would you explain *Mariä Himmelfahrt* or *Pfingsten* in English? Below are English-German translations for the most commonly celebrated official holidays. Their specific dates can be found in the next paragraph:

Holiday	Translation
New Year's Day	Neujahr
Epiphany	Heilige Drei Könige
Carnival	Karneval/Fasching
Good Friday	Karfreitag
Easter	Ostern
Labour Day	Tag der Arbeit
Ascension Day	Christi Himmelfahrt
Whit Sunday	Pfingsten (Pfingstsonntag)

Holiday	Translation
Whit Monday	Pfingstmontag
Corpus Christi	Fronleichnam
Midsummer's Day	Johannistag/Sommersonnenwende
Assumption	Mariä Himmelfahrt
All Saints' Day	Allerheiligen
Christmas Eve	Heiligabend
Christmas Day	Erster Weihnachtsfeiertag
Boxing Day	Zweiter Weihnachtsfeiertag
New Year's Eve	Silvester
National Day	Nationalfeiertag (auch für: Tag der deutschen Einheit)
Liberation Day	Tag der Befreiung

What are bank holidays?
A bank holiday is a public holiday in the United Kingdom and in the Republic of Ireland. Bank holidays are so called because they are the days upon which banks were closed by tradition (since the Bank Holidays Act of 1871). England and Wales share the same days, but Scotland, Northern Ireland and the Republic of Ireland all have their own public holiday.

28.4.3 Country-specific holidays

Besides the commonly celebrated holidays, most countries have specific local public holidays.

Australia
26 January – Australia Day, 25 April – ANZAC Day, second Monday in June – Queen's birthday

Canada
24 May – Victoria Day, 1 July – Canada Day, first Monday in September – Labour Day, second Monday in October – Thanksgiving, 11 November – Remembrance Day

England and Wales

7 May – May Day Bank Holiday, 28 May – Spring Bank Holiday, 27 August – Summer Bank Holiday

Ireland

St. Patrick's Day, first Monday in May, June, August last Monday in October

New Zealand

6 February –Waitangi Day, 25 April – ANZAC Day, first Monday in June – Queen's birthday, fourth Monday in October – Labour Day

Northern Ireland

17 March – St Patrick's Day, 7 May – May Day Bank Holiday, 28 May – Spring Bank Holiday, 12 July – Orangeman's Day, 27 August – Summer Bank Holiday

Scotland

2 January – 2 January, 7 May – May Day Bank Holiday, 28 May – Spring Bank Holiday, 6 August – Summer Bank Holiday, 30 November – St. Andrew's Day

South Africa

21 March – Human Rights Day, 27 April – Freedom Day, 1 May – Workers' Day, 16 June – Youth Day, 9 August – National Women's Day, 24 September – Heritage Day, 16 December – Day of Reconciliation

United States

Traditionally 30 May – Memorial Day, first Monday in September – Labor Day, 4 July – Independence Day – 4th Thursday in November – Thanksgiving Day

28.4.4 Translated geographical names

A number of cities in German-speaking regions have different names in English. The list below helps to prevent misunderstandings when giving address information.

Bayern	Bavaria
Braunschweig	Brunswick
Franken	Franconia
Frankfurt am Main	Frankfort
Hannover	Hanover
Koblenz	Coblenz
Köln	Cologne
Luzern	Lucerne
München	Munich
Niedersachsen	Lower Saxony
Nordrhein	Westfalen
North Rhine	Westphalia
Nürnberg	Nuremberg
Preußen	Prussia
Rheinland Pfalz	Rhineland Palatinate
Ruhrgebiet	Ruhr River Valley
Sachsen	Saxony
Schwaben	Swabia
Steiermark	Styria
Thüringen	Thuringia
Tirol	Tyrol
Westfalen	Westphalia
Wien	Vienna

28.4.5 Temperature conversion table

Fahrenheit (°F)	Celsius (°C)
212 (boiling point)	100 (Siedepunkt)
176	80
122	50
104	40
98.4 (body temperature)	37 (Körpertemperatur)
68	20
50	10
32 (freezing point)	0 (Gefrierpunkt)
14	-10
0	-17,8
-459.67 (absolute zero)	-273,15 (absoluter Nullpunkt)

Conversion of Celsius and Fahrenheit:

- °F – °C: (°F – 32) x 5/9 = °C
- °C – °F: °C x 9/5 + 32 = °F

28.4.6 Weights and measures

Weights	Gewichte
gross weight	Bruttogewicht
net weight	Nettogewicht
1 ounce (oz)	28,35 g
1 pound (lb)	453,6 g
1 stone	6,356 kg
1 short hundredweight (cwt)	45,359 kg (USA)
1 long hundredweight (cwt)	50,802 kg (GB)
1 short ton (tn)	907 kg (USA)
1 long ton (tn)	1016 kg (GB)

1 metric ton	1000 kg
Linear measures	**Längenmaße**
1 inch (in)	2,54 cm
1 foot (ft)	30,48cm (12 in)
1 yard (yd)	91,44cm (3 ft)
1 mile (m)	1,609km (1760 yd)

28.5 Electronic Guidelines on Internet

- Paradigm Online Writing Assistant:
  www.powa.org
  Regeln und Schreibweisen der Europäischen Union: http://publications.europa.eu/code/de/de-000100.htm
- BBC Style guide:
  www.bbctraining.com/pdfs/newsStyleGuide.pdf
- Deutsch-Englisches Wörterbuch:
  http://dict.leo.org

29 False friends game

If you would like to test how much you can remember from reading this book, try the false friends game below. It is a maze, also known as a labyrinth, but with text, and with options to choose from – some of which contain false friends.

Start by reading the text in box number 1, make your decision and then go to the next box that is mentioned. For example: you read box number 1 and decide for the second option. It says ›Go to 9‹, so continue reading at box number 9 and carry on until you are out of the maze.

1 It is Monday morning and a colleague from South Africa has come to Munich for a week to learn about your company and its administration processes. She will then return to SA to start her job there. You welcome her at reception and say to her »Follow me and I'll introduce you to everyone in the bureau.« **Go to 5.**
»Let me bring you to meet my chef.« **Go to 9.**
»Come and meet my colleagues. We have all been looking forward to your arrival.« **Go to 2.**

11 It is now Wednesday and you and your partner are having dinner with Karen in the city centre. You want to ensure that she enjoys her time in Munich. During the conversation, Karen asks you what you do in your spare time. You answer
»I make a lot of sport — cycling, running and wandering.« **Go to 8.**
»I like going out into the nature — every weekend if possible.« **Go to 12.**
»I play the clarinet in a small orchestra and I love badminton.« **Go to 14.**

10 Karen is surprised. It is a bit early in the day for cakes, and she cannot see any on the table, only biscuits/cookies. The meeting starts and Karen is looking forward to learning a lot his week. **Go to 7.**

2 There is a staff meeting every Monday morning and you introduce Karen to colleagues. Afterwards, you say
»I'm responsible for the minutes, so excuse me a moment while I just get organized.« **Go to 7.**
»Would you like some coffee and cakes?« **Go to 10.**
»I normally write the protocol for this meeting. Shall we sit at the front?« **Go to 4.**

12 The correct way to say ich *bin gern draußen in der Natur* is ›I like being outdoors‹ or ›I like spending time in the countryside.‹ **Go to 14.**

16 Congratulations, you have survived the week with an Englishspeaking visitor! If you made any mistakes at any time with false friends, make a note of them for future reference.

15 If someone has to amuse themselves, then it is because their host has no time for them – *sich selbst beschäftigen*. The right thing to say is ›I hope you enjoyed yourself here this week.‹ **Go to 16.**

9 Karen thinks you have your own personal *Chefkoch*. Whoops! Besides this, if you are moving something or someone to a destination further away from your current location, you ›take‹ it or them. So the correct thing to say was »Let me take you to meet my boss.« **Go to 2.**

3 Karen doesn't understand. You have told her that she could be lucky at her new desk (*sie könnte dort Schwein haben*) and she doesn't know why. **Go to 11. Go to 2.**

13 Karen is smiling. A coffer is a large box for holding money, jewels and other treasures, normally something that pirates search for. It is an oldfashioned word. Nowadays, you might hear people use it in the context of the ›state coffers‹ – *die Staatskassen*. **Go to 16.**

14 Friday has arrived. Karen is departing in a few minutes and is waiting for a taxi to take her to the airport. You say »It was nice to meet you, Karen. I hope you will call us if you have any questions when you are back in South Africa.« **Go to 16.**
»Where is your coffer? You mustn't forget it! I hope we see us again soon. Goodbye!« **Go to 13.**
»I hope you amused yourself this week. Have a good journey home!« **Go to 15.**

8 It is that common problem that German speakers have with the verb *machen*. It is correct to say ›I do a lot of sports.‹ If you say you like wandering, you are saying *ich wandere gern herum*, but if you mean you like walking in the hills and mountains, say ›I like hiking.‹ **Go to 14.**

4 Karen is a little confused. You said you write the protocol but this sounds to her like you are responsible for the *Benimmregeln* for the meeting. **Go to 7.**

5 *Büro* is ›office‹ in English. It was a small mistake. You take your visitor, Karen, to meet the people she will be having more contact with in future. **Go to 2.**

6 Karen goes red. She suspects you saw her looking at Dan. He is a goodlooking man, but he is wearing a wedding ring and she does not want a date with him, but she does have to make an appointment to talk with him about finance matters. And what is his job? Controller? Who does he control (*wen steuert er*)? **Go to 11.**

7 While you write the minutes (*Protokoll führen*) Karen agrees on some days and times to go to the other colleagues to learn about their areas of responsibility and their tasks. You ask Karen »Have you a date with Dan, our controller, too? **Go to 6.**
This meeting finishes at 11 o'clock. I'll show you to your desk after that." **Go to 11.**
»After this meeting I'll show you where you can work this week. I'm sure you'll be lucky there.« **Go to 3.**

Die Autoren

Prof. Dr. hc. Sander Schroevers (LL.C.)
ist ein Spezialist im Bereich der internationalen Kommunikation. Derzeit lehrt er Global Business Skills an der Universität für angewandte Wissenschaften in Amsterdam. Schroevers hat bereits achtzig Managementbücher im Bereich der internationalen Kommunikation herausgegeben. Er ist seit mehr als 25 Jahren als Berater in den Bereichen Internationalisierung und Export tätig und hat Angestellte mehrerer deutscher DAX-Unternehmen weitergebildet. Darüber hinaus ist er ein gefragter Sprecher auf internationalen Konferenzen oder Seminaren, und hat bei diversen akademischen und professionellen Institutionen als Professor oder Gastdozent gelehrt. Außer in Deutschland u.a. auch in den Vereinigten Staaten (Harvard), London, Paris, Mumbai, Singapur, Cluj-Napaco, Tiflis, Baku, Tallinn, Kalkutta, Vilnius, Mailand, Teheran, Tokio. Gegenwärtig ist er Präsident des IECIE-Gremiums, dem Europäischen Institut für Internationale Unternehmenskommunikation (l'institut européen de communication internationale d'entreprise) in Paris.

Internet: www.schroevers.eu

Von Sander Schroevers stammen die Kapitel 1, 2 dieses Buches. Zusammen mit Ian R. Lewis hat er Kapitel 5 verfasst.

Jaquie Mary Thomas
stammt aus Oxford, England. Als Diplom-Sozialpädagogin (FH) ist sie auf Erwachsenenbildung spezialisiert. Sie ist von der University of Cambridge (England) als »Teacher of English as a Foreign Language« zertifiziert und von dem International Cultural Institute (Portland, USA) in »Intercultural Foundations« ausgebildet. Ihr Institut »International Communication Training« berät und schult seit 1992 Mitarbeiter und Führungskräfte von internationalen Konzernen.

Die Schwerpunkte sind Trainings in Business English, TOEFL, GMAT, Präsentation, Moderation, interkultureller Kompetenz, Führung und Teambildung. Darüber hinaus ist sie Mitglied in SIETAR (Berufsverband für interkulturelle Zusammenarbeit und Internationalisierung) und war Lehrbeauftragte an der Ludwigs-Maximilians-Universität München.

Kontakt: www.intcomtra.de

Von Jaquie Mary Thomas stammt Kapitel 3 dieses Buches.

Lisa Förster
ist Übersetzerin, Dolmetscherin und Sprachtrainerin für Englisch und Französisch und mit eigenem Übersetzungs- und Sprachtrainingsinstitut selbstständig. Sie arbeitet für Unternehmen und Sprachinstitute und bietet u.a. auch Fachsprachenkurse an. Im Haufe Verlag hat sie zahlreiche, erfolgreiche Bücher zu Business English veröffentlicht.

Annette Pattinson
ist staatlich geprüfte Übersetzerin für Englisch und als Lektorin und Layouterin in der Verlags- und Übersetzungsbranche tätig, mit Schwerpunkt auf mehrsprachigen Büchern und Zeitschriften.

Von Lisa Förster und Annette Pattinson stammt Kapitel 4 dieses Buches.

Ian R. Lewis
Ian R. Lewis stammt aus Irland und ist als Dozent an der Amsterdamer Hochschule für Angewandte Wissenschaften im Fachbereich Economics and Management tätig. Er unterrichtet internationales Verhandeln, Geschichte, Politik, Kultur europäischer und asiatischer Länder sowie Interkulturelle Studien, Studienrichtung Trade Management Asia. Er verfügt über langjährige Erfahrung im internationalen Handel und auf dem Gebiet internationaler Beziehungen.

Von Ian R. Lewis (mit Co-Autor Sander Schroevers) stammt Kapitel 5 dieses Buches.

Stephanie Shellabear
ist selbständige Englisch-Trainerin, Übersetzerin und Korrektorin. Nach ihrem Studium der Betriebswirtschaft und Deutsch in Großbritannien war sie zehn Jahre lang im Bereich Finanzen und Rechnungswesen bei einer renommierten Unternehmensberatung in München tätig sowie einige Jahre am Münchener Sitz eines globalen Computer-Herstellers.

Von Stephanie Shellabear stammt Kapitel 6 dieses Buches.

Weitere Literatur

»Controlling-Fachbegriffe Deutsch-Englisch, Englisch-Deutsch. Wörterbuch, Formulierugshilfen, Vorlagen und Muster«, von Annette Bosewitz, René Bosewitz, Frank Wörner, 280 Seiten, mit CD-ROM, EUR 29,80, ISBN 978-3-448-06030-0, Bestell-Nr. 01418

»Business English für Personaler – Gesprächsleitfäden, Musterdialoge, Fachvokabular«, von Annette Bosewitz und René Bosewitz, 385 Seiten, inkl. Arbeitshilfen online, EUR 39,95, ISBN 978-3-648-11680-7, Bestell-Nr. 04435

»Business Knigge international« von Kai Oppel, 326 Seiten, EUR 19,95, ISBN 978-3-648-06632-4, Bestell-Nr. 00076

»Internationale Personalarbeit in der Praxis – Erfolgsfaktoren und Tools für mittelständische Unternehmen«, von Thomas Batsching, 220 Seiten, EUR 39,95, ISBN 978-3-648-11077-5, Bestell-Nr. 14060